#3

Story by: Atsuko Asano
Art by: Hinoki Kino

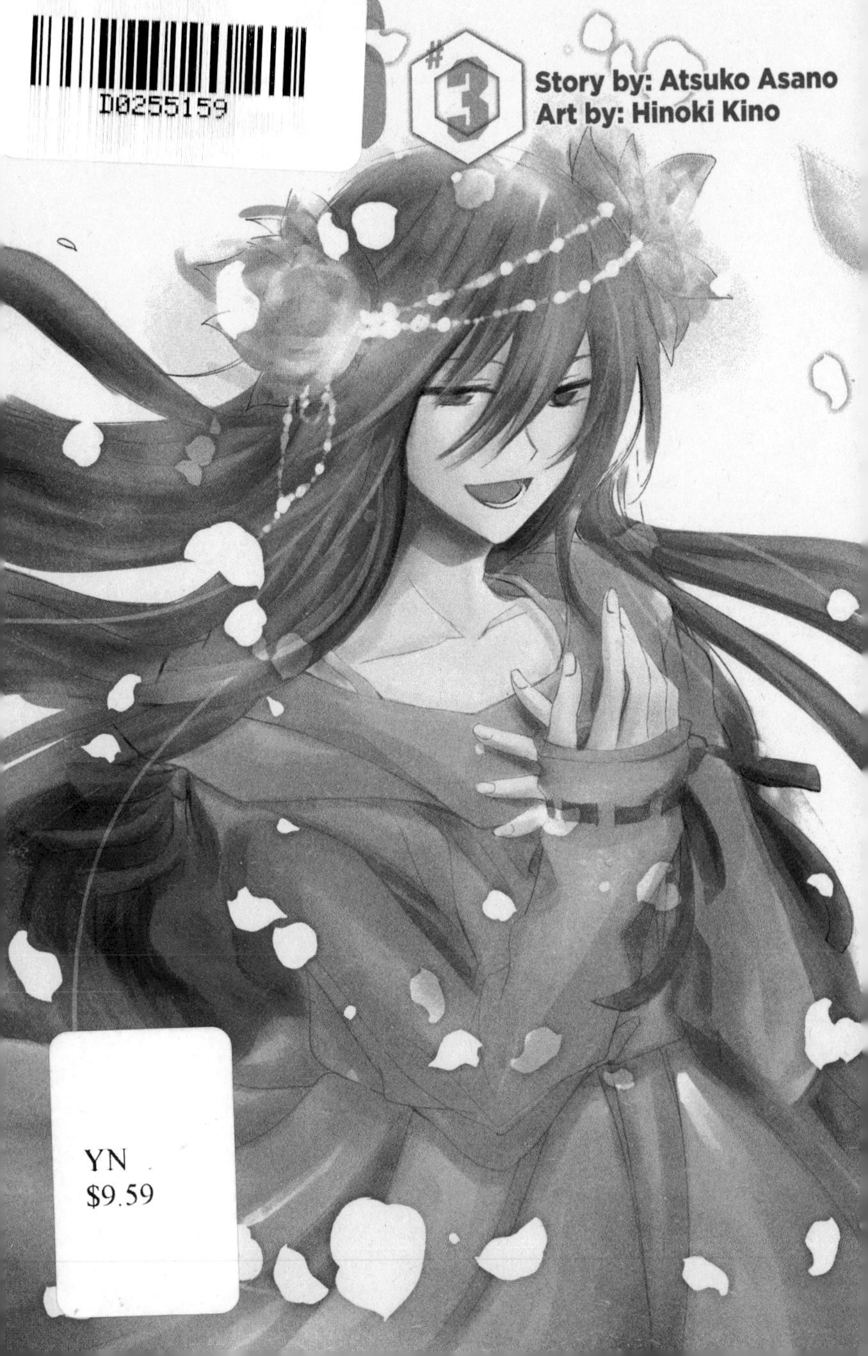

NO.6

#3

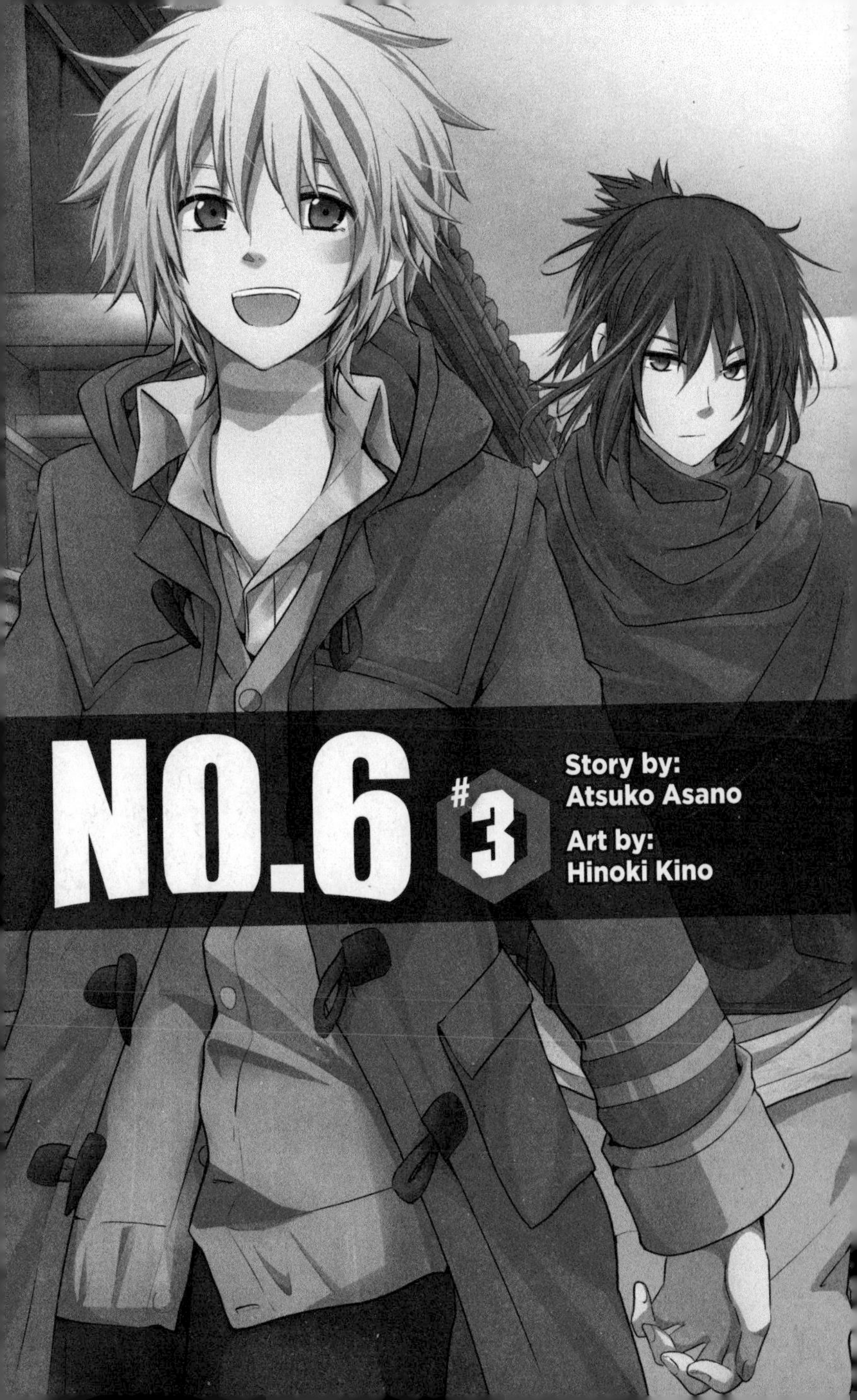
NO.6
#3
Story by:
Atsuko Asano
Art by:
Hinoki Kino

NO.6 STORY and CHARACTERS

SAFU

A childhood
friend with
feelings of love
for Shion. An
elite researcher
who specializes in
neuroscience.

Shion was raised as a privileged elite in the holy city of No. 6. But after sheltering Rat, a fugitive on the run, Shion was stripped of his elite status.

That was four years ago. While eking out a living in Lost Town, Shion was named a murder suspect. As he was being transported to the Correctional Facility, Rat rescued him. Together they escaped No. 6 for West Block, where Shion fell ill, infected by a parasitic bee. After almost dying, his hair turned white and a red snake-like mark wrapped around his body. Amidst the violence and despair of West Block, Shion set out to solve the mystery of the note sent by his mother Karan. Along the way he met Dogkeeper and Rikiga, two citizens of the town.

Meanwhile, Safu returned to No. 6 from overseas, and learned of Shion's fate.

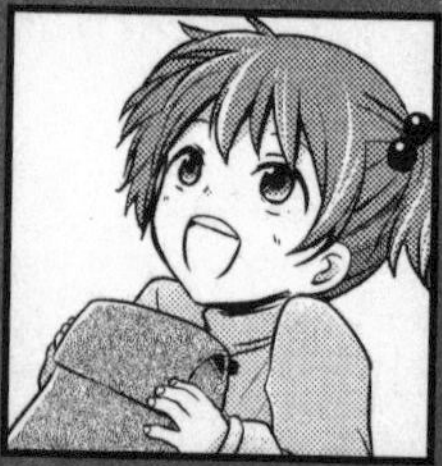

LILY

A little girl and regular customer at Karan's bakery.

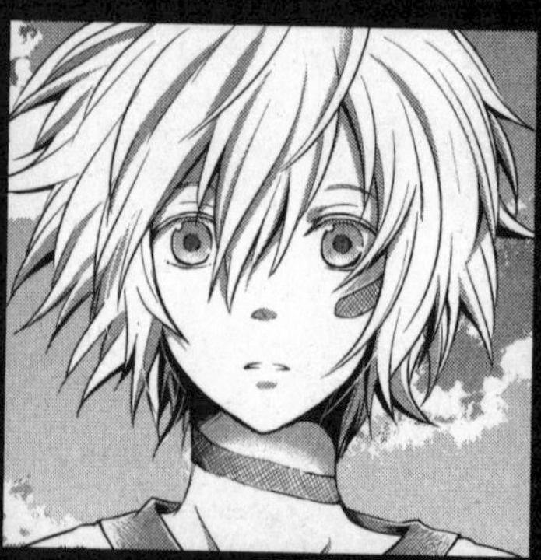

SHION

Fallen from the elite, he escaped to West Block. He was infected by a parasitic bee, but survived.

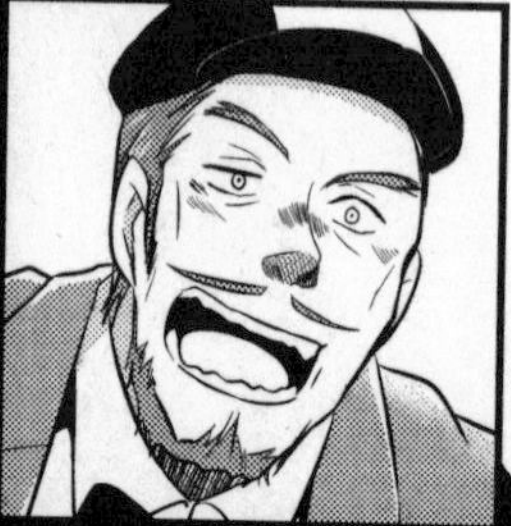

RIKIGA

A former journalist who now publishes a porno magazine in West Block. An old friend of Karan.

THE BEAUTIFUL CITY IN WHICH WE LIVE— NO. 6!
THE MOONDROP (CITY HALL)
LOST TOWN
CHRONOS
FOREST PARK
THE CULMINATION OF HUMAN SCIENCE—THE CITY OF THE FUTURE!

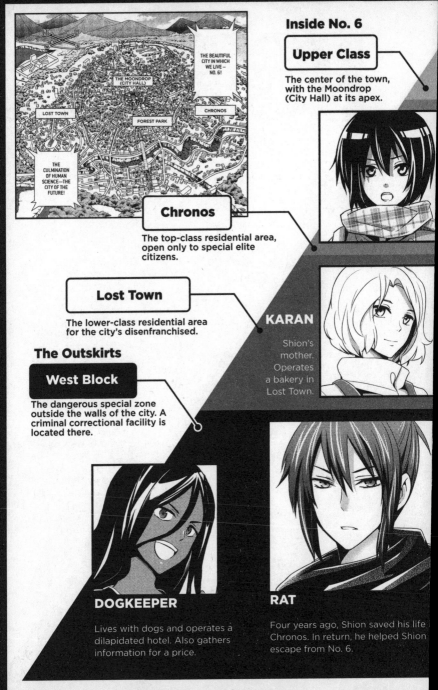

Inside No. 6

Upper Class

The center of the town, with the Moondrop (City Hall) at its apex.

Chronos

The top-class residential area, open only to special elite citizens.

Lost Town

The lower-class residential area for the city's disenfranchised.

KARAN

Shion's mother. Operates a bakery in Lost Town.

The Outskirts

West Block

The dangerous special zone outside the walls of the city. A criminal correctional facility is located there.

DOGKEEPER

Lives with dogs and operates a dilapidated hotel. Also gathers information for a price.

RAT

Four years ago, Shion saved his life i
Chronos. In return, he helped Shion escape from No. 6.

Chapter 8: Angel of Death

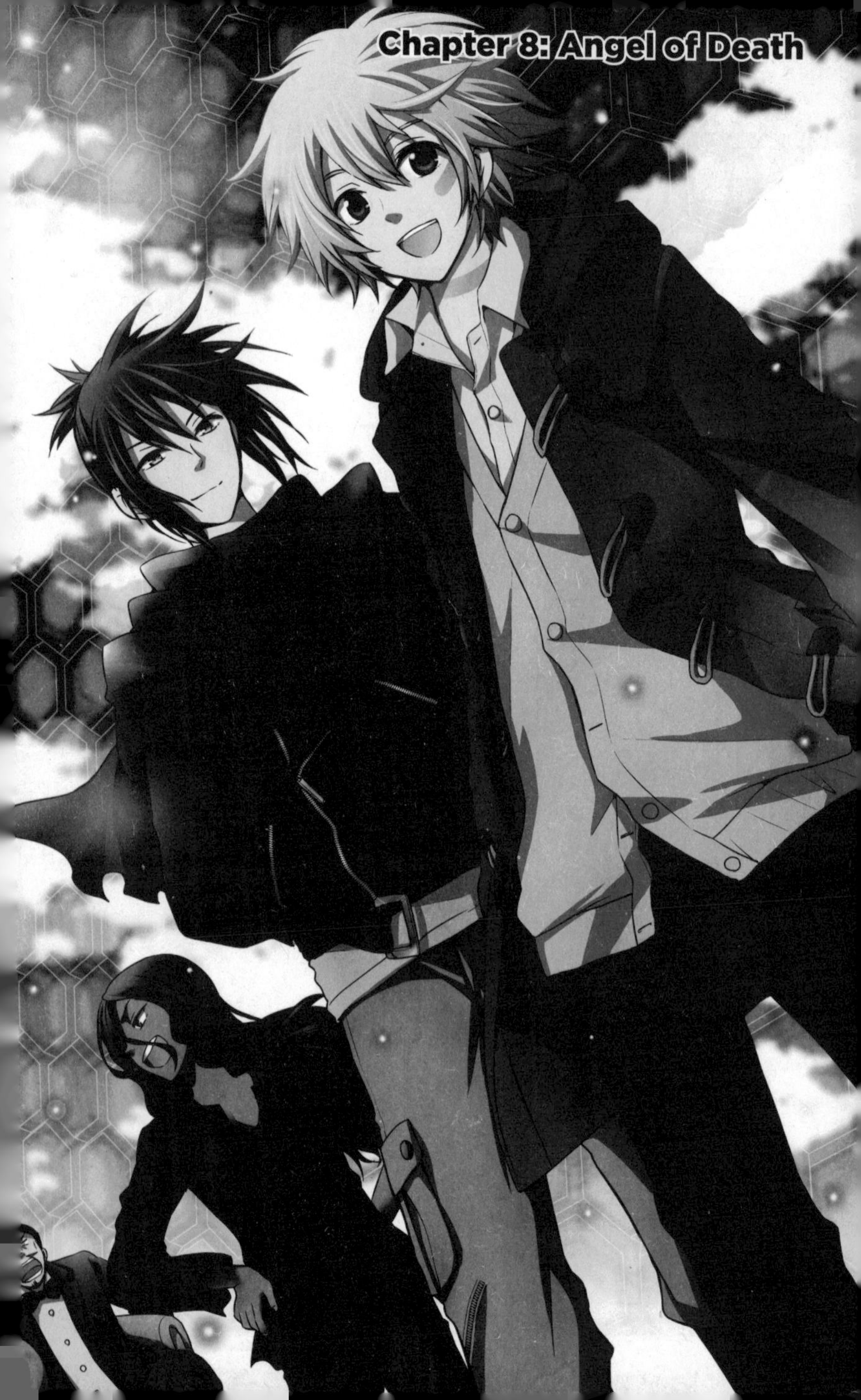

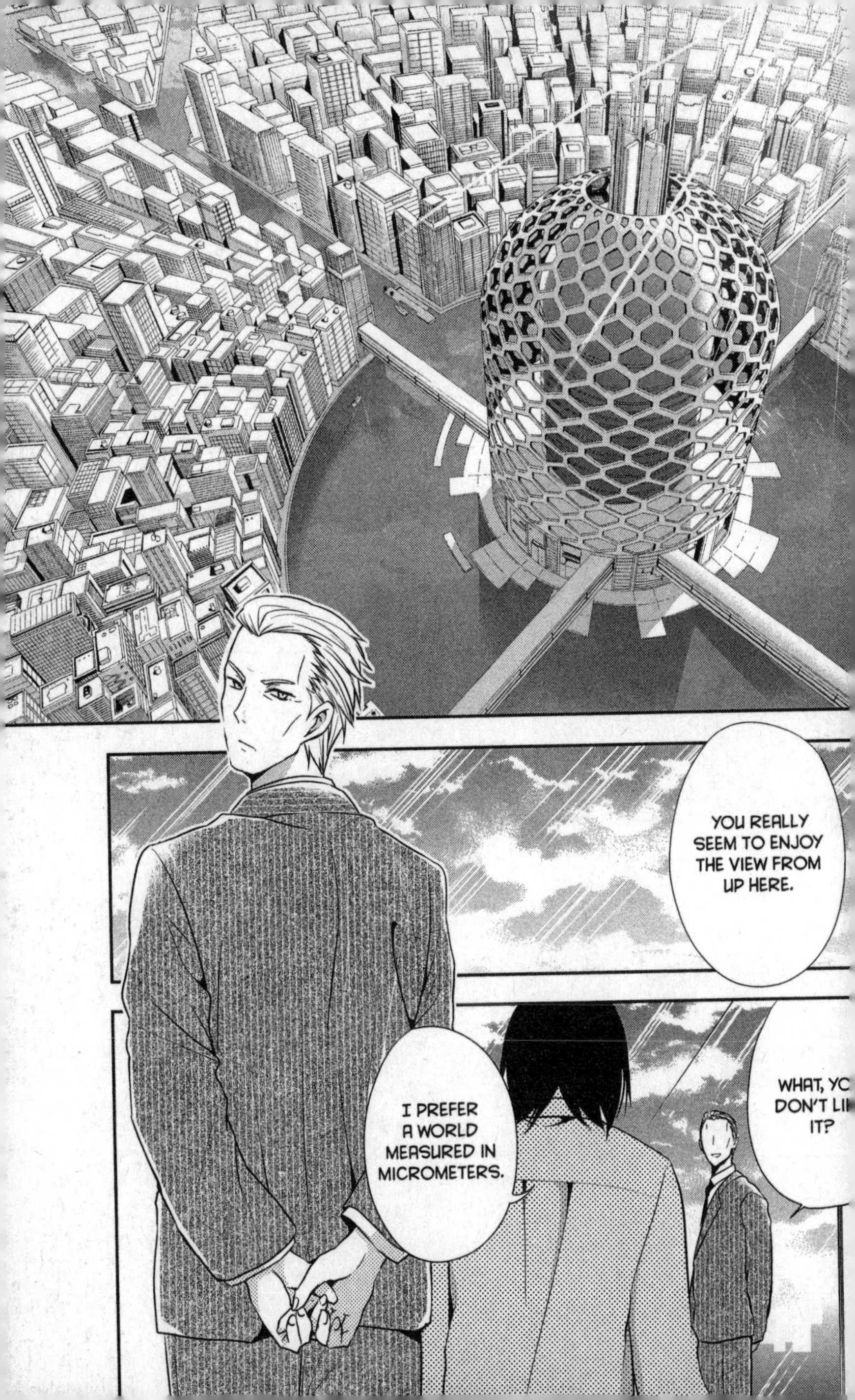
YOU REALLY SEEM TO ENJOY THE VIEW FROM UP HERE.
WHAT, YO DON'T LI IT?
I PREFER A WORLD MEASURED IN MICROMETERS.

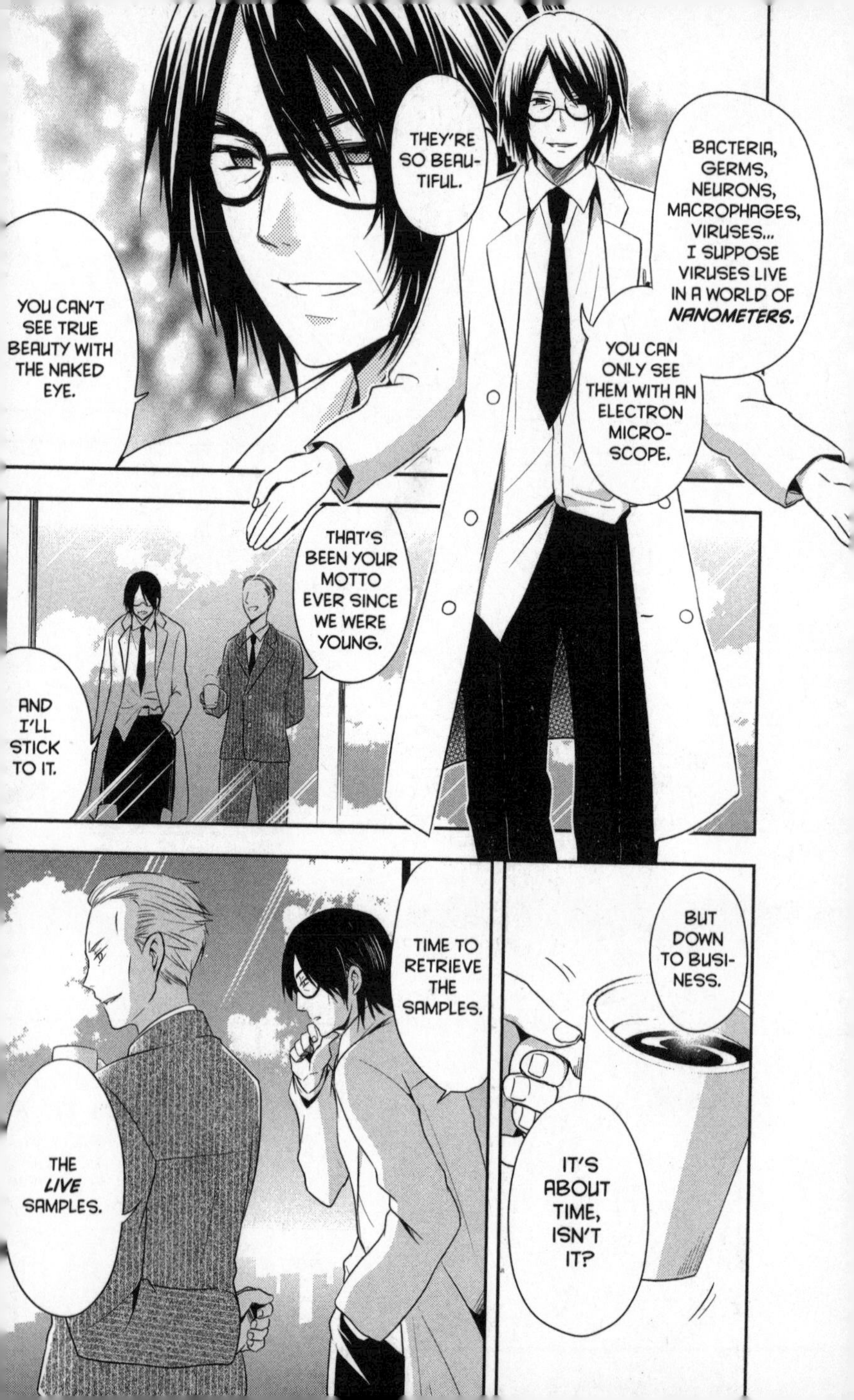
BACTERIA, GERMS, NEURONS, MACROPHAGES, VIRUSES... I SUPPOSE VIRUSES LIVE IN A WORLD OF *NANOMETERS.*
YOU CAN ONLY SEE THEM WITH AN ELECTRON MICROSCOPE.
THEY'RE SO BEAUTIFUL.
YOU CAN'T SEE TRUE BEAUTY WITH THE NAKED EYE.
THAT'S BEEN YOUR MOTTO EVER SINCE WE WERE YOUNG.
AND I'LL STICK TO IT.
BUT DOWN TO BUSINESS.
IT'S ABOUT TIME, ISN'T IT?
TIME TO RETRIEVE THE SAMPLES.
THE *LIVE* SAMPLES.

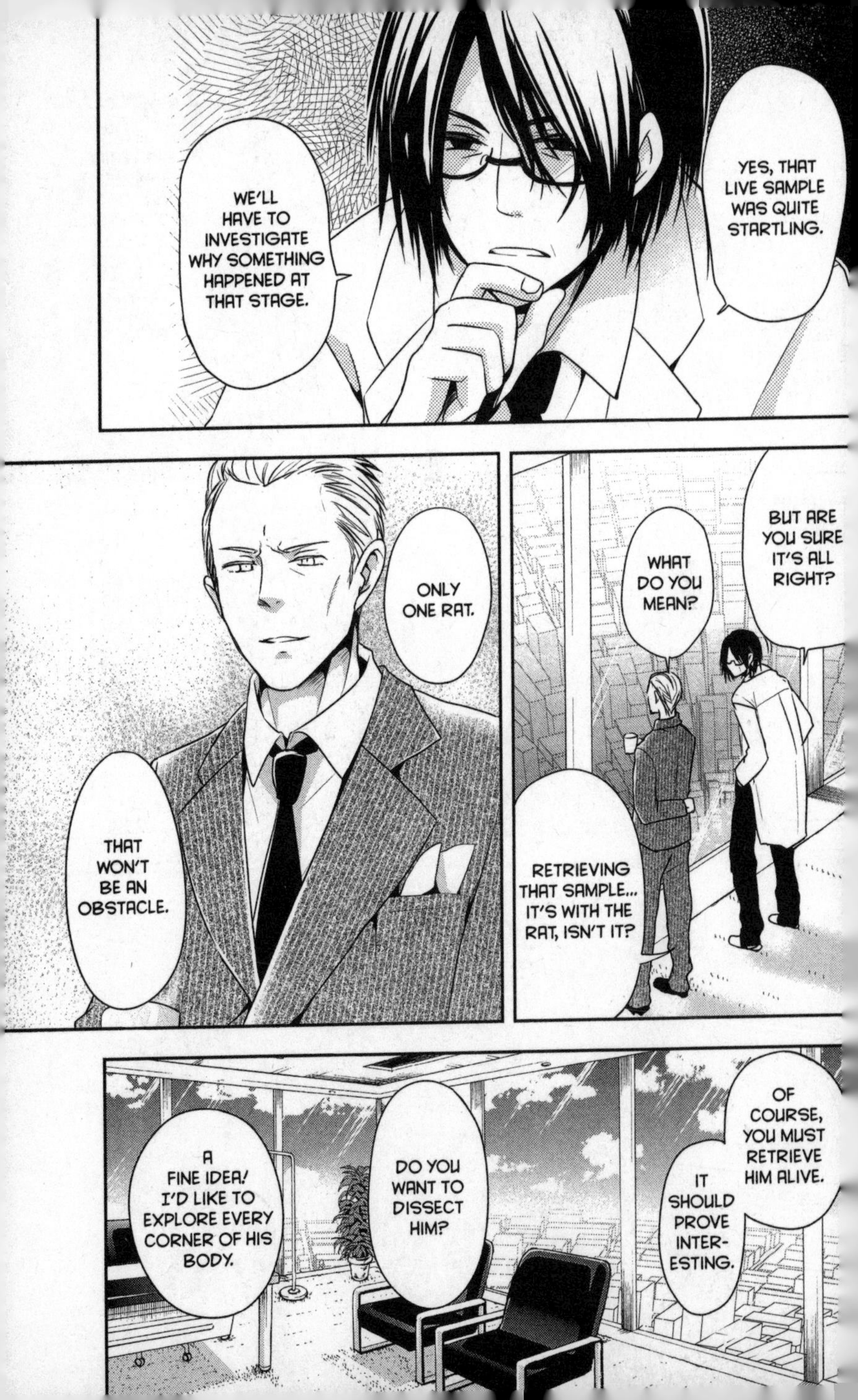
YES, THAT LIVE SAMPLE WAS QUITE STARTLING.
WE'LL HAVE TO INVESTIGATE WHY SOMETHING HAPPENED AT THAT STAGE.
BUT ARE YOU SURE IT'S ALL RIGHT?
WHAT DO YOU MEAN?
RETRIEVING THAT SAMPLE... IT'S WITH THE RAT, ISN'T IT?
ONLY ONE RAT.
THAT WON'T BE AN OBSTACLE.
OF COURSE, YOU MUST RETRIEVE HIM ALIVE.
IT SHOULD PROVE INTER-ESTING.
DO YOU WANT TO DISSECT HIM?
A FINE IDEA! I'D LIKE TO EXPLORE EVERY CORNER OF HIS BODY.

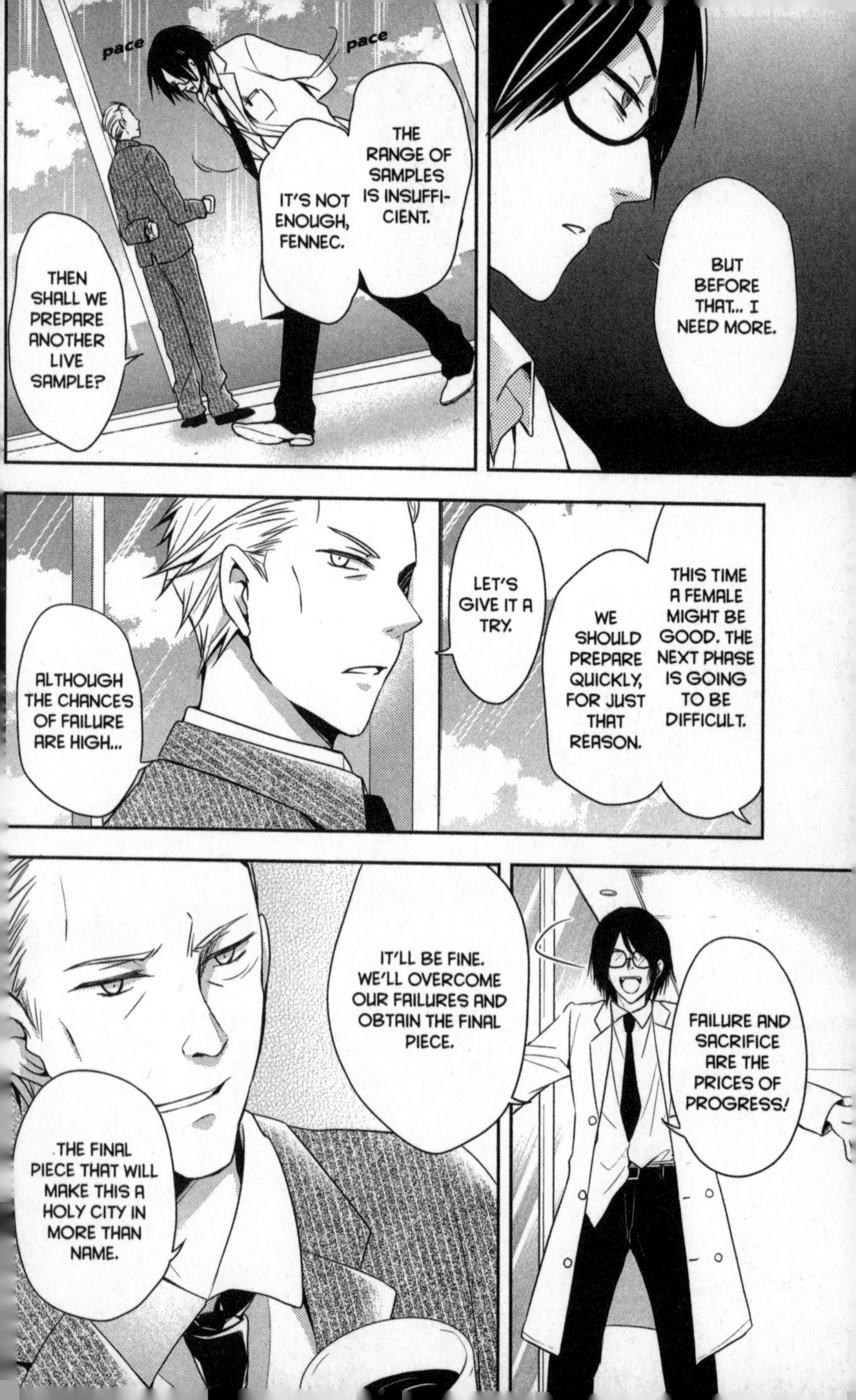
BUT BEFORE THAT... I NEED MORE.
pace
pace
THE RANGE OF SAMPLES IS INSUFFICIENT.
IT'S NOT ENOUGH, FENNEC.
THEN SHALL WE PREPARE ANOTHER LIVE SAMPLE?
THIS TIME A FEMALE MIGHT BE GOOD. THE NEXT PHASE IS GOING TO BE DIFFICULT.
WE SHOULD PREPARE QUICKLY, FOR JUST THAT REASON.
LET'S GIVE IT A TRY.
ALTHOUGH THE CHANCES OF FAILURE ARE HIGH...
FAILURE AND SACRIFICE ARE THE PRICES OF PROGRESS!
IT'LL BE FINE. WE'LL OVERCOME OUR FAILURES AND OBTAIN THE FINAL PIECE.
THE FINAL PIECE THAT WILL MAKE THIS A HOLY CITY IN MORE THAN NAME.

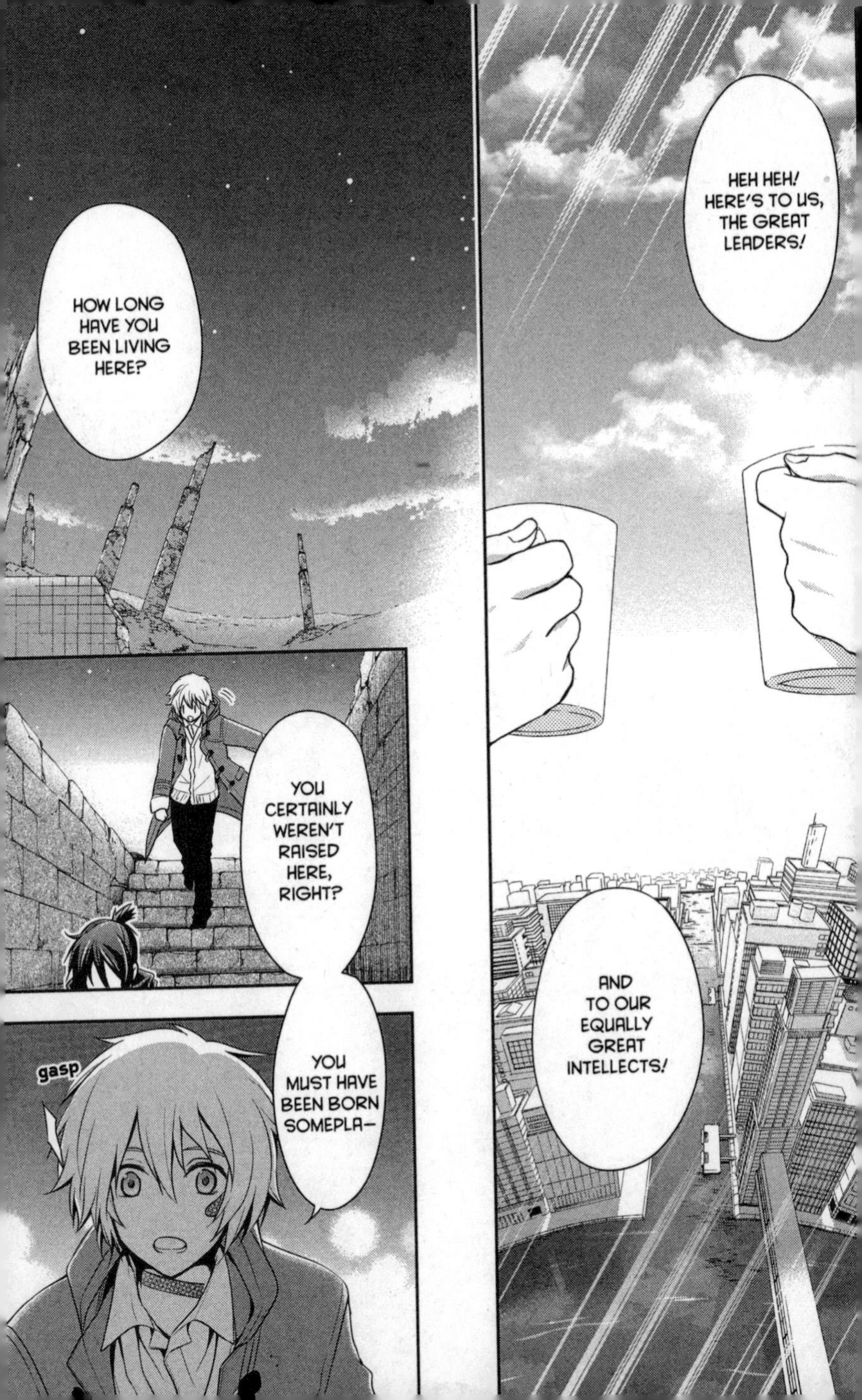
HEH HEH! HERE'S TO US, THE GREAT LEADERS!
AND TO OUR EQUALLY GREAT INTELLECTS!
HOW LONG HAVE YOU BEEN LIVING HERE?
YOU CERTAINLY WEREN'T RAISED HERE, RIGHT?
YOU MUST HAVE BEEN BORN SOMEPLA—
gasp

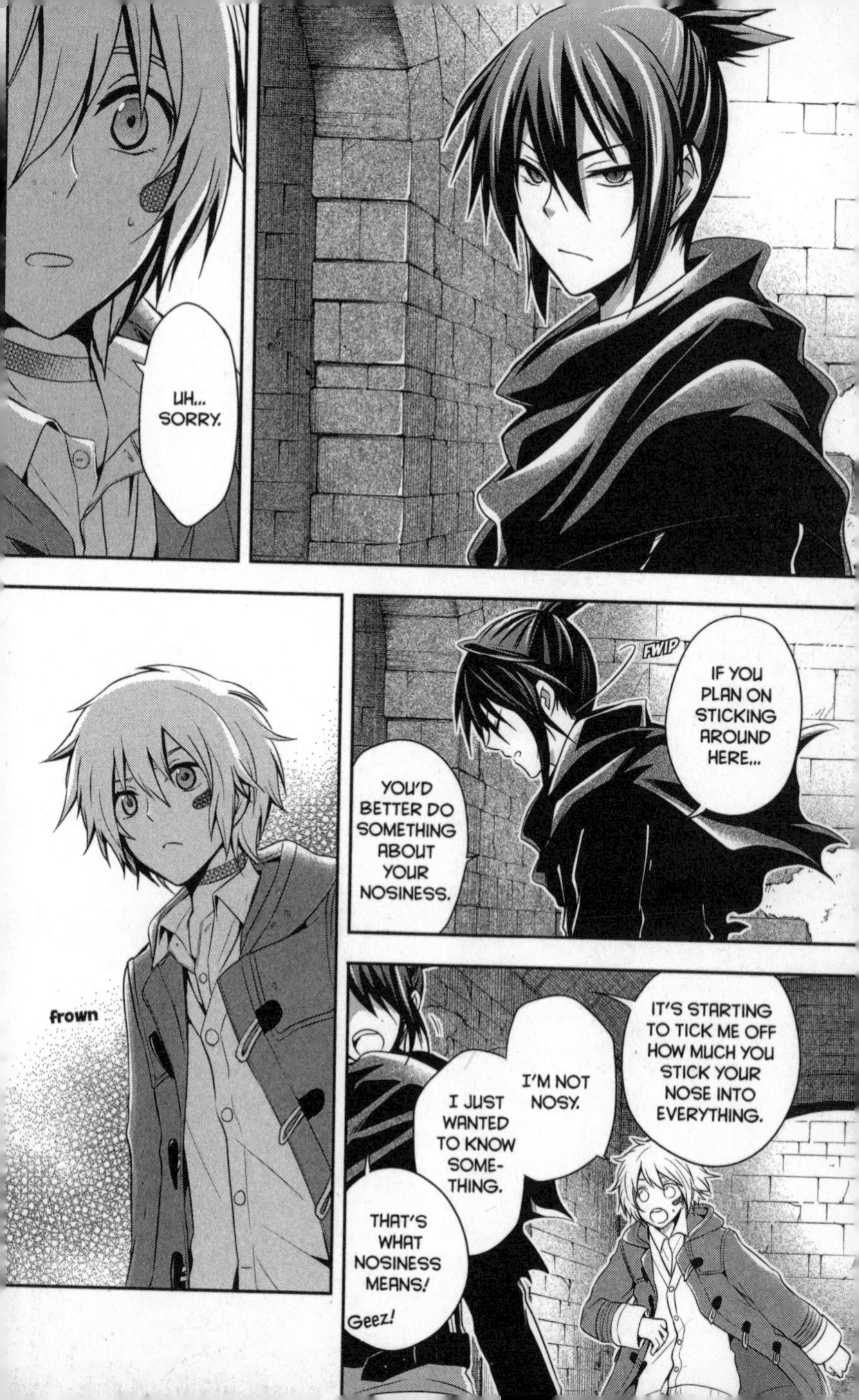
UH... SORRY.
FWIP
IF YOU PLAN ON STICKING AROUND HERE...
YOU'D BETTER DO SOMETHING ABOUT YOUR NOSINESS.
IT'S STARTING TO TICK ME OFF HOW MUCH YOU STICK YOUR NOSE INTO EVERYTHING.
I'M NOT NOSY.
I JUST WANTED TO KNOW SOME-THING.
THAT'S WHAT NOSINESS MEANS!
Geez!
frown

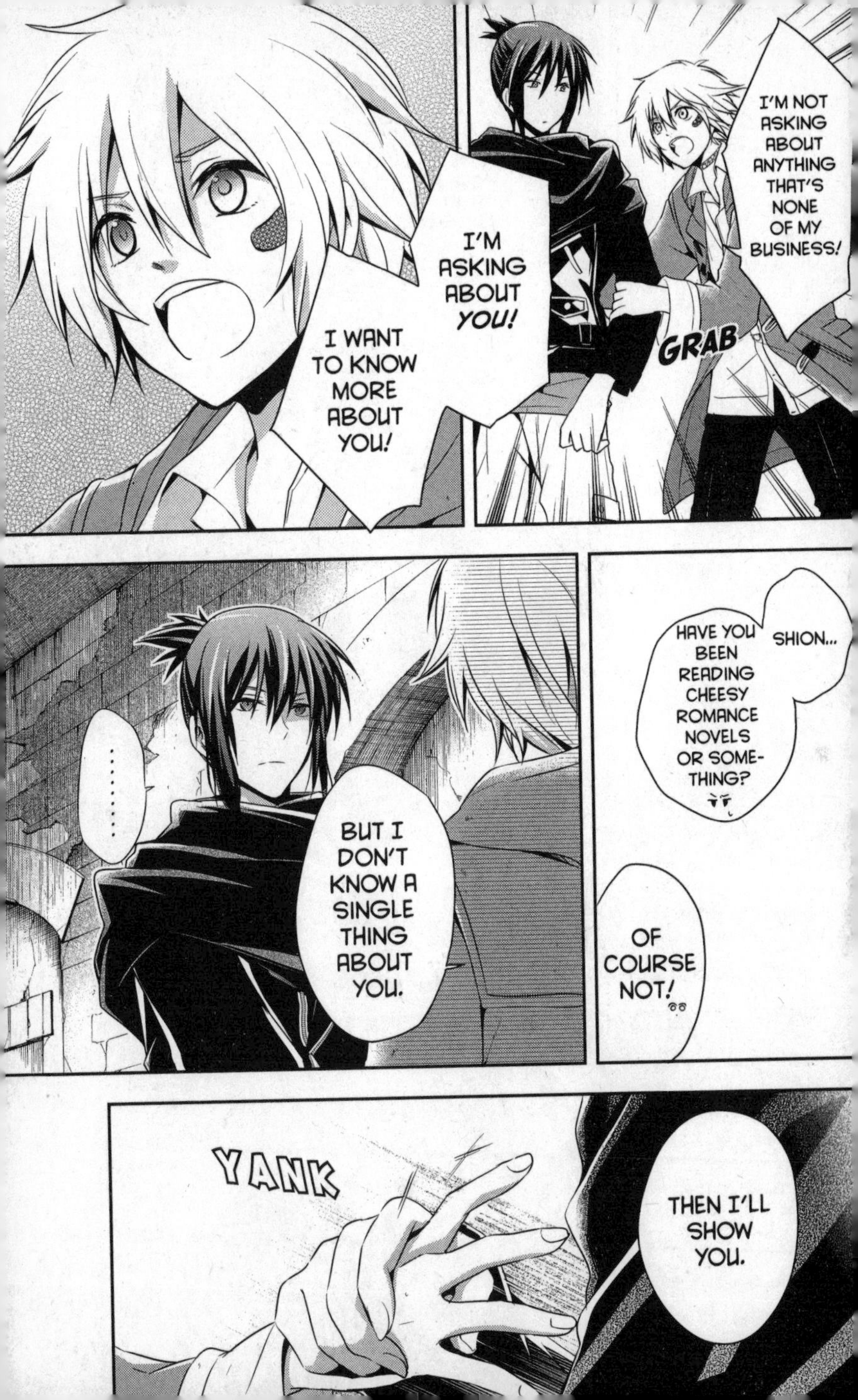
I'M NOT ASKING ABOUT ANYTHING THAT'S NONE OF MY BUSINESS!
GRAB
I'M ASKING ABOUT *YOU!*
I WANT TO KNOW MORE ABOUT YOU!
SHION...
HAVE YOU BEEN READING CHEESY ROMANCE NOVELS OR SOMETHING?
OF COURSE NOT!
BUT I DON'T KNOW A SINGLE THING ABOUT YOU.
....
THEN I'LL SHOW YOU.
YANK

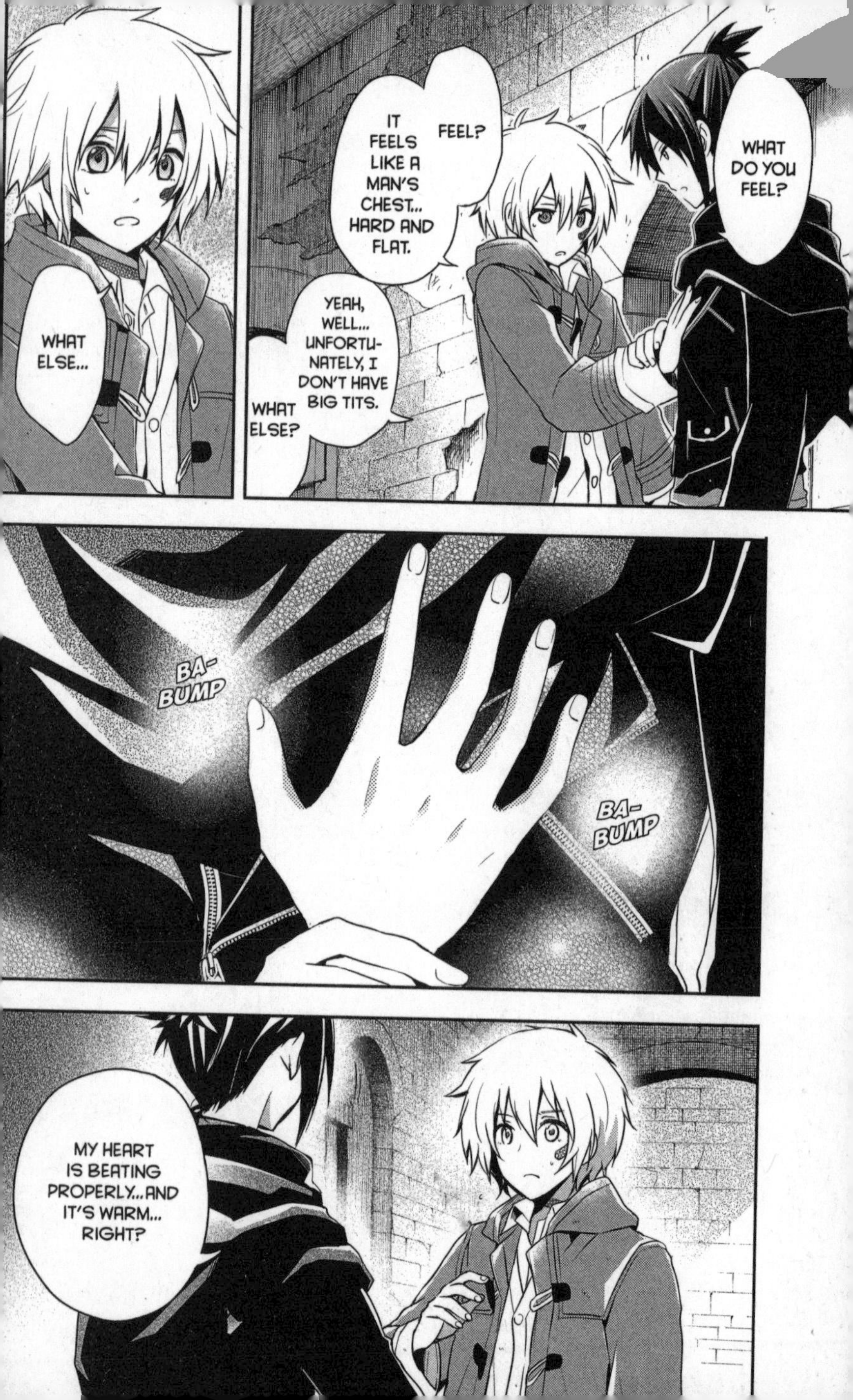
WHAT DO YOU FEEL?
FEEL?
IT FEELS LIKE A MAN'S CHEST... HARD AND FLAT.
YEAH, WELL... UNFORTU-NATELY, I DON'T HAVE BIG TITS.
WHAT ELSE?
WHAT ELSE...
BA-BUMP
BA-BUMP
MY HEART IS BEATING PROPERLY...AND IT'S WARM... RIGHT?

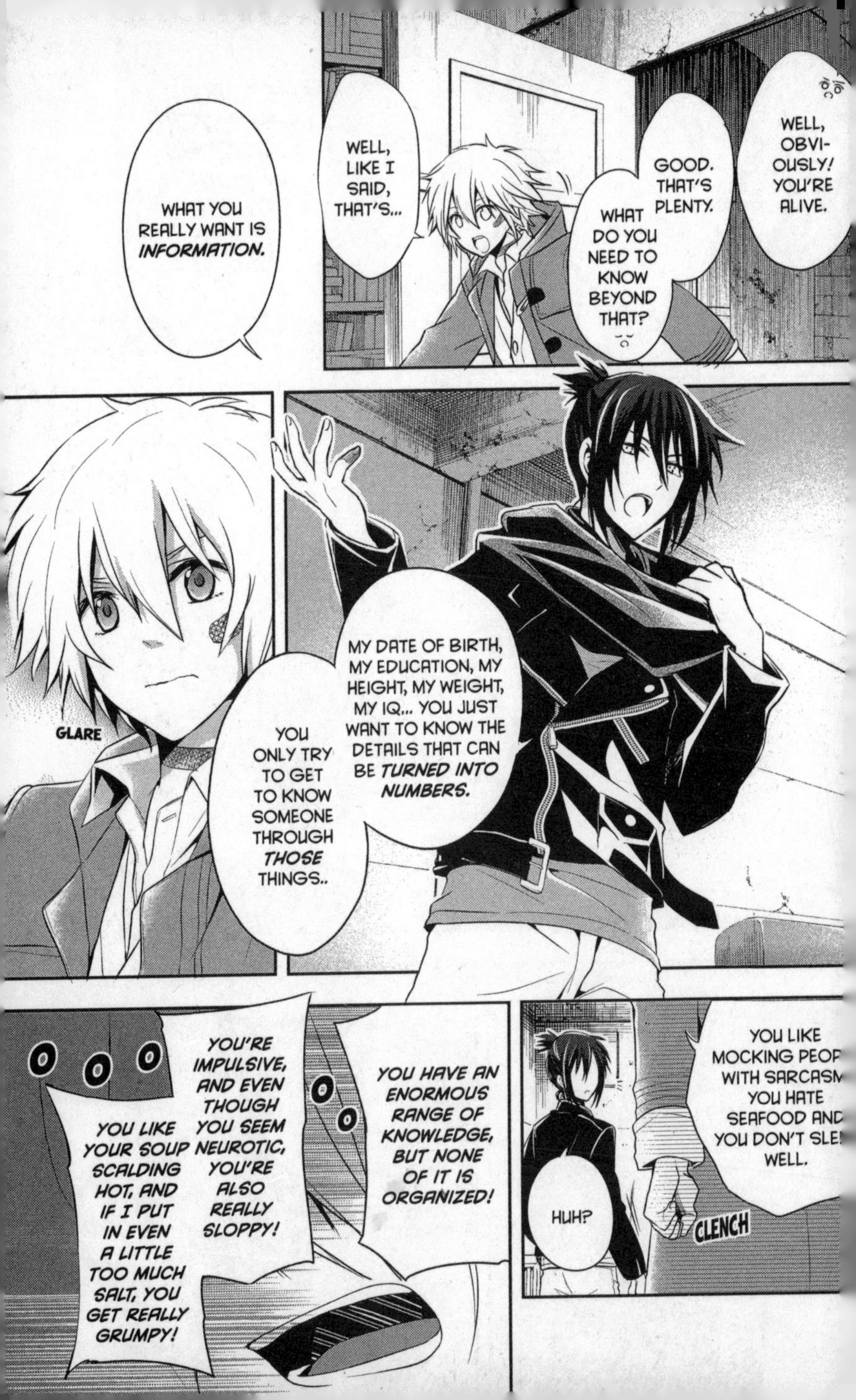
WELL, OBVI-OUSLY! YOU'RE ALIVE.
GOOD. THAT'S PLENTY.
WHAT DO YOU NEED TO KNOW BEYOND THAT?
WELL, LIKE I SAID, THAT'S...
WHAT YOU REALLY WANT IS *INFORMATION.*
MY DATE OF BIRTH, MY EDUCATION, MY HEIGHT, MY WEIGHT, MY IQ... YOU JUST WANT TO KNOW THE DETAILS THAT CAN BE *TURNED INTO NUMBERS.*
YOU ONLY TRY TO GET TO KNOW SOMEONE THROUGH *THOSE* THINGS..
GLARE
YOU LIKE MOCKING PEOP WITH SARCASM YOU HATE SEAFOOD AND YOU DON'T SLE WELL.
HUH?
CLENCH
YOU HAVE AN ENORMOUS RANGE OF KNOWLEDGE, BUT NONE OF IT IS ORGANIZED!
YOU'RE IMPULSIVE, AND EVEN THOUGH YOU SEEM NEUROTIC, YOU'RE ALSO REALLY SLOPPY!
YOU LIKE YOUR SOUP SCALDING HOT, AND IF I PUT IN EVEN A LITTLE TOO MUCH SALT, YOU GET REALLY GRUMPY!

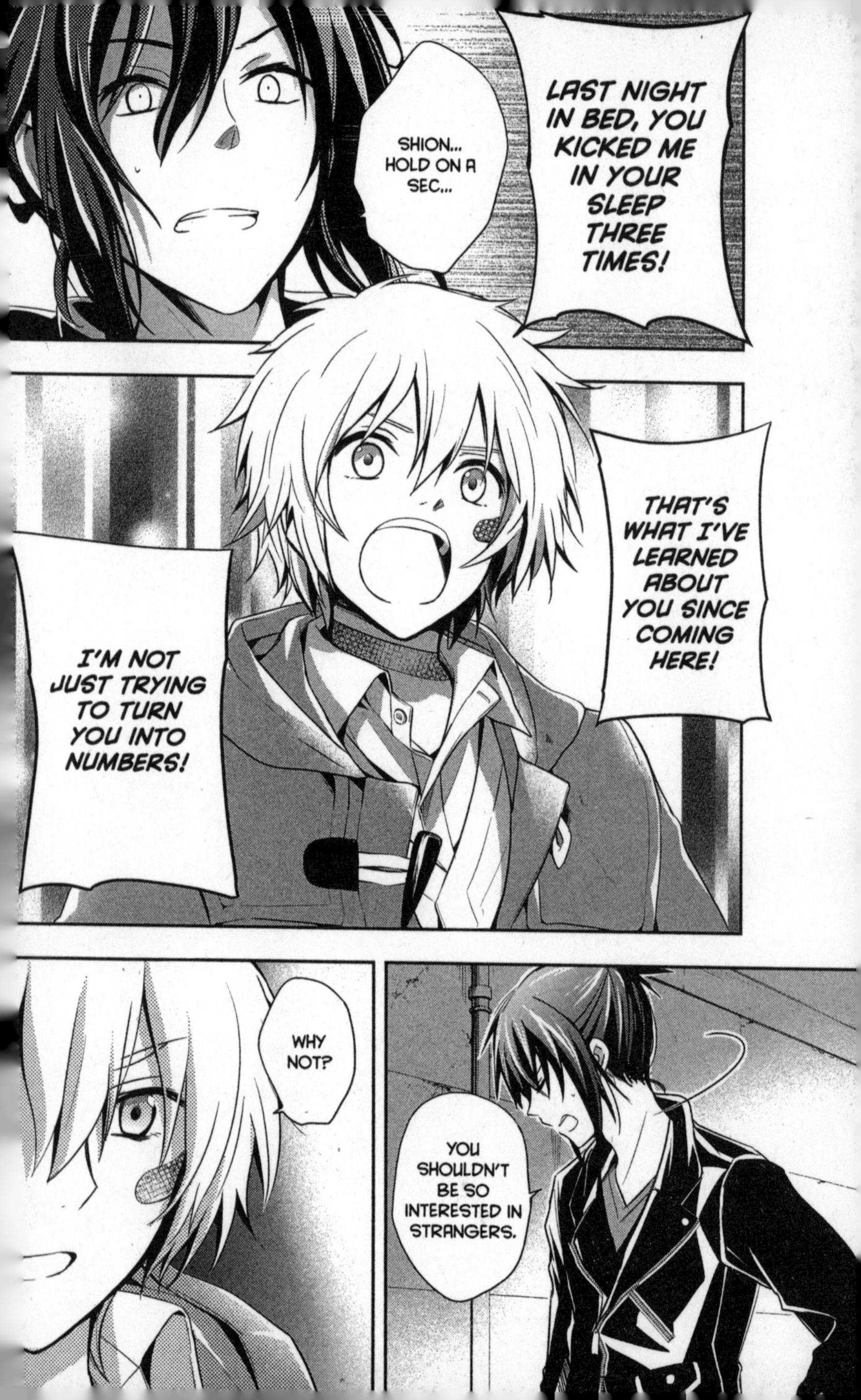
LAST NIGHT IN BED, YOU KICKED ME IN YOUR SLEEP THREE TIMES!
SHION... HOLD ON A SEC...
THAT'S WHAT I'VE LEARNED ABOUT YOU SINCE COMING HERE!
I'M NOT JUST TRYING TO TURN YOU INTO NUMBERS!
YOU SHOULDN'T BE SO INTERESTED IN STRANGERS.
WHY NOT?

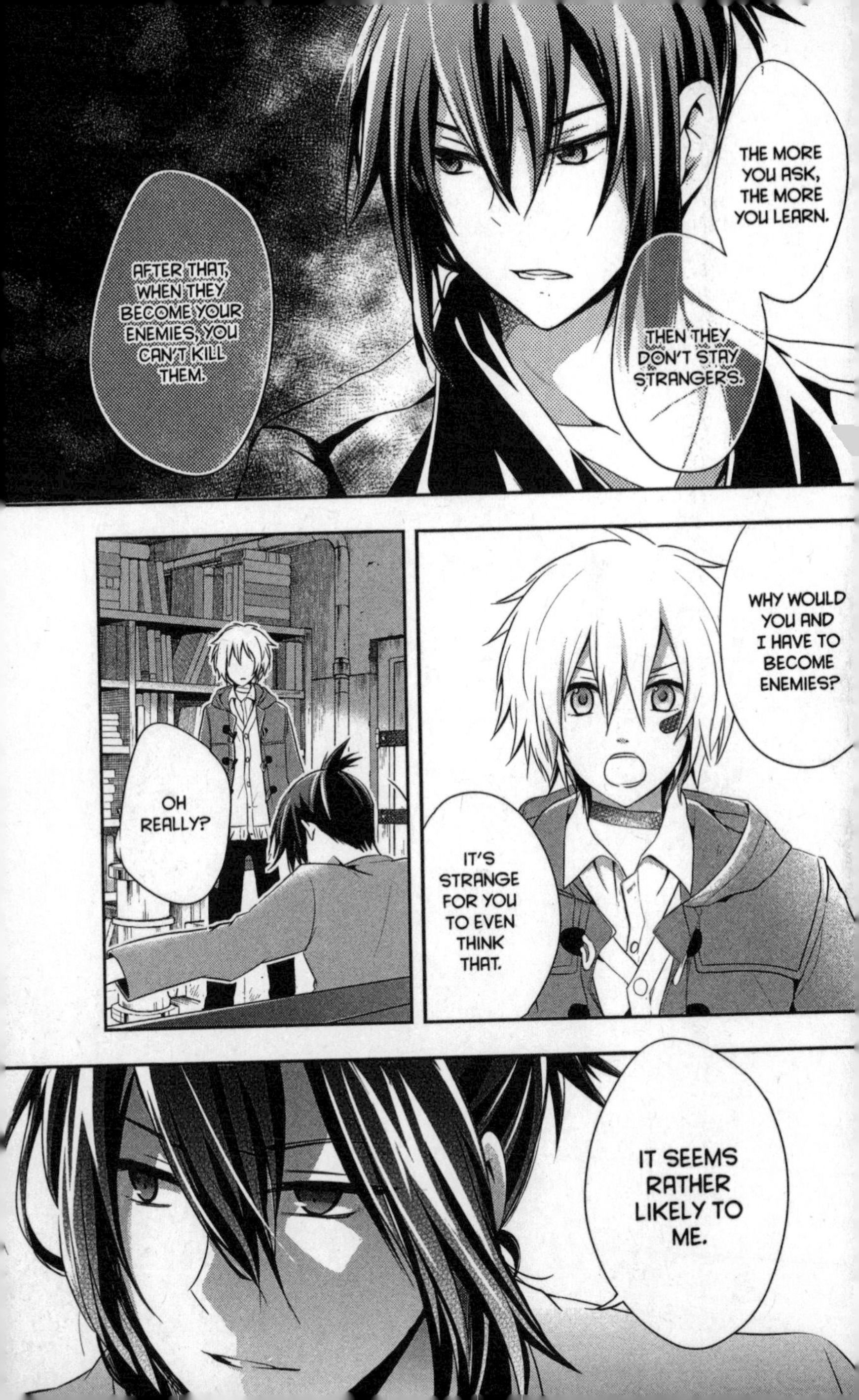
THE MORE YOU ASK, THE MORE YOU LEARN.
THEN THEY DON'T STAY STRANGERS.
AFTER THAT, WHEN THEY BECOME YOUR ENEMIES, YOU CAN'T KILL THEM.
WHY WOULD YOU AND I HAVE TO BECOME ENEMIES?
IT'S STRANGE FOR YOU TO EVEN THINK THAT.
OH REALLY?
IT SEEMS RATHER LIKELY TO ME.

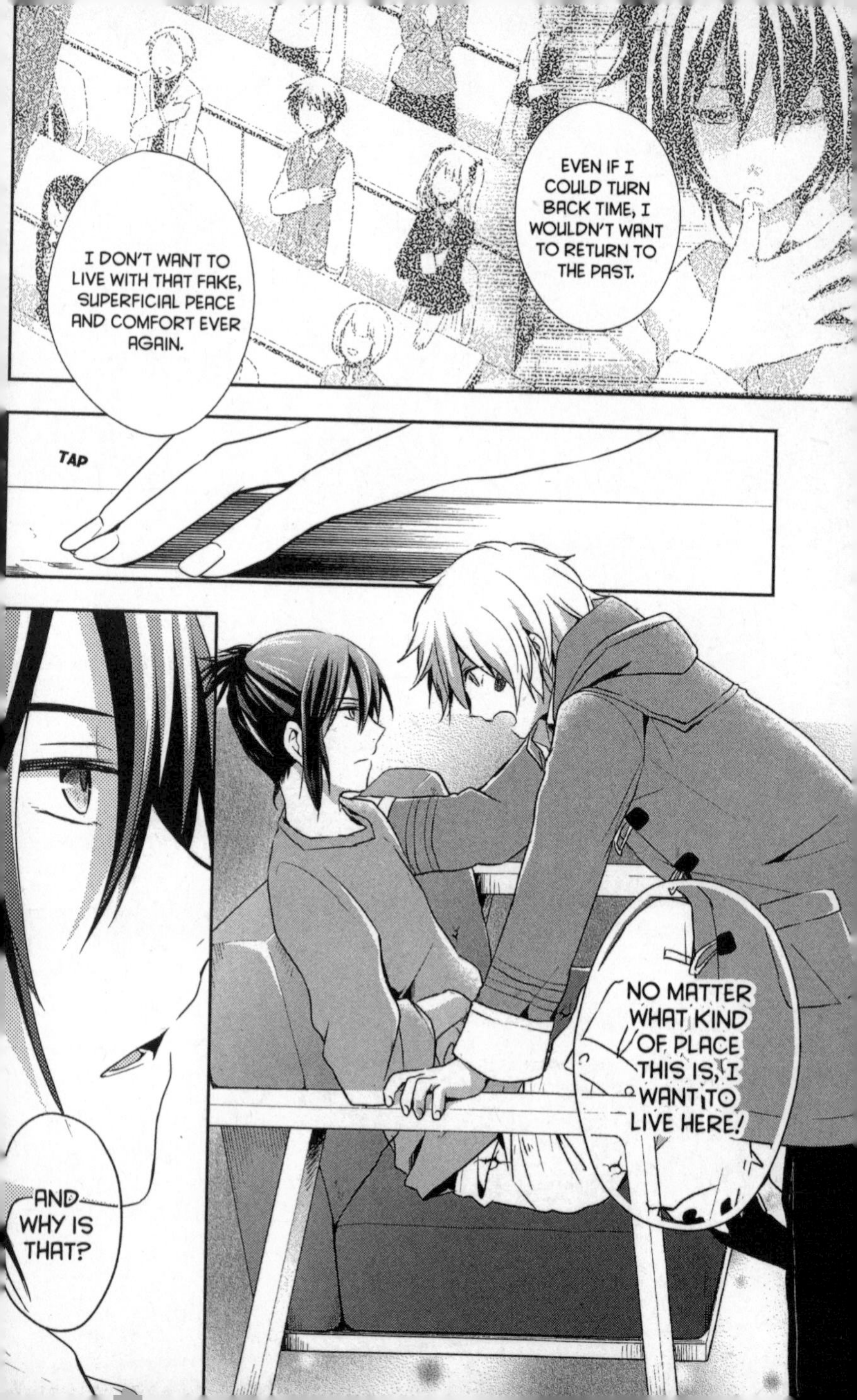
EVEN IF I COULD TURN BACK TIME, I WOULDN'T WANT TO RETURN TO THE PAST.
I DON'T WANT TO LIVE WITH THAT FAKE, SUPERFICIAL PEACE AND COMFORT EVER AGAIN.
TAP
NO MATTER WHAT KIND OF PLACE THIS IS, I WANT TO LIVE HERE!
AND WHY IS THAT?

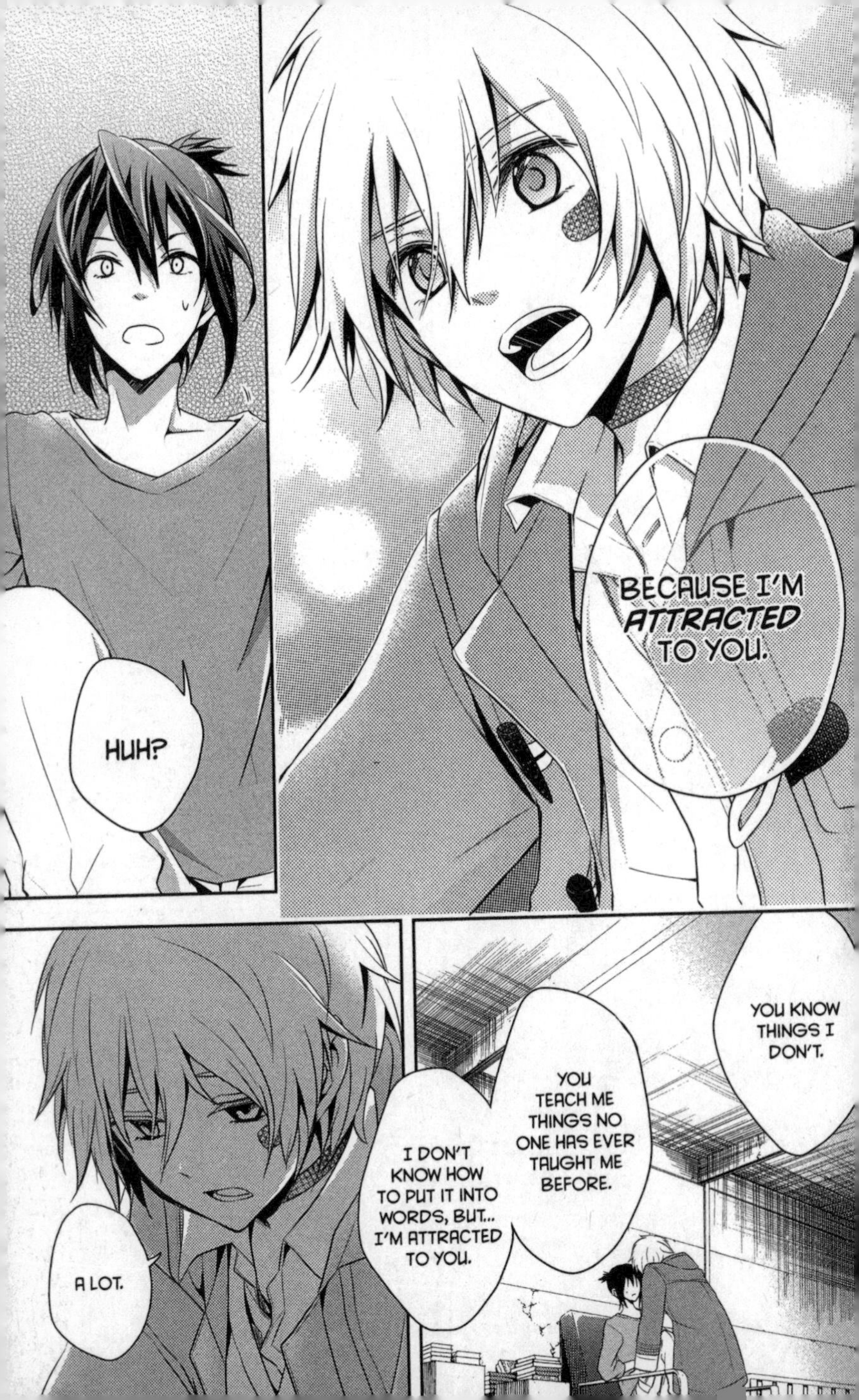
BECAUSE I'M *ATTRACTED* TO YOU.
HUH?
YOU KNOW THINGS I DON'T.
YOU TEACH ME THINGS NO ONE HAS EVER TAUGHT ME BEFORE.
I DON'T KNOW HOW TO PUT IT INTO WORDS, BUT... I'M ATTRACTED TO YOU.
A LOT.

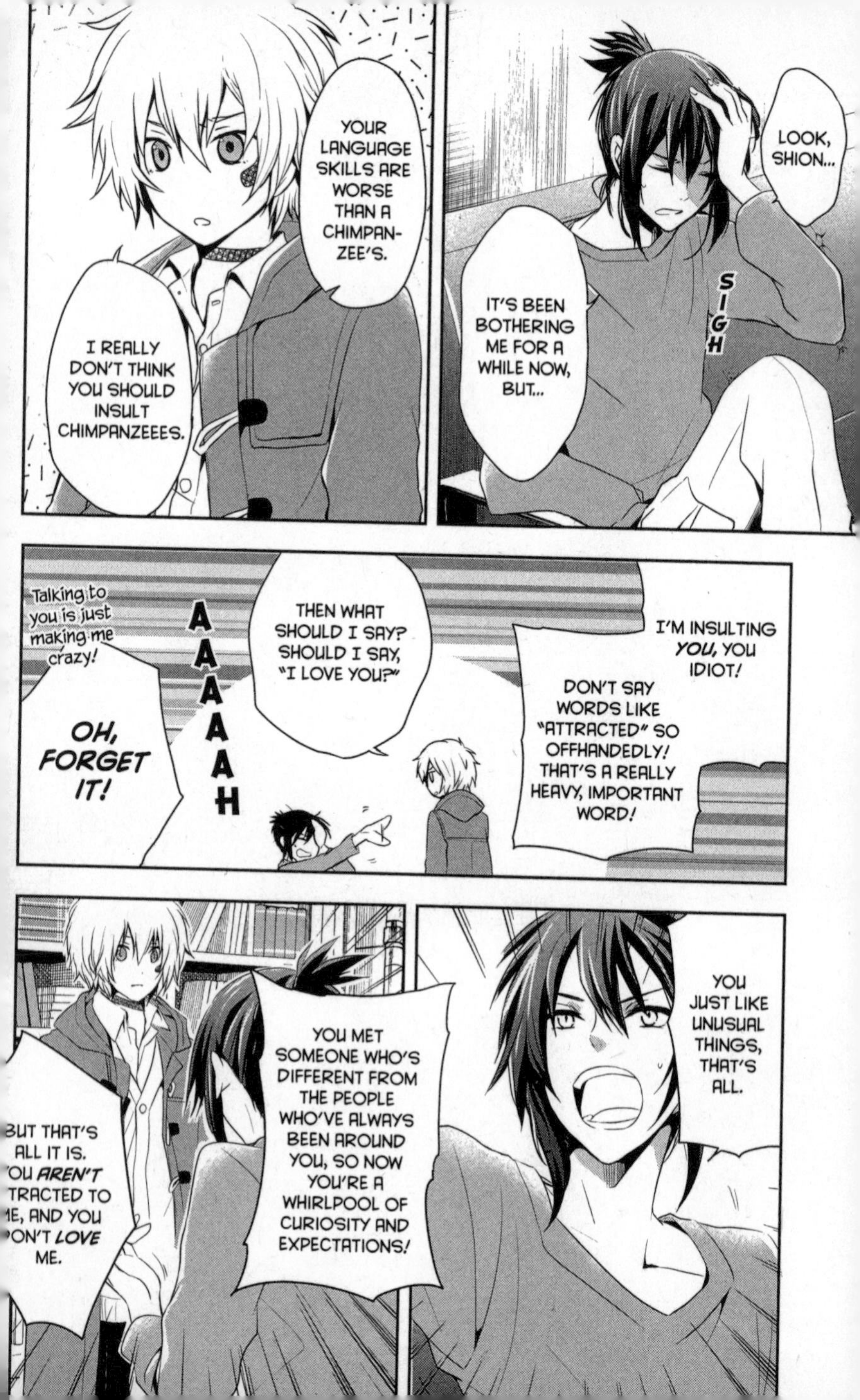
LOOK, SHION...
SIGH
IT'S BEEN BOTHERING ME FOR A WHILE NOW, BUT...
YOUR LANGUAGE SKILLS ARE WORSE THAN A CHIMPANZEE'S.
I REALLY DON'T THINK YOU SHOULD INSULT CHIMPANZEEES.
I'M INSULTING YOU, YOU IDIOT!
DON'T SAY WORDS LIKE "ATTRACTED" SO OFFHANDEDLY! THAT'S A REALLY HEAVY, IMPORTANT WORD!
THEN WHAT SHOULD I SAY? SHOULD I SAY, "I LOVE YOU?"
AAAAAH
Talking to you is just making me crazy!
OH, FORGET IT!
YOU JUST LIKE UNUSUAL THINGS, THAT'S ALL.
YOU MET SOMEONE WHO'S DIFFERENT FROM THE PEOPLE WHO'VE ALWAYS BEEN AROUND YOU, SO NOW YOU'RE A WHIRLPOOL OF CURIOSITY AND EXPECTATIONS!
BUT THAT'S ALL IT IS. OU AREN'T TRACTED TO IE, AND YOU ON'T LOVE ME.

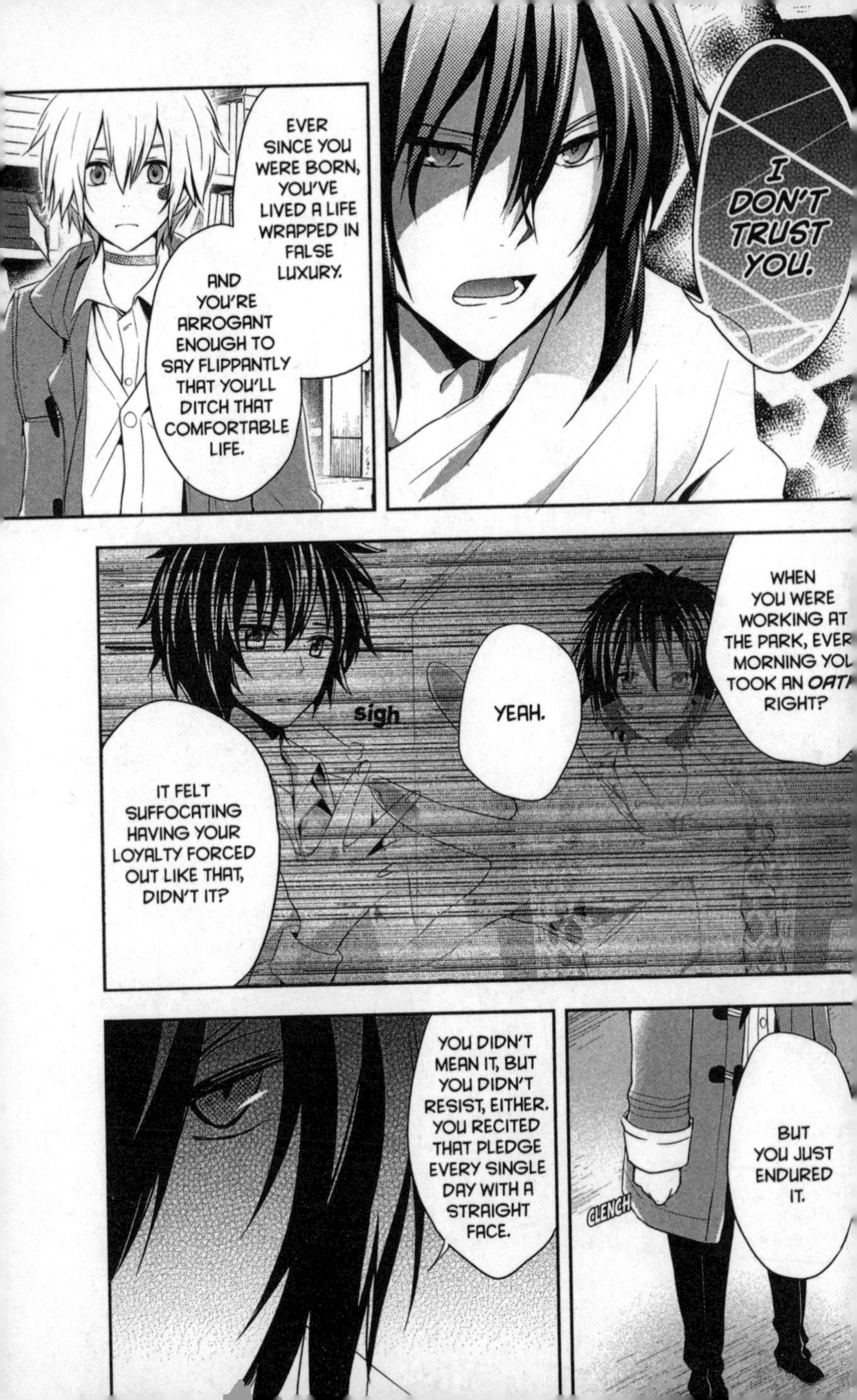
I DON'T TRUST YOU.
EVER SINCE YOU WERE BORN, YOU'VE LIVED A LIFE WRAPPED IN FALSE LUXURY.
AND YOU'RE ARROGANT ENOUGH TO SAY FLIPPANTLY THAT YOU'LL DITCH THAT COMFORTABLE LIFE.
WHEN YOU WERE WORKING AT THE PARK, EVER MORNING YOU TOOK AN OAT RIGHT?
YEAH.
sigh
IT FELT SUFFOCATING HAVING YOUR LOYALTY FORCED OUT LIKE THAT, DIDN'T IT?
BUT YOU JUST ENDURED IT.
CLENCH
YOU DIDN'T MEAN IT, BUT YOU DIDN'T RESIST, EITHER. YOU RECITED THAT PLEDGE EVERY SINGLE DAY WITH A STRAIGHT FACE.

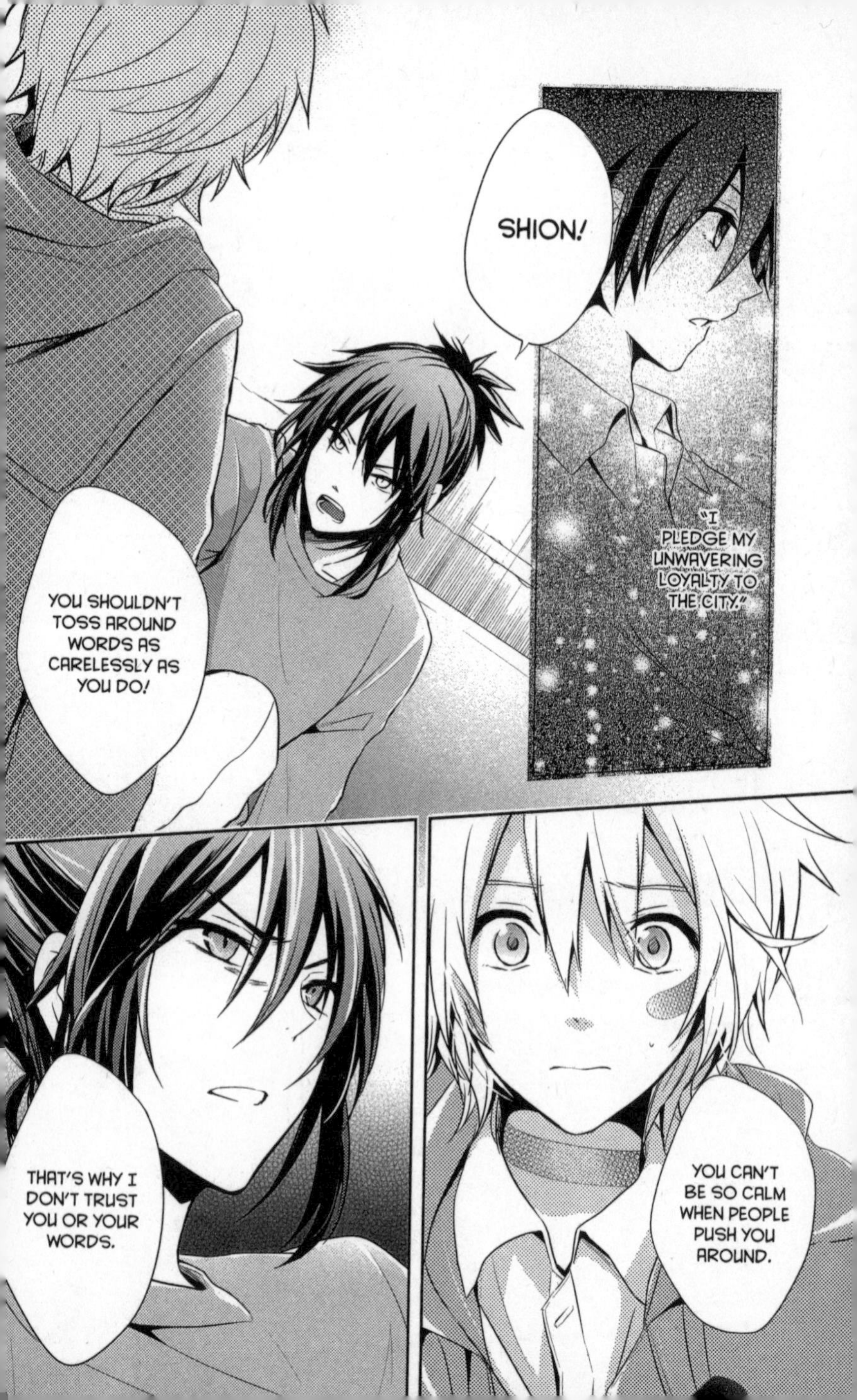
SHION!
"I PLEDGE MY UNWAVERING LOYALTY TO THE CITY."
YOU SHOULDN'T TOSS AROUND WORDS AS CARELESSLY AS YOU DO!
YOU CAN'T BE SO CALM WHEN PEOPLE PUSH YOU AROUND.
THAT'S WHY I DON'T TRUST YOU OR YOUR WORDS.

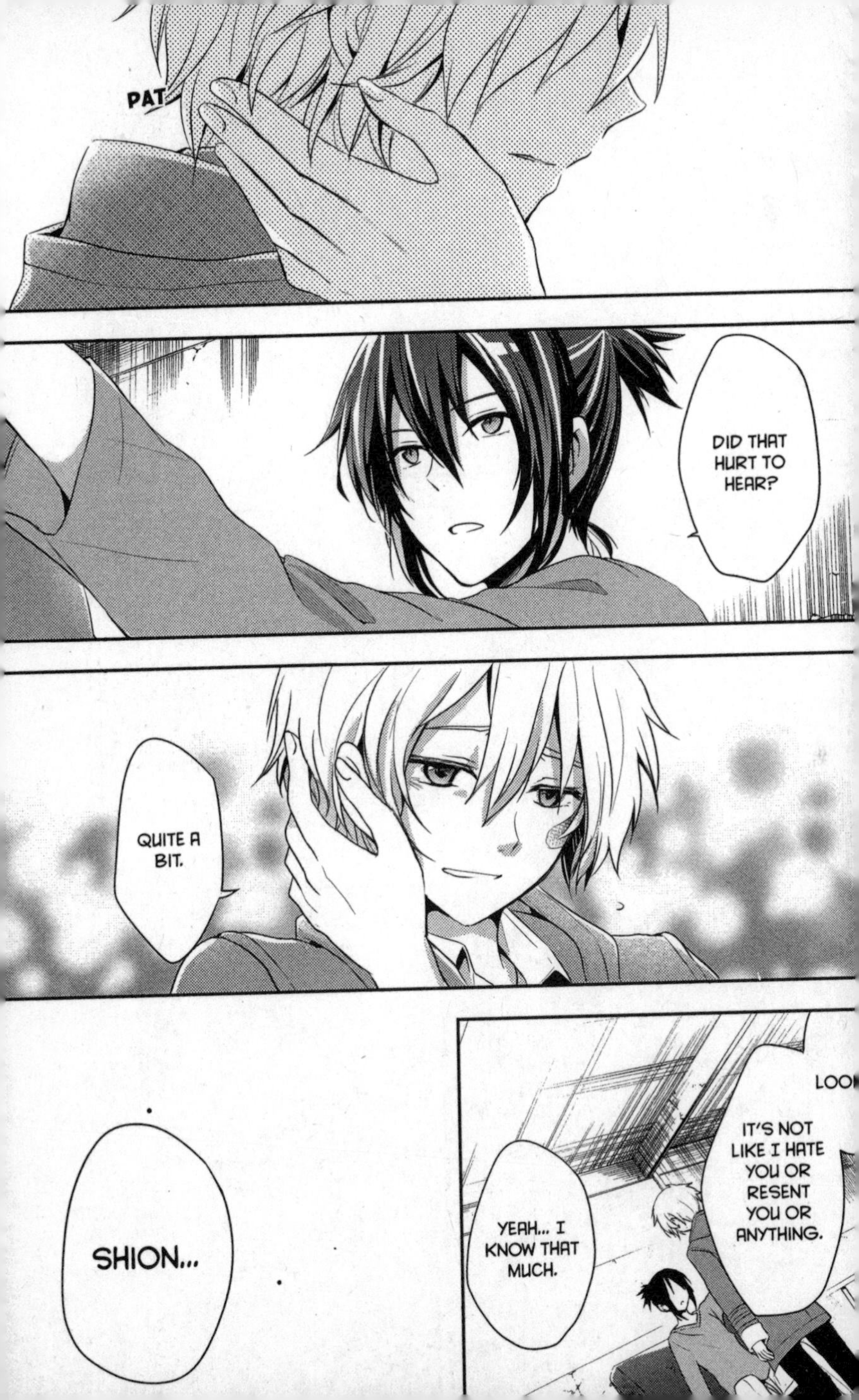
PAT
DID THAT HURT TO HEAR?
QUITE A BIT.
LOO
IT'S NOT LIKE I HATE YOU OR RESENT YOU OR ANYTHING.
YEAH... I KNOW THAT MUCH.
SHION...

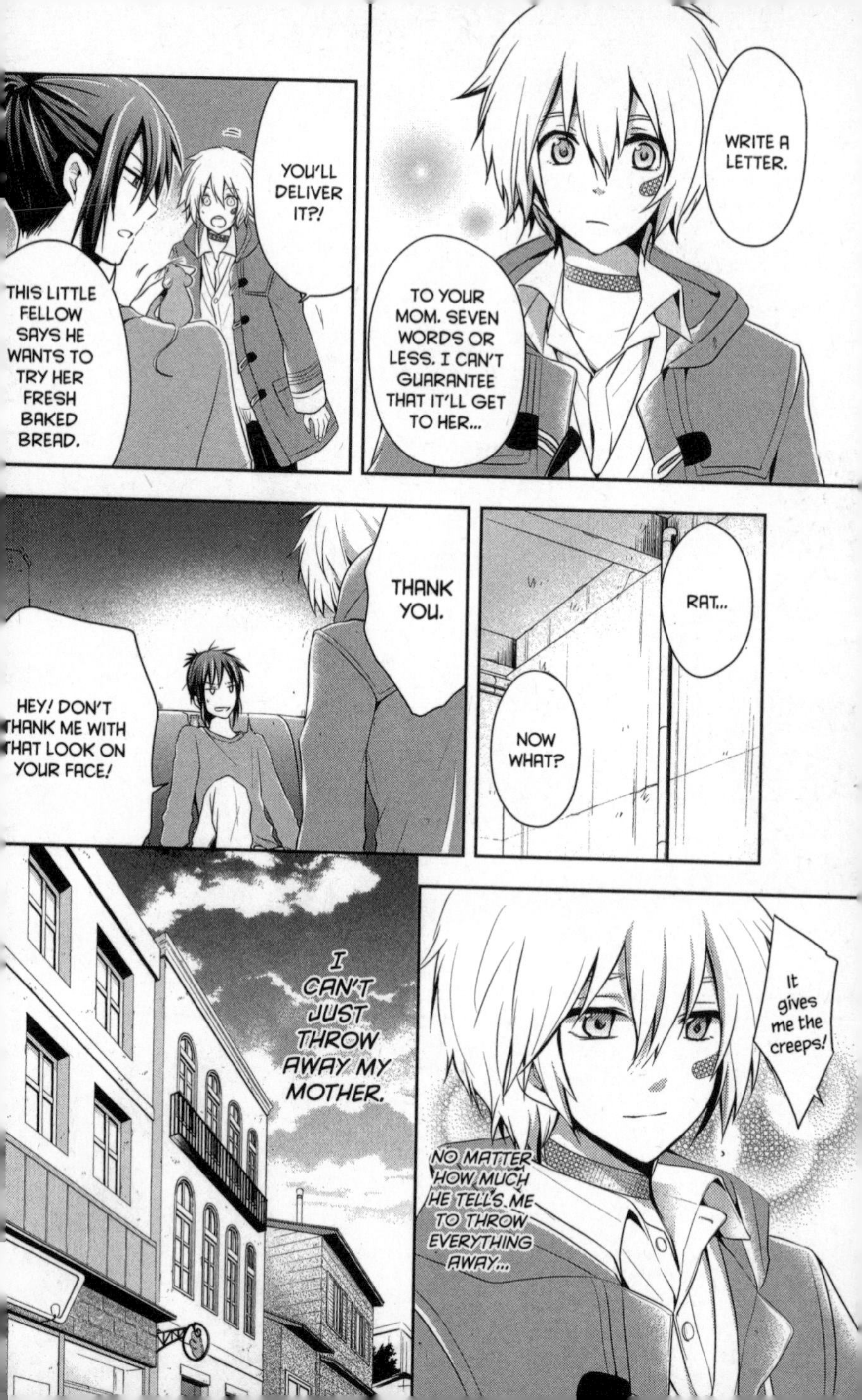
WRITE A LETTER.
TO YOUR MOM. SEVEN WORDS OR LESS. I CAN'T GUARANTEE THAT IT'LL GET TO HER...
YOU'LL DELIVER IT?!
THIS LITTLE FELLOW SAYS HE WANTS TO TRY HER FRESH BAKED BREAD.
RAT...
NOW WHAT?
THANK YOU.
HEY! DON'T THANK ME WITH THAT LOOK ON YOUR FACE!
It gives me the creeps!
NO MATTER HOW MUCH HE TELLS ME TO THROW EVERYTHING AWAY...
I CAN'T JUST THROW AWAY MY MOTHER.

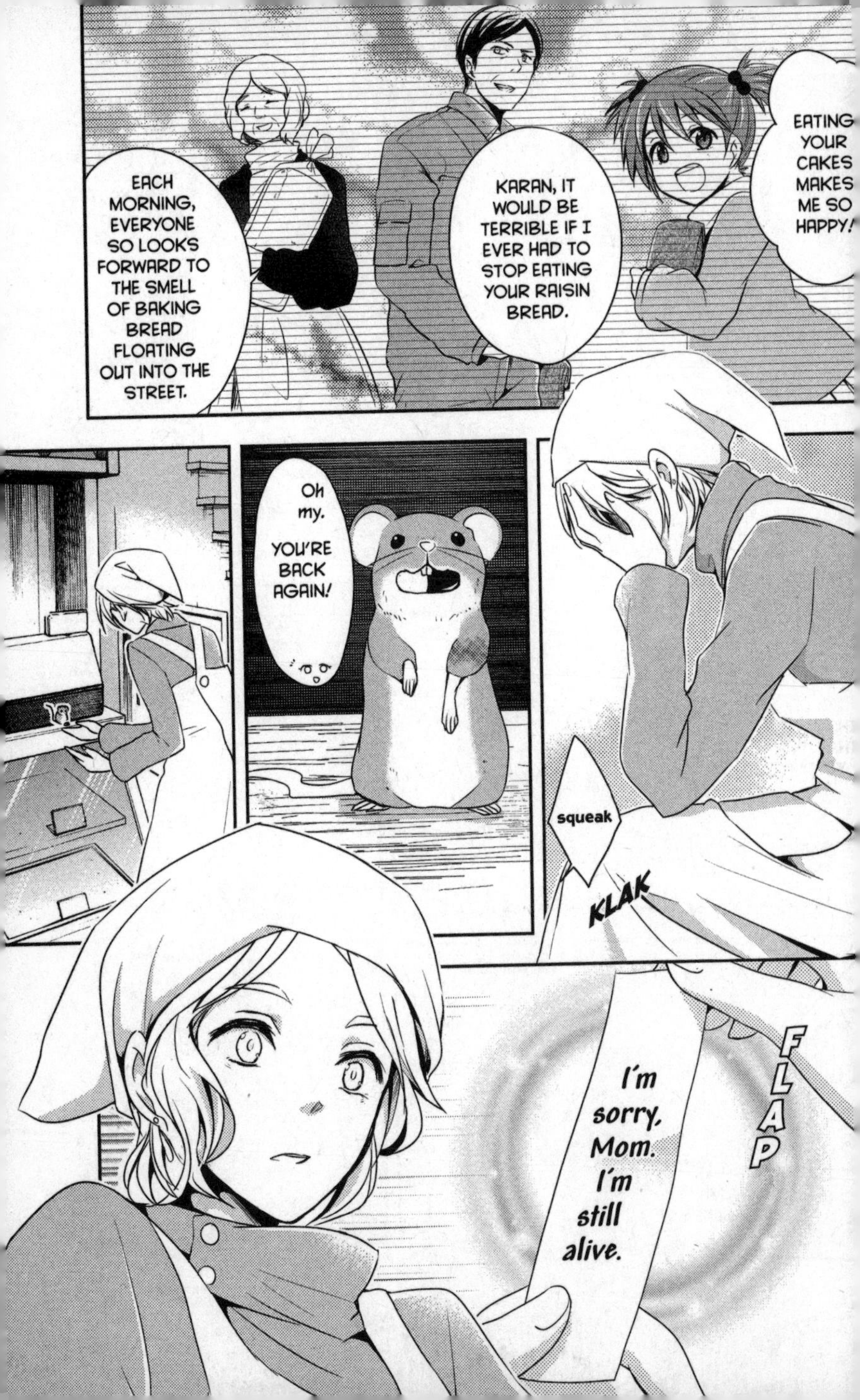
EATING YOUR CAKES MAKES ME SO HAPPY!
KARAN, IT WOULD BE TERRIBLE IF I EVER HAD TO STOP EATING YOUR RAISIN BREAD.
EACH MORNING, EVERYONE SO LOOKS FORWARD TO THE SMELL OF BAKING BREAD FLOATING OUT INTO THE STREET.
squeak
KLAK
Oh my.
YOU'RE BACK AGAIN!
FLAP
I'm sorry, Mom. I'm still alive.

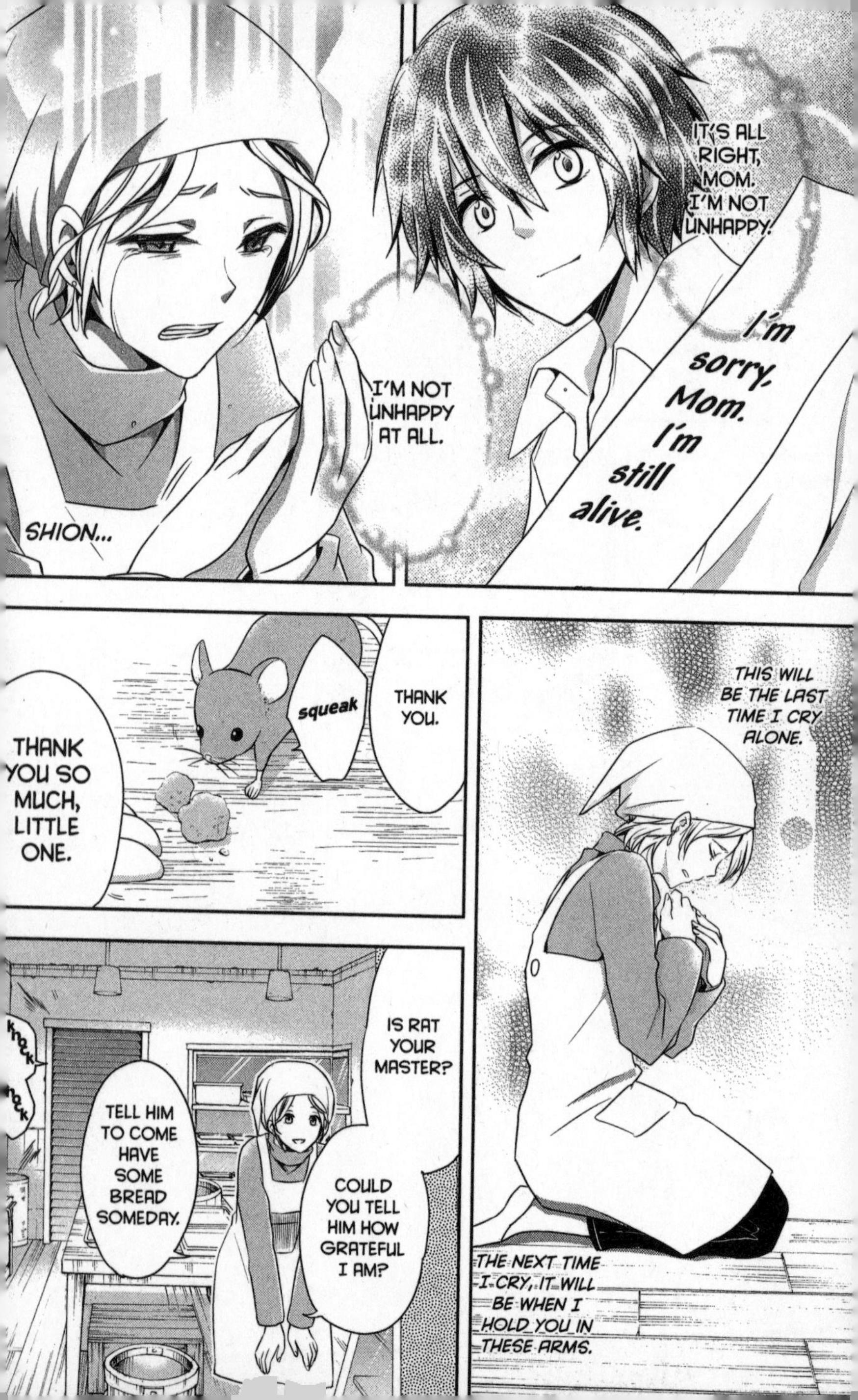
IT'S ALL RIGHT, MOM. I'M NOT UNHAPPY.
I'm sorry, Mom. I'm still alive.
I'M NOT UNHAPPY AT ALL.
SHION...
THIS WILL BE THE LAST TIME I CRY ALONE.
THE NEXT TIME I CRY, IT WILL BE WHEN I HOLD YOU IN THESE ARMS.
THANK YOU.
squeak
THANK YOU SO MUCH, LITTLE ONE.
IS RAT YOUR MASTER?
COULD YOU TELL HIM HOW GRATEFUL I AM?
knock
knock
TELL HIM TO COME HAVE SOME BREAD SOMEDAY.

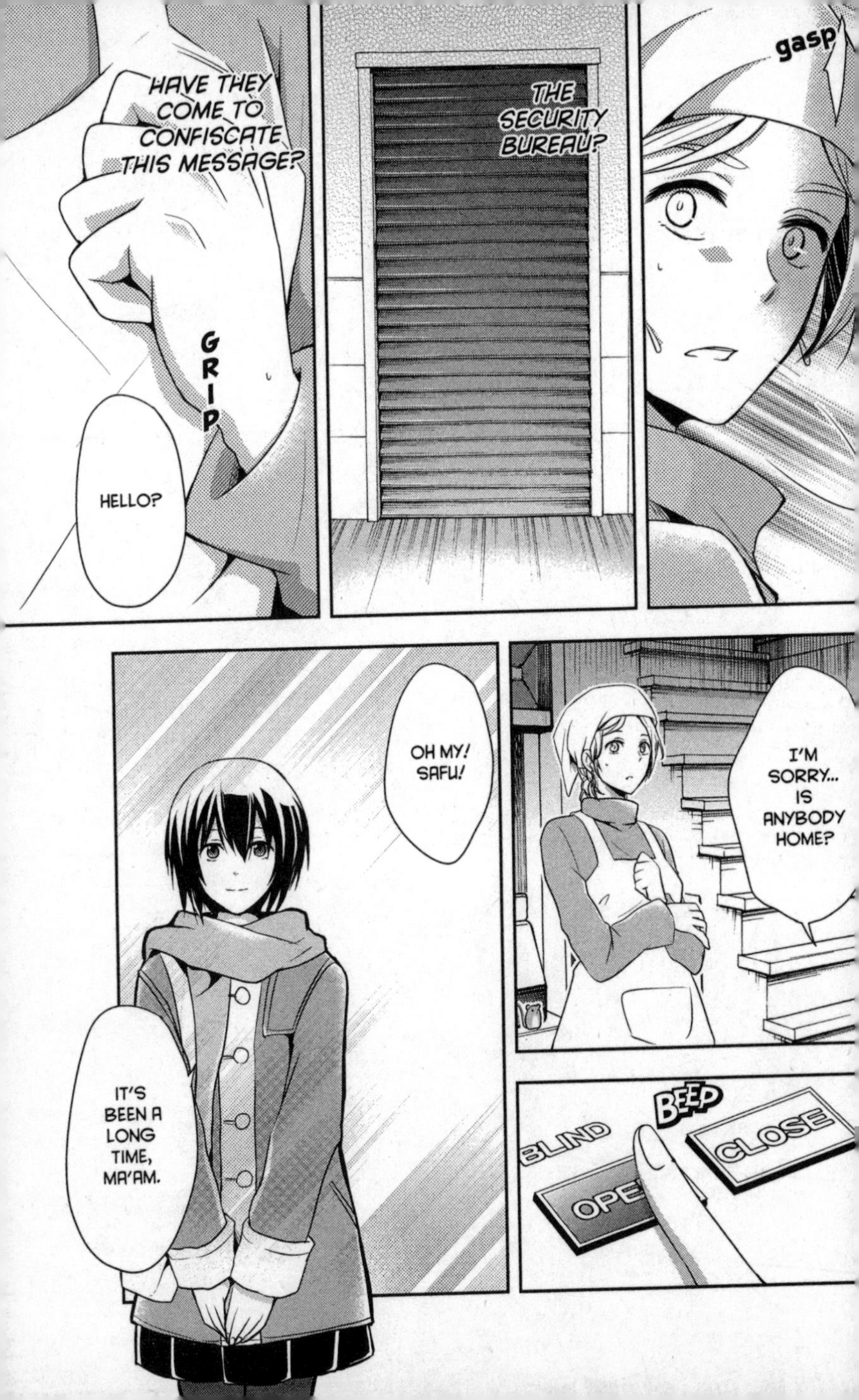
gasp
THE SECURITY BUREAU?
HAVE THEY COME TO CONFISCATE THIS MESSAGE?
GRIP
HELLO?
I'M SORRY... IS ANYBODY HOME?
BEEP
BLIND
CLOSE
OH MY! SAFU!
IT'S BEEN A LONG TIME, MA'AM.

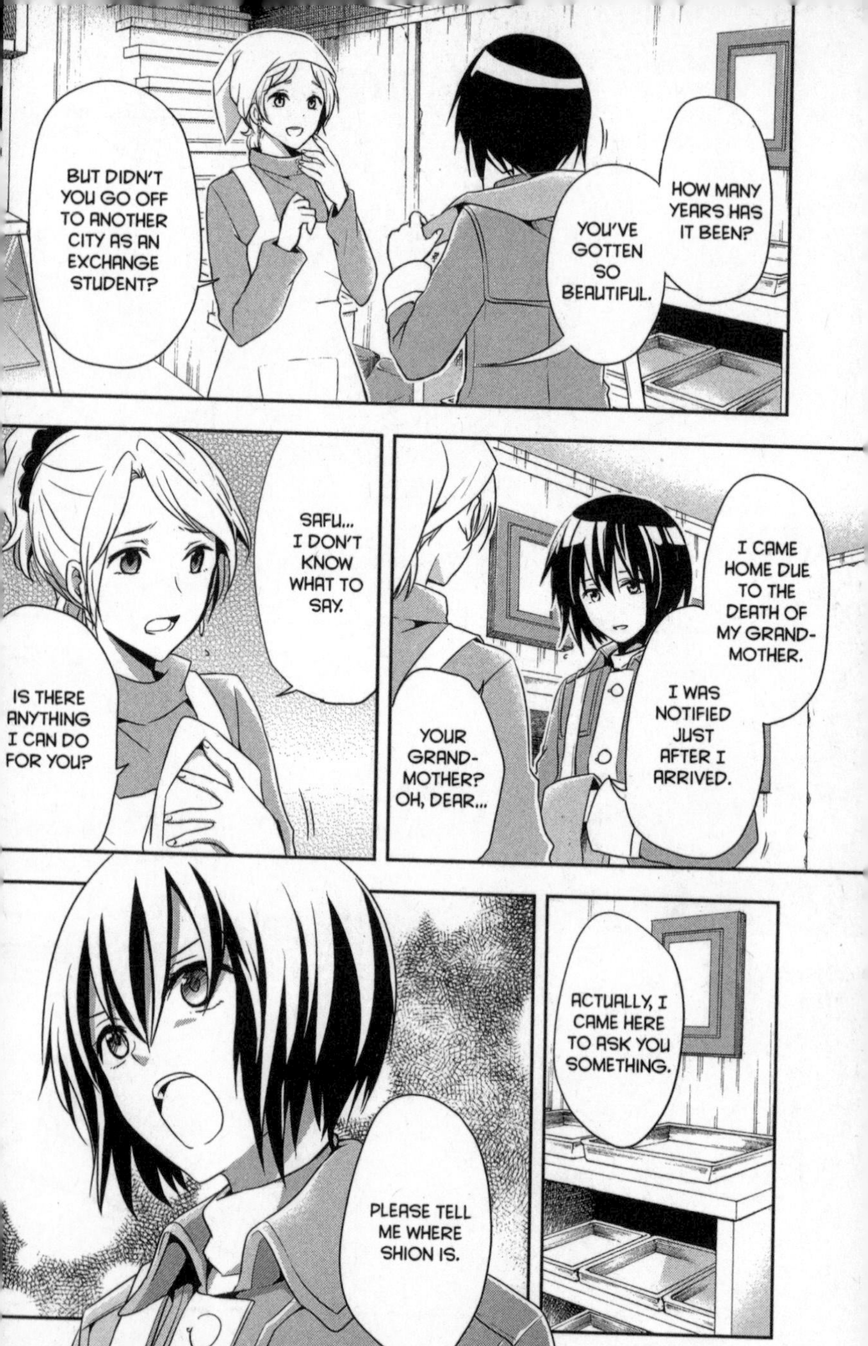
HOW MANY YEARS HAS IT BEEN?
YOU'VE GOTTEN SO BEAUTIFUL.
BUT DIDN'T YOU GO OFF TO ANOTHER CITY AS AN EXCHANGE STUDENT?
I CAME HOME DUE TO THE DEATH OF MY GRAND-MOTHER.
I WAS NOTIFIED JUST AFTER I ARRIVED.
YOUR GRAND-MOTHER? OH, DEAR...
SAFU... I DON'T KNOW WHAT TO SAY.
IS THERE ANYTHING I CAN DO FOR YOU?
ACTUALLY, I CAME HERE TO ASK YOU SOMETHING.
PLEASE TELL ME WHERE SHION IS.

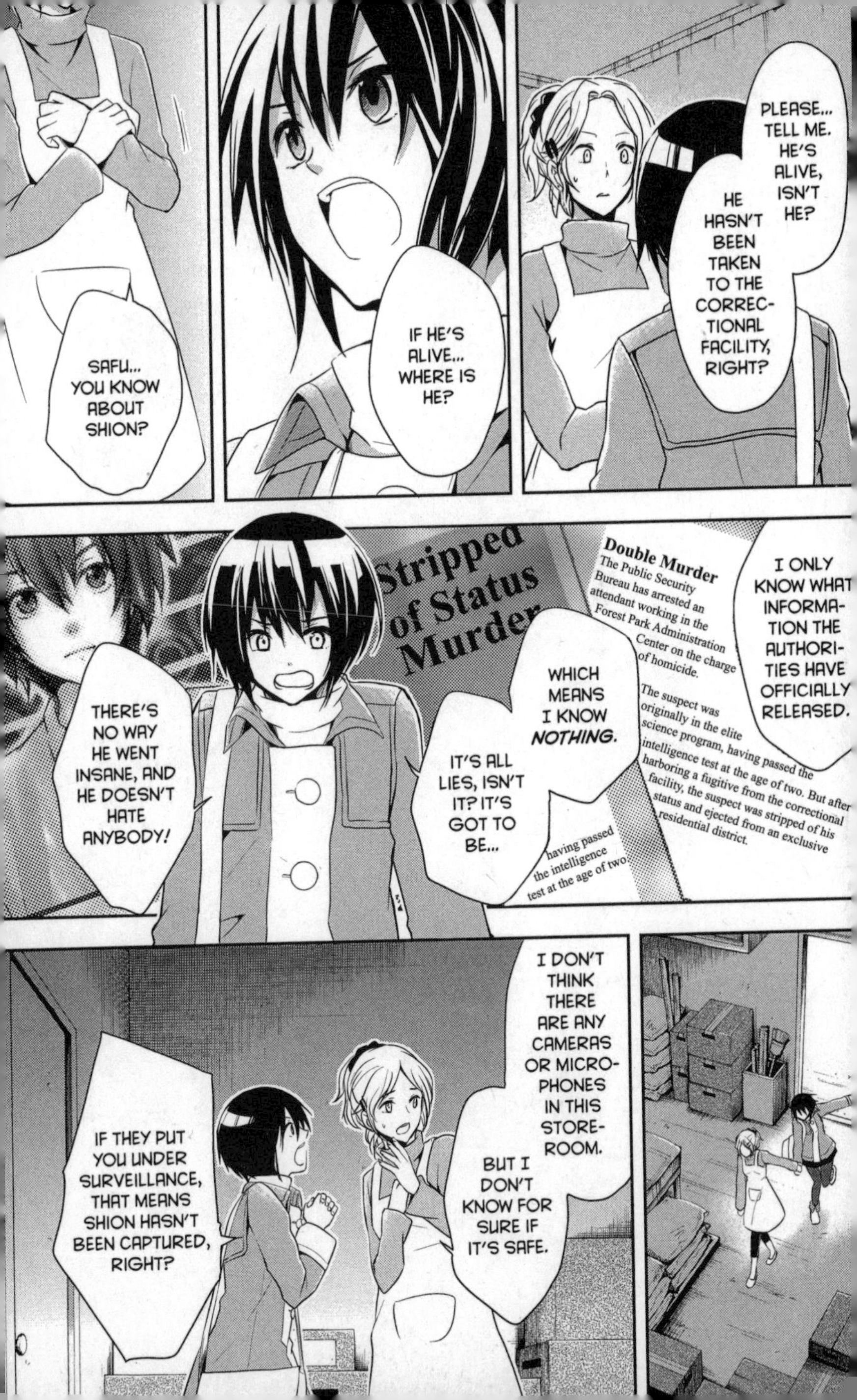
PLEASE... TELL ME. HE'S ALIVE, ISN'T HE?
HE HASN'T BEEN TAKEN TO THE CORREC-TIONAL FACILITY, RIGHT?
IF HE'S ALIVE... WHERE IS HE?
SAFU... YOU KNOW ABOUT SHION?
I ONLY KNOW WHAT INFORMA-TION THE AUTHORI-TIES HAVE OFFICIALLY RELEASED.
Double Murder
The Public Security Bureau has arrested an attendant working in the Forest Park Administration Center on the charge of homicide.
The suspect was originally in the elite science program, having passed the intelligence test at the age of two. But after harboring a fugitive from the correctional facility, the suspect was stripped of his status and ejected from an exclusive residential district.
Stripped of Status Murder
having passed the intelligence test at the age of two
WHICH MEANS I KNOW *NOTHING.*
IT'S ALL LIES, ISN'T IT? IT'S GOT TO BE...
THERE'S NO WAY HE WENT INSANE, AND HE DOESN'T HATE ANYBODY!
I DON'T THINK THERE ARE ANY CAMERAS OR MICRO-PHONES IN THIS STORE-ROOM.
BUT I DON'T KNOW FOR SURE IF IT'S SAFE.
IF THEY PUT YOU UNDER SURVEILLANCE, THAT MEANS SHION HASN'T BEEN CAPTURED, RIGHT?

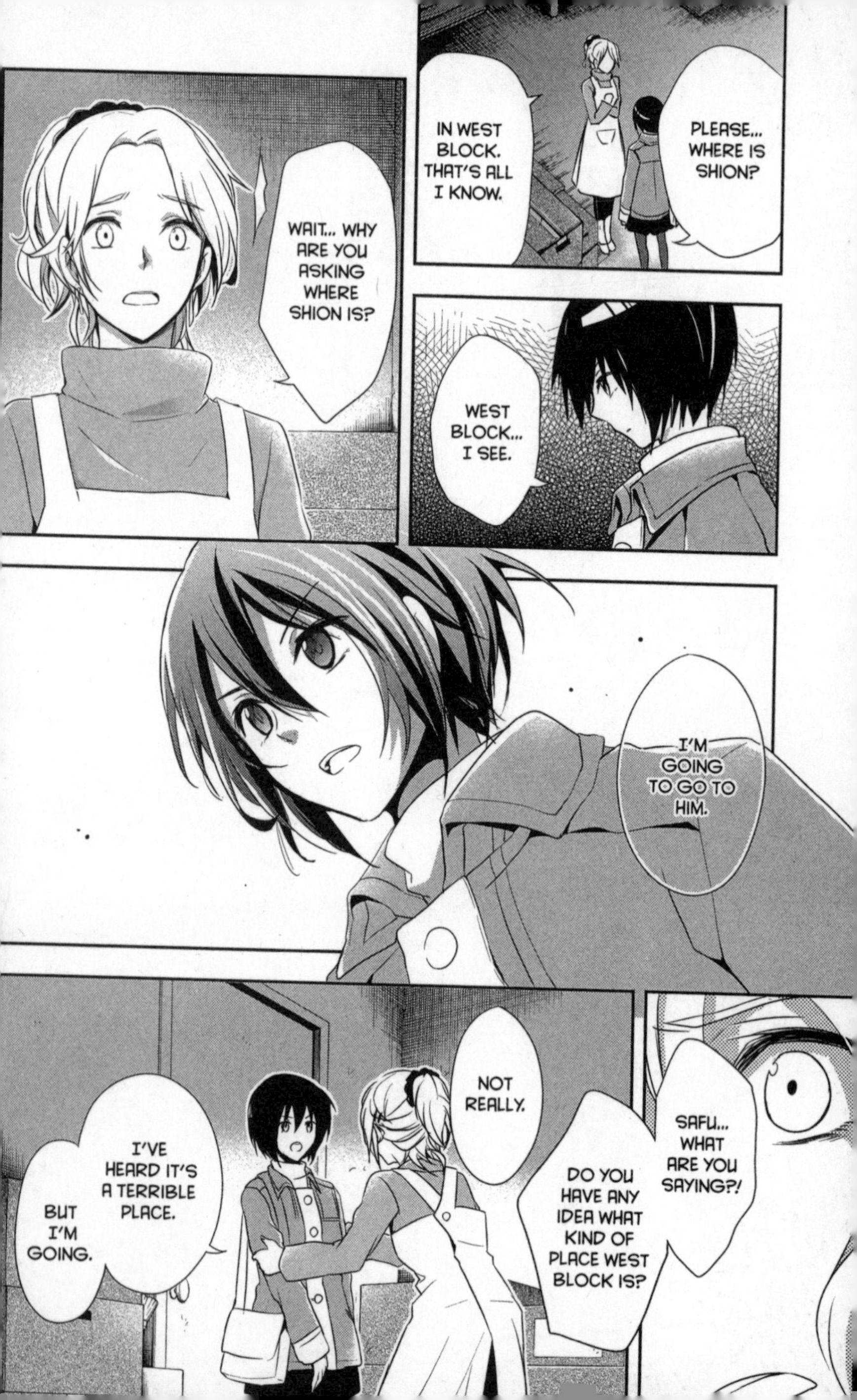

PLEASE... WHERE IS SHION?
IN WEST BLOCK. THAT'S ALL I KNOW.
WEST BLOCK... I SEE.
WAIT... WHY ARE YOU ASKING WHERE SHION IS?
I'M GOING TO GO TO HIM.
SAFU... WHAT ARE YOU SAYING?!
DO YOU HAVE ANY IDEA WHAT KIND OF PLACE WEST BLOCK IS?
NOT REALLY.
I'VE HEARD IT'S A TERRIBLE PLACE.
BUT I'M GOING.

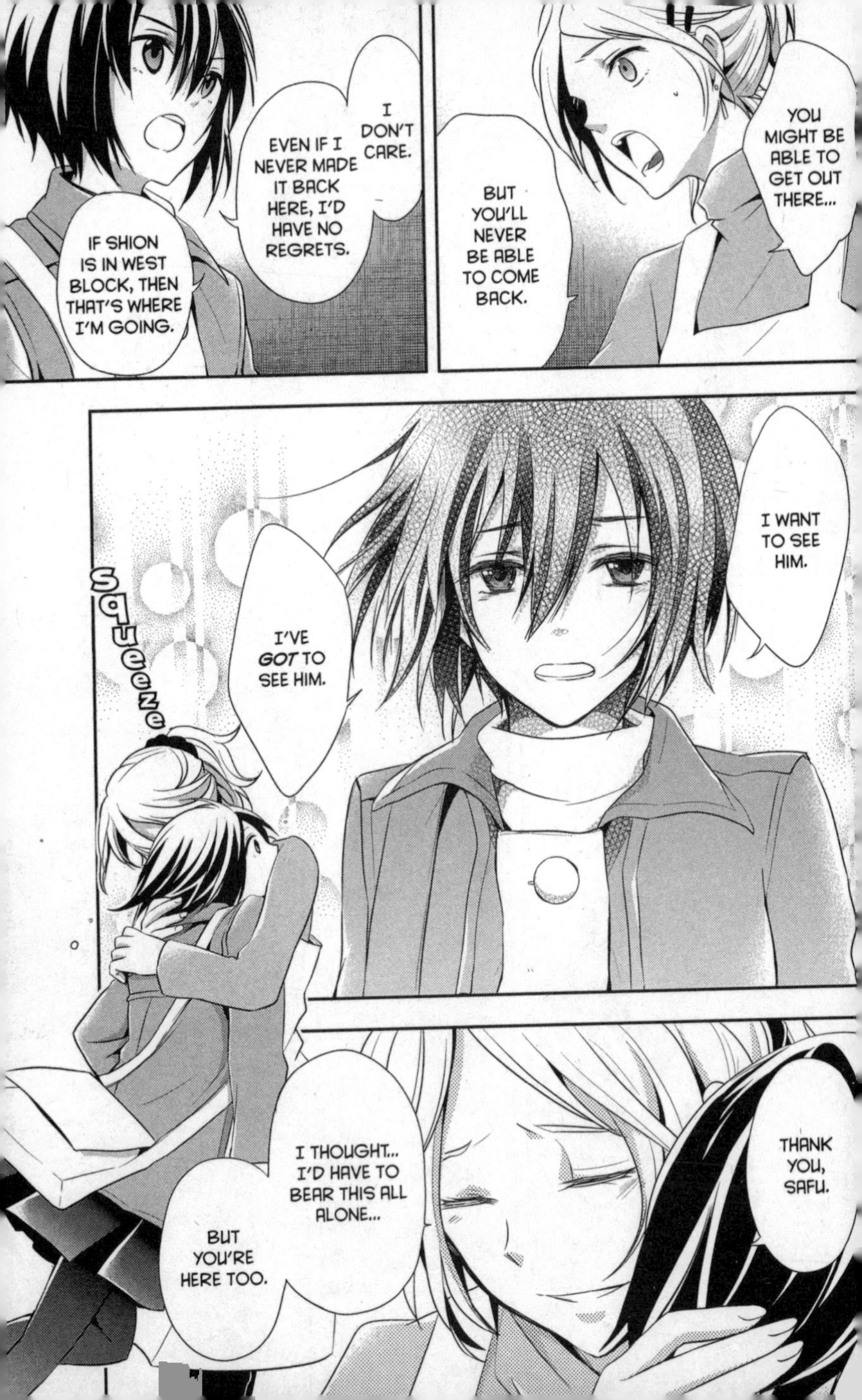
YOU MIGHT BE ABLE TO GET OUT THERE...
BUT YOU'LL NEVER BE ABLE TO COME BACK.
I DON'T CARE.
EVEN IF I NEVER MADE IT BACK HERE, I'D HAVE NO REGRETS.
IF SHION IS IN WEST BLOCK, THEN THAT'S WHERE I'M GOING.
I WANT TO SEE HIM.
I'VE *GOT* TO SEE HIM.
squeeze
THANK YOU, SAFU.
I THOUGHT... I'D HAVE TO BEAR THIS ALL ALONE...
BUT YOU'RE HERE TOO.

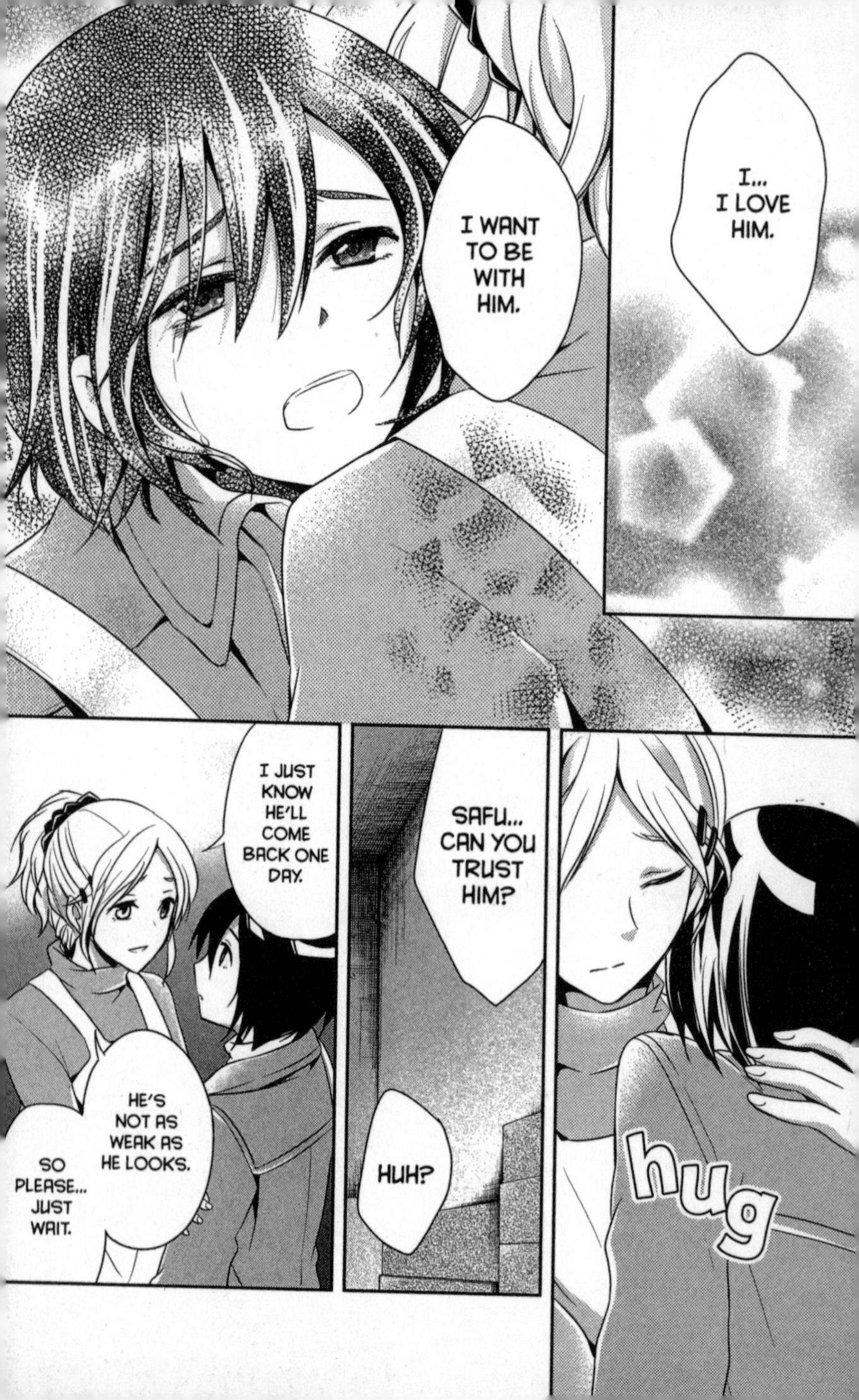
I...
I LOVE
HIM.
I WANT
TO BE
WITH
HIM.
hug
SAFU...
CAN YOU
TRUST
HIM?
HUH?
I JUST
KNOW
HE'LL
COME
BACK ONE
DAY.
HE'S
NOT AS
WEAK AS
HE LOOKS.
SO
PLEASE...
JUST
WAIT.

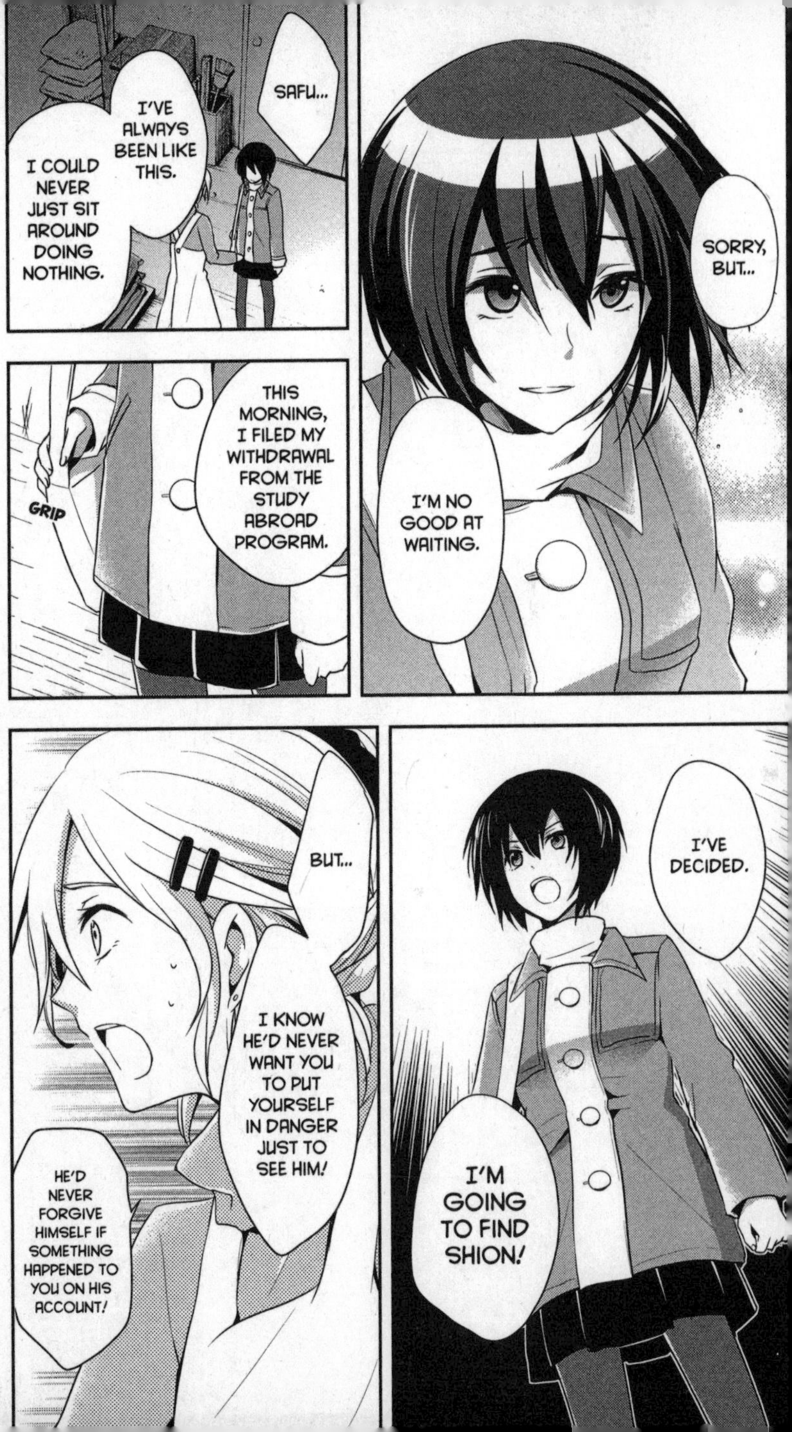
SORRY, BUT...
I'M NO GOOD AT WAITING.
SAFU...
I'VE ALWAYS BEEN LIKE THIS.
I COULD NEVER JUST SIT AROUND DOING NOTHING.
THIS MORNING, I FILED MY WITHDRAWAL FROM THE STUDY ABROAD PROGRAM.
GRIP
I'VE DECIDED.
I'M GOING TO FIND SHION!
BUT...
I KNOW HE'D NEVER WANT YOU TO PUT YOURSELF IN DANGER JUST TO SEE HIM!
HE'D NEVER FORGIVE HIMSELF IF SOMETHING HAPPENED TO YOU ON HIS ACCOUNT!

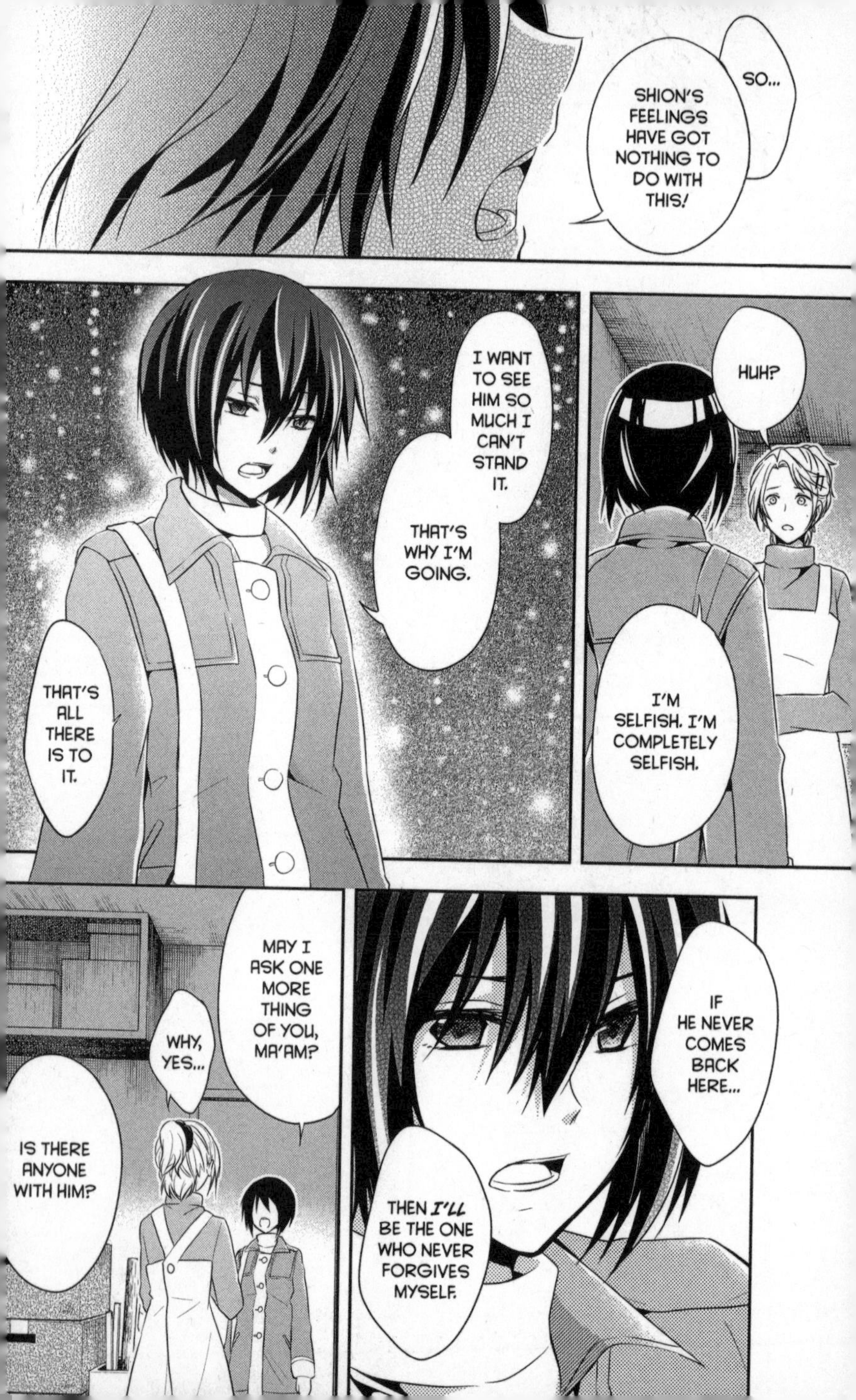
SO...
SHION'S FEELINGS HAVE GOT NOTHING TO DO WITH THIS!
HUH?
I'M SELFISH. I'M COMPLETELY SELFISH.
I WANT TO SEE HIM SO MUCH I CAN'T STAND IT.
THAT'S WHY I'M GOING.
THAT'S ALL THERE IS TO IT.
IF HE NEVER COMES BACK HERE...
THEN *I'LL* BE THE ONE WHO NEVER FORGIVES MYSELF.
MAY I ASK ONE MORE THING OF YOU, MA'AM?
WHY, YES...
IS THERE ANYONE WITH HIM?

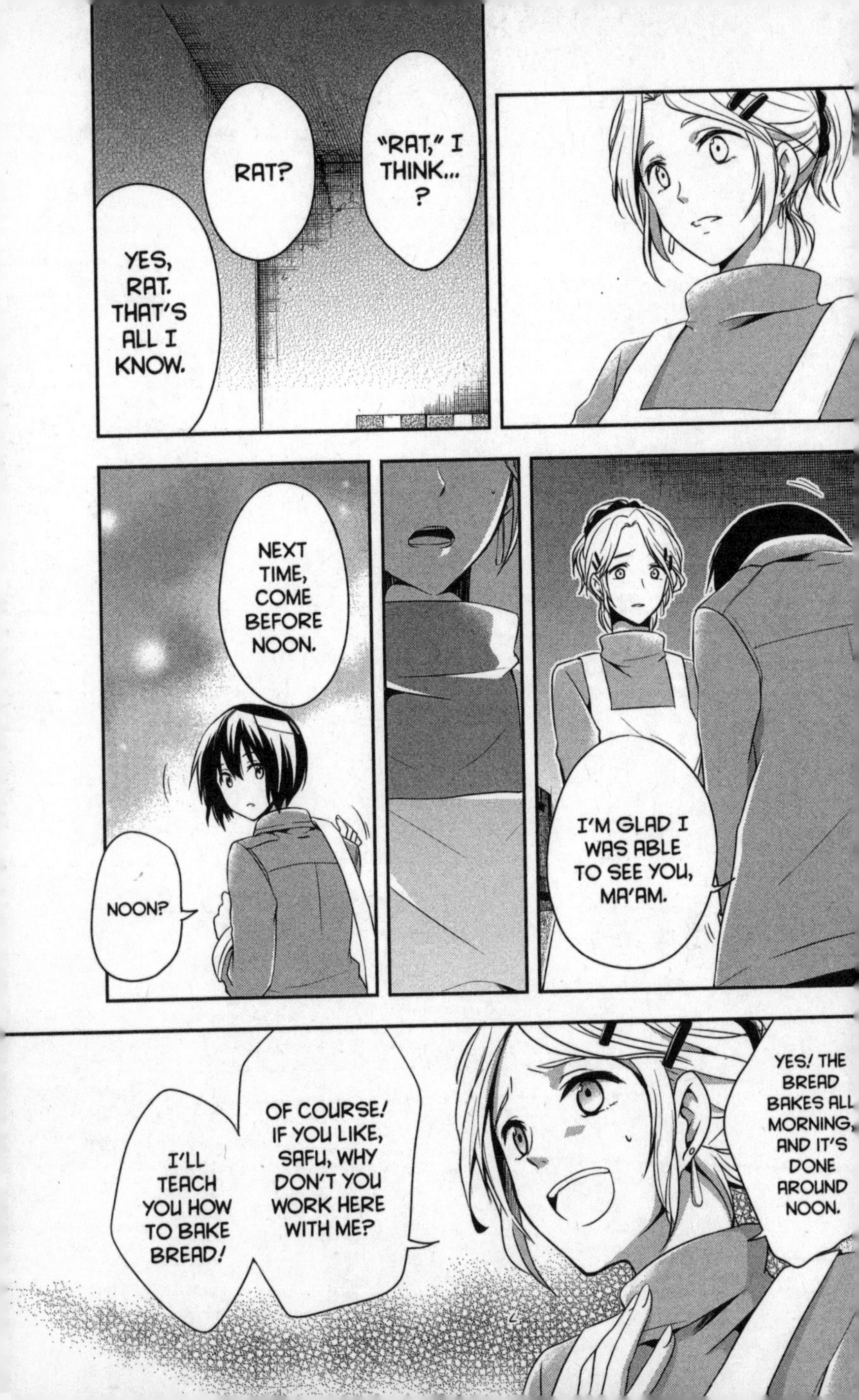
"RAT," I THINK... ?
RAT?
YES, RAT. THAT'S ALL I KNOW.
I'M GLAD I WAS ABLE TO SEE YOU, MA'AM.
NEXT TIME, COME BEFORE NOON.
NOON?
YES! THE BREAD BAKES ALL MORNING, AND IT'S DONE AROUND NOON.
OF COURSE! IF YOU LIKE, SAFU, WHY DON'T YOU WORK HERE WITH ME?
I'LL TEACH YOU HOW TO BAKE BREAD!

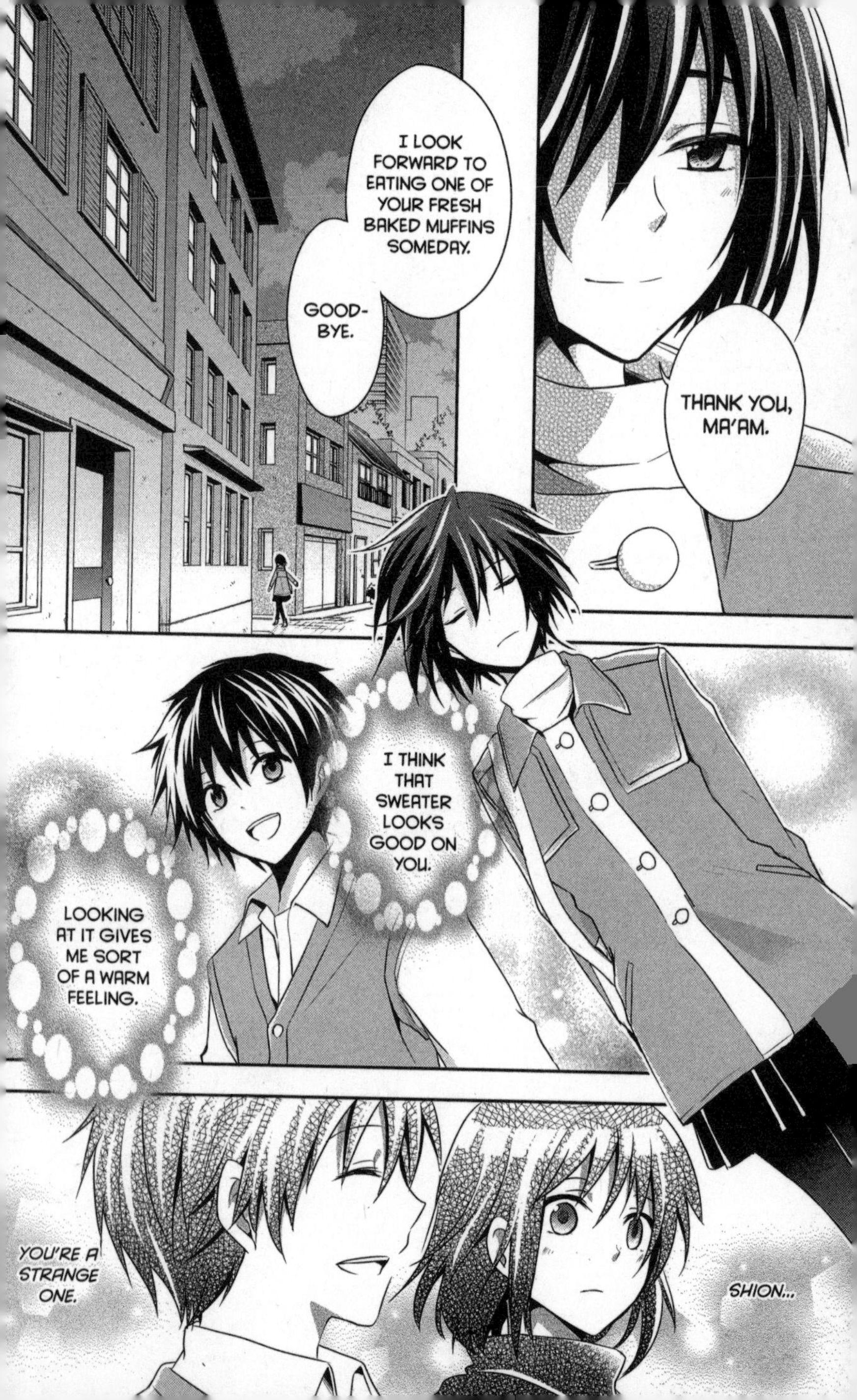
THANK YOU, MA'AM.
I LOOK FORWARD TO EATING ONE OF YOUR FRESH BAKED MUFFINS SOMEDAY.
GOOD-BYE.
I THINK THAT SWEATER LOOKS GOOD ON YOU.
LOOKING AT IT GIVES ME SORT OF A WARM FEELING.
SHION...
YOU'RE A STRANGE ONE.

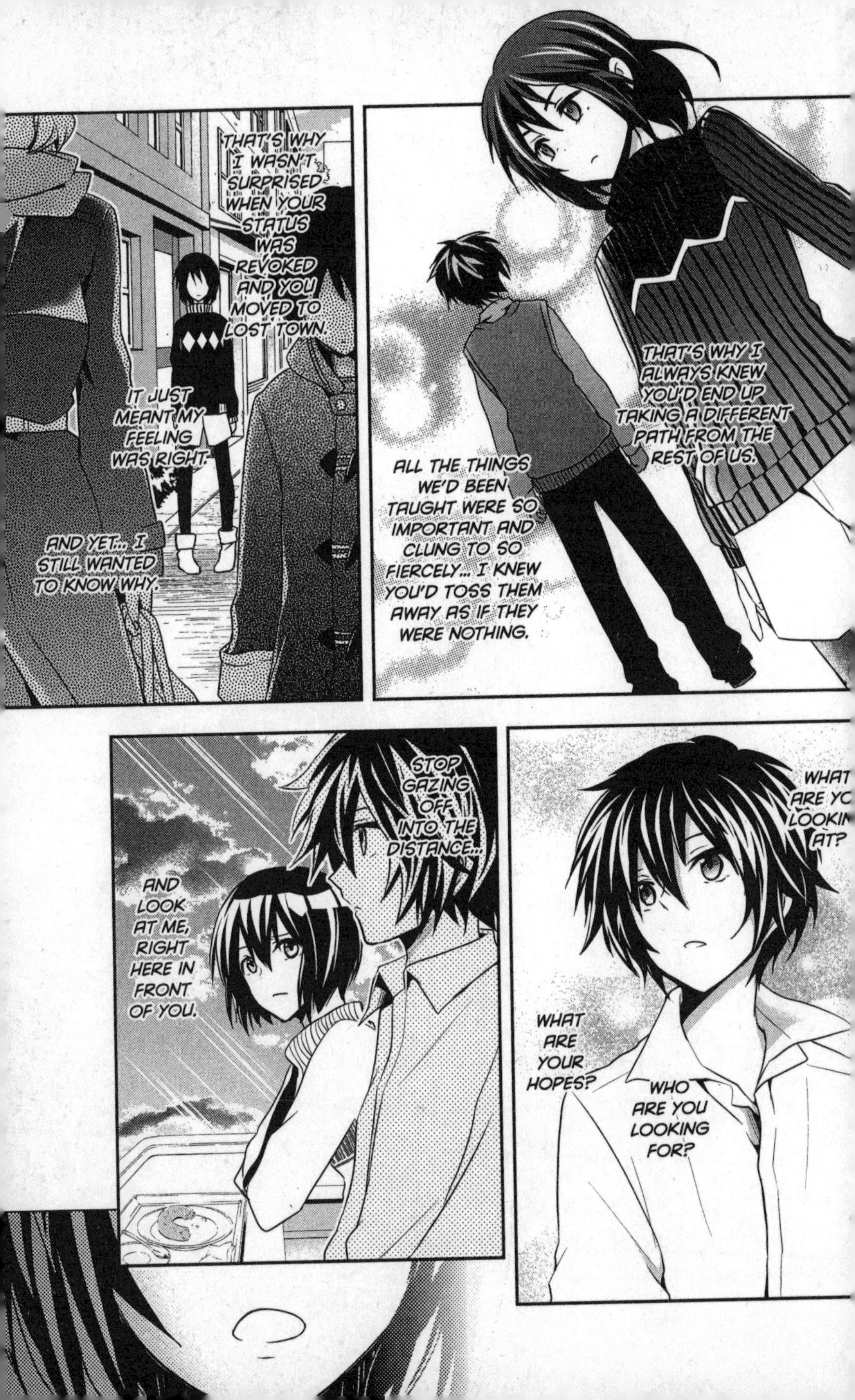
THAT'S WHY I ALWAYS KNEW YOU'D END UP TAKING A DIFFERENT PATH FROM THE REST OF US.
ALL THE THINGS WE'D BEEN TAUGHT WERE SO IMPORTANT AND CLUNG TO SO FIERCELY... I KNEW YOU'D TOSS THEM AWAY AS IF THEY WERE NOTHING.
THAT'S WHY I WASN'T SURPRISED WHEN YOUR STATUS WAS REVOKED AND YOU MOVED TO LOST TOWN.
IT JUST MEANT MY FEELING WAS RIGHT.
AND YET... I STILL WANTED TO KNOW WHY.
WHAT ARE YO LOOKIN AT?
WHAT ARE YOUR HOPES?
WHO ARE YOU LOOKING FOR?
STOP GAZING OFF INTO THE DISTANCE...
AND LOOK AT ME, RIGHT HERE IN FRONT OF YOU.

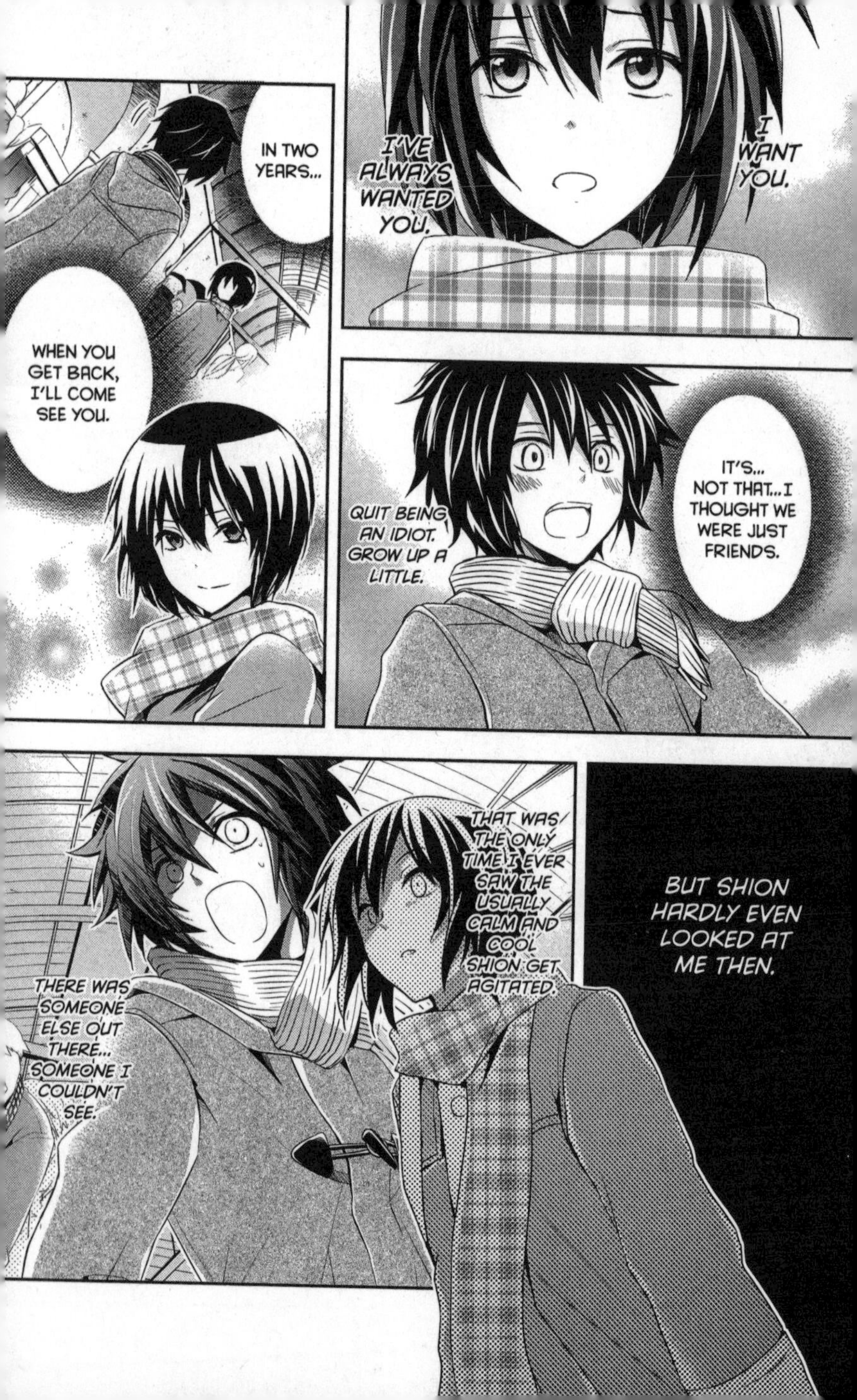
I WANT YOU.
I'VE ALWAYS WANTED YOU.
IT'S... NOT THAT...I THOUGHT WE WERE JUST FRIENDS.
QUIT BEING AN IDIOT. GROW UP A LITTLE.
IN TWO YEARS...
WHEN YOU GET BACK, I'LL COME SEE YOU.
BUT SHION HARDLY EVEN LOOKED AT ME THEN.
THAT WAS THE ONLY TIME I EVER SAW THE USUALLY CALM AND COOL SHION GET AGITATED.
THERE WAS SOMEONE ELSE OUT THERE... SOMEONE I COULDN'T SEE.

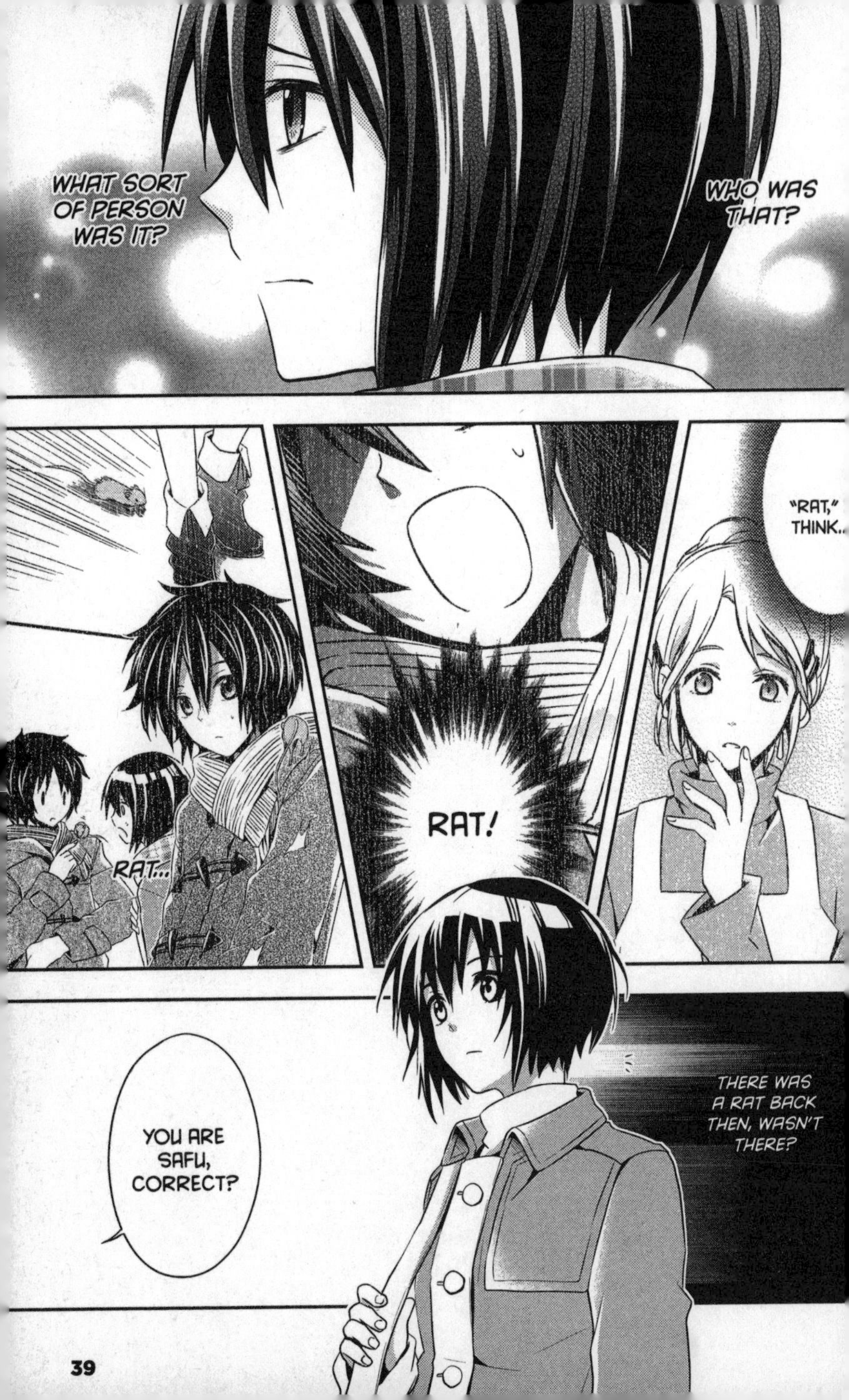
WHO WAS THAT?
WHAT SORT OF PERSON WAS IT?
"RAT," THINK..
RAT!
RAT...
THERE WAS A RAT BACK THEN, WASN'T THERE?
YOU ARE SAFU, CORRECT?

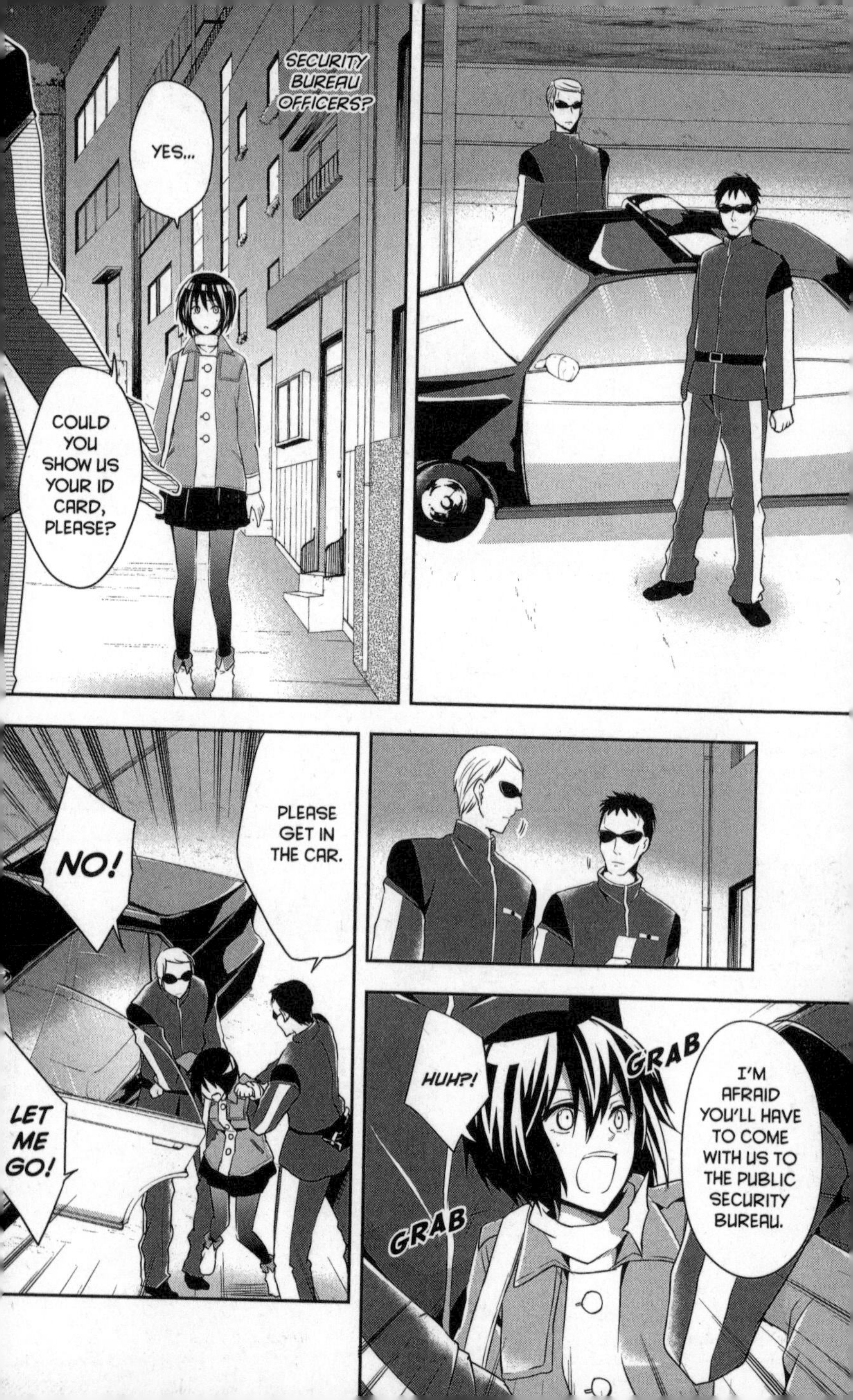
SECURITY BUREAU OFFICERS?
YES...
COULD YOU SHOW US YOUR ID CARD, PLEASE?
I'M AFRAID YOU'LL HAVE TO COME WITH US TO THE PUBLIC SECURITY BUREAU.
GRAB
HUH?!
GRAB
PLEASE GET IN THE CAR.
NO!
LET ME GO!

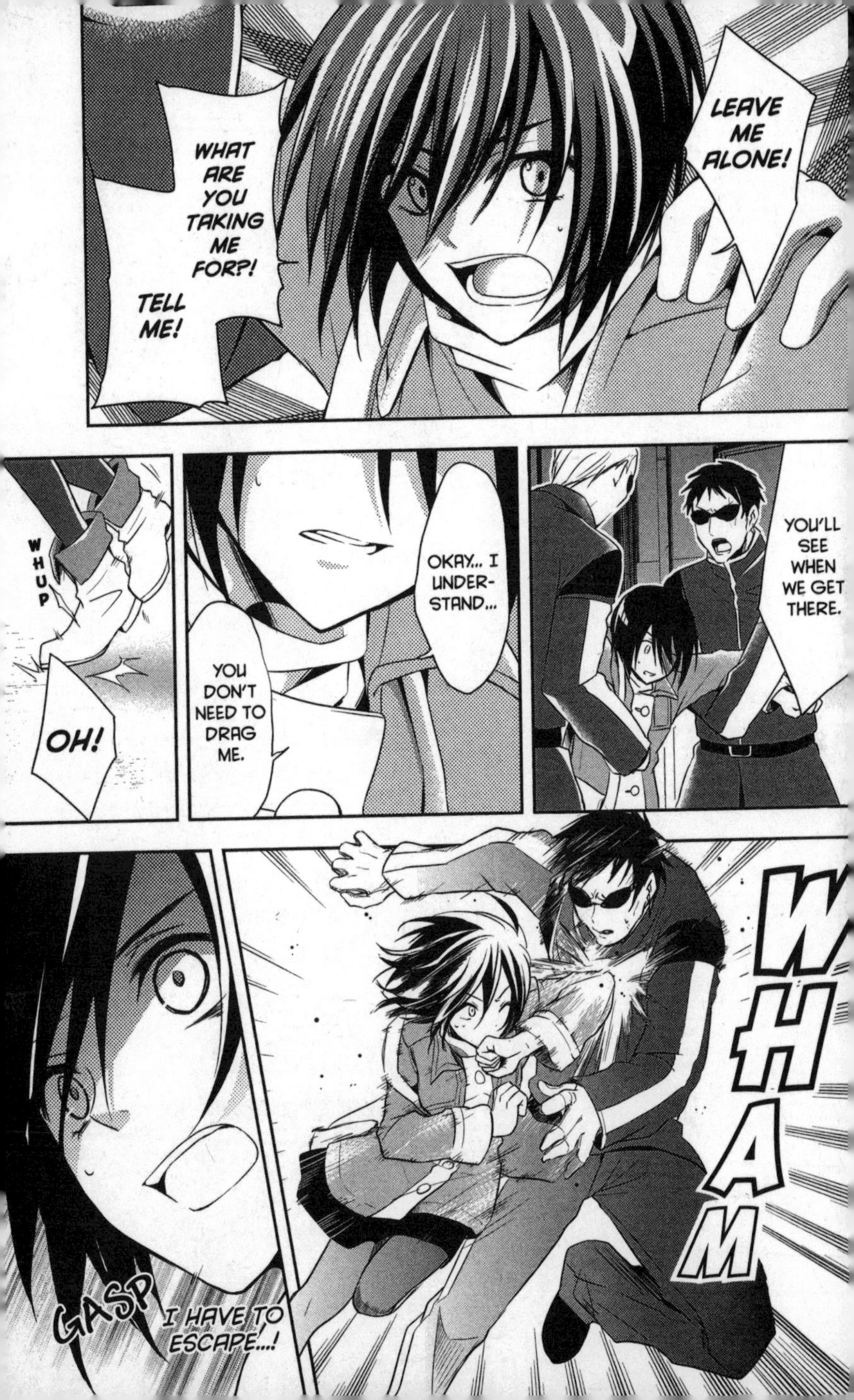
LEAVE ME ALONE!
WHAT ARE YOU TAKING ME FOR?!
TELL ME!
YOU'LL SEE WHEN WE GET THERE.
OKAY... I UNDER-STAND...
YOU DON'T NEED TO DRAG ME.
WHUP
OH!
WHAM
GASP
I HAVE TO ESCAPE...!

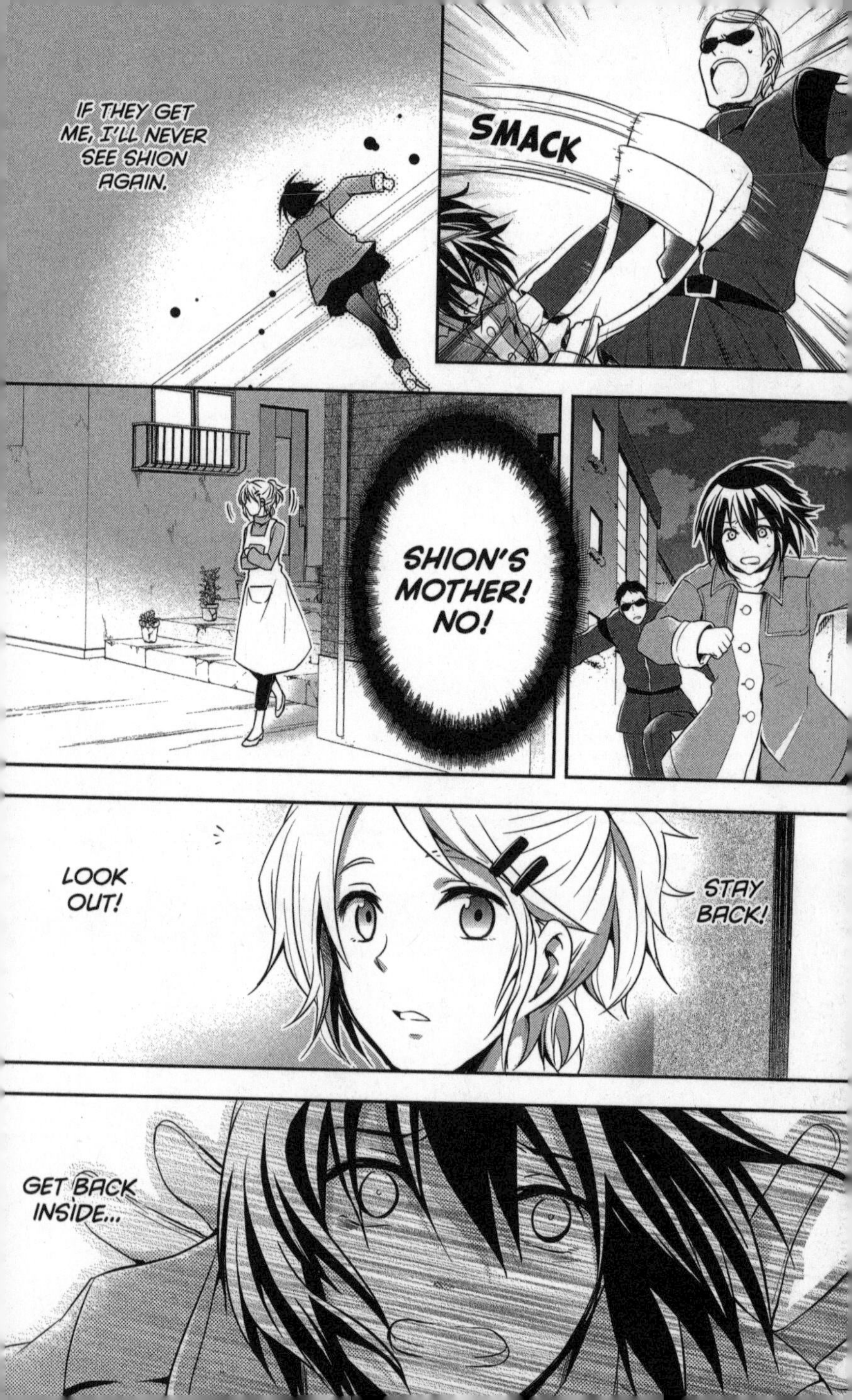
SMACK
IF THEY GET ME, I'LL NEVER SEE SHION AGAIN.
SHION'S MOTHER! NO!
STAY BACK!
LOOK OUT!
GET BACK INSIDE...

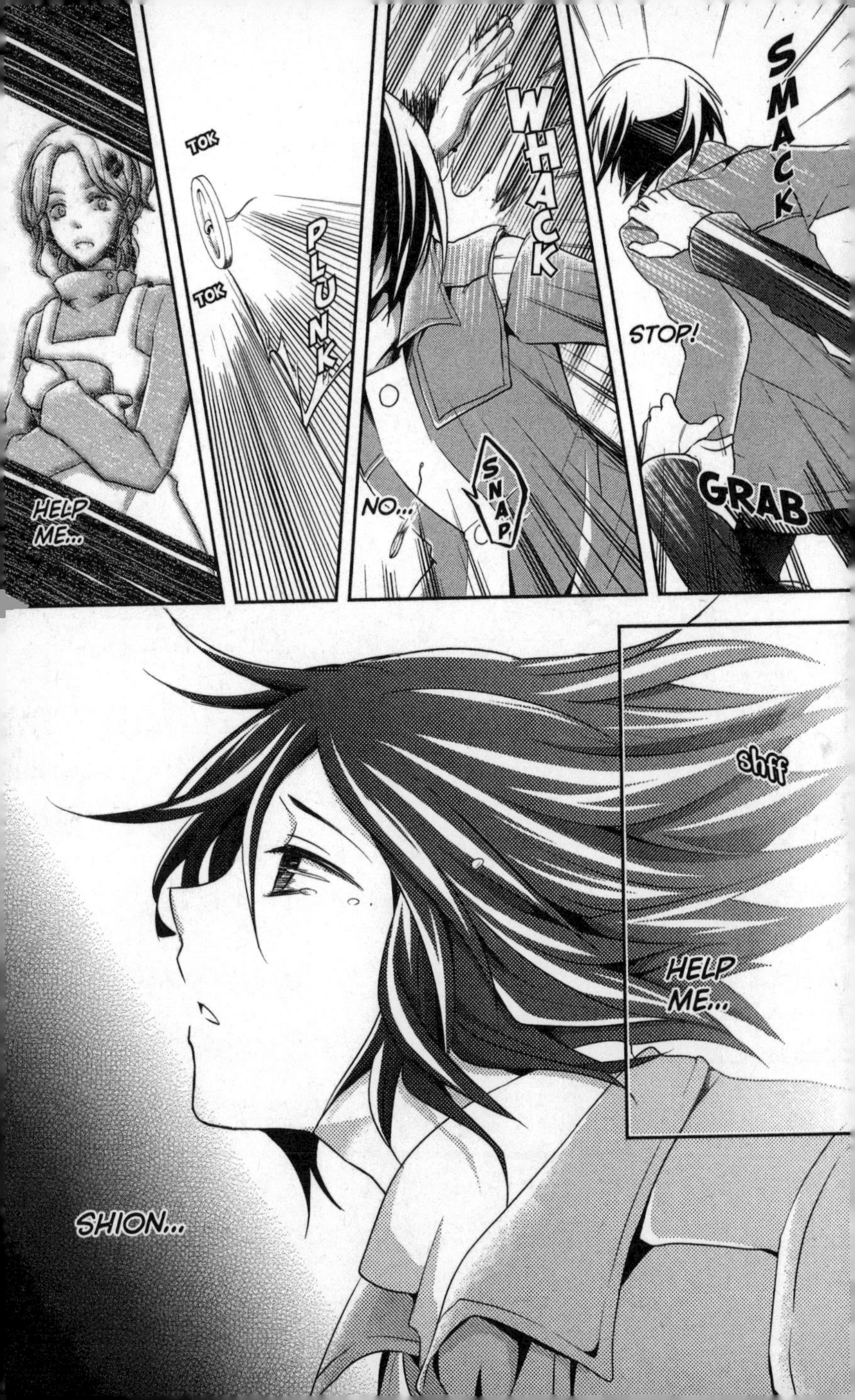
SMACK
STOP!
GRAB
WHACK
SNAP
NO...
TOK
TOK
PLUNK
HELP ME...
shff
HELP ME...
SHION...

Chapter 9: These Beautiful Things

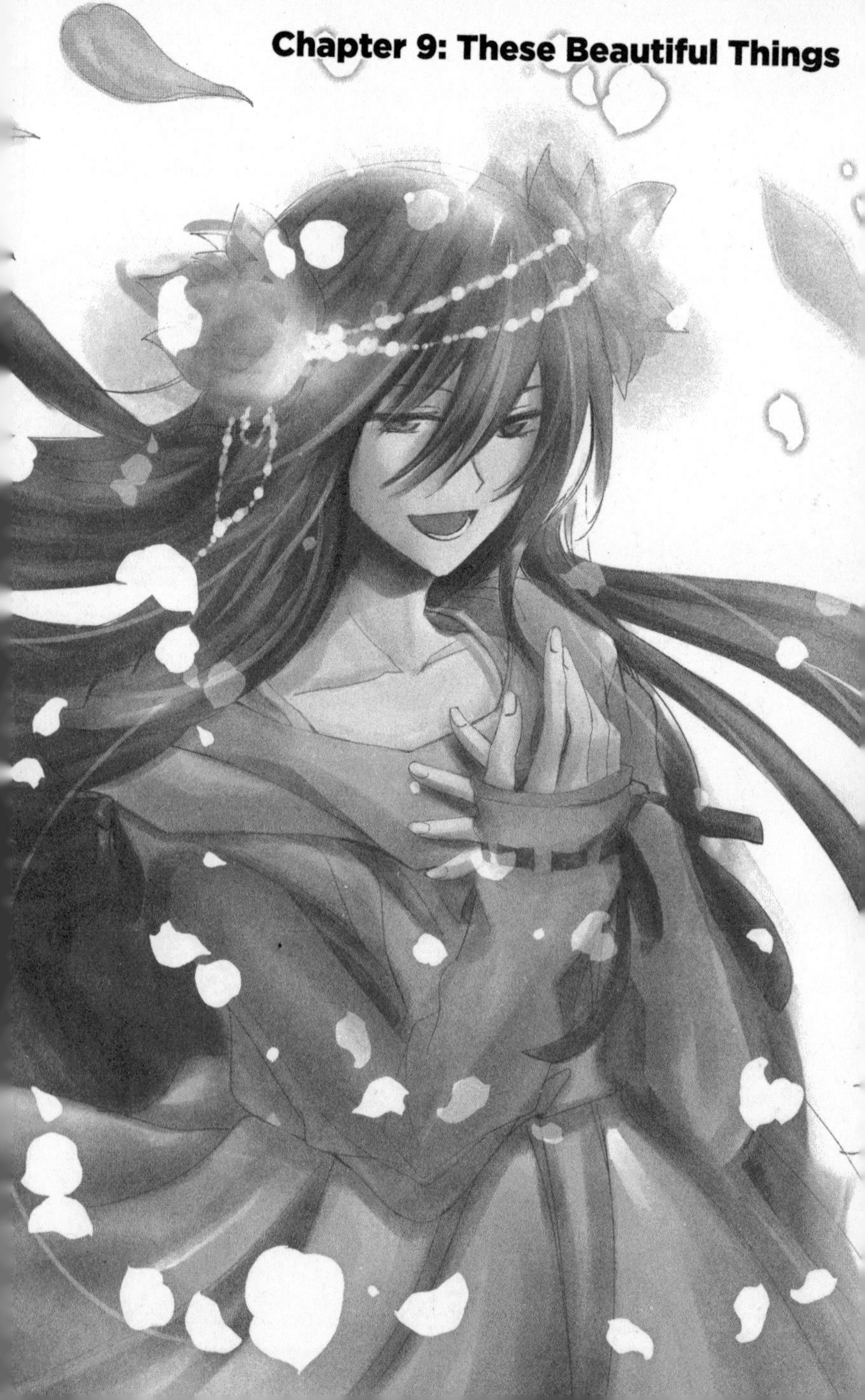

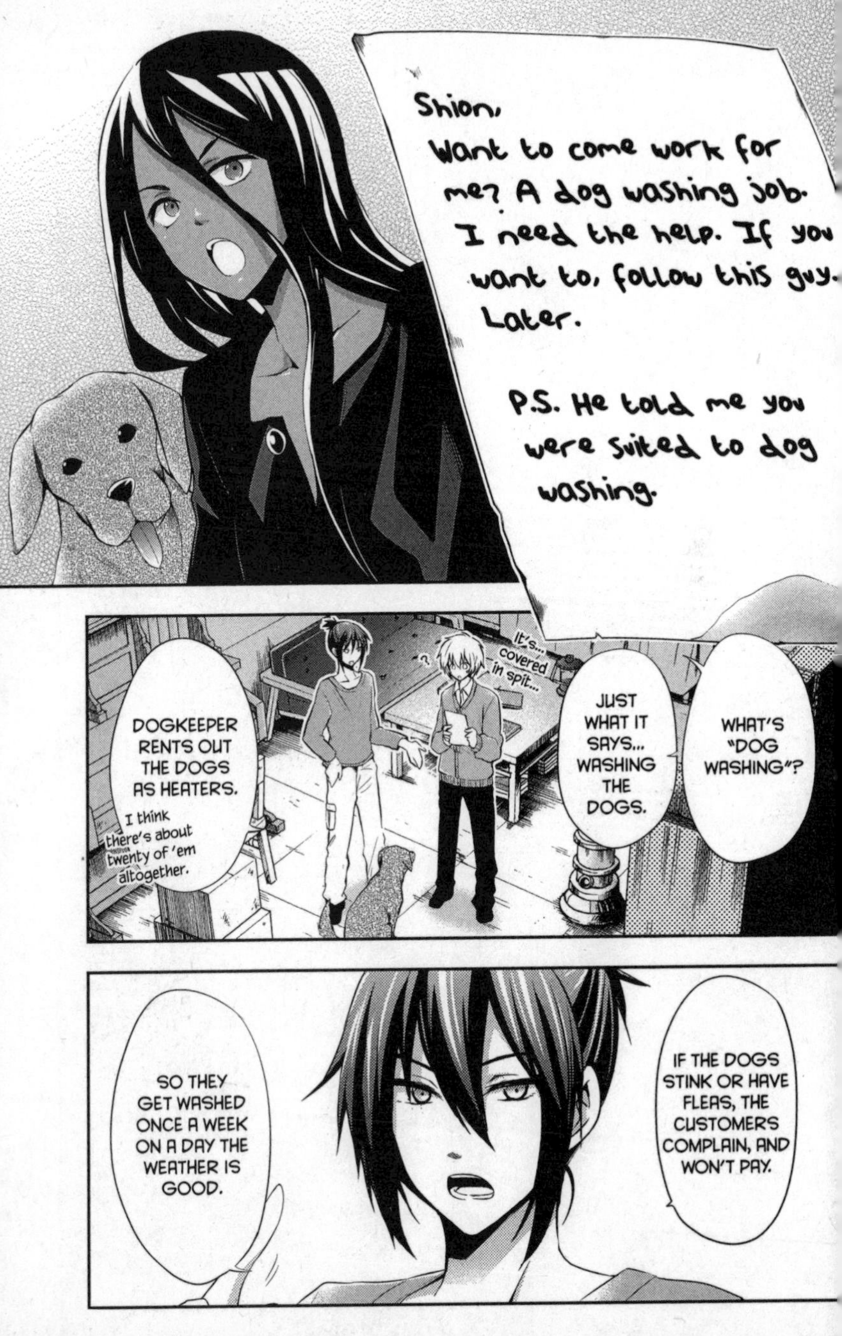
Shion,
Want to come work for me? A dog washing job. I need the help. If you want to, follow this guy. Later.
P.S. He told me you were suited to dog washing.
WHAT'S "DOG WASHING"?
JUST WHAT IT SAYS... WASHING THE DOGS.
It's... covered in spit...
DOGKEEPER RENTS OUT THE DOGS AS HEATERS.
I think there's about twenty of 'em altogether.
IF THE DOGS STINK OR HAVE FLEAS, THE CUSTOMERS COMPLAIN, AND WON'T PAY.
SO THEY GET WASHED ONCE A WEEK ON A DAY THE WEATHER IS GOOD.

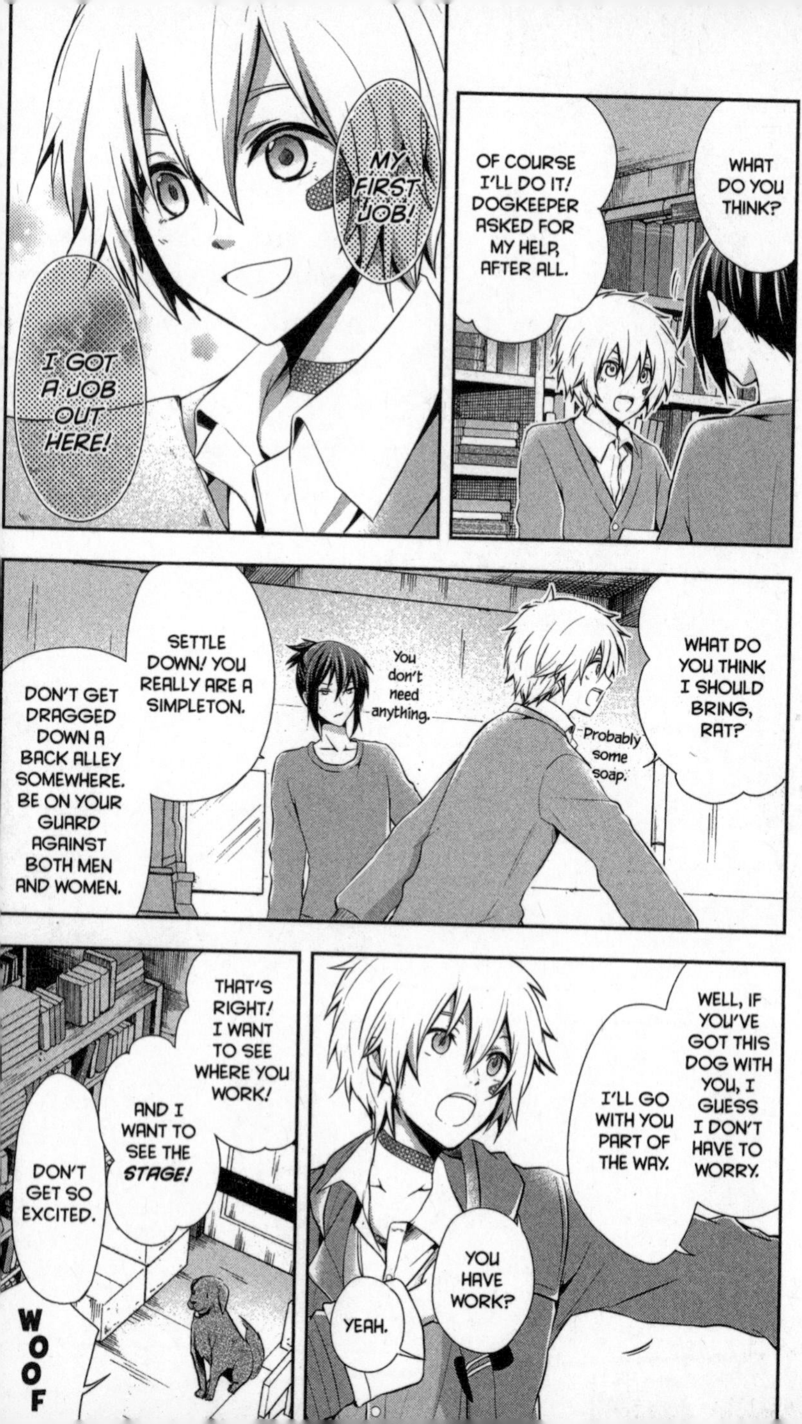
WHAT DO YOU THINK?
OF COURSE I'LL DO IT! DOGKEEPER ASKED FOR MY HELP, AFTER ALL.
MY FIRST JOB!
I GOT A JOB OUT HERE!
WHAT DO YOU THINK I SHOULD BRING, RAT?
Probably some soap.
You don't need anything.
SETTLE DOWN! YOU REALLY ARE A SIMPLETON.
DON'T GET DRAGGED DOWN A BACK ALLEY SOMEWHERE. BE ON YOUR GUARD AGAINST BOTH MEN AND WOMEN.
WELL, IF YOU'VE GOT THIS DOG WITH YOU, I GUESS I DON'T HAVE TO WORRY.
I'LL GO WITH YOU PART OF THE WAY.
YOU HAVE WORK?
YEAH.
THAT'S RIGHT! I WANT TO SEE WHERE YOU WORK!
AND I WANT TO SEE THE *STAGE!*
DON'T GET SO EXCITED.
WOOF

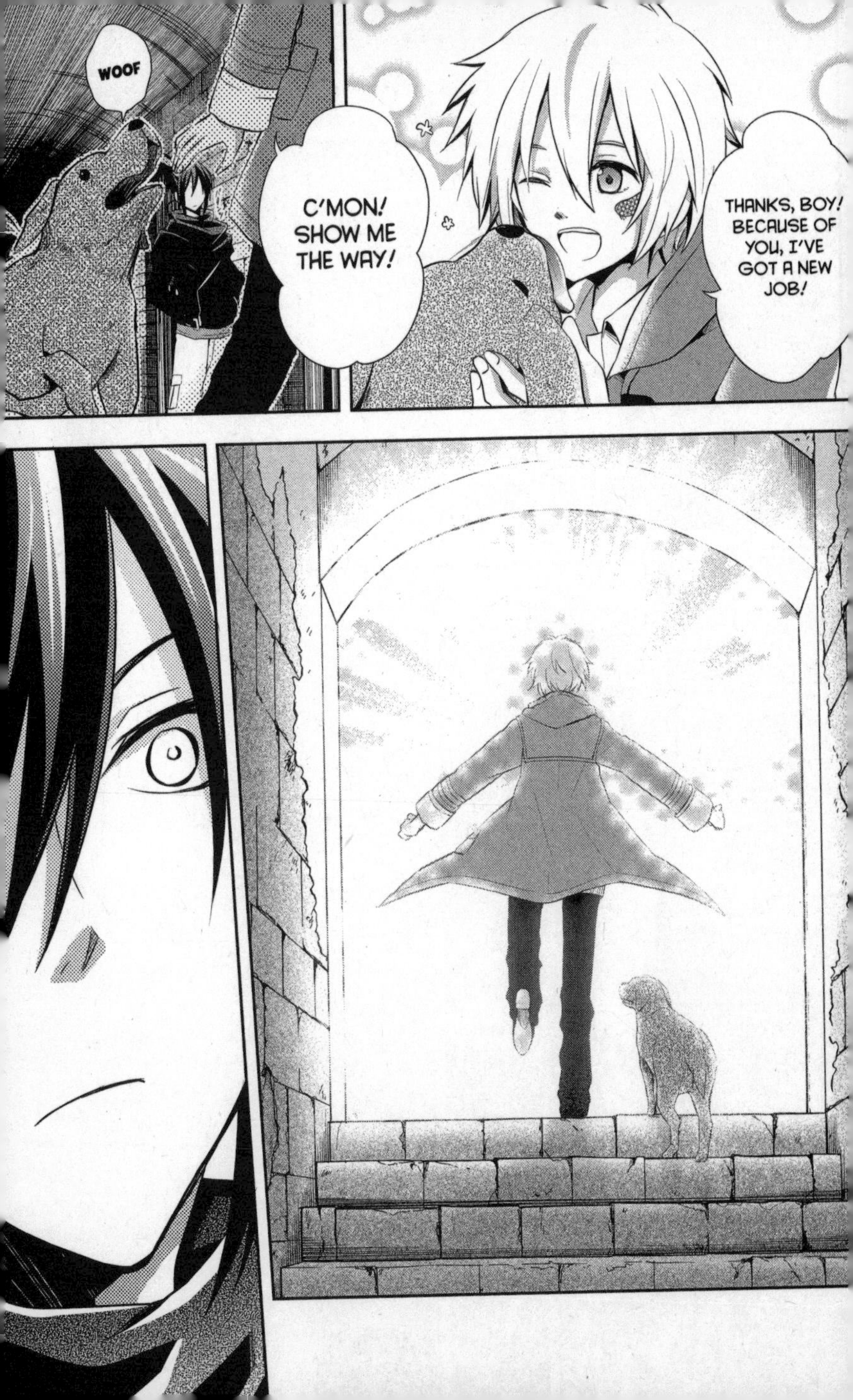
THANKS, BOY! BECAUSE OF YOU, I'VE GOT A NEW JOB!
C'MON! SHOW ME THE WAY!
WOOF

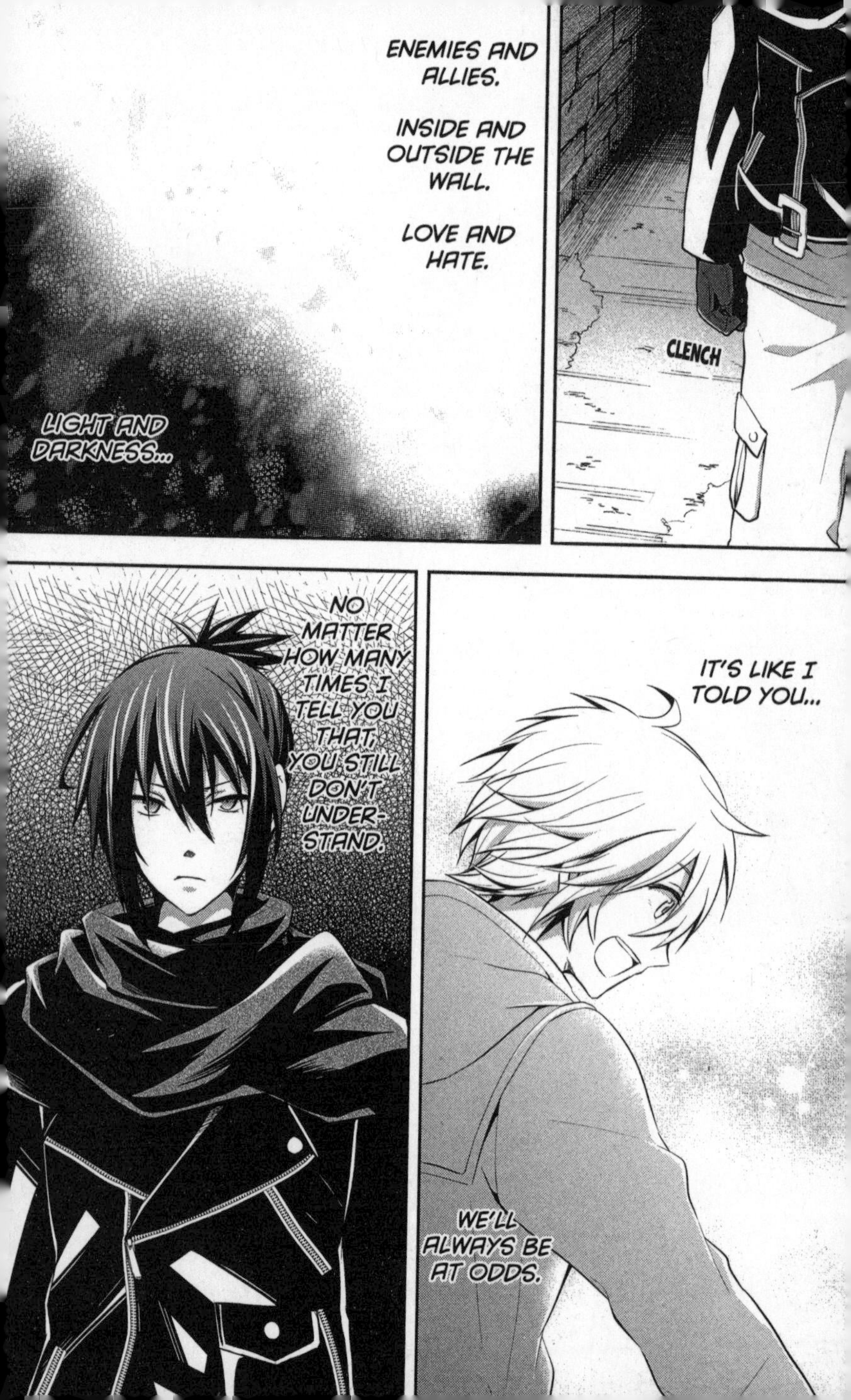
CLENCH
ENEMIES AND ALLIES.
INSIDE AND OUTSIDE THE WALL.
LOVE AND HATE.
LIGHT AND DARKNESS...
IT'S LIKE I TOLD YOU...
WE'LL ALWAYS BE AT ODDS.
NO MATTER HOW MANY TIMES I TELL YOU THAT, YOU STILL DON'T UNDER-STAND.

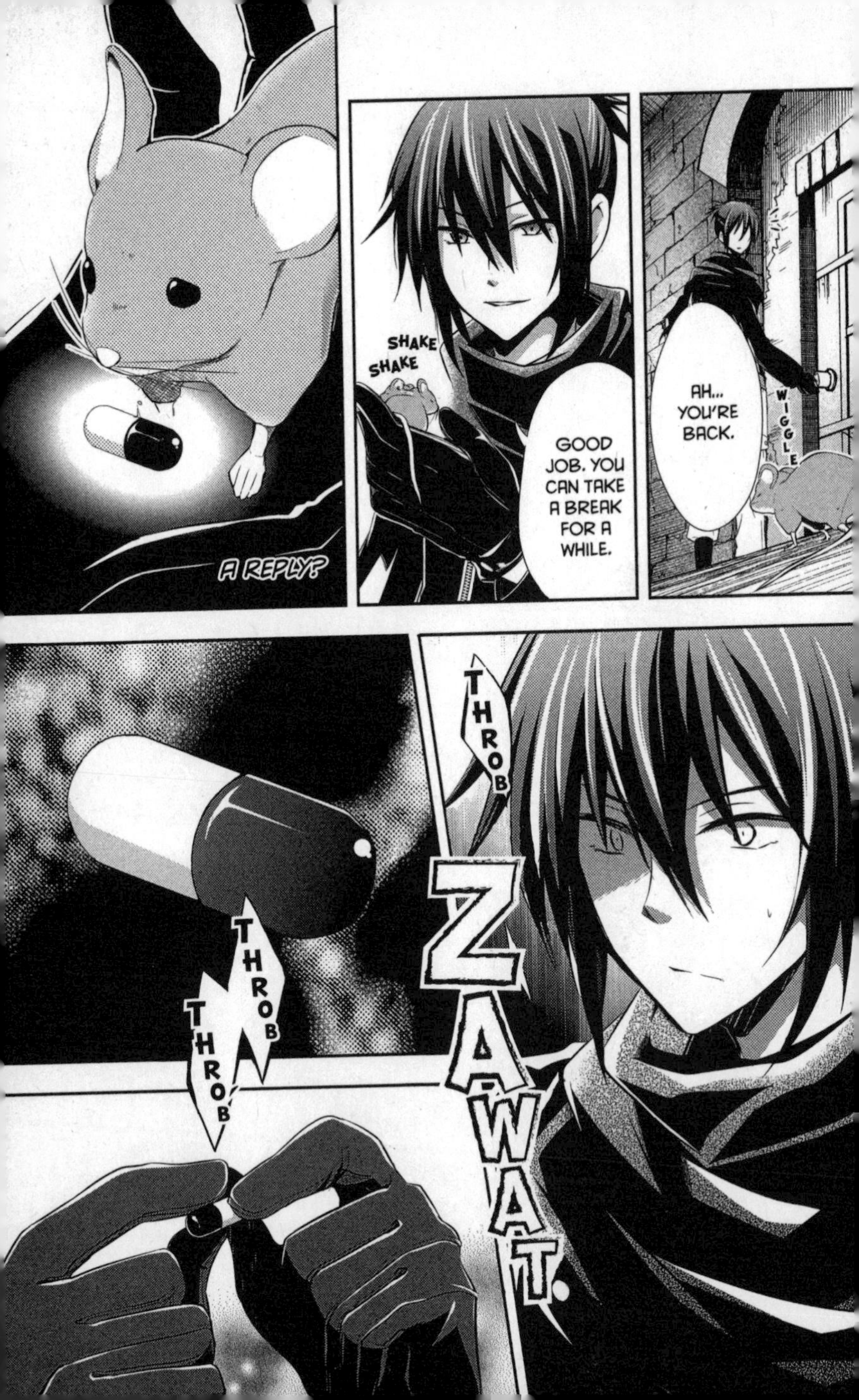
AH... YOU'RE BACK.
WIGGLE
SHAKE SHAKE
GOOD JOB. YOU CAN TAKE A BREAK FOR A WHILE.
A REPLY?
THROB
ZAWAT.
THROB
THROB

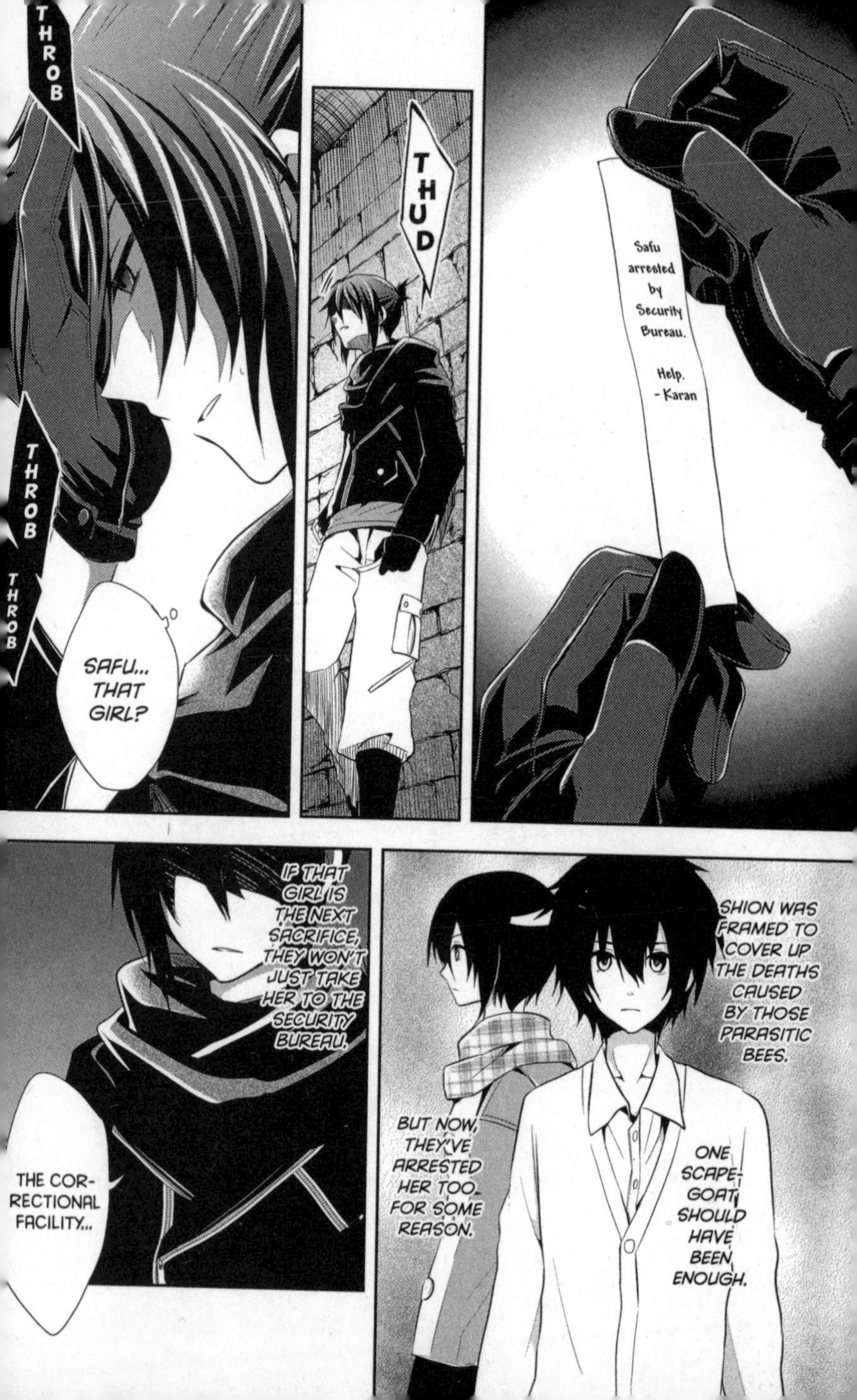
Safu arrested by Security Bureau.
Help.
- Karan
THUD
THROB
THROB
THROB
THROB
SAFU... THAT GIRL?
SHION WAS FRAMED TO COVER UP THE DEATHS CAUSED BY THOSE PARASITIC BEES.
ONE SCAPE-GOAT SHOULD HAVE BEEN ENOUGH.
BUT NOW, THEY'VE ARRESTED HER TOO. FOR SOME REASON.
IF THAT GIRL IS THE NEXT SACRIFICE, THEY WON'T JUST TAKE HER TO THE SECURITY BUREAU.
THE COR-RECTIONAL FACILITY...

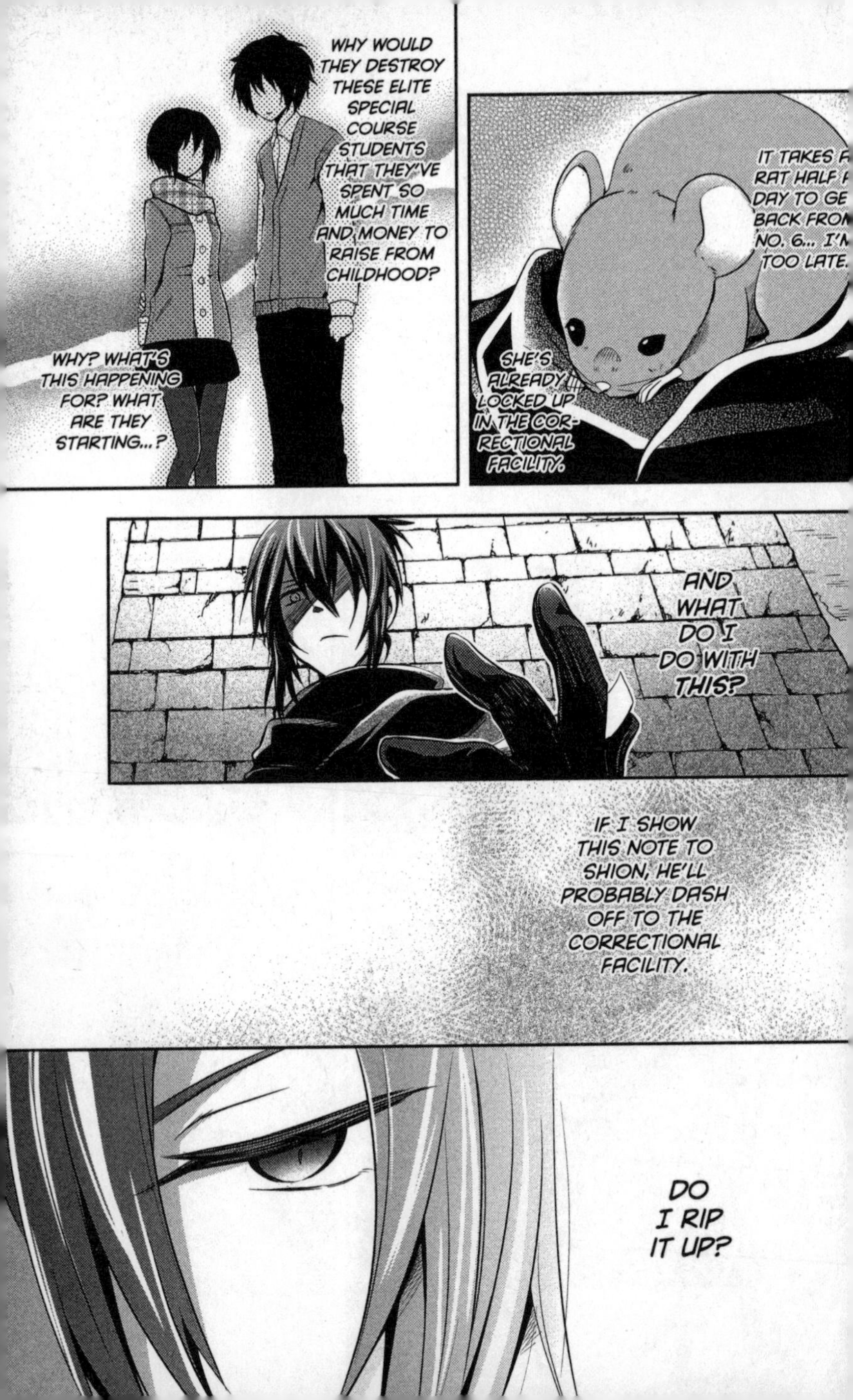
IT TAKES A RAT HALF A DAY TO GE BACK FROM NO. 6... I'M TOO LATE.
SHE'S ALREADY LOCKED UP IN THE COR-RECTIONAL FACILITY.
WHY WOULD THEY DESTROY THESE ELITE SPECIAL COURSE STUDENTS THAT THEY'VE SPENT SO MUCH TIME AND MONEY TO RAISE FROM CHILDHOOD?
WHY? WHAT'S THIS HAPPENING FOR? WHAT ARE THEY STARTING...?
AND WHAT DO I DO WITH THIS?
IF I SHOW THIS NOTE TO SHION, HE'LL PROBABLY DASH OFF TO THE CORRECTIONAL FACILITY.
DO I RIP IT UP?

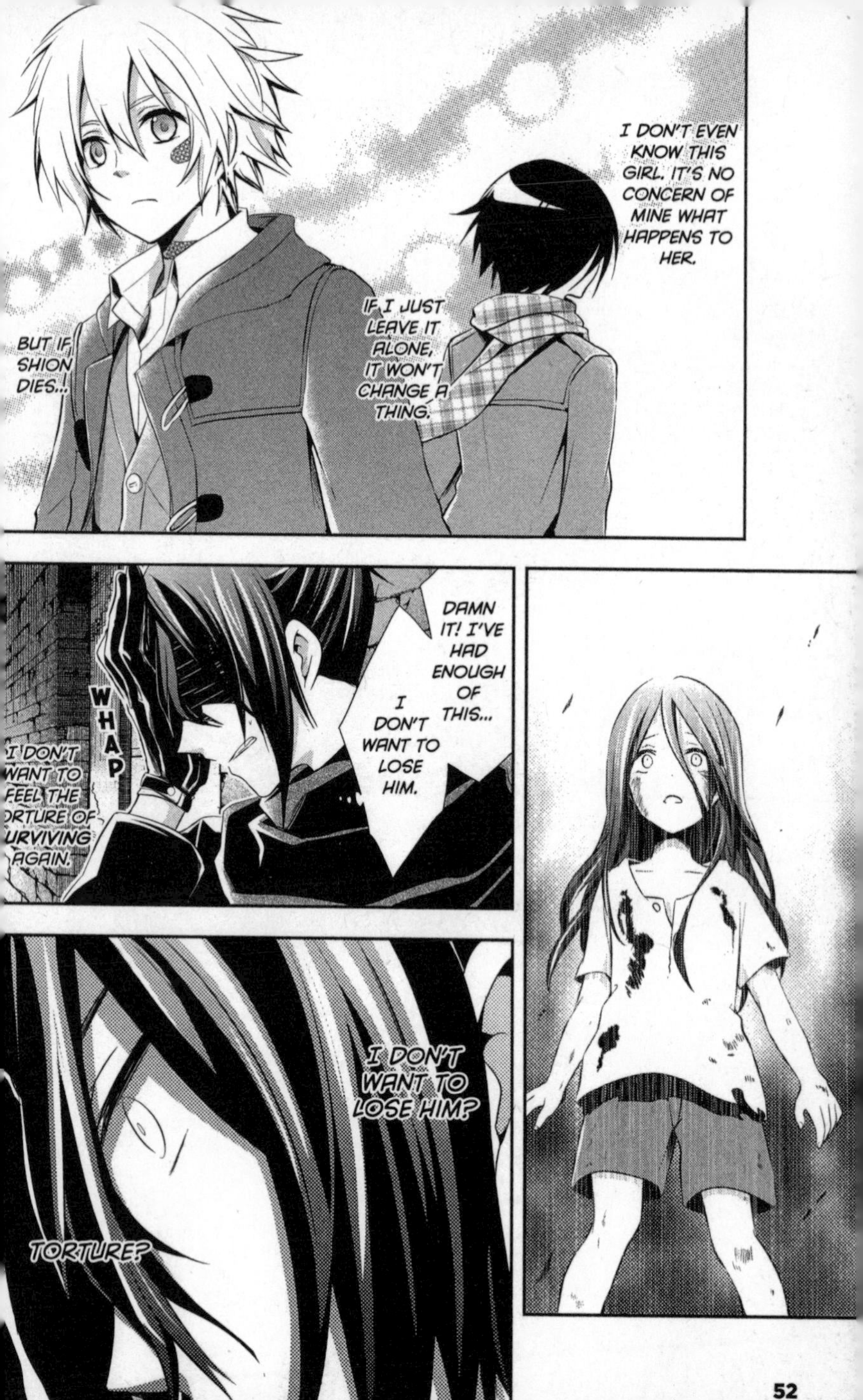
I DON'T EVEN KNOW THIS GIRL. IT'S NO CONCERN OF MINE WHAT HAPPENS TO HER.
IF I JUST LEAVE IT ALONE, IT WON'T CHANGE A THING.
BUT IF SHION DIES...
!
DAMN IT! I'VE HAD ENOUGH OF THIS...
I DON'T WANT TO LOSE HIM.
WHAP
I DON'T WANT TO FEEL THE ORTURE OF URVIVING AGAIN.
I DON'T WANT TO LOSE HIM?
TORTURE?

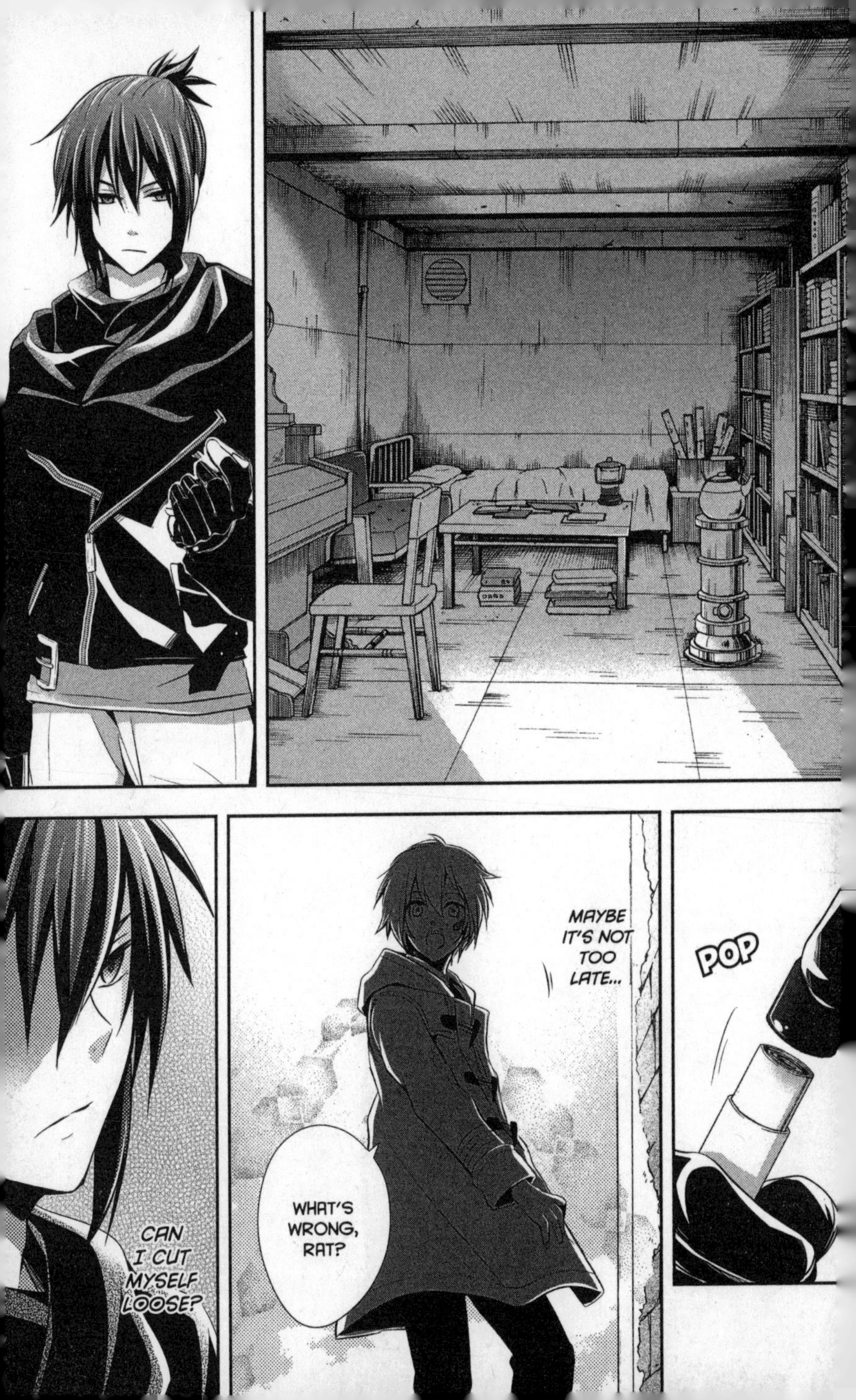
POP
MAYBE IT'S NOT TOO LATE...
WHAT'S WRONG, RAT?
CAN I CUT MYSELF LOOSE?

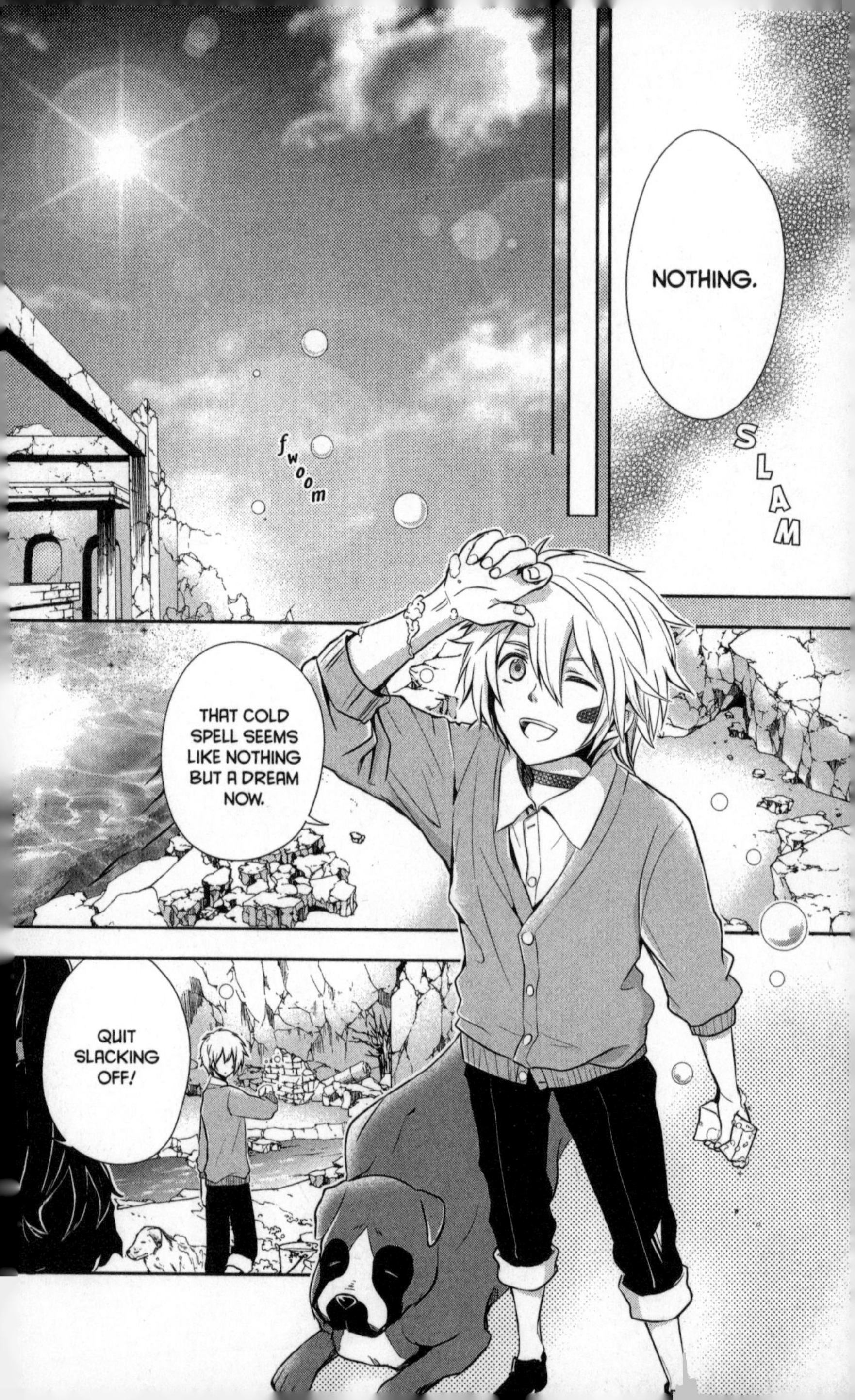
NOTHING.
SLAM
fwoom
THAT COLD SPELL SEEMS LIKE NOTHING BUT A DREAM NOW.
QUIT SLACKING OFF!

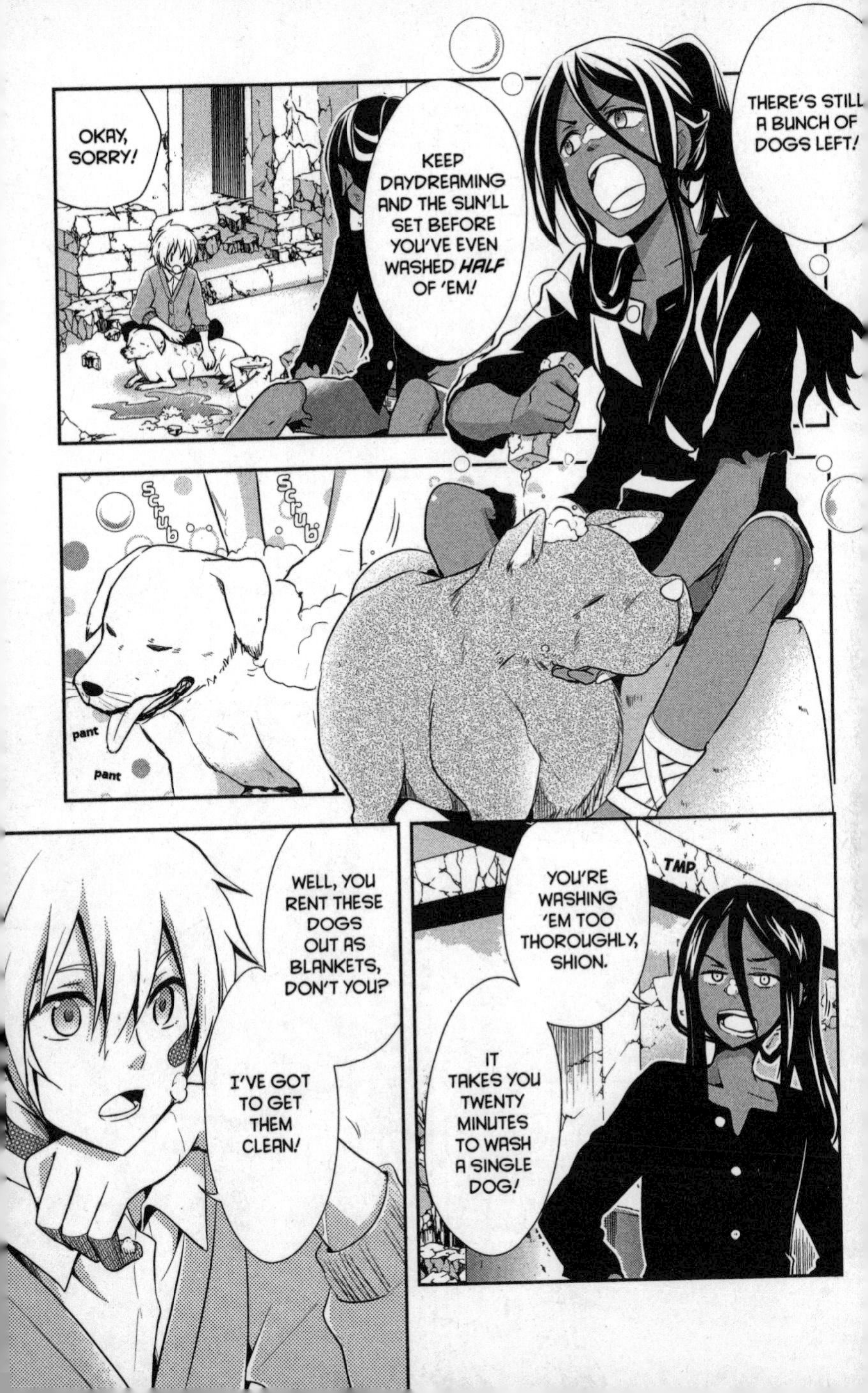
THERE'S STILL A BUNCH OF DOGS LEFT!
KEEP DAYDREAMING AND THE SUN'LL SET BEFORE YOU'VE EVEN WASHED *HALF* OF 'EM!
OKAY, SORRY!
SCRUB
SCRUB
PANT
PANT
TMP
YOU'RE WASHING 'EM TOO THOROUGHLY, SHION.
IT TAKES YOU TWENTY MINUTES TO WASH A SINGLE DOG!
WELL, YOU RENT THESE DOGS OUT AS BLANKETS, DON'T YOU?
I'VE GOT TO GET THEM CLEAN!

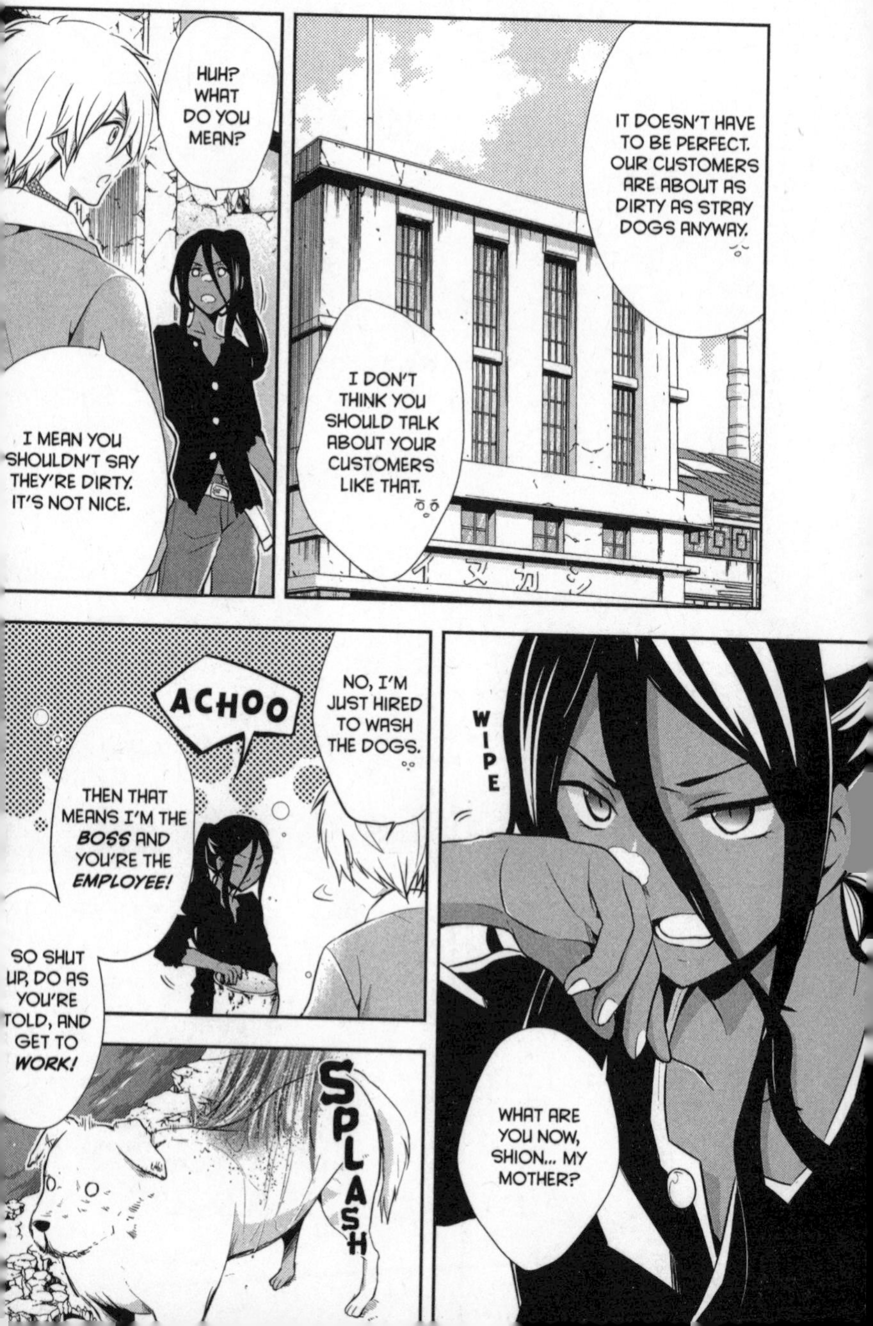
IT DOESN'T HAVE TO BE PERFECT. OUR CUSTOMERS ARE ABOUT AS DIRTY AS STRAY DOGS ANYWAY.
I DON'T THINK YOU SHOULD TALK ABOUT YOUR CUSTOMERS LIKE THAT.
HUH? WHAT DO YOU MEAN?
I MEAN YOU SHOULDN'T SAY THEY'RE DIRTY. IT'S NOT NICE.
WIPE
WHAT ARE YOU NOW, SHION... MY MOTHER?
NO, I'M JUST HIRED TO WASH THE DOGS.
ACHOO
THEN THAT MEANS I'M THE *BOSS* AND YOU'RE THE *EMPLOYEE!*
SO SHUT UP, DO AS YOU'RE TOLD, AND GET TO *WORK!*
SPLASH

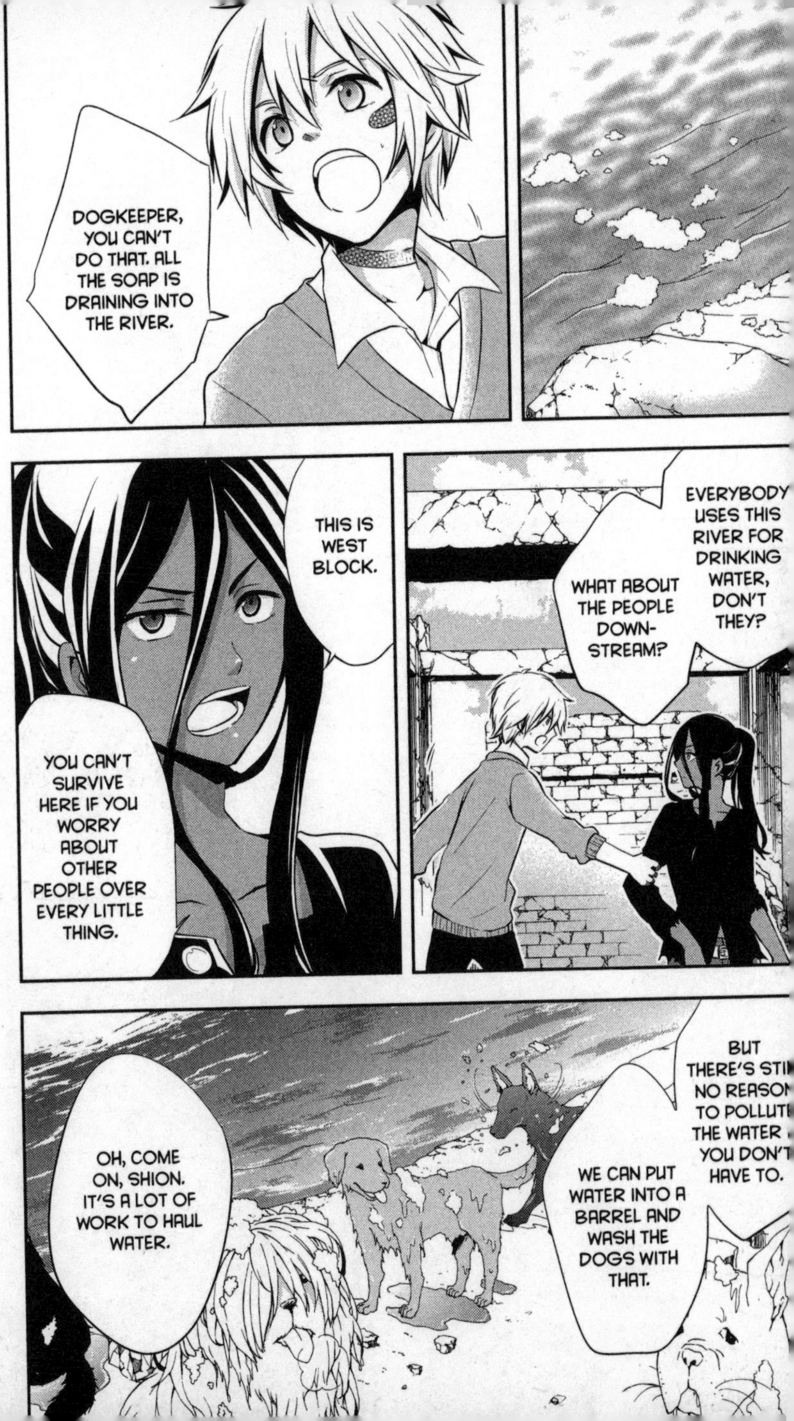
DOGKEEPER, YOU CAN'T DO THAT. ALL THE SOAP IS DRAINING INTO THE RIVER.
EVERYBODY USES THIS RIVER FOR DRINKING WATER, DON'T THEY?
WHAT ABOUT THE PEOPLE DOWN-STREAM?
THIS IS WEST BLOCK.
YOU CAN'T SURVIVE HERE IF YOU WORRY ABOUT OTHER PEOPLE OVER EVERY LITTLE THING.
BUT THERE'S STI NO REASON TO POLLUT THE WATER YOU DON'T HAVE TO.
WE CAN PUT WATER INTO A BARREL AND WASH THE DOGS WITH THAT.
OH, COME ON, SHION. IT'S A LOT OF WORK TO HAUL WATER.

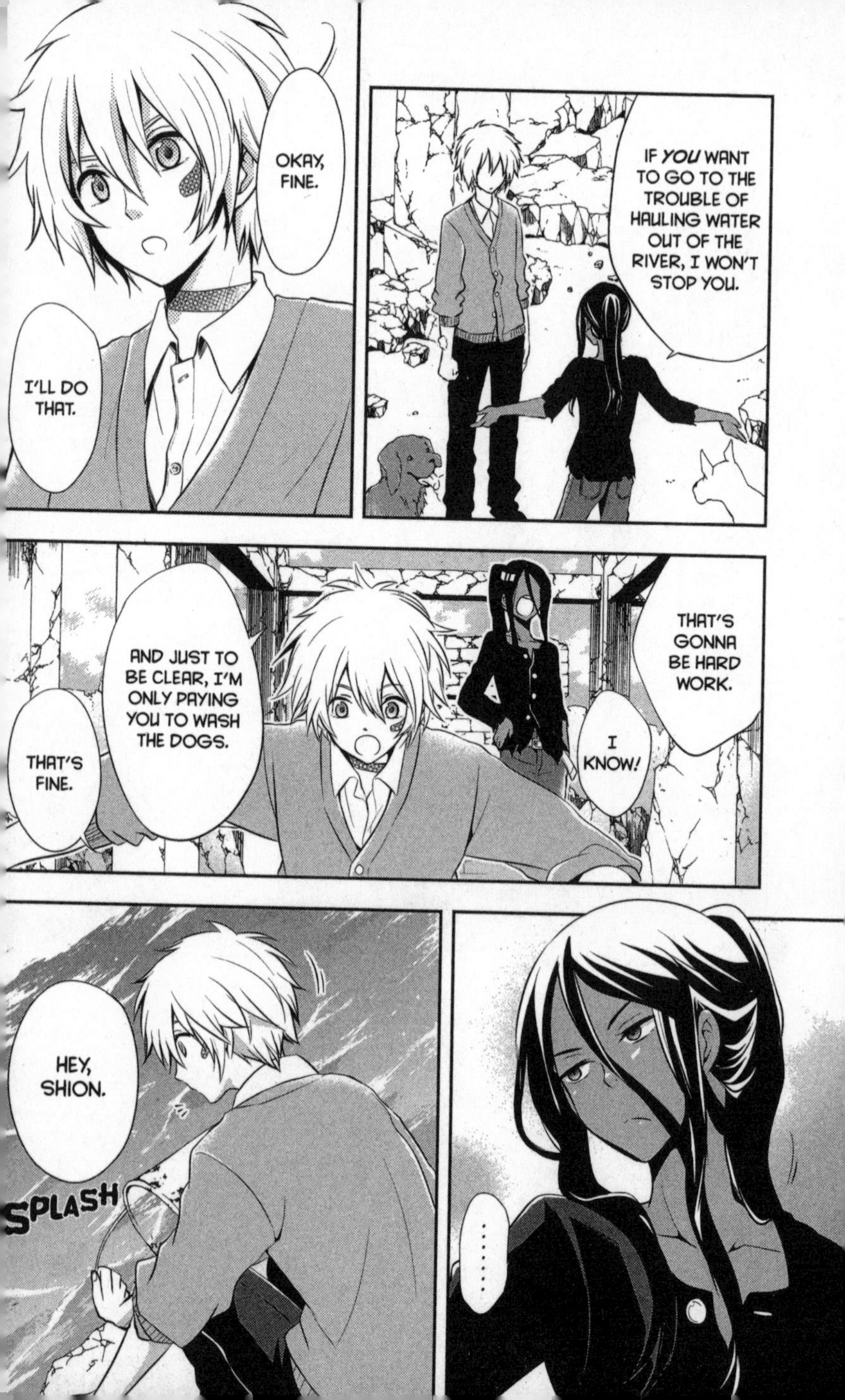
IF *YOU* WANT TO GO TO THE TROUBLE OF HAULING WATER OUT OF THE RIVER, I WON'T STOP YOU.
OKAY, FINE.
I'LL DO THAT.
THAT'S GONNA BE HARD WORK.
I KNOW!
AND JUST TO BE CLEAR, I'M ONLY PAYING YOU TO WASH THE DOGS.
THAT'S FINE.
......
HEY, SHION.
SPLASH

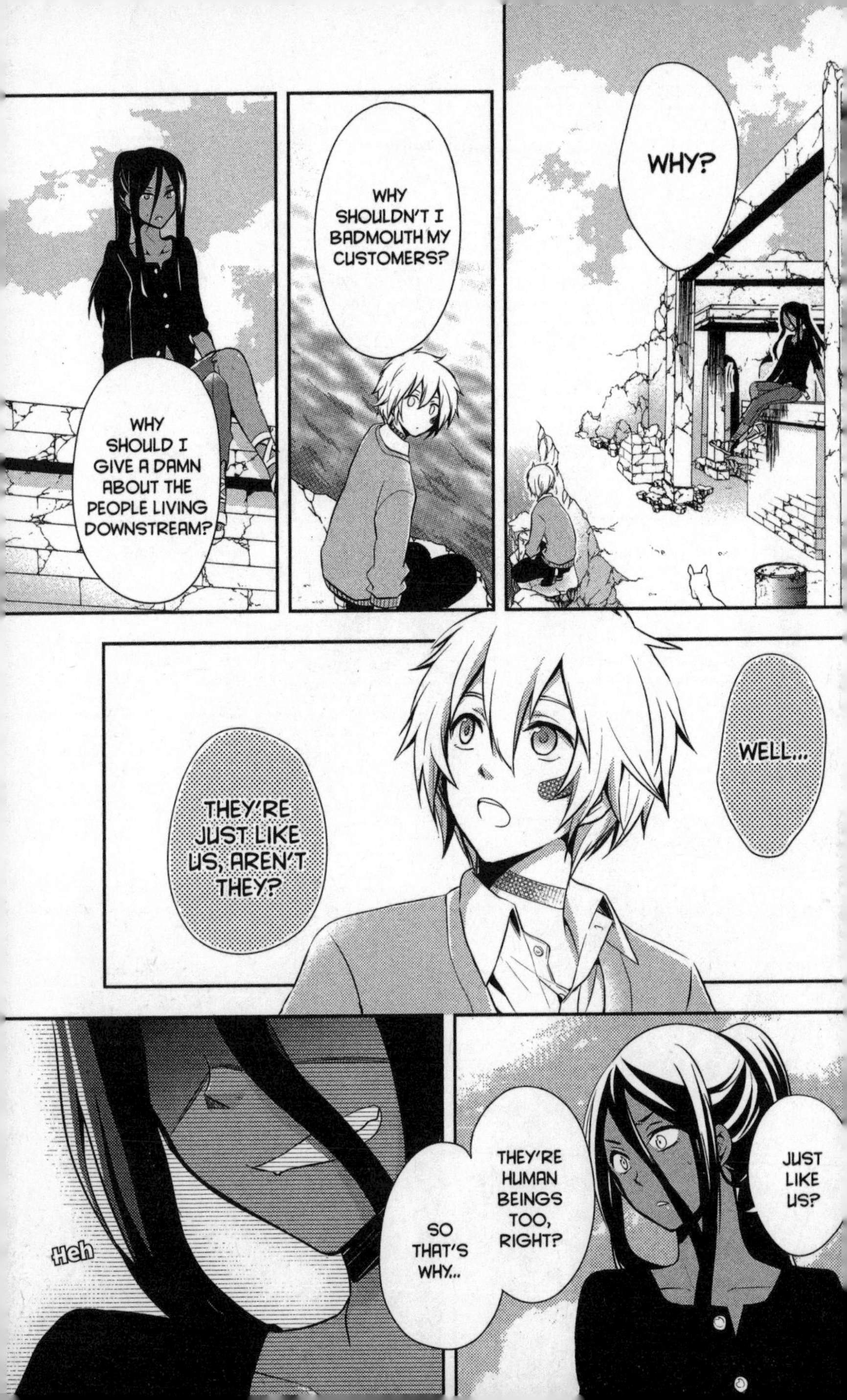
WHY?
WHY SHOULDN'T I BADMOUTH MY CUSTOMERS?
WHY SHOULD I GIVE A DAMN ABOUT THE PEOPLE LIVING DOWNSTREAM?
WELL...
THEY'RE JUST LIKE US, AREN'T THEY?
JUST LIKE US?
THEY'RE HUMAN BEINGS TOO, RIGHT?
SO THAT'S WHY...
Heh

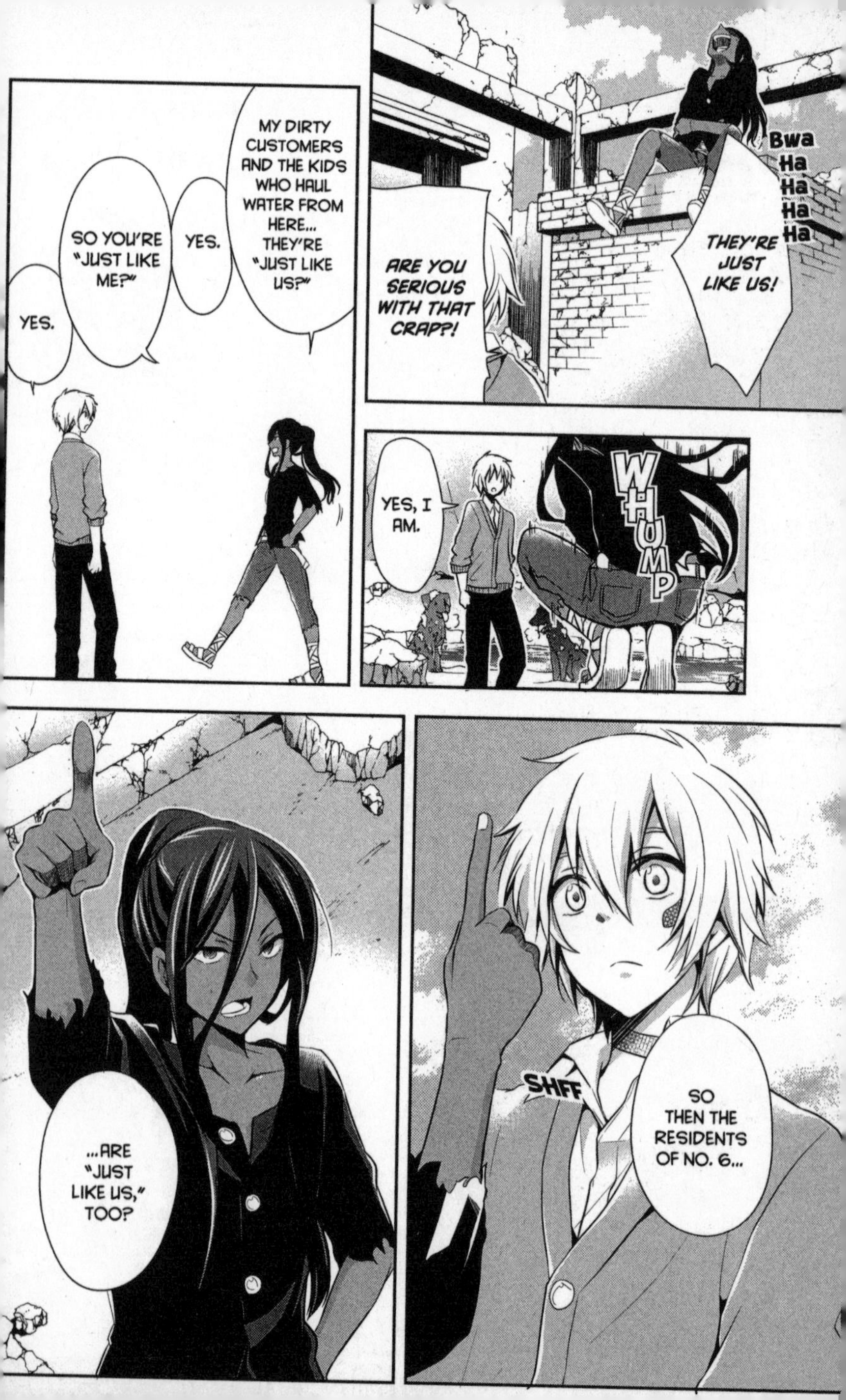
Bwa Ha Ha Ha Ha
THEY'RE JUST LIKE US!
ARE YOU SERIOUS WITH THAT CRAP?!
WHUMP
YES, I AM.
MY DIRTY CUSTOMERS AND THE KIDS WHO HAUL WATER FROM HERE... THEY'RE "JUST LIKE US?"
YES.
SO YOU'RE "JUST LIKE ME?"
YES.
SHFF
SO THEN THE RESIDENTS OF NO. 6...
...ARE "JUST LIKE US," TOO?

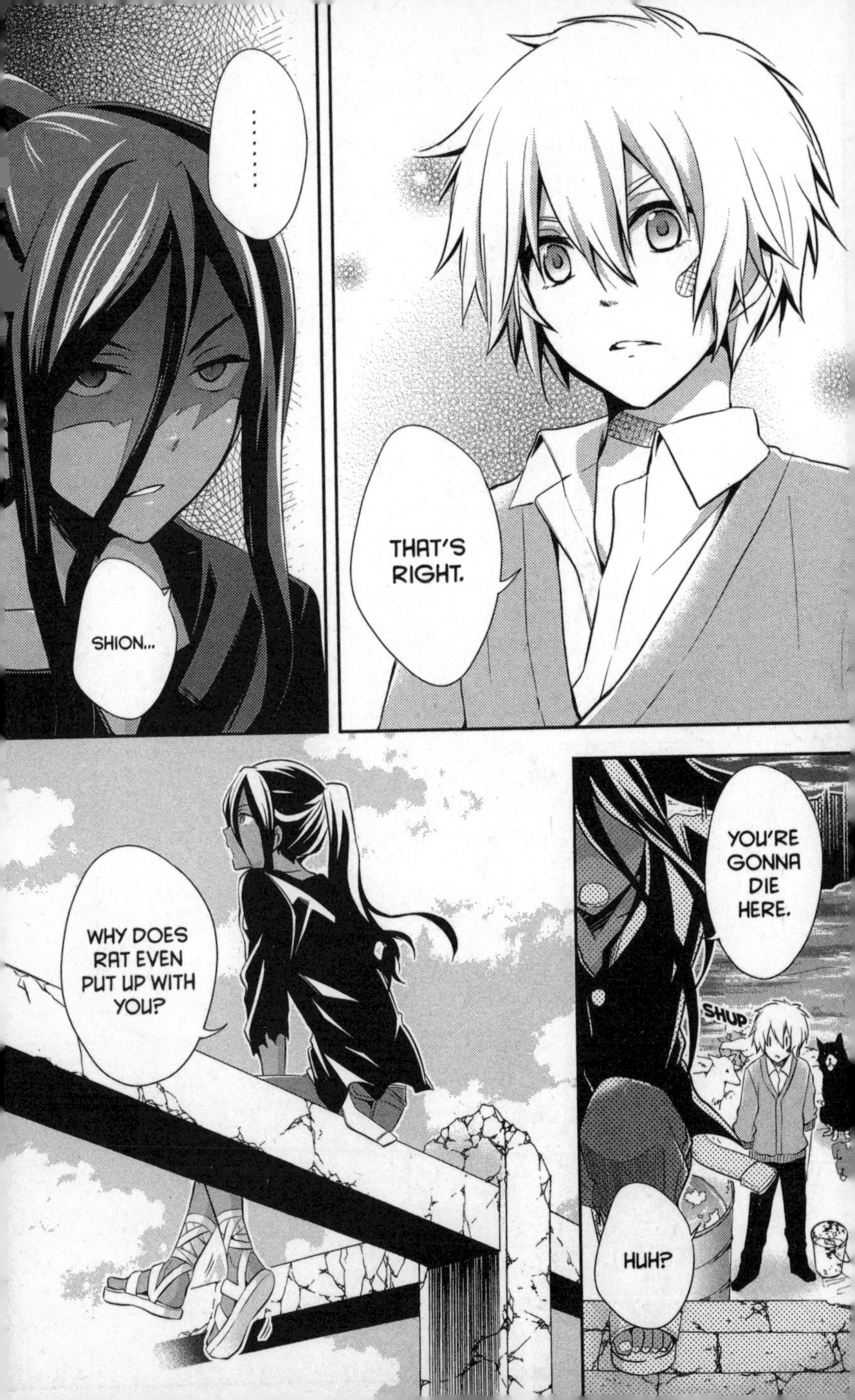
THAT'S RIGHT.
......
SHION...
YOU'RE GONNA DIE HERE.
SHUP
HUH?
WHY DOES RAT EVEN PUT UP WITH YOU?

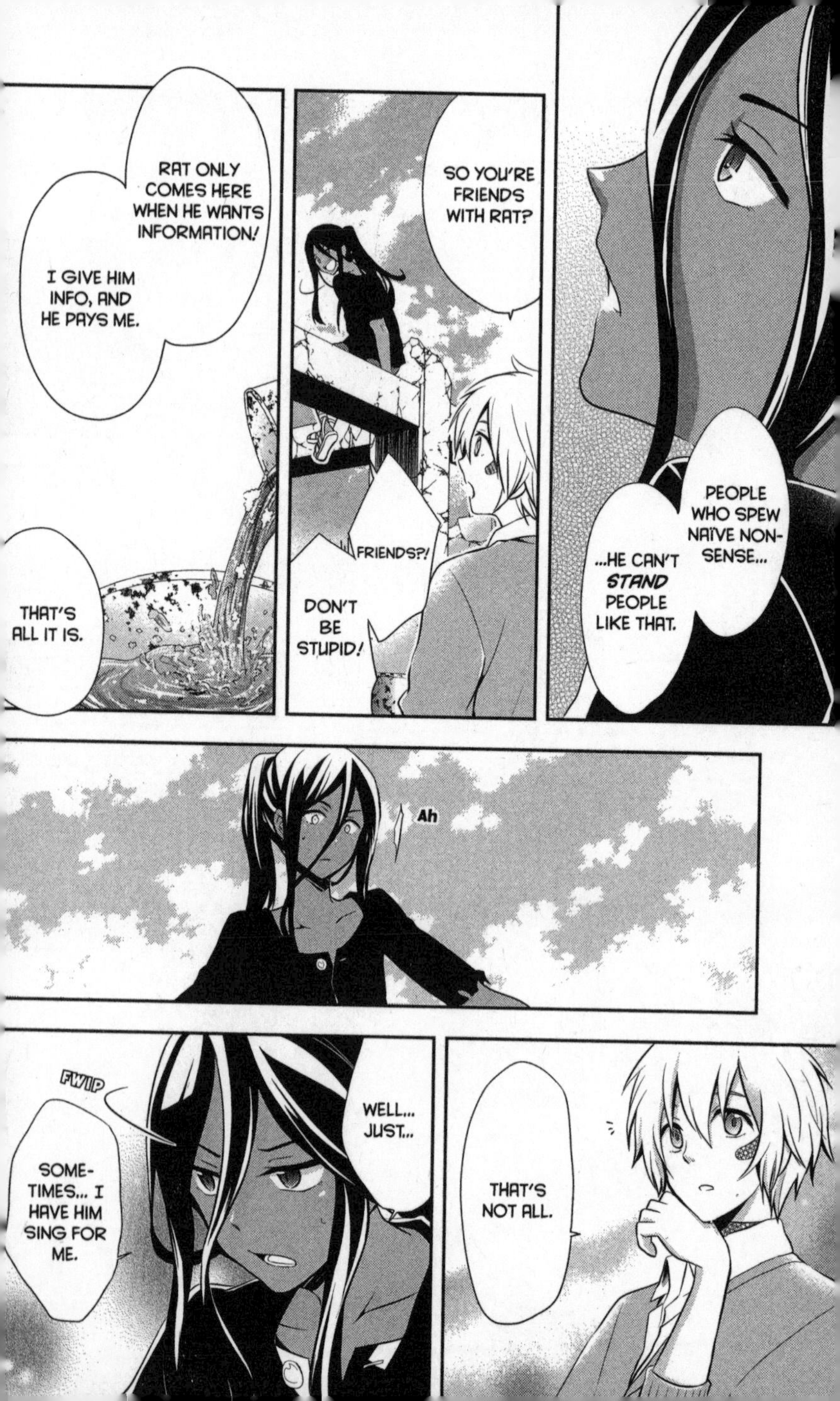
PEOPLE WHO SPEW NAÏVE NON-SENSE...
...HE CAN'T *STAND* PEOPLE LIKE THAT.
SO YOU'RE FRIENDS WITH RAT?
FRIENDS?!
DON'T BE STUPID!
RAT ONLY COMES HERE WHEN HE WANTS INFORMATION!
I GIVE HIM INFO, AND HE PAYS ME.
THAT'S ALL IT IS.
Ah
THAT'S NOT ALL.
WELL... JUST...
FWIP
SOME-TIMES... I HAVE HIM SING FOR ME.

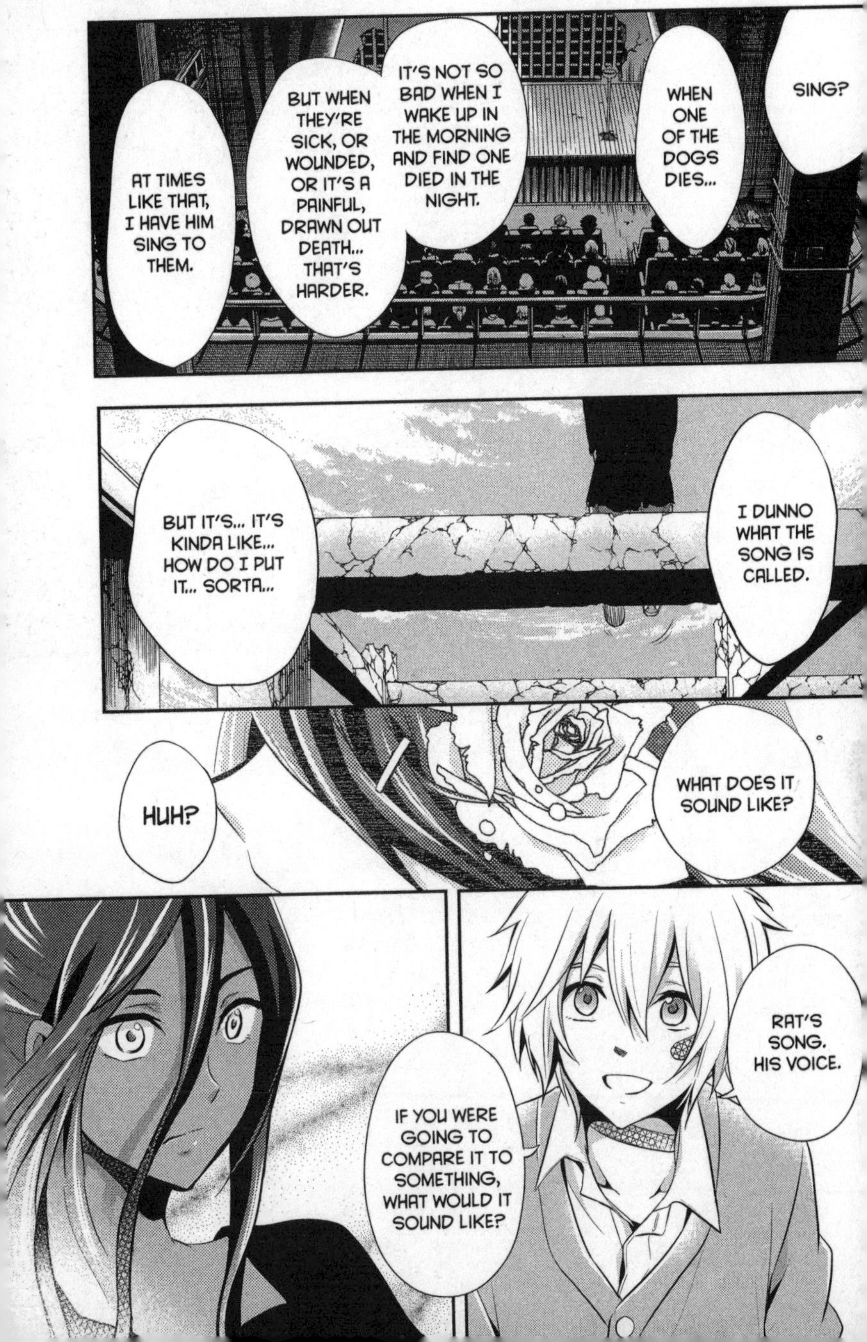
SING?
WHEN ONE OF THE DOGS DIES...
IT'S NOT SO BAD WHEN I WAKE UP IN THE MORNING AND FIND ONE DIED IN THE NIGHT.
BUT WHEN THEY'RE SICK, OR WOUNDED, OR IT'S A PAINFUL, DRAWN OUT DEATH... THAT'S HARDER.
AT TIMES LIKE THAT, I HAVE HIM SING TO THEM.
I DUNNO WHAT THE SONG IS CALLED.
BUT IT'S... IT'S KINDA LIKE... HOW DO I PUT IT... SORTA...
WHAT DOES IT SOUND LIKE?
HUH?
RAT'S SONG. HIS VOICE.
IF YOU WERE GOING TO COMPARE IT TO SOMETHING, WHAT WOULD IT SOUND LIKE?

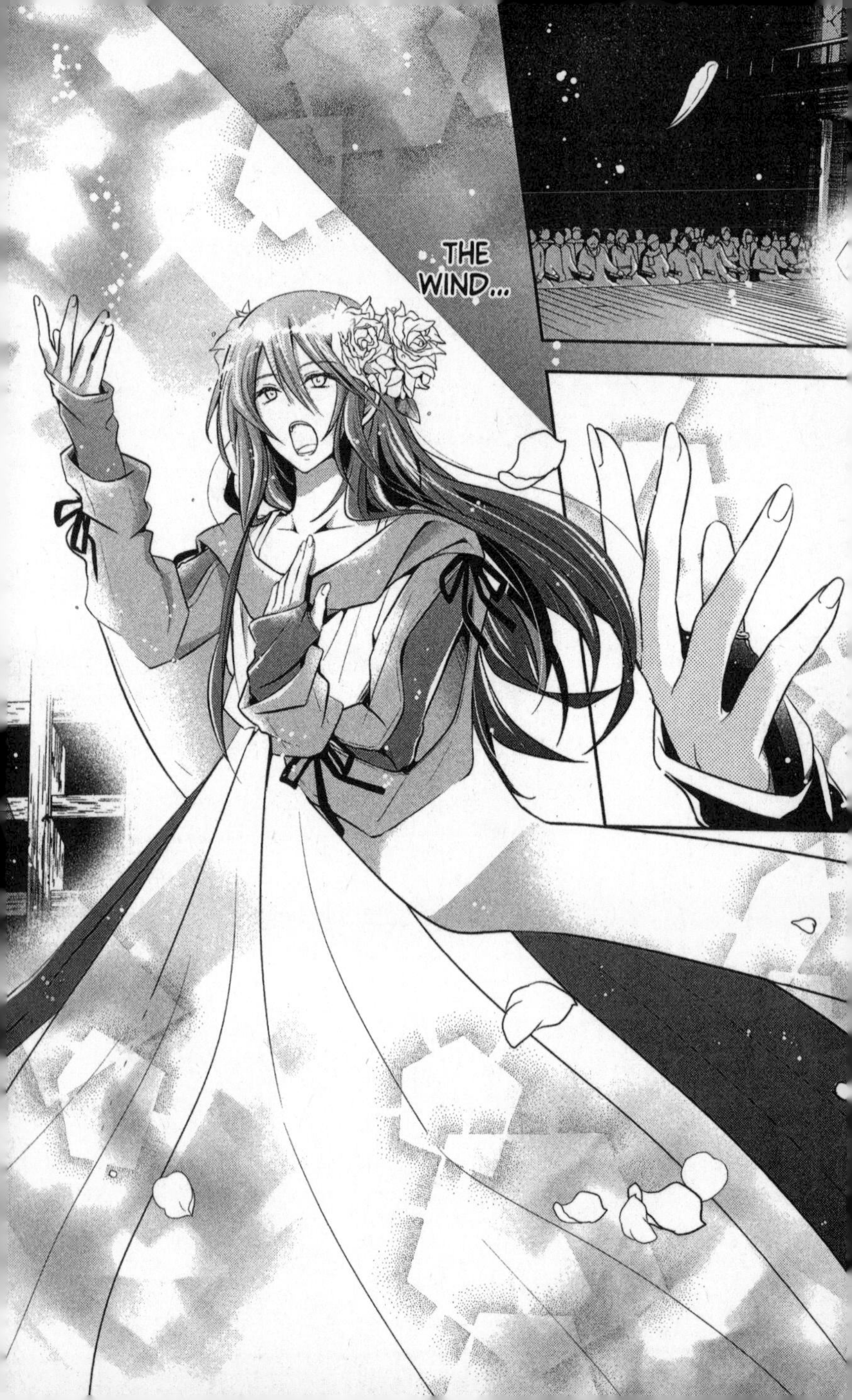
THE WIND...

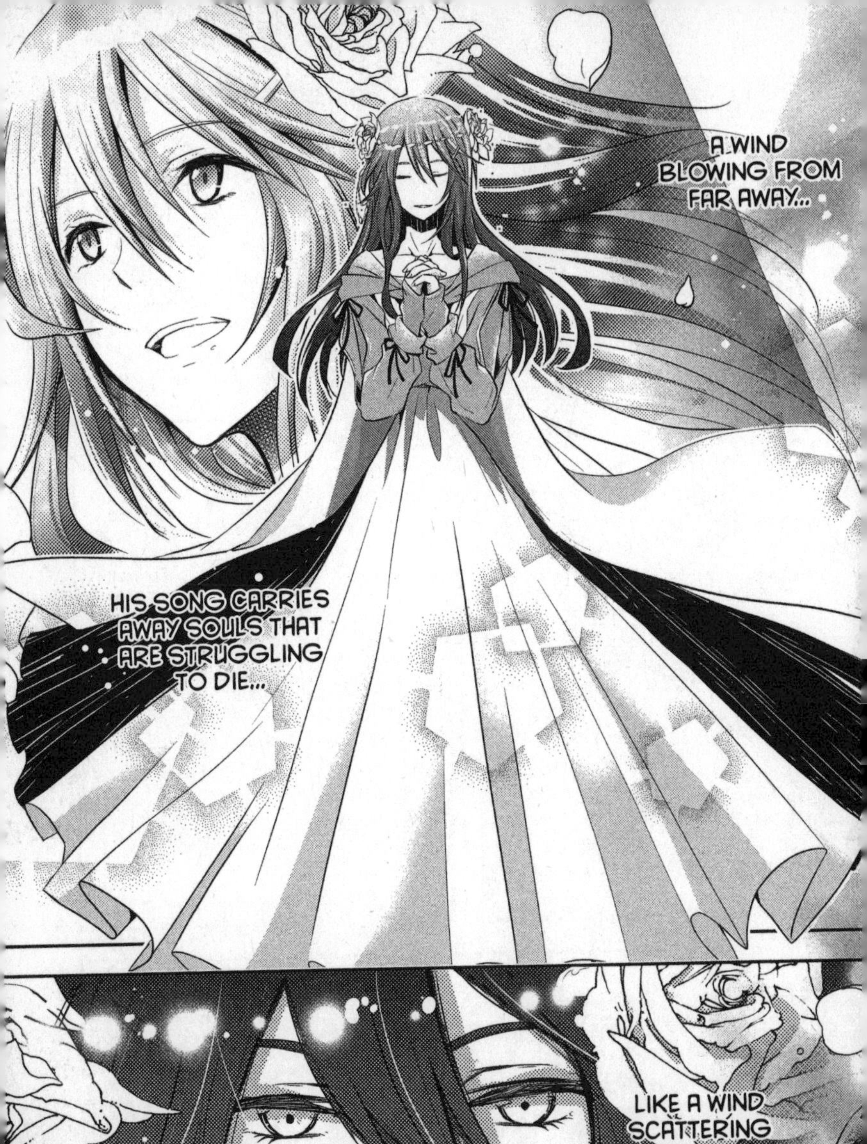
A WIND BLOWING FROM FAR AWAY...
HIS SONG CARRIES AWAY SOULS THAT ARE STRUGGLING TO DIE...
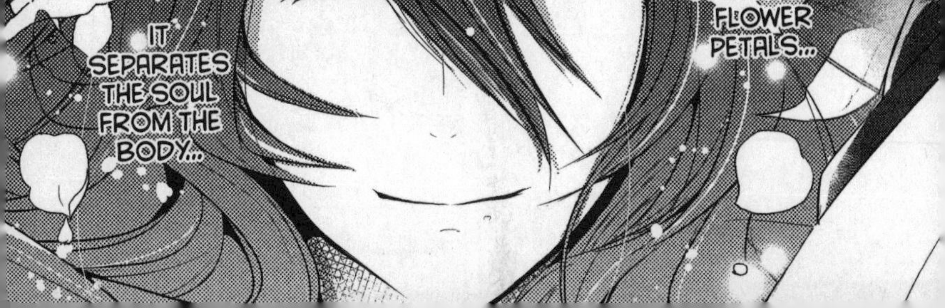
LIKE A WIND SCATTERING FLOWER PETALS...
IT SEPARATES THE SOUL FROM THE BODY...

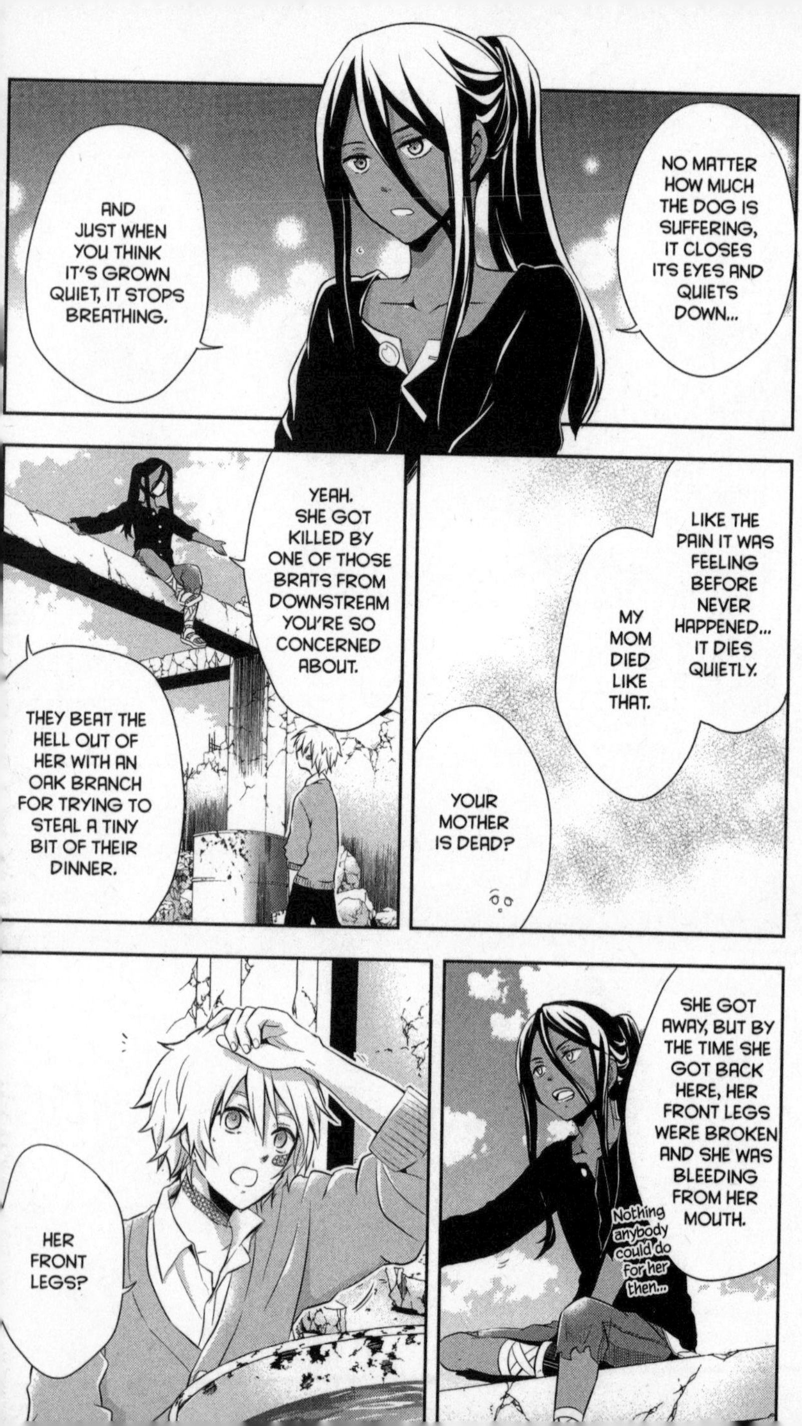

NO MATTER HOW MUCH THE DOG IS SUFFERING, IT CLOSES ITS EYES AND QUIETS DOWN...
AND JUST WHEN YOU THINK IT'S GROWN QUIET, IT STOPS BREATHING.
LIKE THE PAIN IT WAS FEELING BEFORE NEVER HAPPENED... IT DIES QUIETLY.
MY MOM DIED LIKE THAT.
YOUR MOTHER IS DEAD?
YEAH. SHE GOT KILLED BY ONE OF THOSE BRATS FROM DOWNSTREAM YOU'RE SO CONCERNED ABOUT.
THEY BEAT THE HELL OUT OF HER WITH AN OAK BRANCH FOR TRYING TO STEAL A TINY BIT OF THEIR DINNER.
SHE GOT AWAY, BUT BY THE TIME SHE GOT BACK HERE, HER FRONT LEGS WERE BROKEN AND SHE WAS BLEEDING FROM HER MOUTH.
Nothing anybody could do for her then...
HER FRONT LEGS?

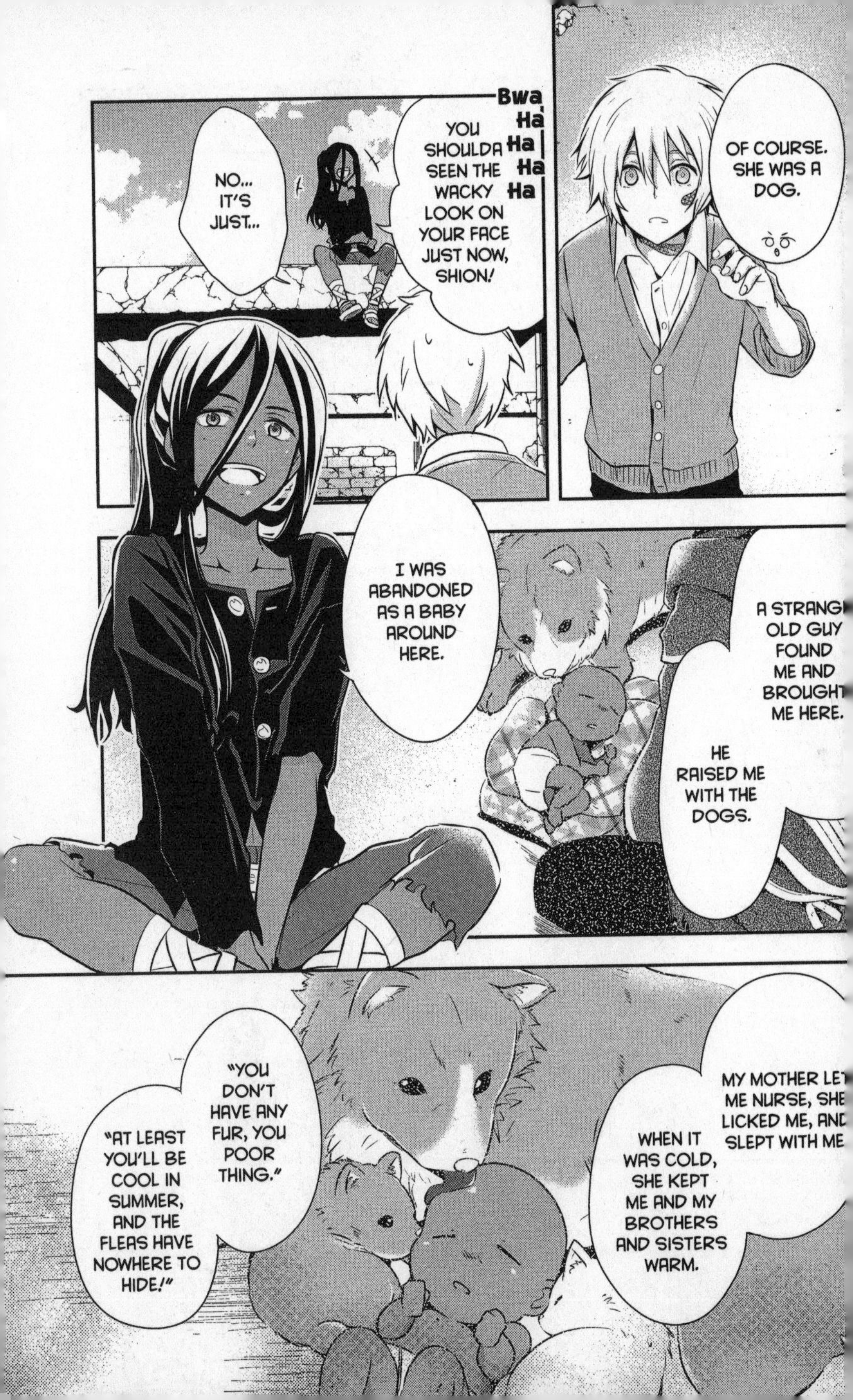
OF COURSE. SHE WAS A DOG.
Bwa Ha Ha Ha Ha
YOU SHOULDA SEEN THE WACKY LOOK ON YOUR FACE JUST NOW, SHION!
NO... IT'S JUST...
I WAS ABANDONED AS A BABY AROUND HERE.
A STRANG OLD GUY FOUND ME AND BROUGHT ME HERE.
HE RAISED ME WITH THE DOGS.
MY MOTHER LET ME NURSE, SHE LICKED ME, AND SLEPT WITH ME.
WHEN IT WAS COLD, SHE KEPT ME AND MY BROTHERS AND SISTERS WARM.
"YOU DON'T HAVE ANY FUR, YOU POOR THING."
"AT LEAST YOU'LL BE COOL IN SUMMER, AND THE FLEAS HAVE NOWHERE TO HIDE!"

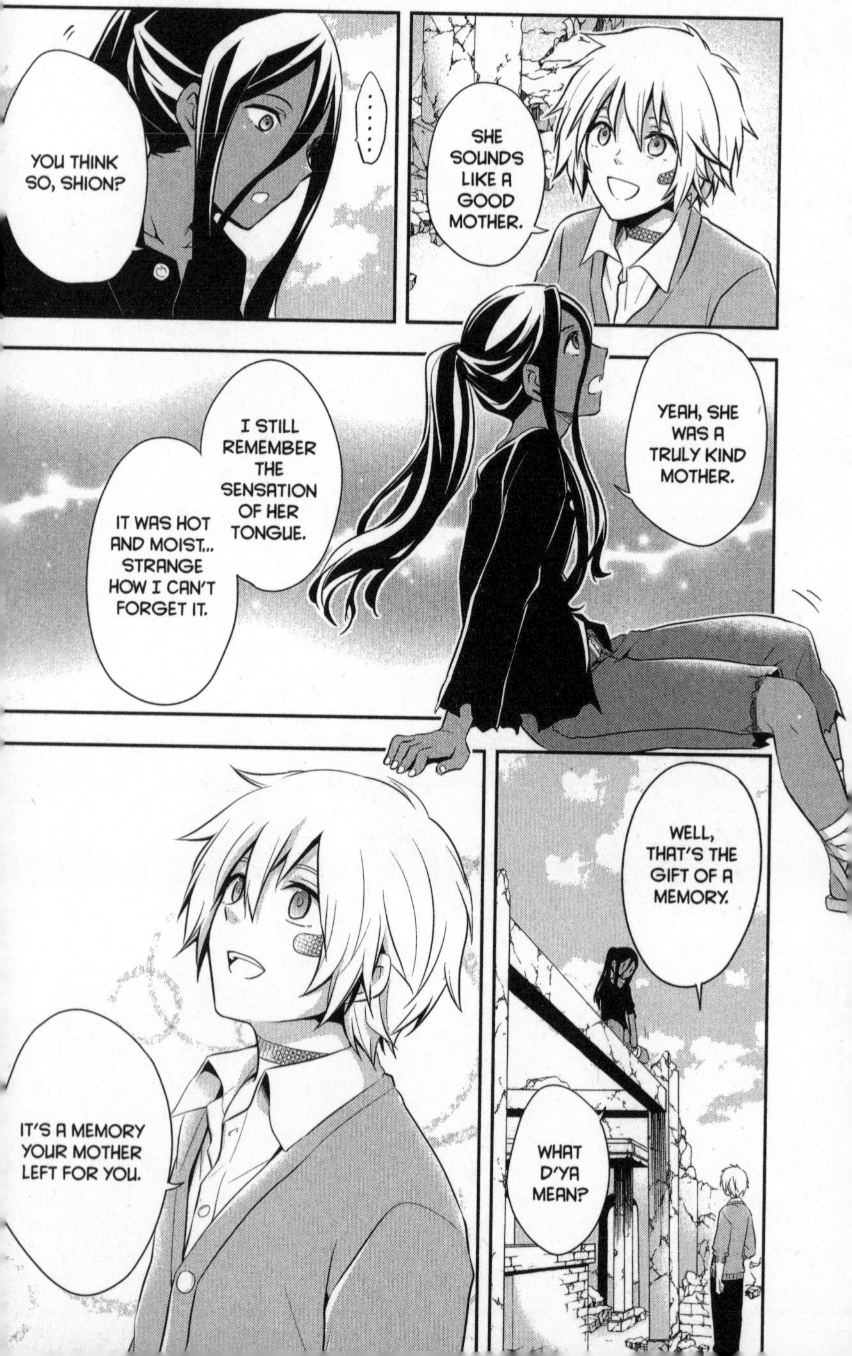
SHE SOUNDS LIKE A GOOD MOTHER.
......
YOU THINK SO, SHION?
YEAH, SHE WAS A TRULY KIND MOTHER.
I STILL REMEMBER THE SENSATION OF HER TONGUE.
IT WAS HOT AND MOIST... STRANGE HOW I CAN'T FORGET IT.
WELL, THAT'S THE GIFT OF A MEMORY.
WHAT D'YA MEAN?
IT'S A MEMORY YOUR MOTHER LEFT FOR YOU.

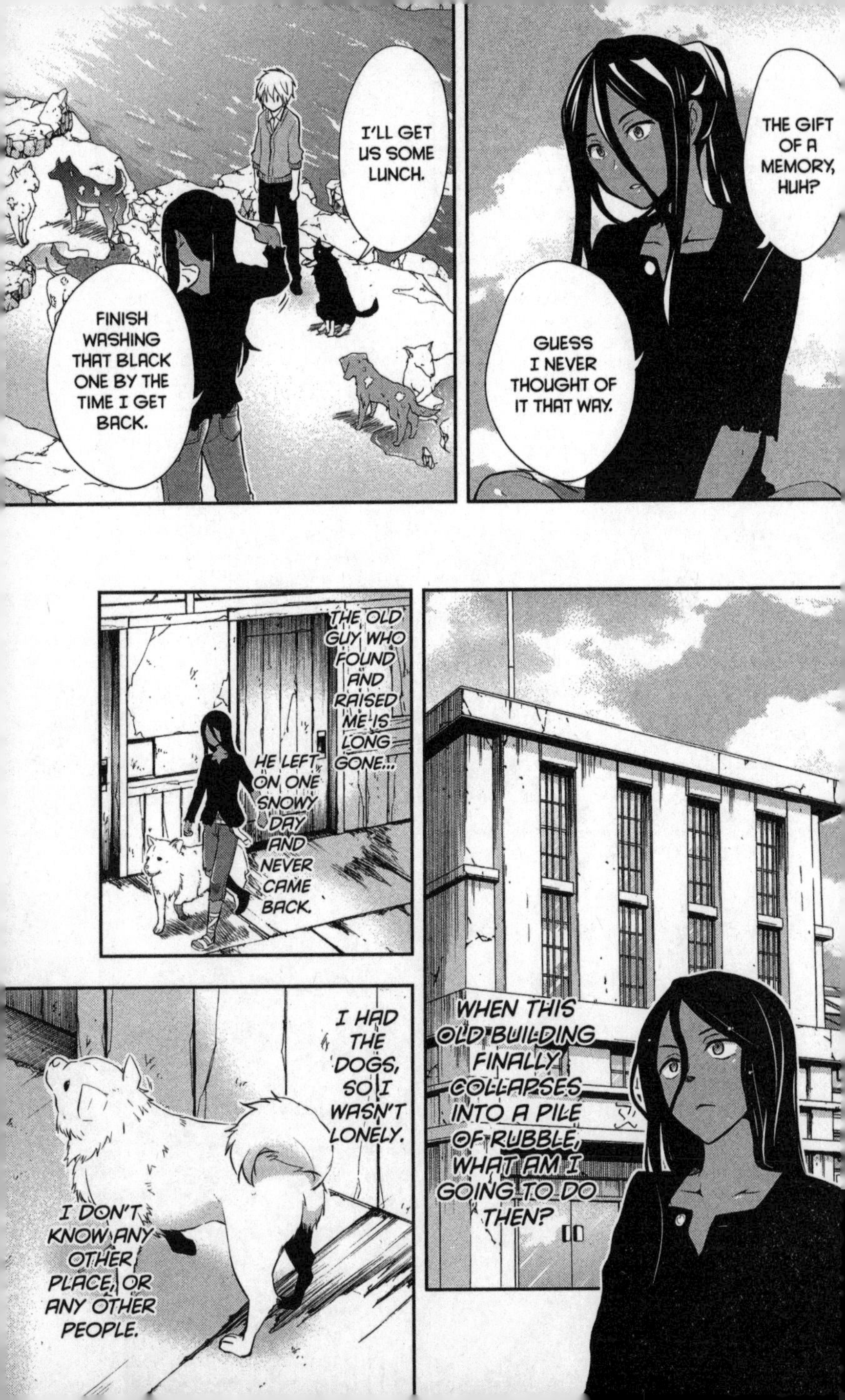
THE GIFT OF A MEMORY, HUH?
GUESS I NEVER THOUGHT OF IT THAT WAY.
I'LL GET US SOME LUNCH.
FINISH WASHING THAT BLACK ONE BY THE TIME I GET BACK.
WHEN THIS OLD BUILDING FINALLY COLLAPSES INTO A PILE OF RUBBLE, WHAT AM I GOING TO DO THEN?
THE OLD GUY WHO FOUND AND RAISED ME IS LONG GONE...
HE LEFT ON ONE SNOWY DAY AND NEVER CAME BACK.
I HAD THE DOGS, SO I WASN'T LONELY.
I DON'T KNOW ANY OTHER PLACE, OR ANY OTHER PEOPLE.

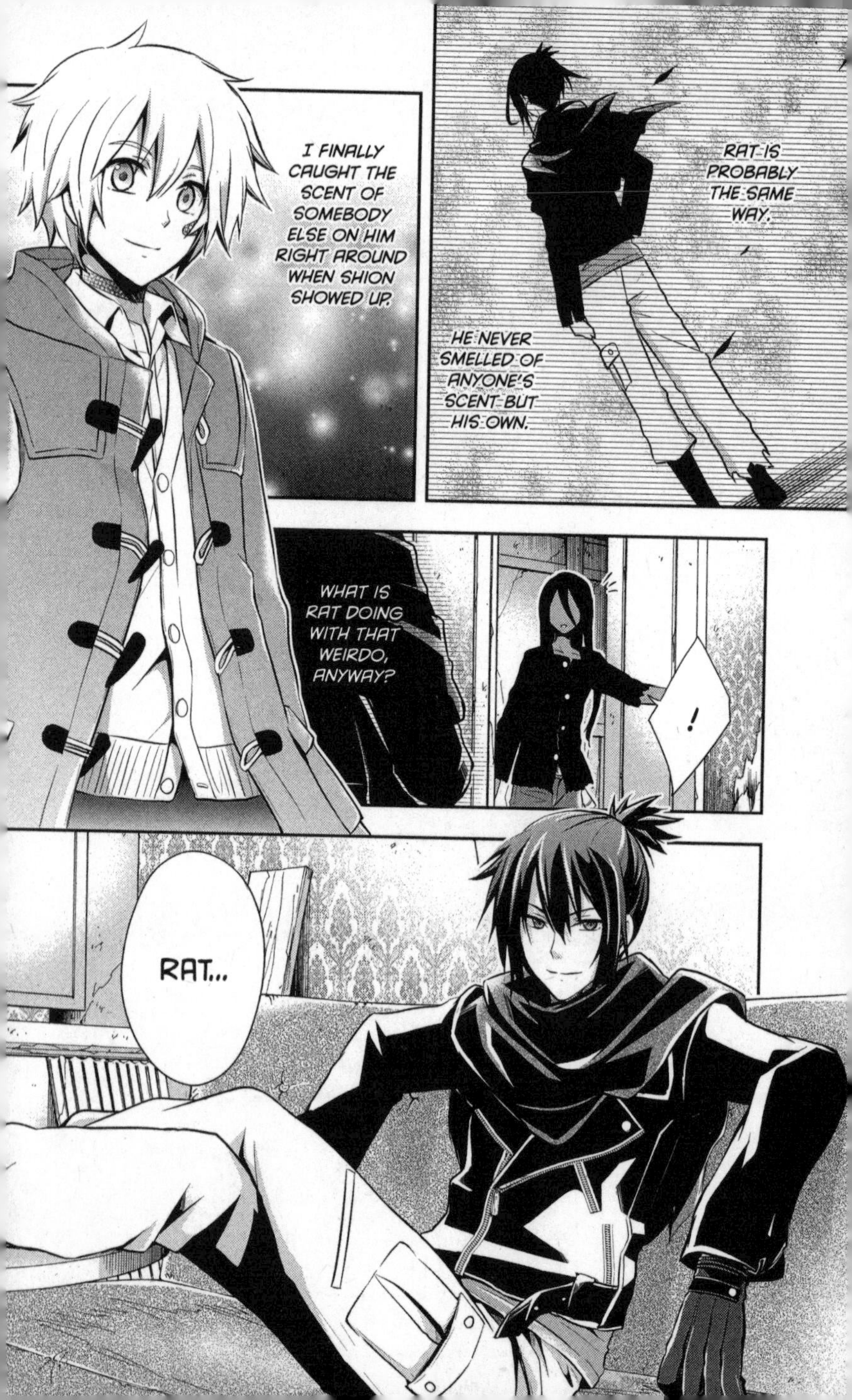
RAT IS PROBABLY THE SAME WAY.
HE NEVER SMELLED OF ANYONE'S SCENT BUT HIS OWN.
I FINALLY CAUGHT THE SCENT OF SOMEBODY ELSE ON HIM RIGHT AROUND WHEN SHION SHOWED UP.
WHAT IS RAT DOING WITH THAT WEIRDO, ANYWAY?
!
RAT...

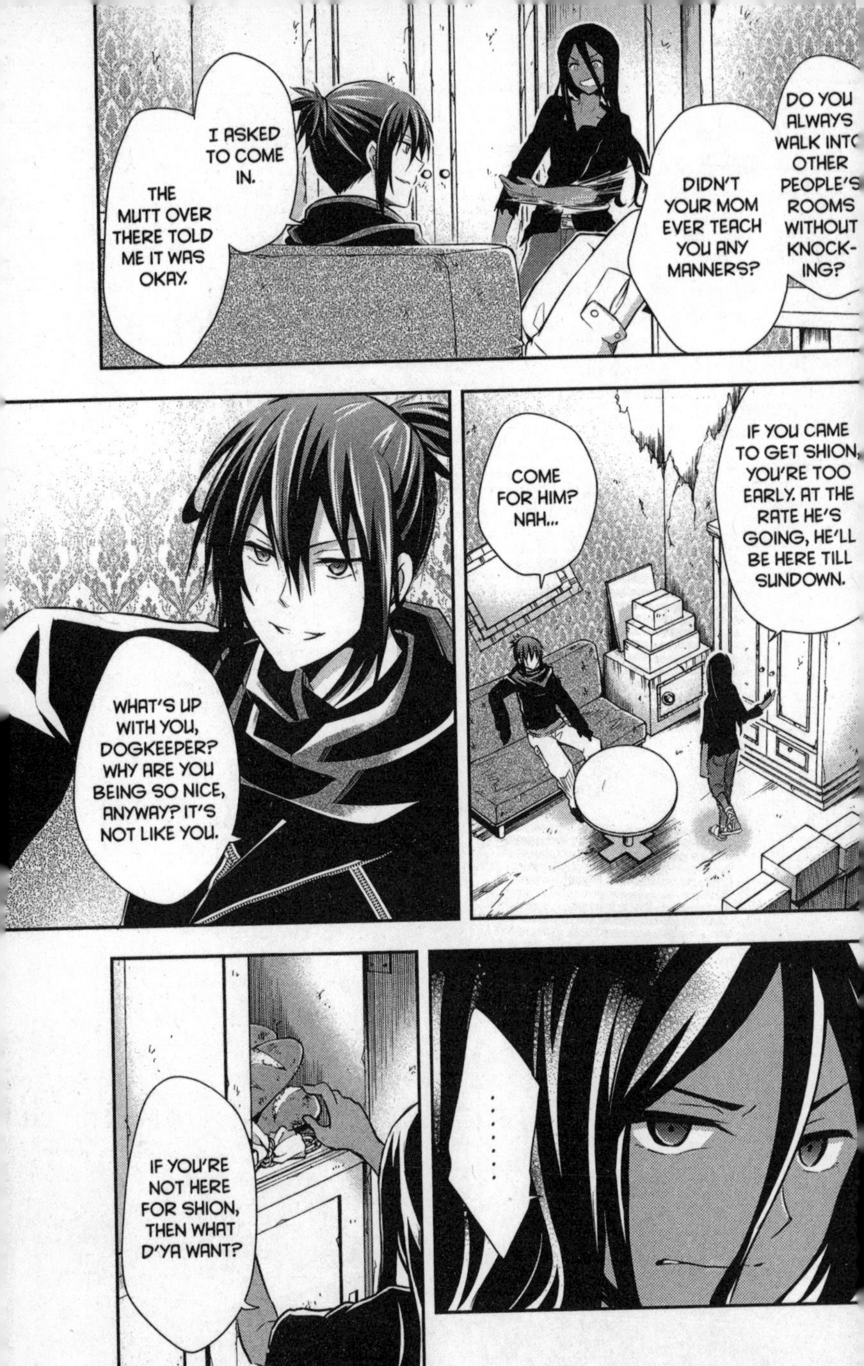
DO YOU ALWAYS WALK INTO OTHER PEOPLE'S ROOMS WITHOUT KNOCK-ING?
DIDN'T YOUR MOM EVER TEACH YOU ANY MANNERS?
I ASKED TO COME IN.
THE MUTT OVER THERE TOLD ME IT WAS OKAY.
IF YOU CAME TO GET SHION, YOU'RE TOO EARLY. AT THE RATE HE'S GOING, HE'LL BE HERE TILL SUNDOWN.
COME FOR HIM? NAH...
WHAT'S UP WITH YOU, DOGKEEPER? WHY ARE YOU BEING SO NICE, ANYWAY? IT'S NOT LIKE YOU.
......
IF YOU'RE NOT HERE FOR SHION, THEN WHAT D'YA WANT?

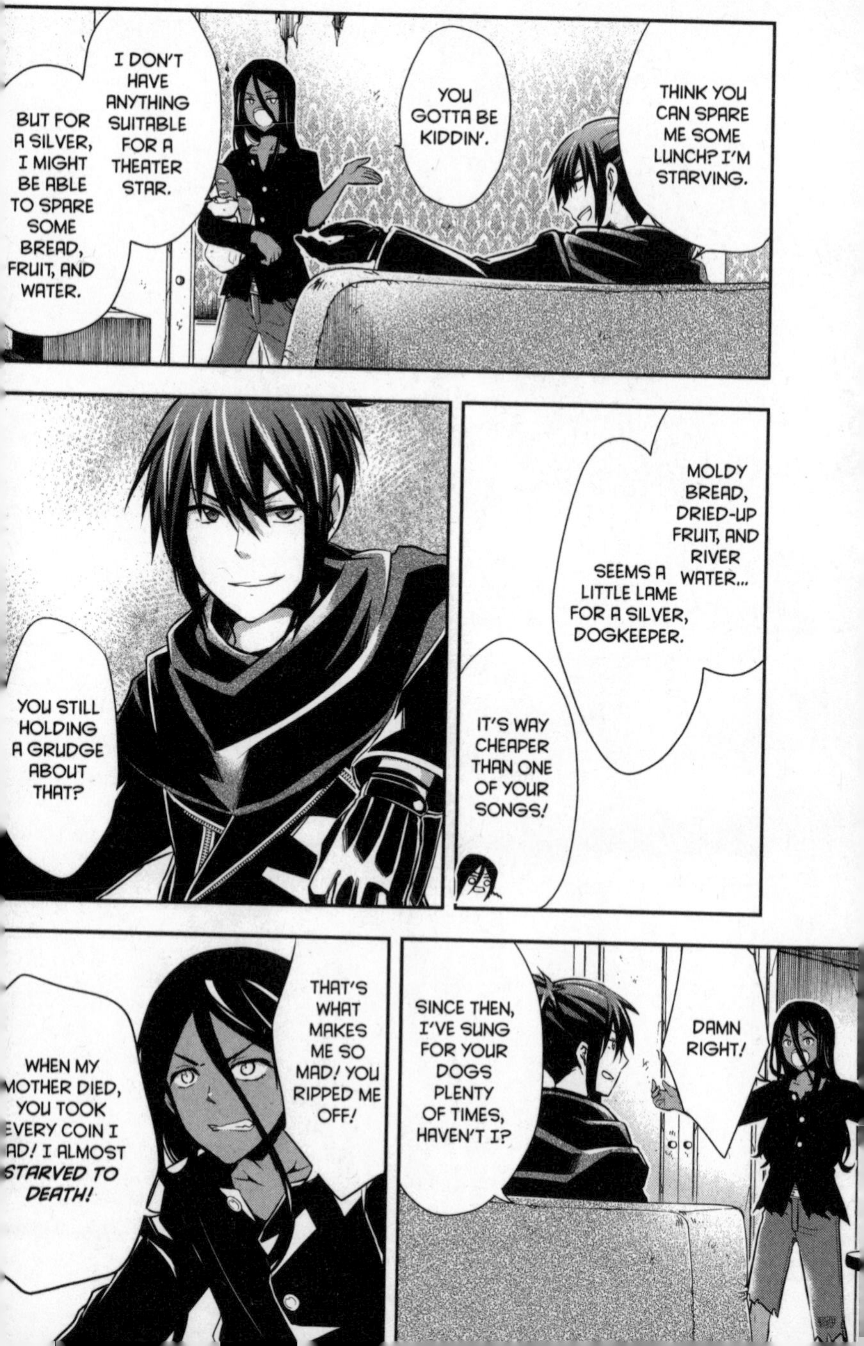
THINK YOU CAN SPARE ME SOME LUNCH? I'M STARVING.
YOU GOTTA BE KIDDIN'.
I DON'T HAVE ANYTHING SUITABLE FOR A THEATER STAR.
BUT FOR A SILVER, I MIGHT BE ABLE TO SPARE SOME BREAD, FRUIT, AND WATER.
MOLDY BREAD, DRIED-UP FRUIT, AND RIVER WATER...
SEEMS A LITTLE LAME FOR A SILVER, DOGKEEPER.
IT'S WAY CHEAPER THAN ONE OF YOUR SONGS!
YOU STILL HOLDING A GRUDGE ABOUT THAT?
DAMN RIGHT!
SINCE THEN, I'VE SUNG FOR YOUR DOGS PLENTY OF TIMES, HAVEN'T I?
THAT'S WHAT MAKES ME SO MAD! YOU RIPPED ME OFF!
WHEN MY MOTHER DIED, YOU TOOK EVERY COIN I HAD! I ALMOST *STARVED TO DEATH!*

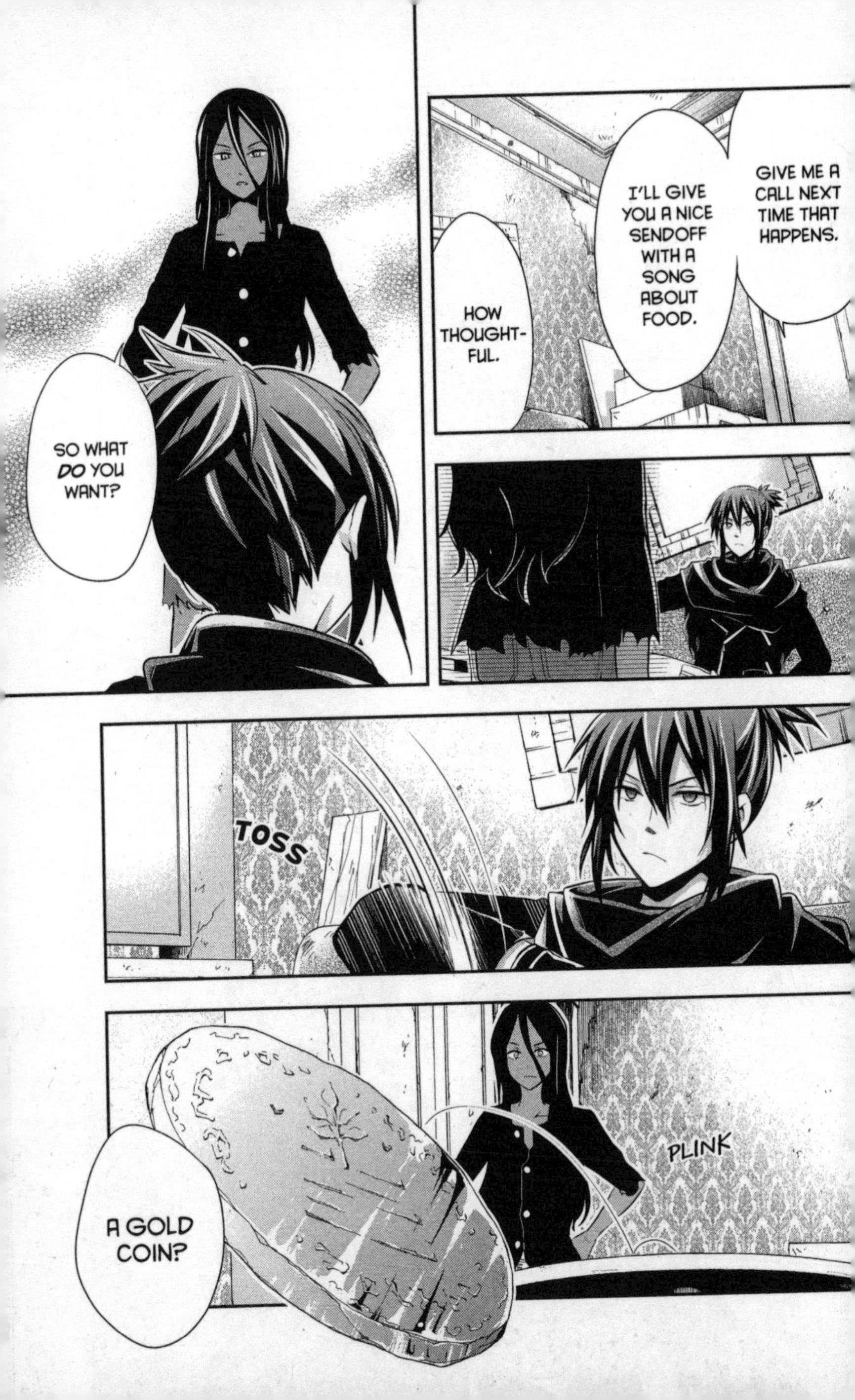
GIVE ME A CALL NEXT TIME THAT HAPPENS.
I'LL GIVE YOU A NICE SENDOFF WITH A SONG ABOUT FOOD.
HOW THOUGHT-FUL.
SO WHAT DO YOU WANT?
TOSS
PLINK
A GOLD COIN?

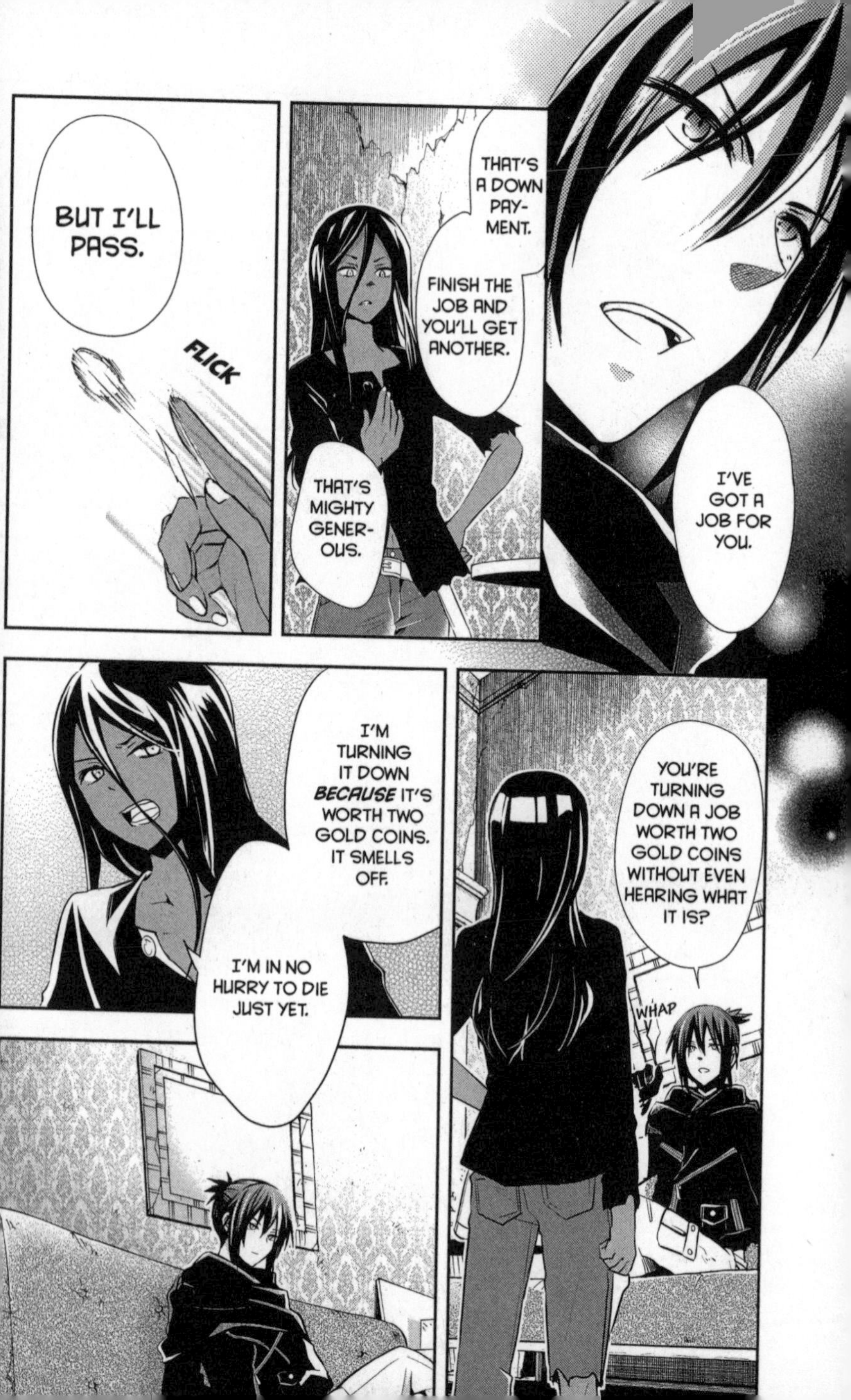
I'VE GOT A JOB FOR YOU.
THAT'S A DOWN PAY-MENT.
FINISH THE JOB AND YOU'LL GET ANOTHER.
THAT'S MIGHTY GENER-OUS.
BUT I'LL PASS.
FLICK
YOU'RE TURNING DOWN A JOB WORTH TWO GOLD COINS WITHOUT EVEN HEARING WHAT IT IS?
WHAP
I'M TURNING IT DOWN *BECAUSE* IT'S WORTH TWO GOLD COINS. IT SMELLS OFF.
I'M IN NO HURRY TO DIE JUST YET.

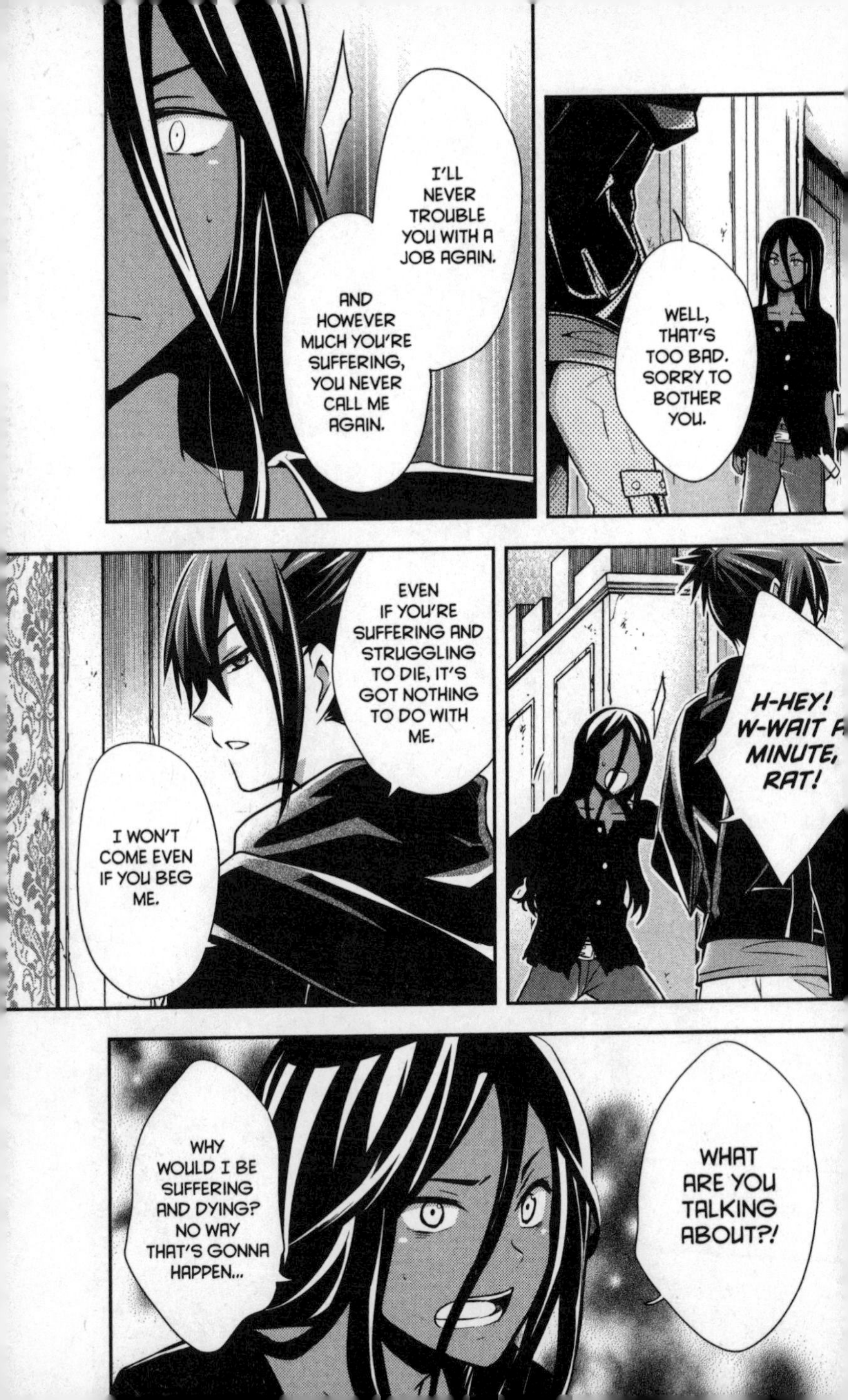
WELL, THAT'S TOO BAD. SORRY TO BOTHER YOU.
I'LL NEVER TROUBLE YOU WITH A JOB AGAIN.
AND HOWEVER MUCH YOU'RE SUFFERING, YOU NEVER CALL ME AGAIN.
H-HEY! W-WAIT A MINUTE, RAT!
EVEN IF YOU'RE SUFFERING AND STRUGGLING TO DIE, IT'S GOT NOTHING TO DO WITH ME.
I WON'T COME EVEN IF YOU BEG ME.
WHAT ARE YOU TALKING ABOUT?!
WHY WOULD I BE SUFFERING AND DYING? NO WAY THAT'S GONNA HAPPEN...

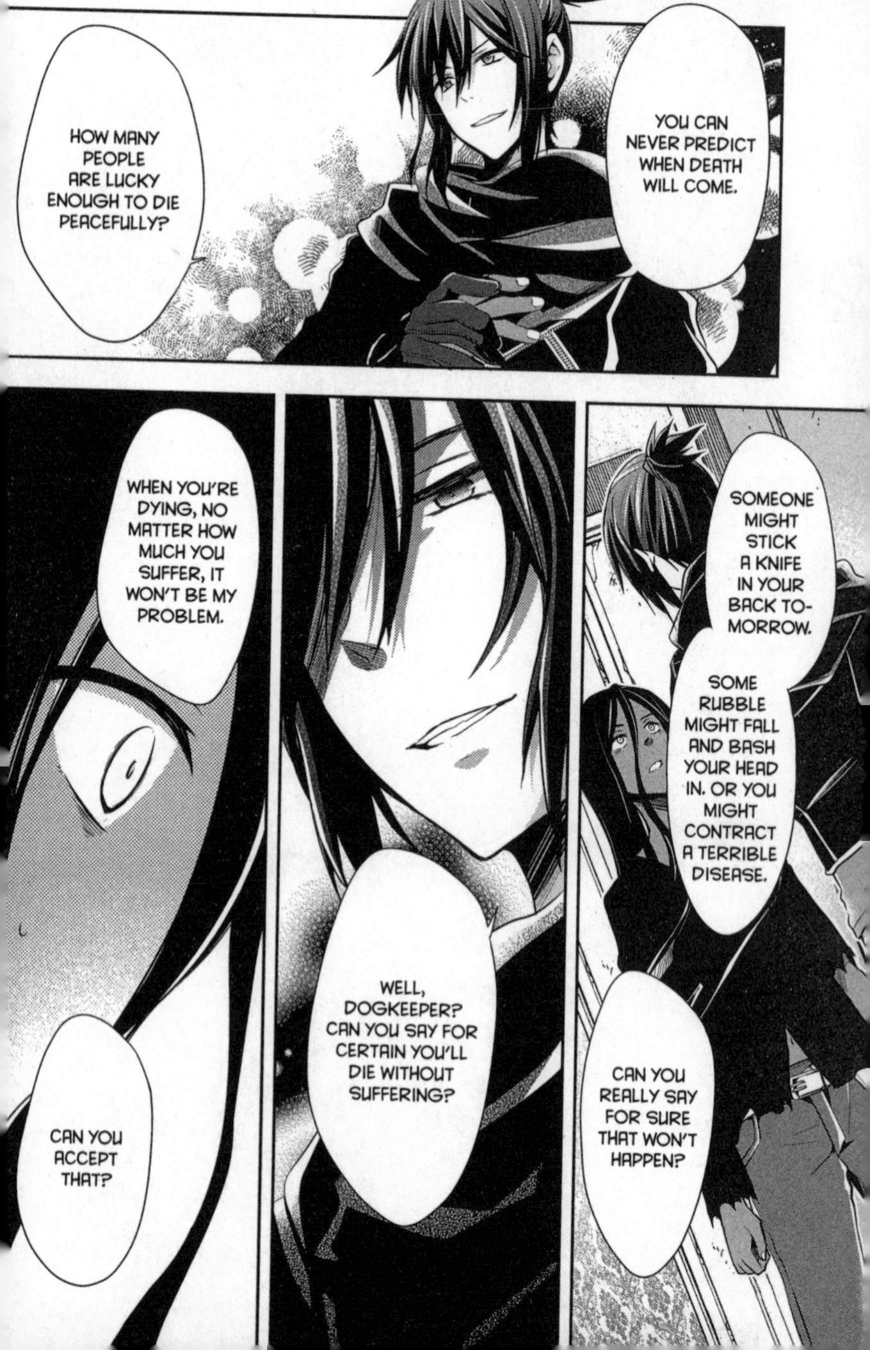
YOU CAN NEVER PREDICT WHEN DEATH WILL COME.
HOW MANY PEOPLE ARE LUCKY ENOUGH TO DIE PEACEFULLY?
SOMEONE MIGHT STICK A KNIFE IN YOUR BACK TO-MORROW.
SOME RUBBLE MIGHT FALL AND BASH YOUR HEAD IN. OR YOU MIGHT CONTRACT A TERRIBLE DISEASE.
CAN YOU REALLY SAY FOR SURE THAT WON'T HAPPEN?
WELL, DOGKEEPER? CAN YOU SAY FOR CERTAIN YOU'LL DIE WITHOUT SUFFERING?
WHEN YOU'RE DYING, NO MATTER HOW MUCH YOU SUFFER, IT WON'T BE MY PROBLEM.
CAN YOU ACCEPT THAT?

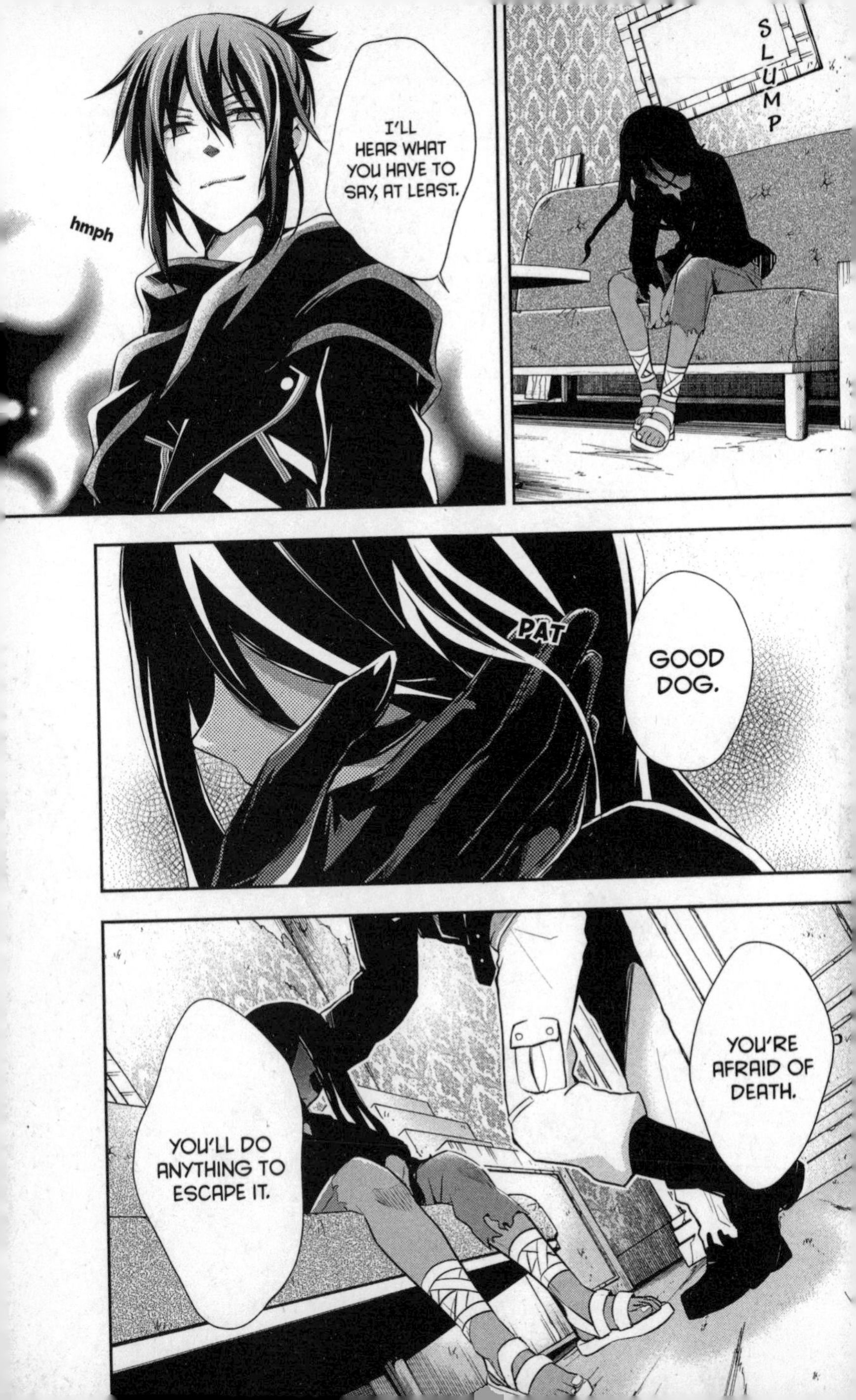
SLUMP
hmph
I'LL HEAR WHAT YOU HAVE TO SAY, AT LEAST.
PAT
GOOD DOG.
YOU'RE AFRAID OF DEATH.
YOU'LL DO ANYTHING TO ESCAPE IT.

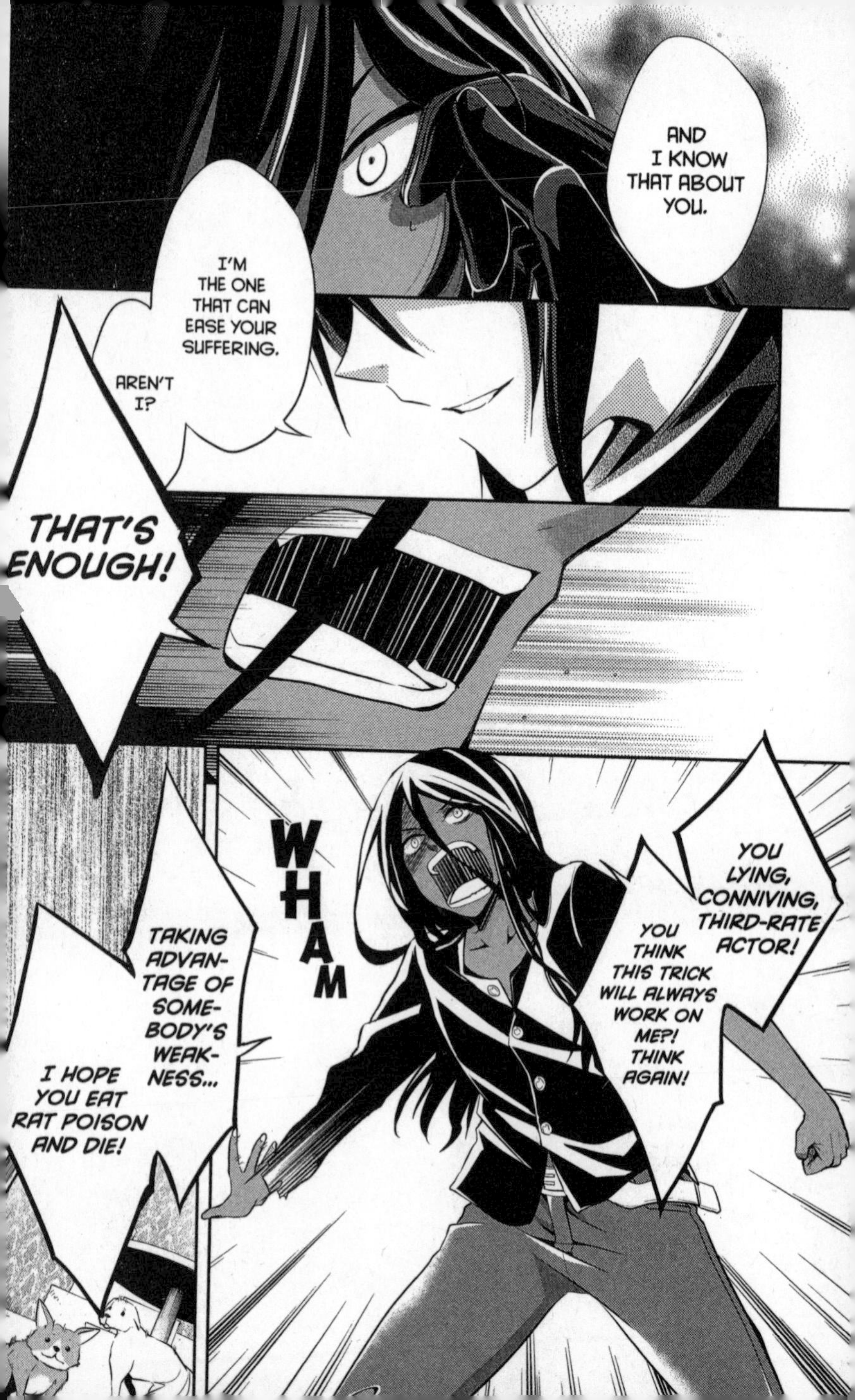
AND I KNOW THAT ABOUT YOU.
I'M THE ONE THAT CAN EASE YOUR SUFFERING.
AREN'T I?
THAT'S ENOUGH!
YOU LYING, CONNIVING, THIRD-RATE ACTOR!
YOU THINK THIS TRICK WILL ALWAYS WORK ON ME?! THINK AGAIN!
WHAM
TAKING ADVANTAGE OF SOMEBODY'S WEAKNESS...
I HOPE YOU EAT RAT POISON AND DIE!

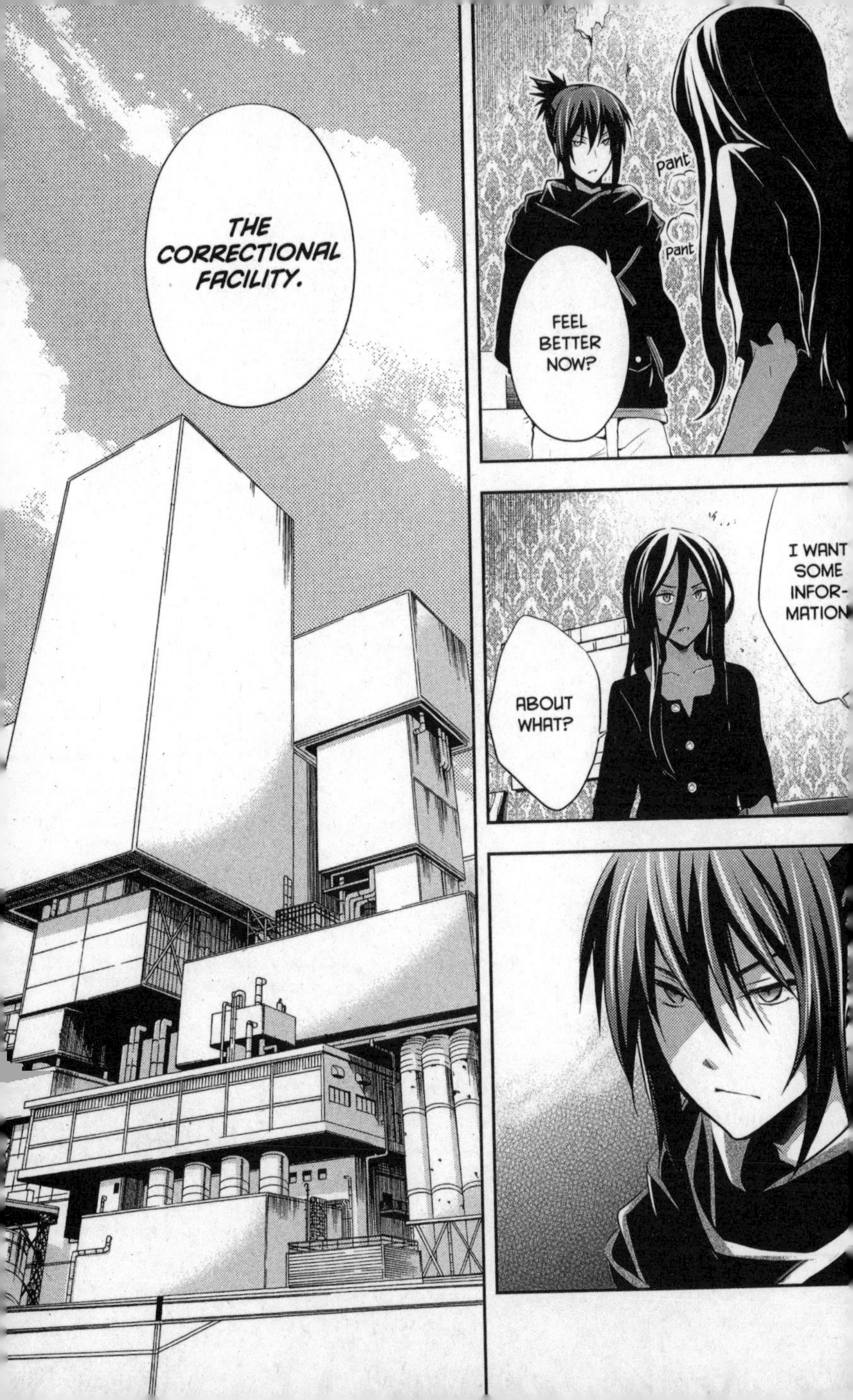
pant
pant
FEEL BETTER NOW?
I WANT SOME INFOR-MATION
ABOUT WHAT?
THE CORRECTIONAL FACILITY.

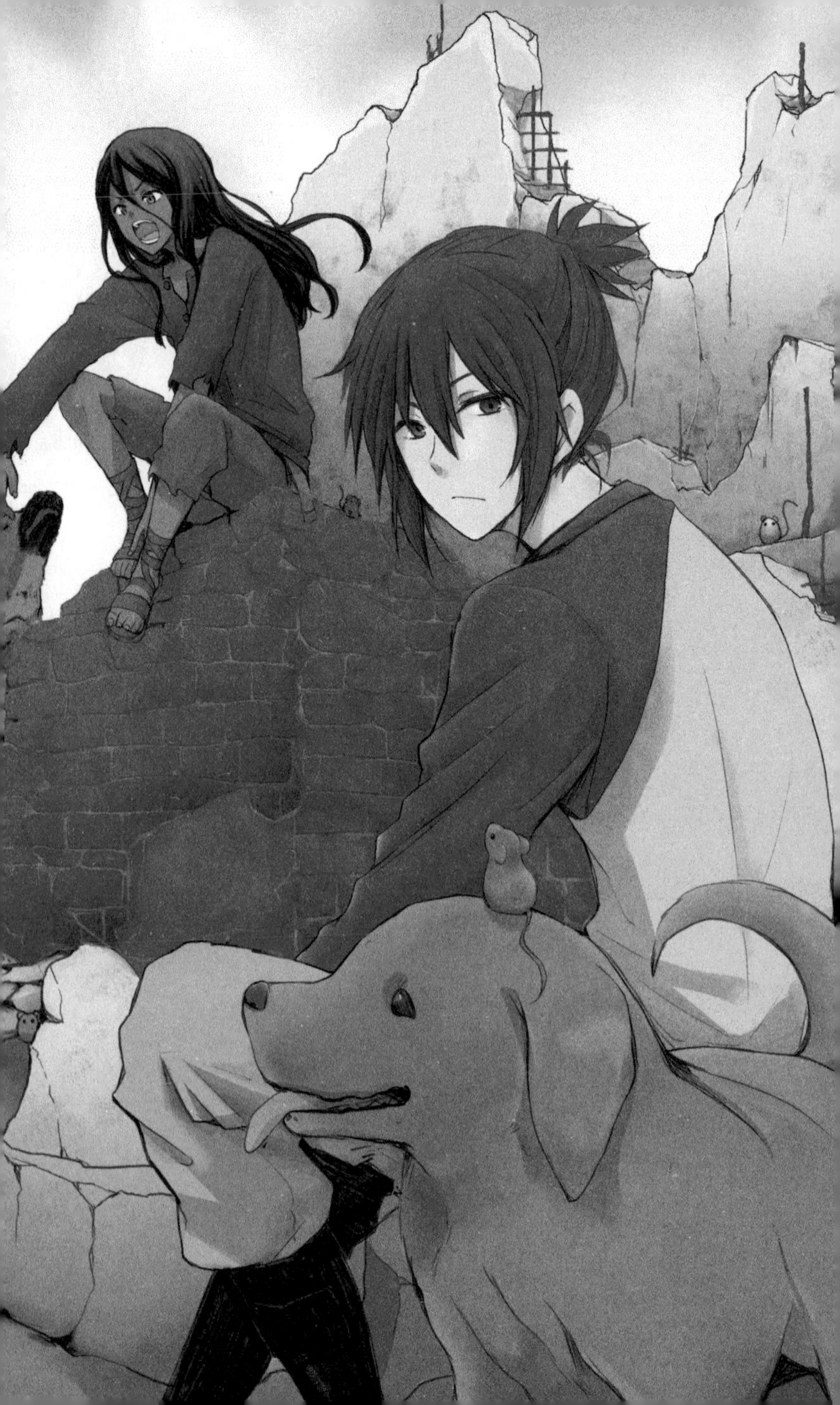

Chapter 10: Hidden Dangers

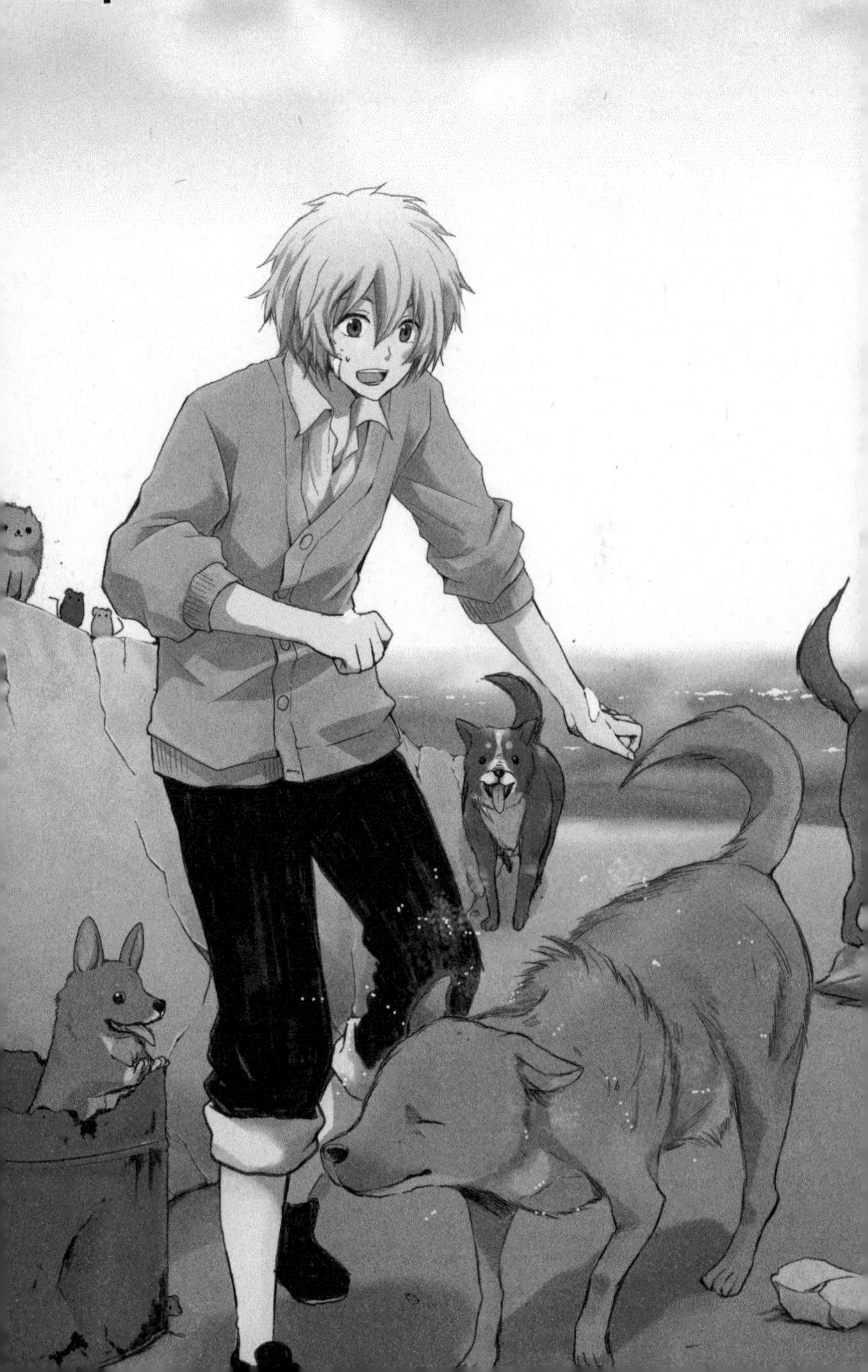

NO.6

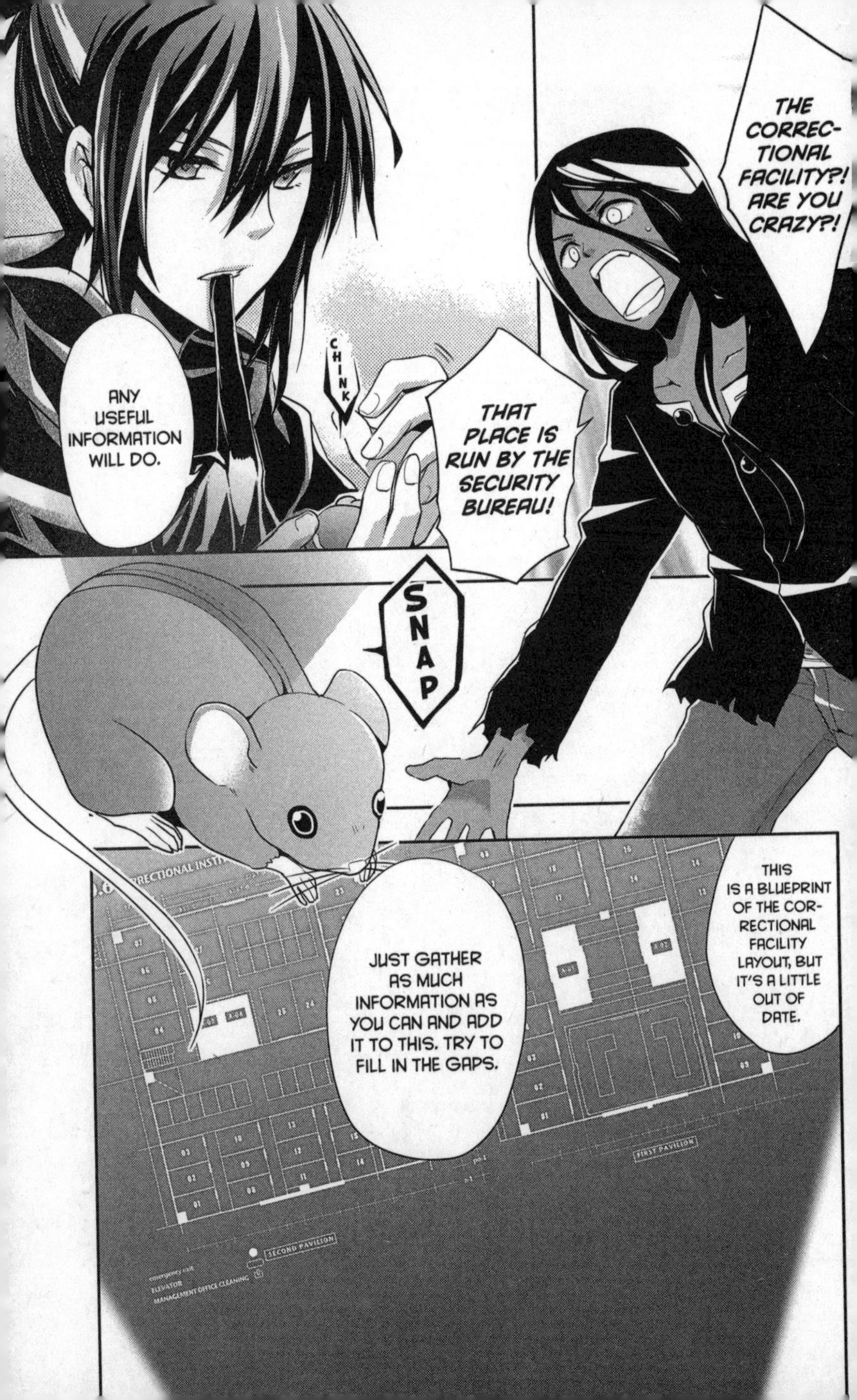
THE CORRECTIONAL FACILITY?! ARE YOU CRAZY?!
THAT PLACE IS RUN BY THE SECURITY BUREAU!
CHINK
ANY USEFUL INFORMATION WILL DO.
SNAP
THIS IS A BLUEPRINT OF THE CORRECTIONAL FACILITY LAYOUT, BUT IT'S A LITTLE OUT OF DATE.
JUST GATHER AS MUCH INFORMATION AS YOU CAN AND ADD IT TO THIS. TRY TO FILL IN THE GAPS.
FIRST PAVILION
SECOND PAVILION
ELEVATOR
MANAGEMENT OFFICE CLEANING

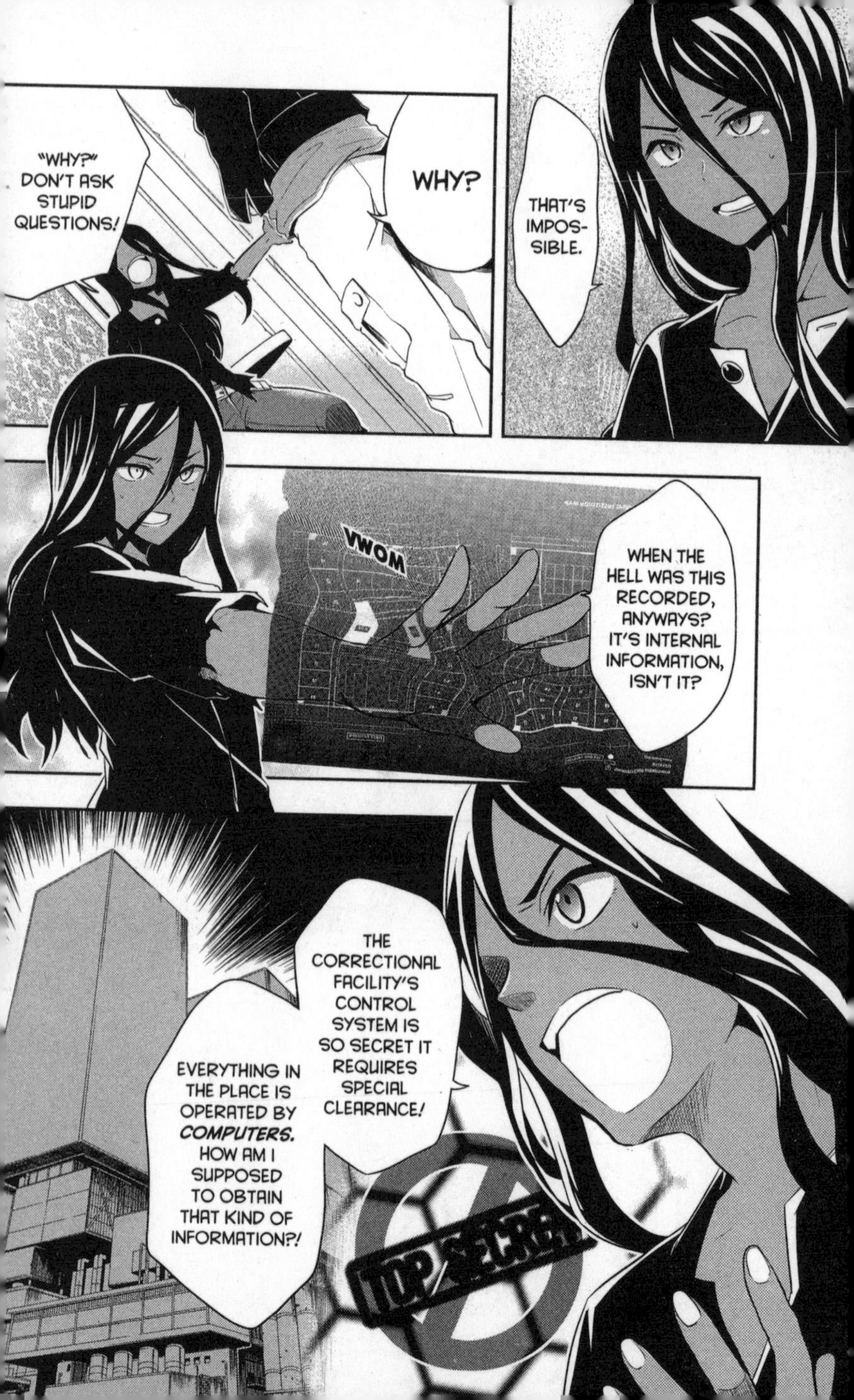
THAT'S IMPOS-SIBLE.
WHY?
"WHY?" DON'T ASK STUPID QUESTIONS!
WHEN THE HELL WAS THIS RECORDED, ANYWAYS? IT'S INTERNAL INFORMATION, ISN'T IT?
VWOM
THE CORRECTIONAL FACILITY'S CONTROL SYSTEM IS SO SECRET IT REQUIRES SPECIAL CLEARANCE!
EVERYTHING IN THE PLACE IS OPERATED BY *COMPUTERS.* HOW AM I SUPPOSED TO OBTAIN THAT KIND OF INFORMATION?!
TOP SECRET

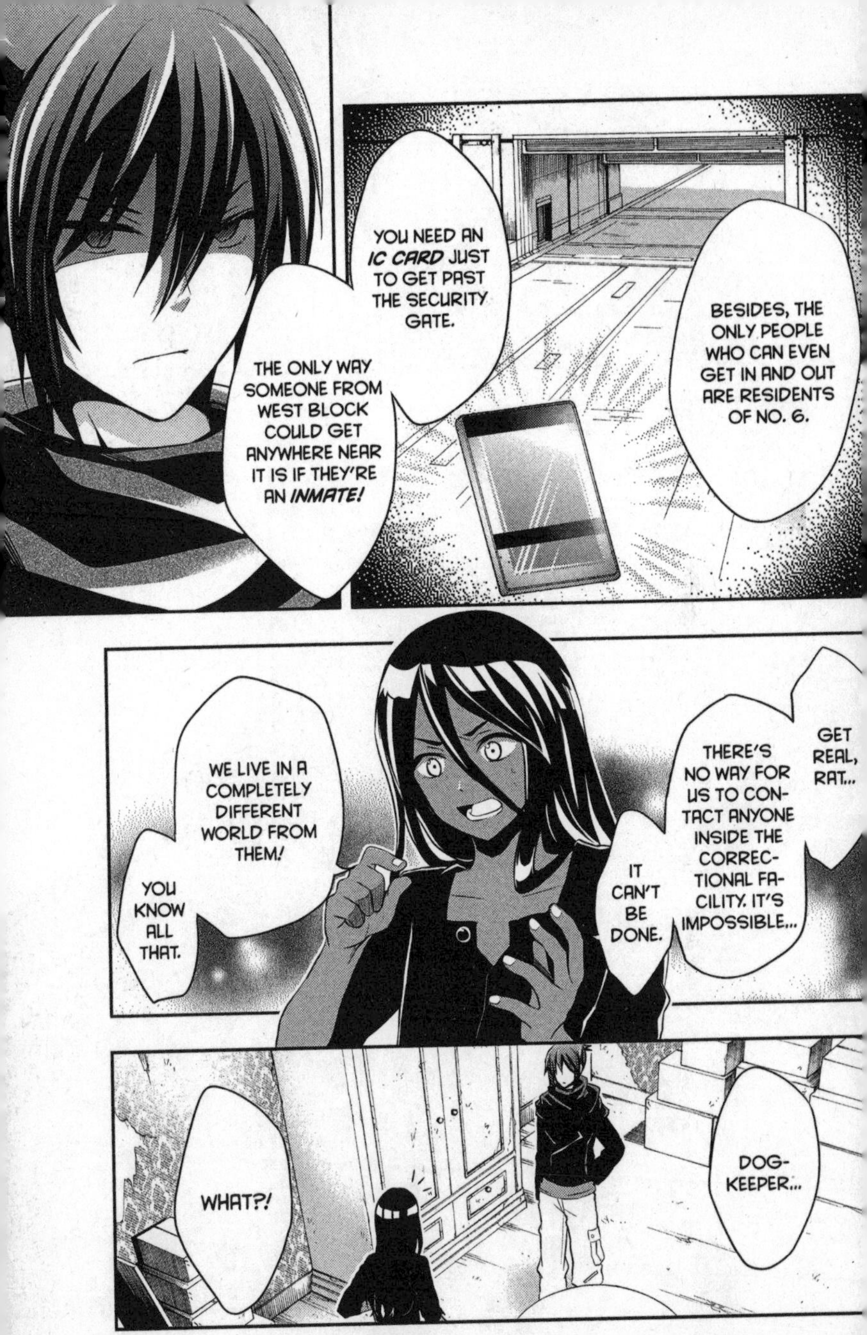
BESIDES, THE ONLY PEOPLE WHO CAN EVEN GET IN AND OUT ARE RESIDENTS OF NO. 6.
YOU NEED AN *IC CARD* JUST TO GET PAST THE SECURITY GATE.
THE ONLY WAY SOMEONE FROM WEST BLOCK COULD GET ANYWHERE NEAR IT IS IF THEY'RE AN *INMATE!*
GET REAL, RAT...
THERE'S NO WAY FOR US TO CONTACT ANYONE INSIDE THE CORRECTIONAL FACILITY. IT'S IMPOSSIBLE...
IT CAN'T BE DONE.
WE LIVE IN A COMPLETELY DIFFERENT WORLD FROM THEM!
YOU KNOW ALL THAT.
DOG-KEEPER...
WHAT?!

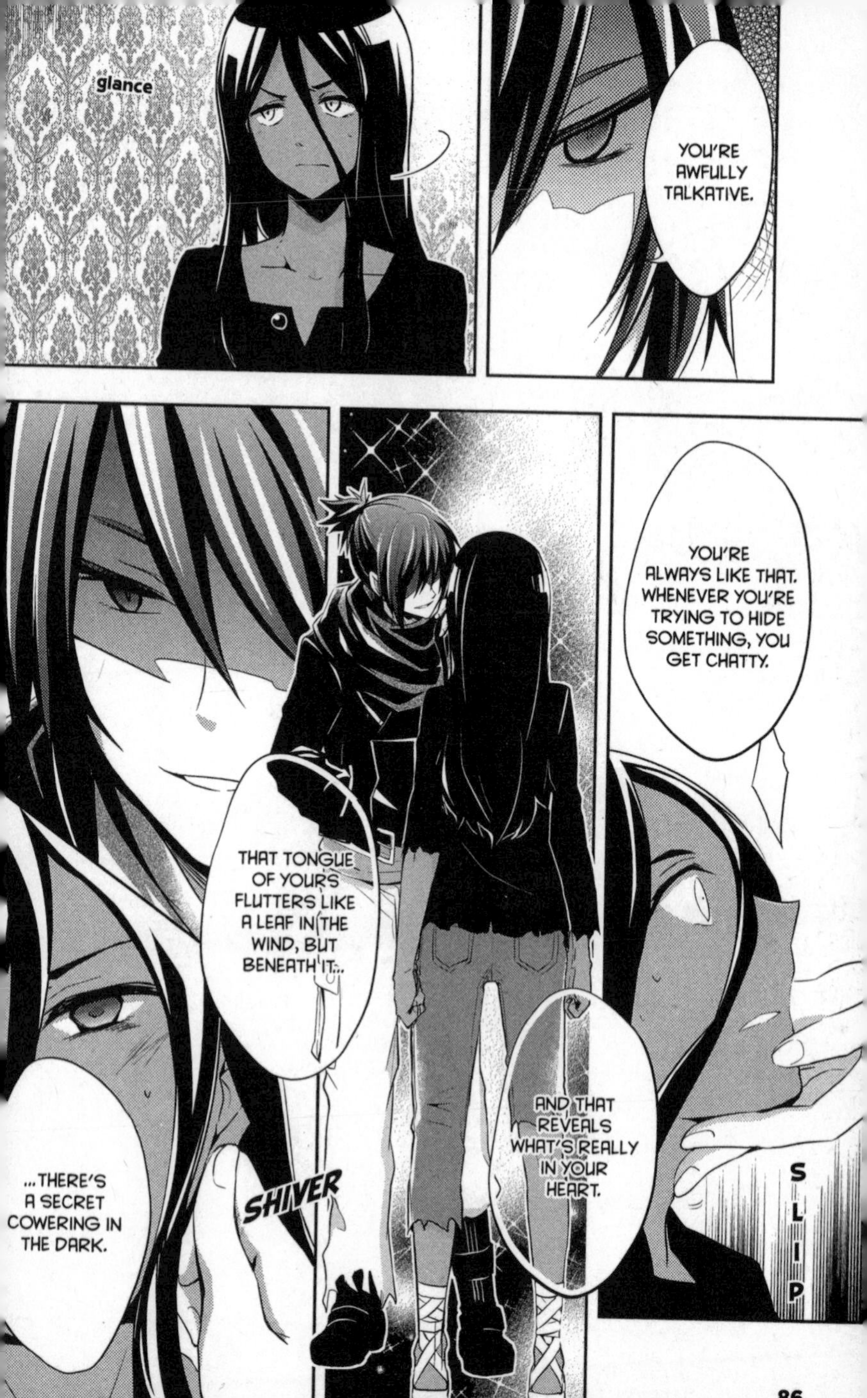
YOU'RE AWFULLY TALKATIVE.
glance
YOU'RE ALWAYS LIKE THAT. WHENEVER YOU'RE TRYING TO HIDE SOMETHING, YOU GET CHATTY.
THAT TONGUE OF YOURS FLUTTERS LIKE A LEAF IN THE WIND, BUT BENEATH IT...
AND THAT REVEALS WHAT'S REALLY IN YOUR HEART.
SLIP
...THERE'S A SECRET COWERING IN THE DARK.
SHIVER

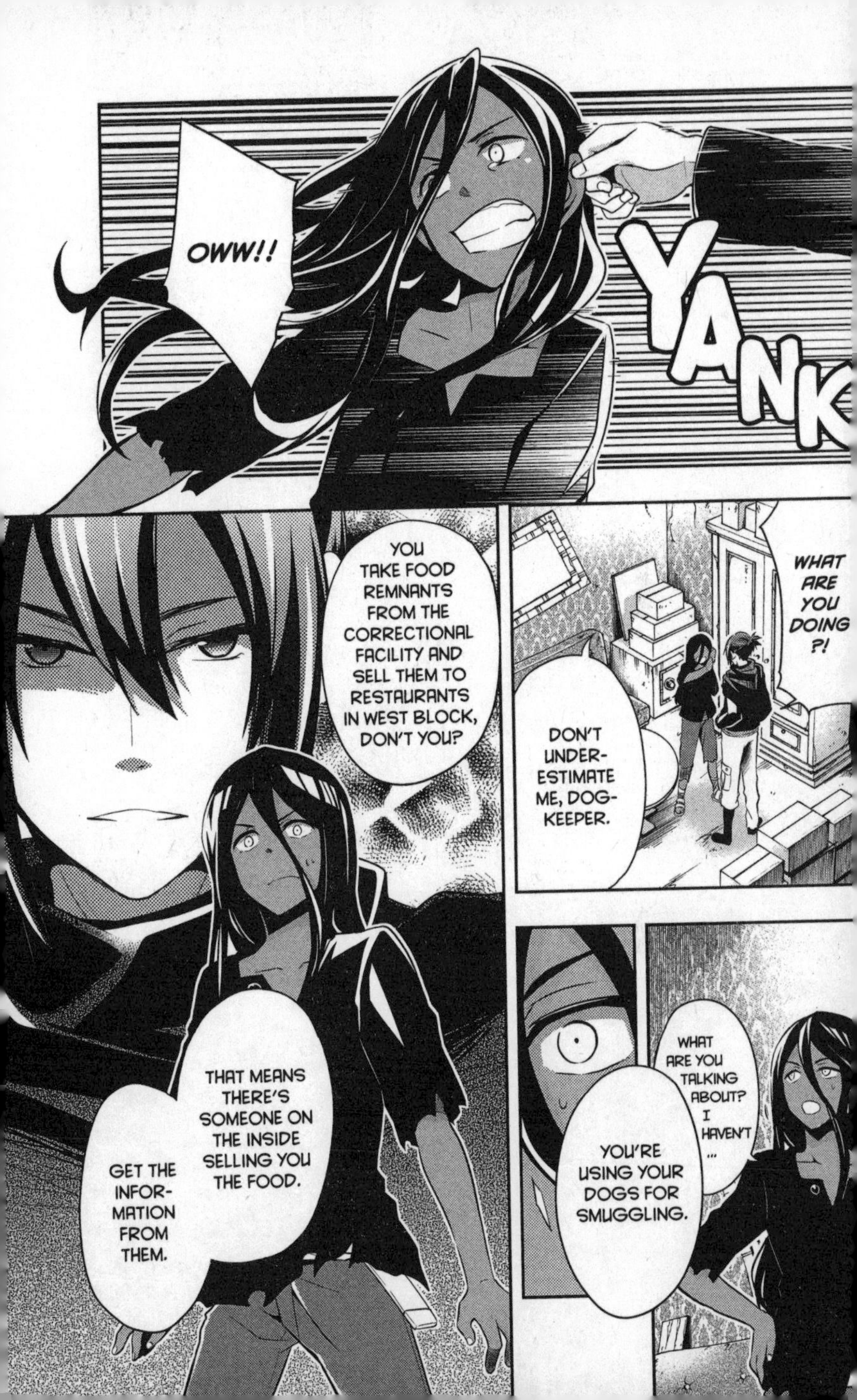
YANK
OWW!!
WHAT ARE YOU DOING?!
DON'T UNDER-ESTIMATE ME, DOG-KEEPER.
WHAT ARE YOU TALKING ABOUT? I HAVEN'T...
YOU'RE USING YOUR DOGS FOR SMUGGLING.
YOU TAKE FOOD REMNANTS FROM THE CORRECTIONAL FACILITY AND SELL THEM TO RESTAURANTS IN WEST BLOCK, DON'T YOU?
THAT MEANS THERE'S SOMEONE ON THE INSIDE SELLING YOU THE FOOD.
GET THE INFOR-MATION FROM THEM.

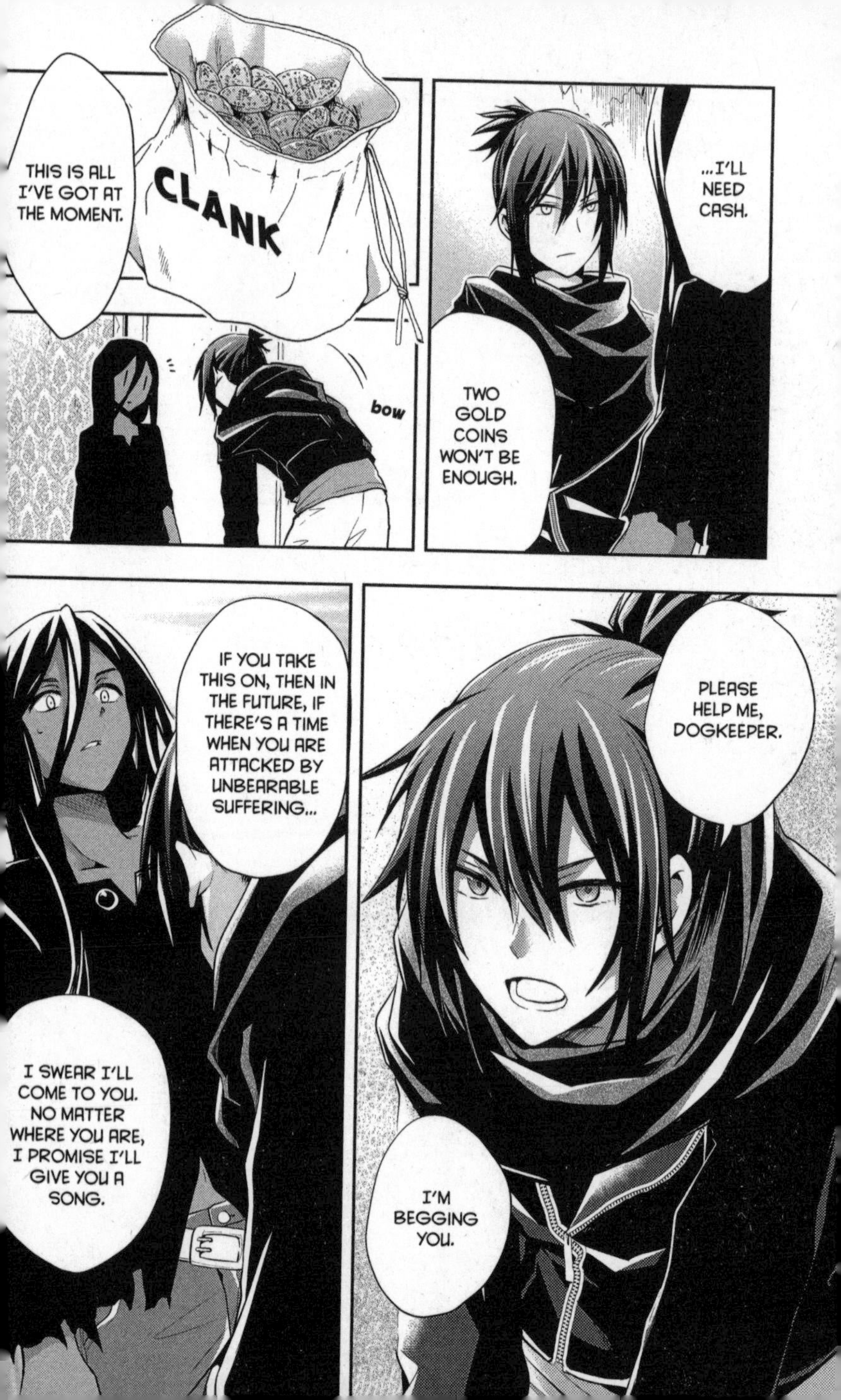
...I'LL NEED CASH.
TWO GOLD COINS WON'T BE ENOUGH.
THIS IS ALL I'VE GOT AT THE MOMENT.
CLANK
bow
PLEASE HELP ME, DOGKEEPER.
I'M BEGGING YOU.
IF YOU TAKE THIS ON, THEN IN THE FUTURE, IF THERE'S A TIME WHEN YOU ARE ATTACKED BY UNBEARABLE SUFFERING...
I SWEAR I'LL COME TO YOU. NO MATTER WHERE YOU ARE, I PROMISE I'LL GIVE YOU A SONG.

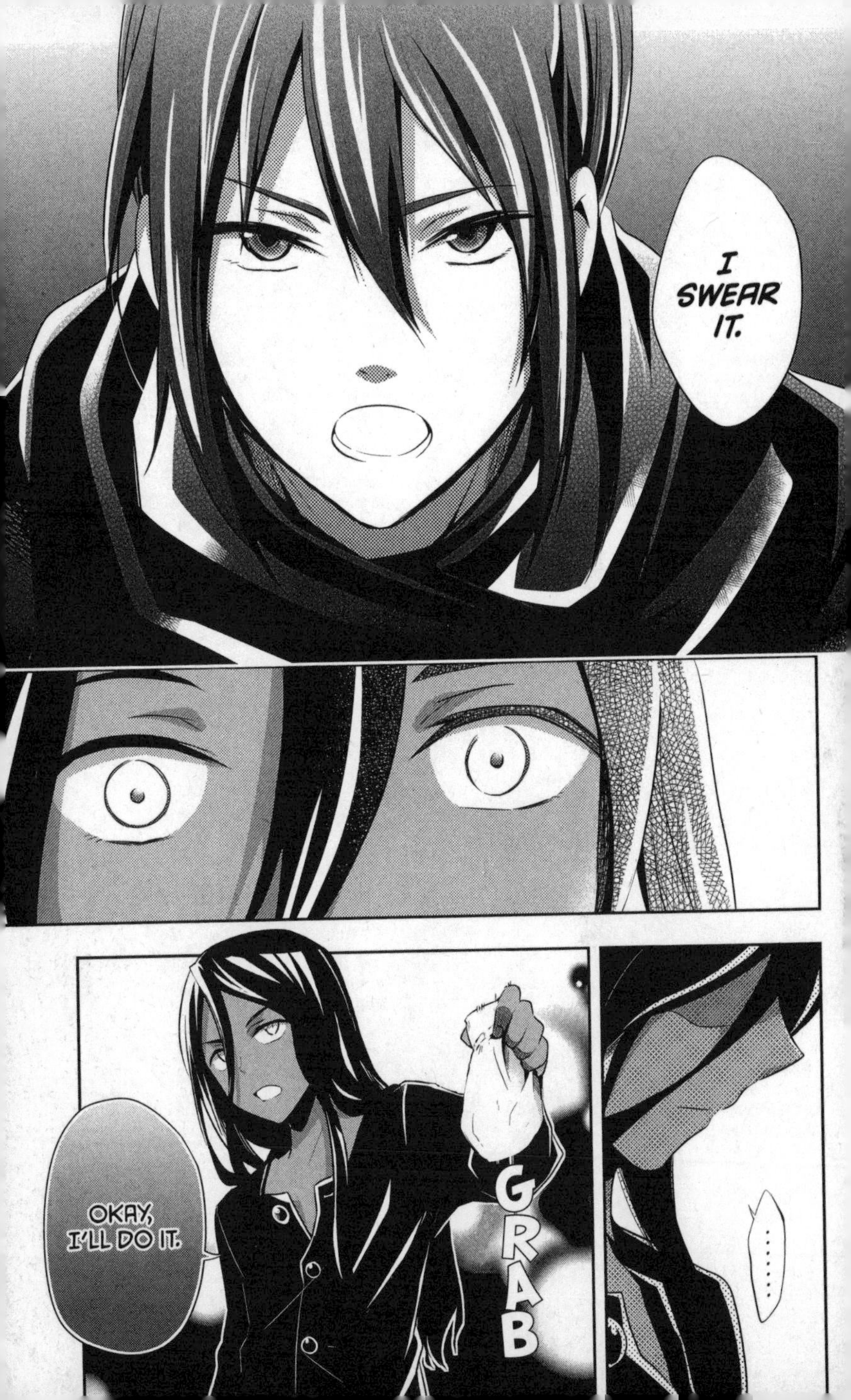
I SWEAR IT.
......
GRAB
OKAY, I'LL DO IT.

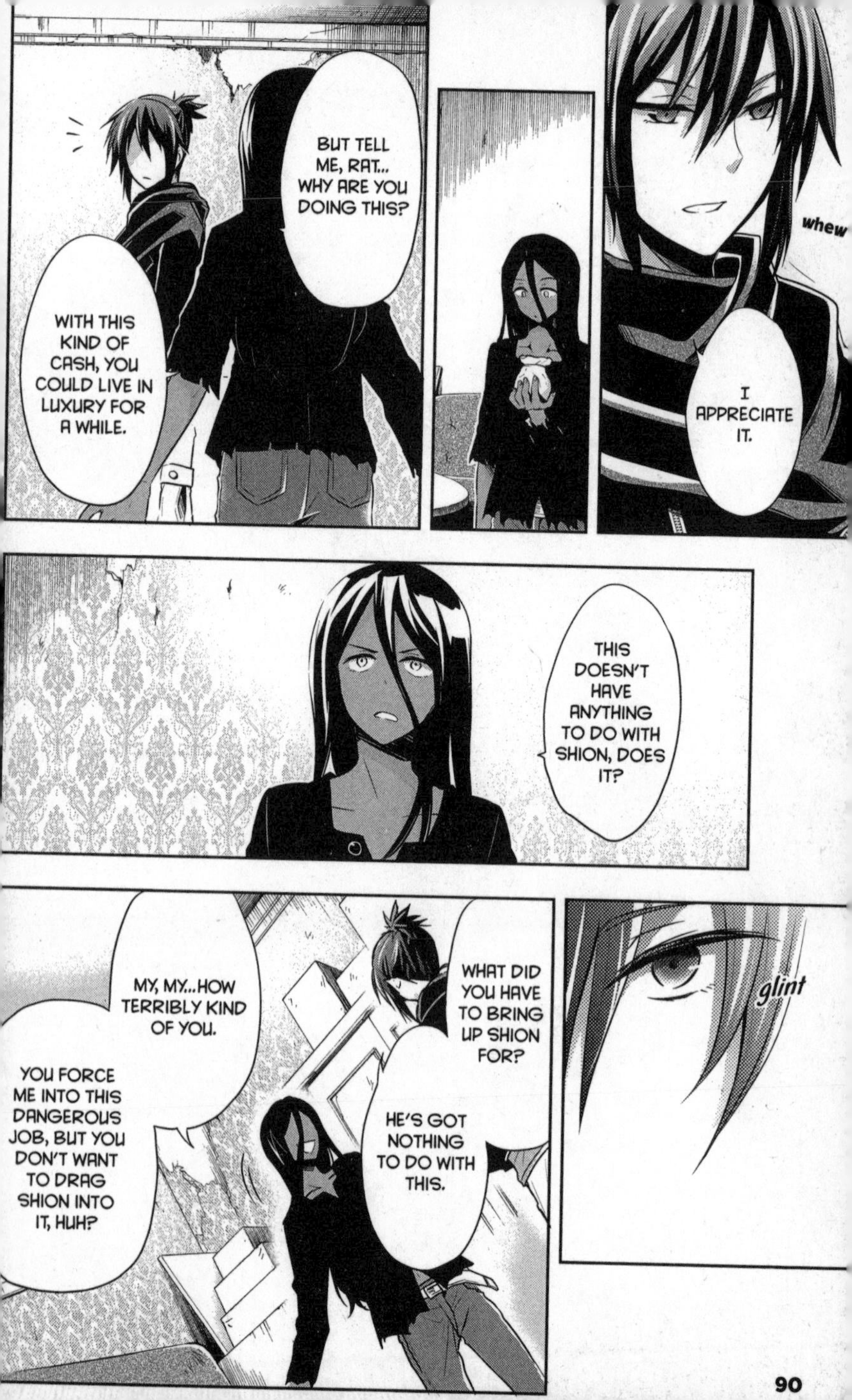
whew
I APPRECIATE IT.
BUT TELL ME, RAT... WHY ARE YOU DOING THIS?
WITH THIS KIND OF CASH, YOU COULD LIVE IN LUXURY FOR A WHILE.
THIS DOESN'T HAVE ANYTHING TO DO WITH SHION, DOES IT?
glint
WHAT DID YOU HAVE TO BRING UP SHION FOR?
HE'S GOT NOTHING TO DO WITH THIS.
MY, MY...HOW TERRIBLY KIND OF YOU.
YOU FORCE ME INTO THIS DANGEROUS JOB, BUT YOU DON'T WANT TO DRAG SHION INTO IT, HUH?

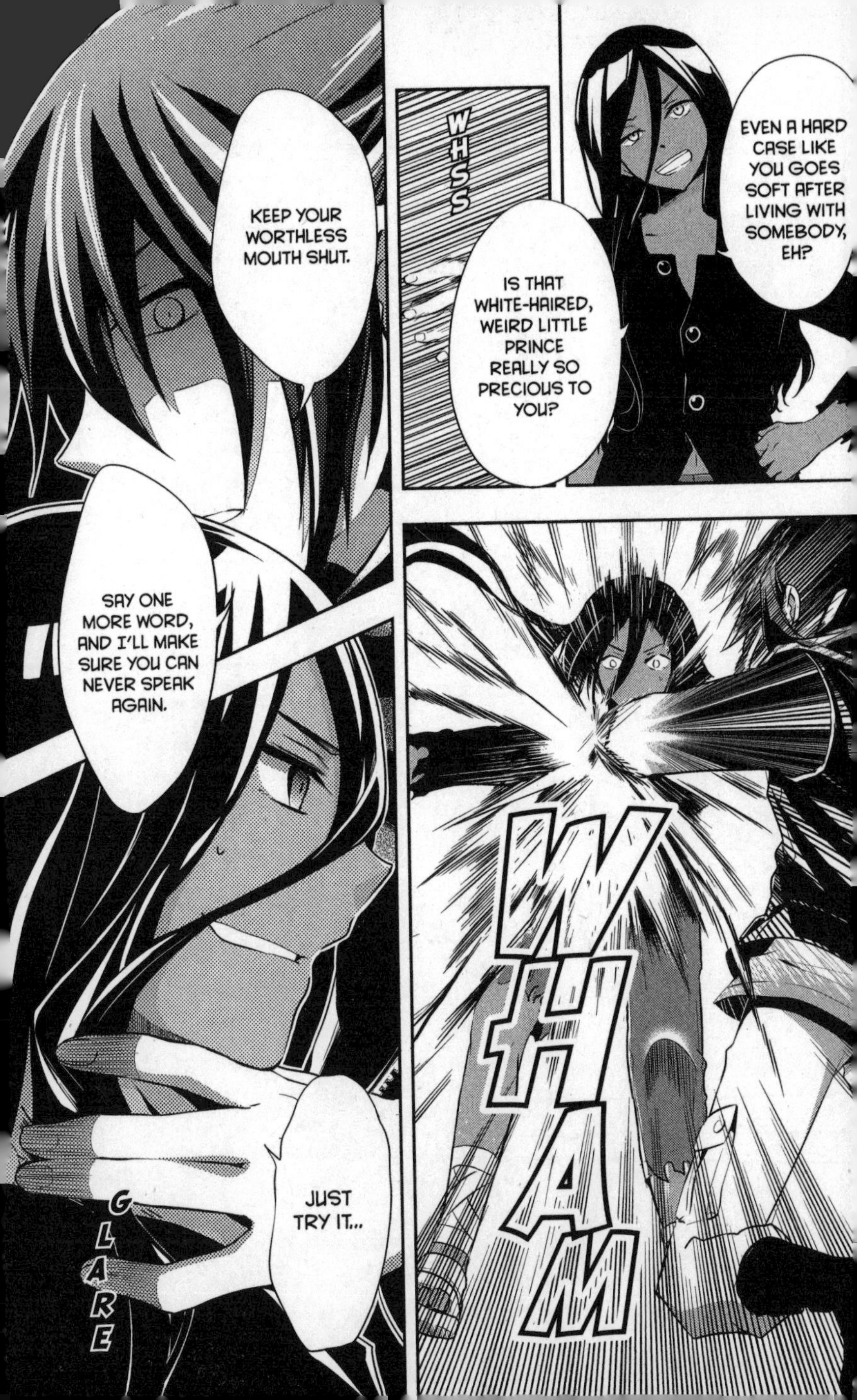
EVEN A HARD CASE LIKE YOU GOES SOFT AFTER LIVING WITH SOMEBODY, EH?
IS THAT WHITE-HAIRED, WEIRD LITTLE PRINCE REALLY SO PRECIOUS TO YOU?
WHSS
KEEP YOUR WORTHLESS MOUTH SHUT.
WHAM
SAY ONE MORE WORD, AND I'LL MAKE SURE YOU CAN NEVER SPEAK AGAIN.
JUST TRY IT...
GLARE

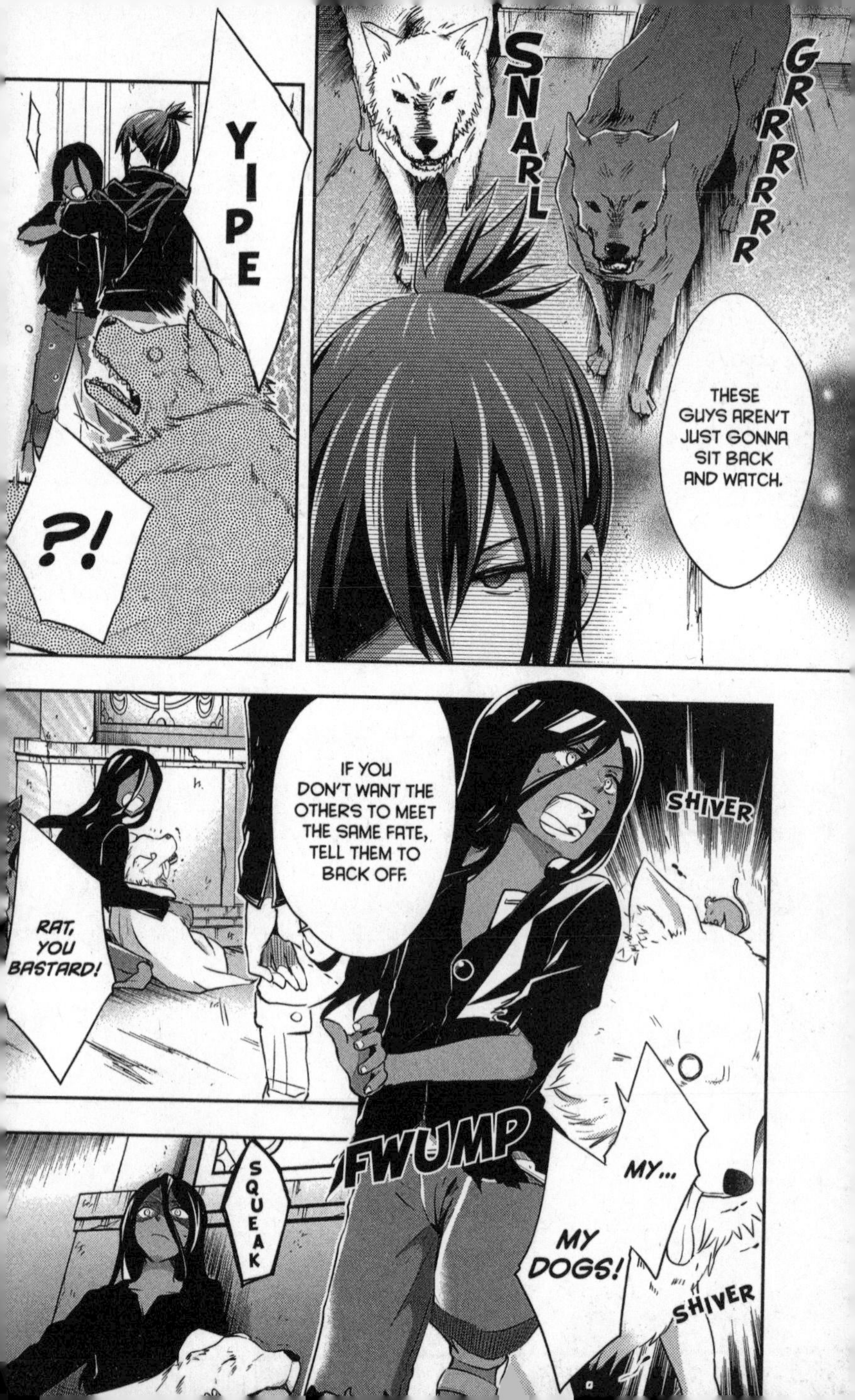
SNARL
GRRRRRR
THESE GUYS AREN'T JUST GONNA SIT BACK AND WATCH.
YIPE
?!
IF YOU DON'T WANT THE OTHERS TO MEET THE SAME FATE, TELL THEM TO BACK OFF.
SHIVER
FWUMP
MY...
MY DOGS!
SHIVER
RAT, YOU BASTARD!
SQUEAK

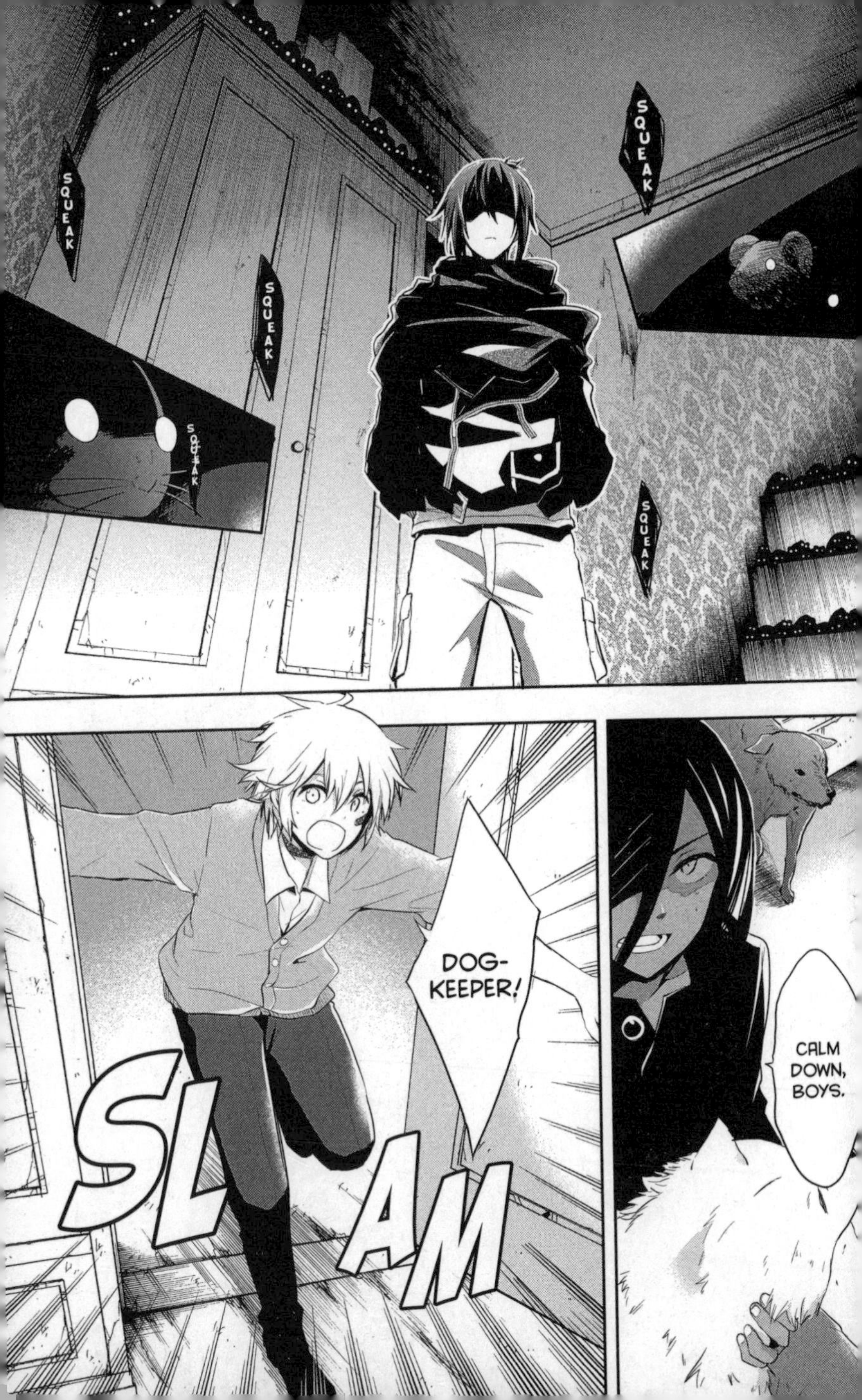
SQUEAK
SQUEAK
SQUEAK
SQUEAK
SQUEAK
CALM DOWN, BOYS.
DOG-KEEPER!
SLAM

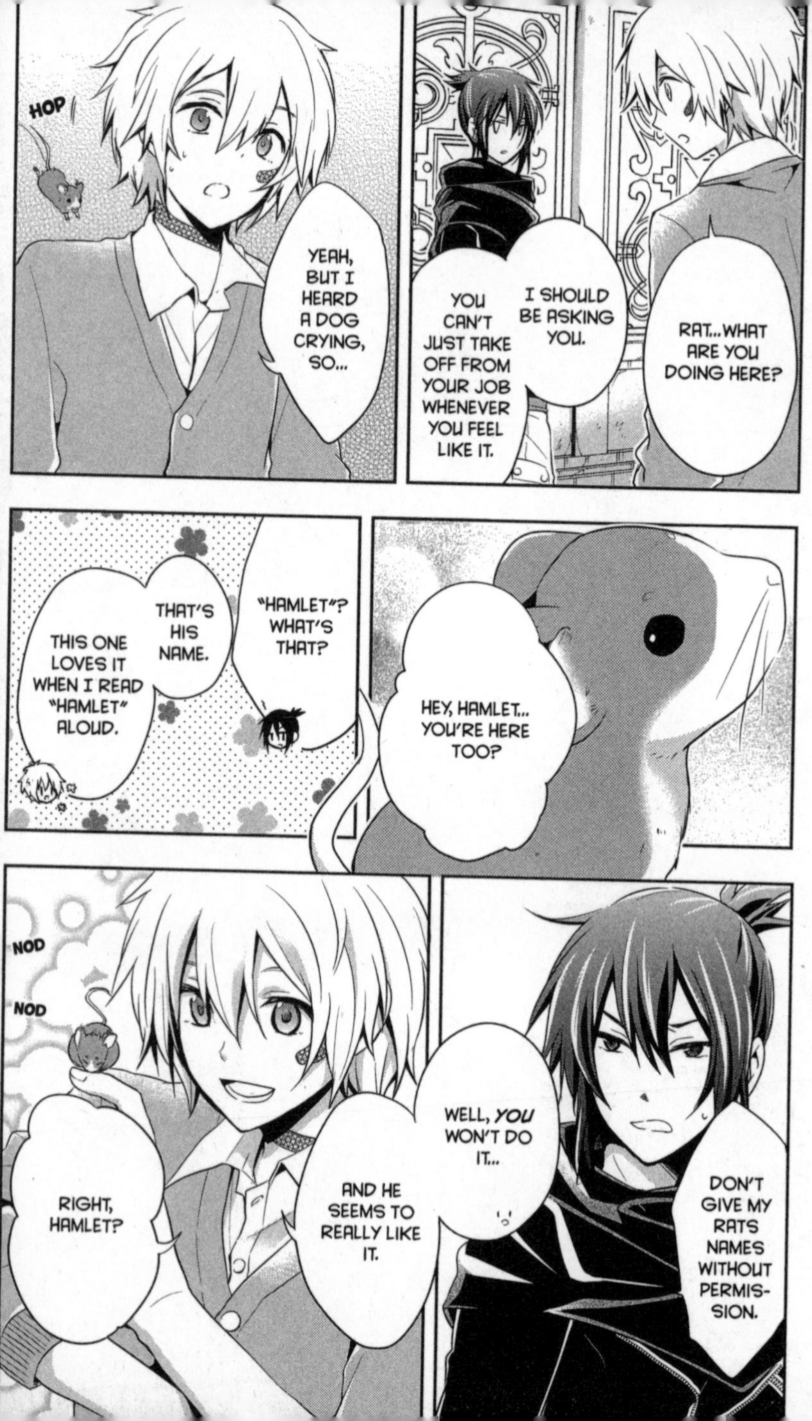
RAT...WHAT ARE YOU DOING HERE?
I SHOULD BE ASKING YOU.
YOU CAN'T JUST TAKE OFF FROM YOUR JOB WHENEVER YOU FEEL LIKE IT.
HOP
YEAH, BUT I HEARD A DOG CRYING, SO...
HEY, HAMLET... YOU'RE HERE TOO?
"HAMLET"? WHAT'S THAT?
THAT'S HIS NAME.
THIS ONE LOVES IT WHEN I READ "HAMLET" ALOUD.
DON'T GIVE MY RATS NAMES WITHOUT PERMIS-SION.
WELL, *YOU* WON'T DO IT...
AND HE SEEMS TO REALLY LIKE IT.
NOD
NOD
RIGHT, HAMLET?

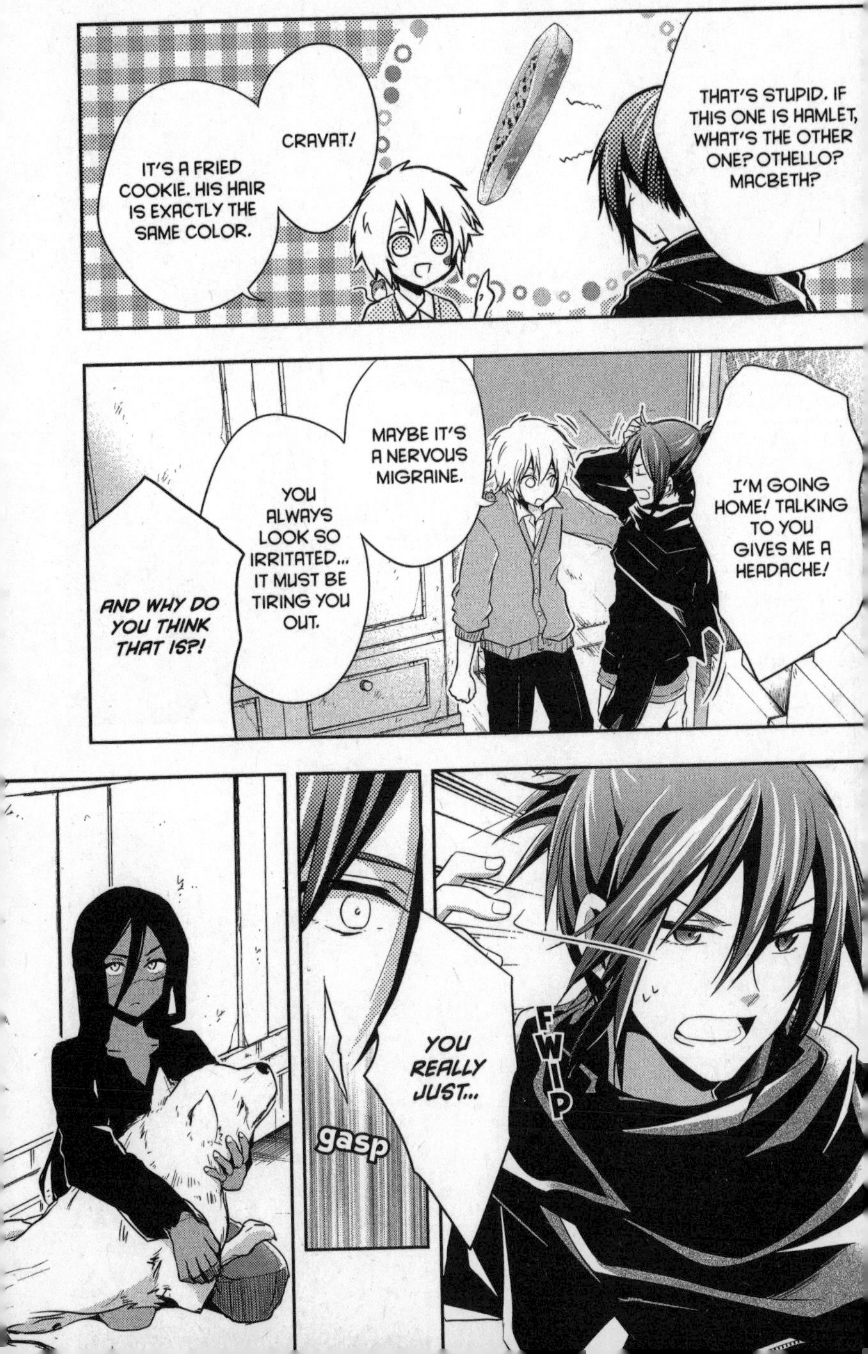
THAT'S STUPID. IF THIS ONE IS HAMLET, WHAT'S THE OTHER ONE? OTHELLO? MACBETH?
CRAVAT!
IT'S A FRIED COOKIE. HIS HAIR IS EXACTLY THE SAME COLOR.
I'M GOING HOME! TALKING TO YOU GIVES ME A HEADACHE!
MAYBE IT'S A NERVOUS MIGRAINE.
YOU ALWAYS LOOK SO IRRITATED... IT MUST BE TIRING YOU OUT.
AND WHY DO YOU THINK THAT IS?!
FWIP
YOU REALLY JUST...
gasp

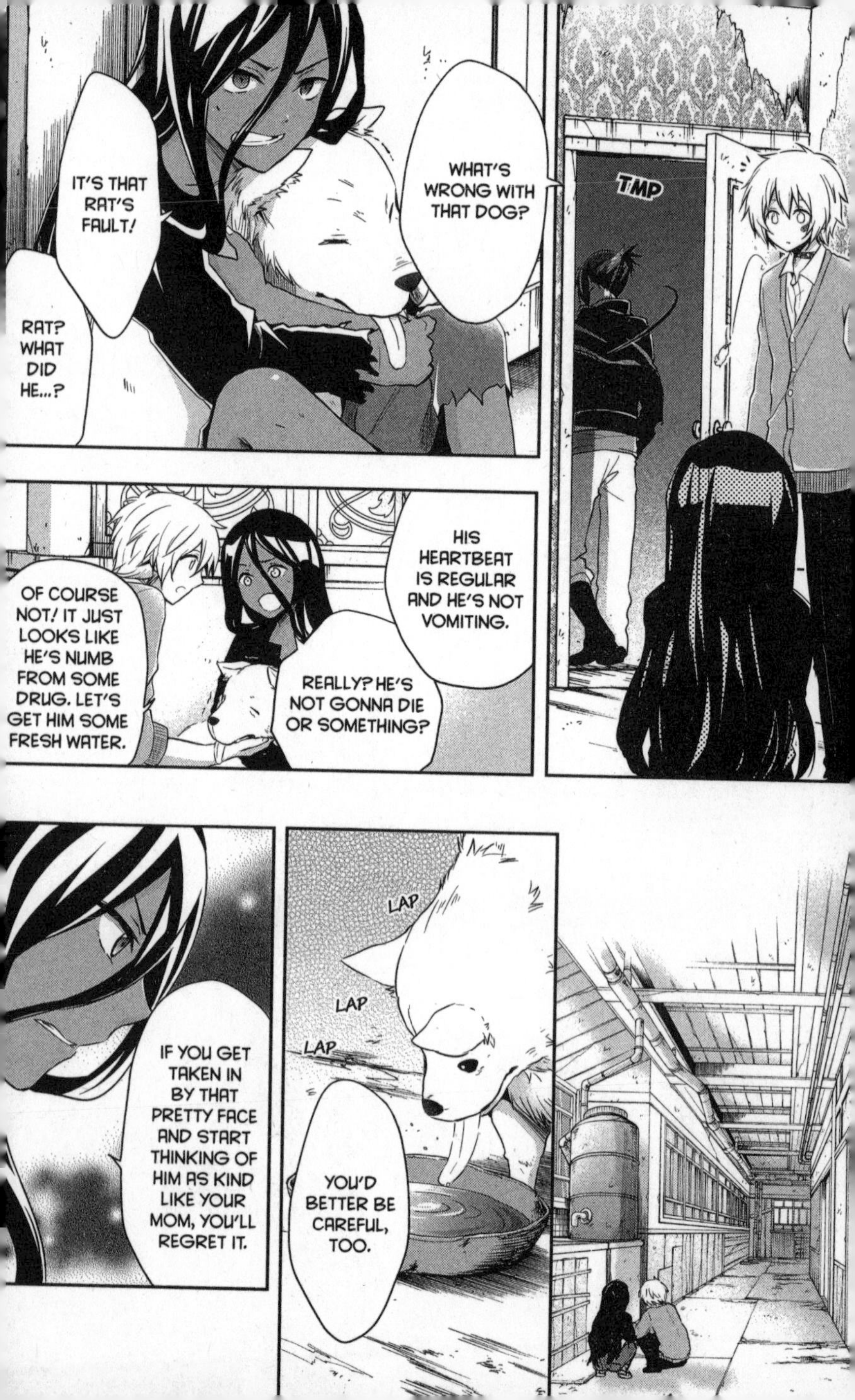
TMP
WHAT'S WRONG WITH THAT DOG?
IT'S THAT RAT'S FAULT!
RAT? WHAT DID HE...?
HIS HEARTBEAT IS REGULAR AND HE'S NOT VOMITING.
REALLY? HE'S NOT GONNA DIE OR SOMETHING?
OF COURSE NOT! IT JUST LOOKS LIKE HE'S NUMB FROM SOME DRUG. LET'S GET HIM SOME FRESH WATER.
LAP
LAP
LAP
YOU'D BETTER BE CAREFUL, TOO.
IF YOU GET TAKEN IN BY THAT PRETTY FACE AND START THINKING OF HIM AS KIND LIKE YOUR MOM, YOU'LL REGRET IT.

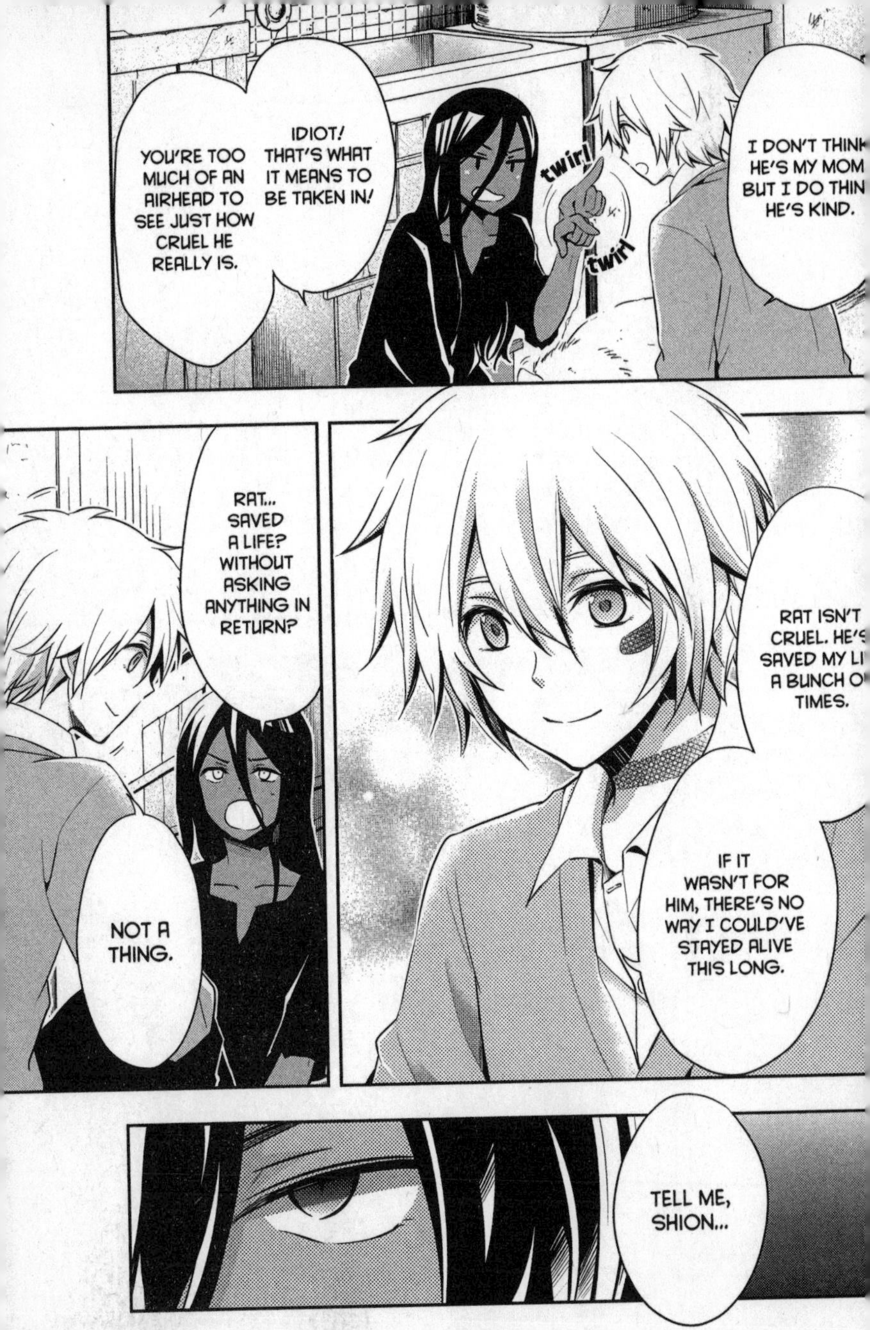
I DON'T THINK HE'S MY MOM BUT I DO THIN HE'S KIND.
IDIOT! THAT'S WHAT IT MEANS TO BE TAKEN IN!
twirl
twirl
YOU'RE TOO MUCH OF AN AIRHEAD TO SEE JUST HOW CRUEL HE REALLY IS.
RAT ISN'T CRUEL. HE'S SAVED MY LI A BUNCH O TIMES.
IF IT WASN'T FOR HIM, THERE'S NO WAY I COULD'VE STAYED ALIVE THIS LONG.
RAT... SAVED A LIFE? WITHOUT ASKING ANYTHING IN RETURN?
NOT A THING.
TELL ME, SHION...

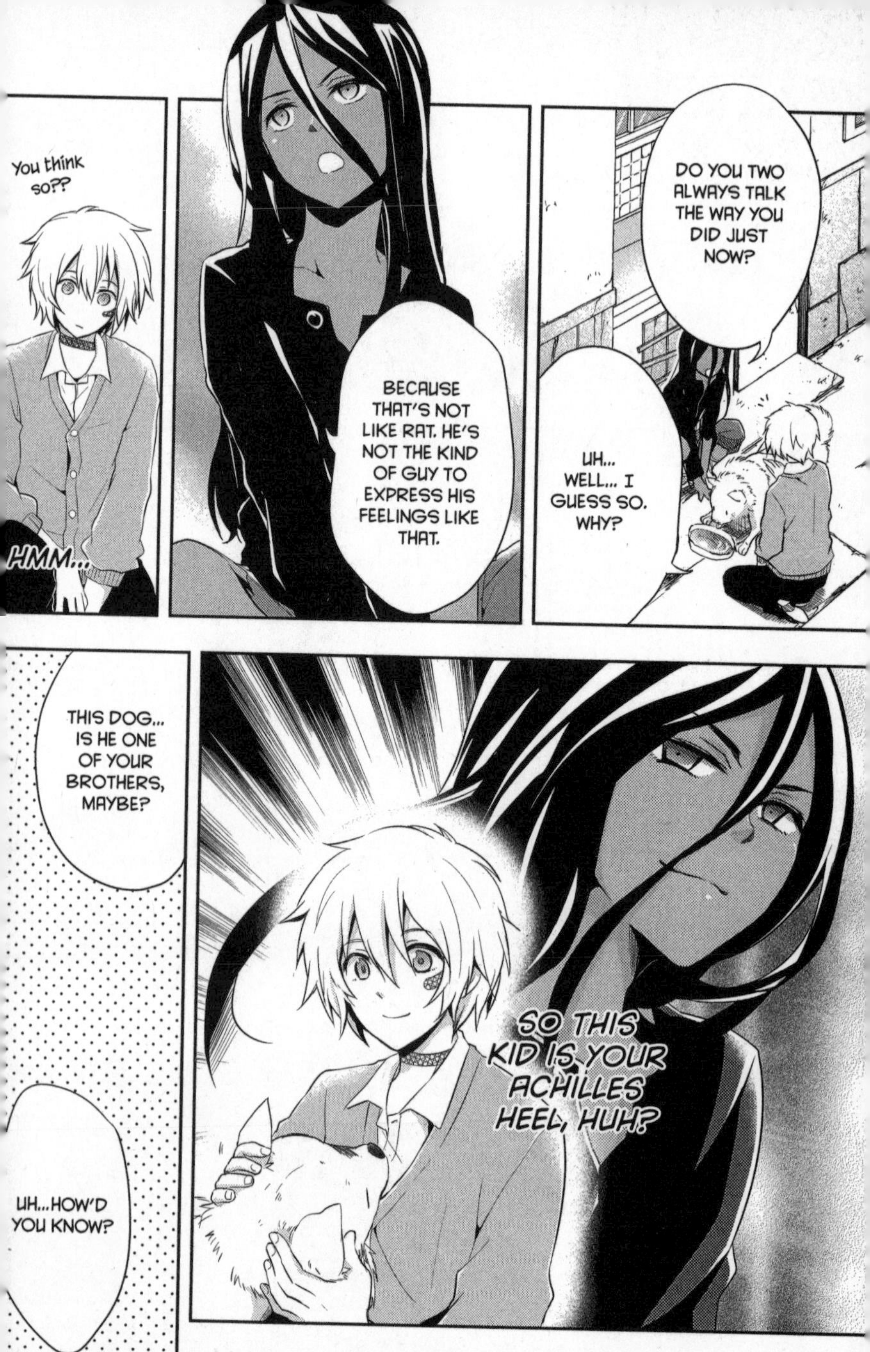
DO YOU TWO ALWAYS TALK THE WAY YOU DID JUST NOW?
UH... WELL... I GUESS SO. WHY?
BECAUSE THAT'S NOT LIKE RAT. HE'S NOT THE KIND OF GUY TO EXPRESS HIS FEELINGS LIKE THAT.
You think so??
HMM...
SO THIS KID IS YOUR ACHILLES HEEL, HUH?
THIS DOG... IS HE ONE OF YOUR BROTHERS, MAYBE?
UH...HOW'D YOU KNOW?

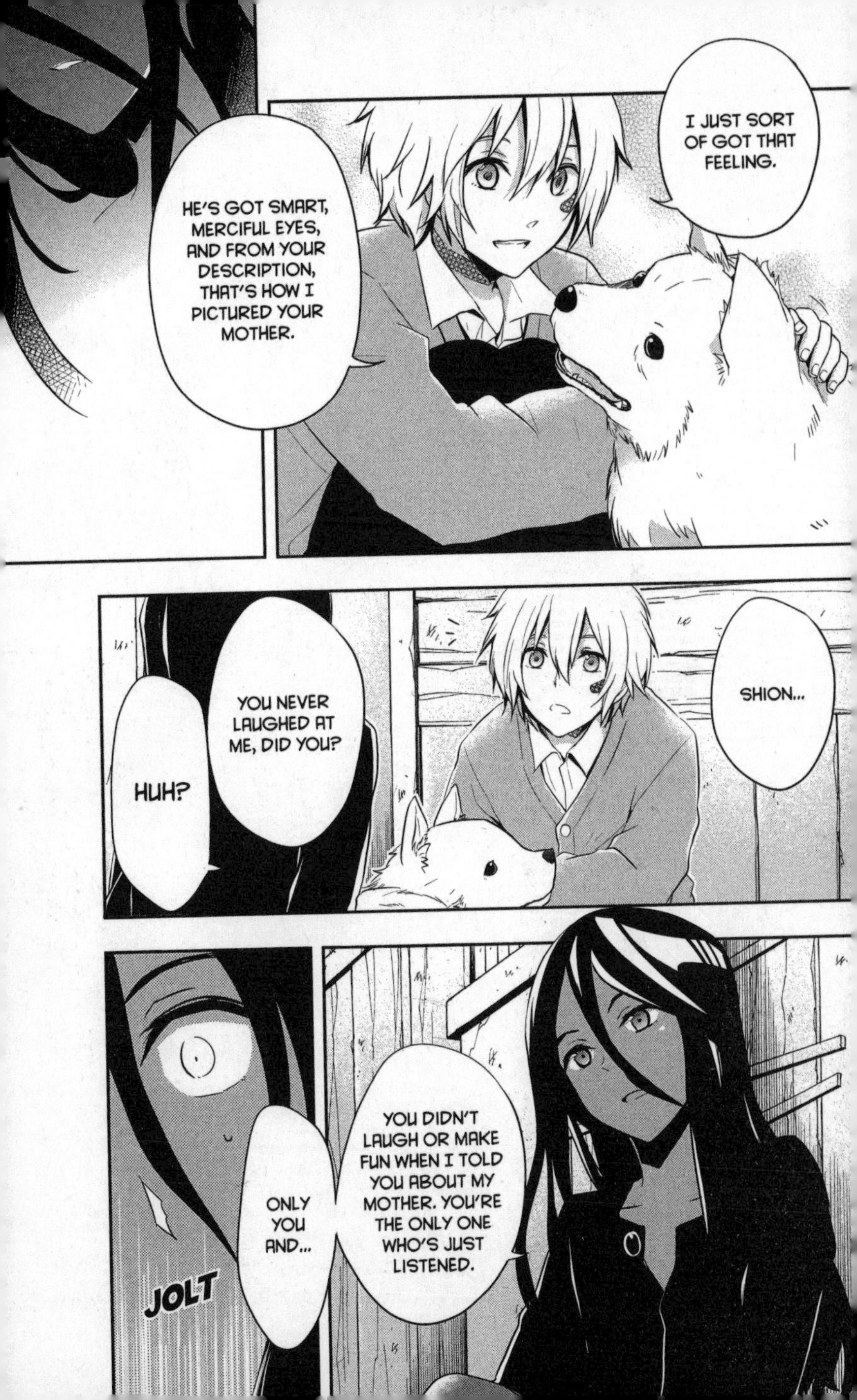
I JUST SORT OF GOT THAT FEELING.
HE'S GOT SMART, MERCIFUL EYES, AND FROM YOUR DESCRIPTION, THAT'S HOW I PICTURED YOUR MOTHER.
SHION...
YOU NEVER LAUGHED AT ME, DID YOU?
HUH?
YOU DIDN'T LAUGH OR MAKE FUN WHEN I TOLD YOU ABOUT MY MOTHER. YOU'RE THE ONLY ONE WHO'S JUST LISTENED.
ONLY YOU AND...
JOLT

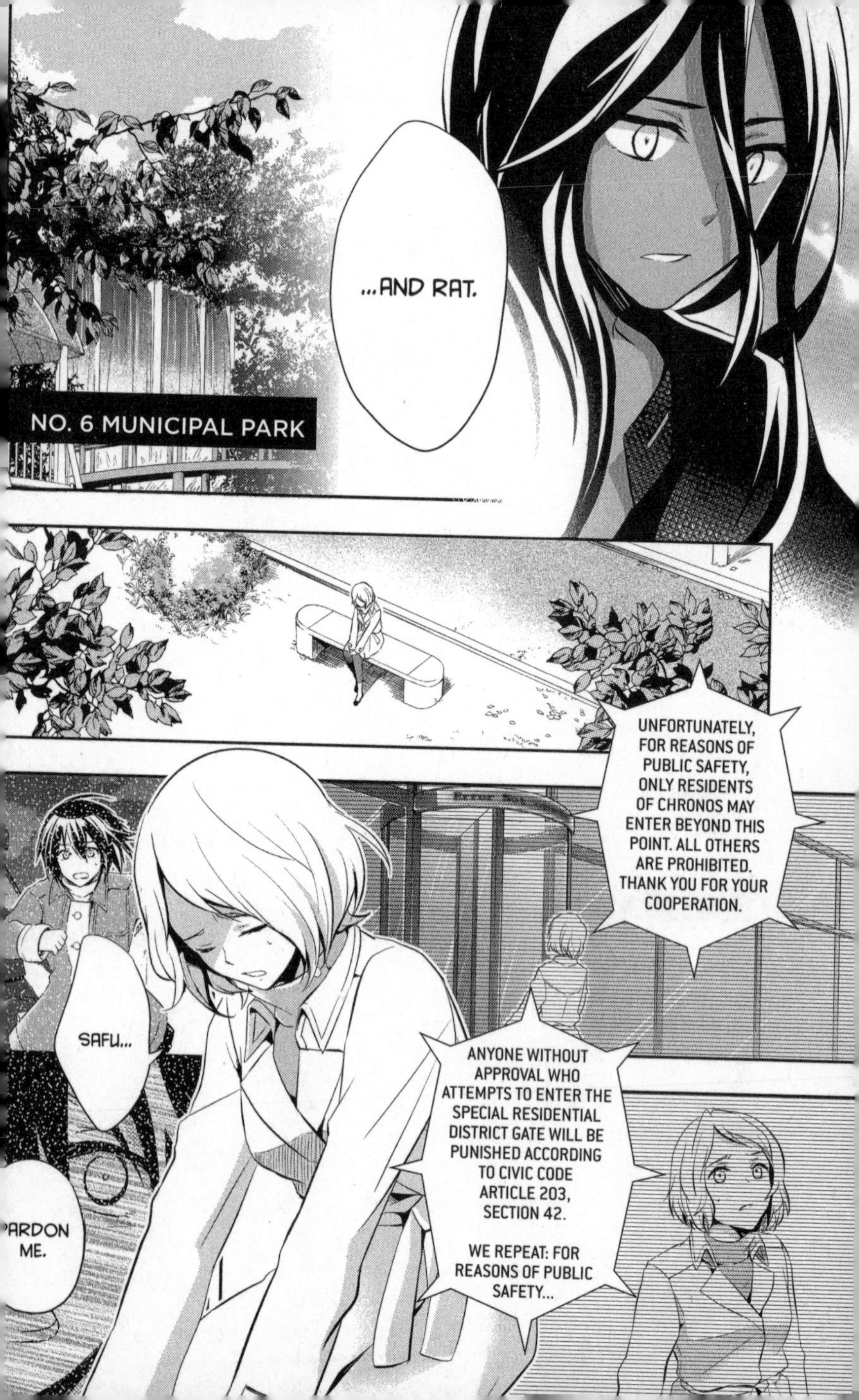
...AND RAT.
NO. 6 MUNICIPAL PARK
UNFORTUNATELY, FOR REASONS OF PUBLIC SAFETY, ONLY RESIDENTS OF CHRONOS MAY ENTER BEYOND THIS POINT. ALL OTHERS ARE PROHIBITED. THANK YOU FOR YOUR COOPERATION.
ANYONE WITHOUT APPROVAL WHO ATTEMPTS TO ENTER THE SPECIAL RESIDENTIAL DISTRICT GATE WILL BE PUNISHED ACCORDING TO CIVIC CODE ARTICLE 203, SECTION 42.
WE REPEAT: FOR REASONS OF PUBLIC SAFETY...
SAFU...
PARDON ME.

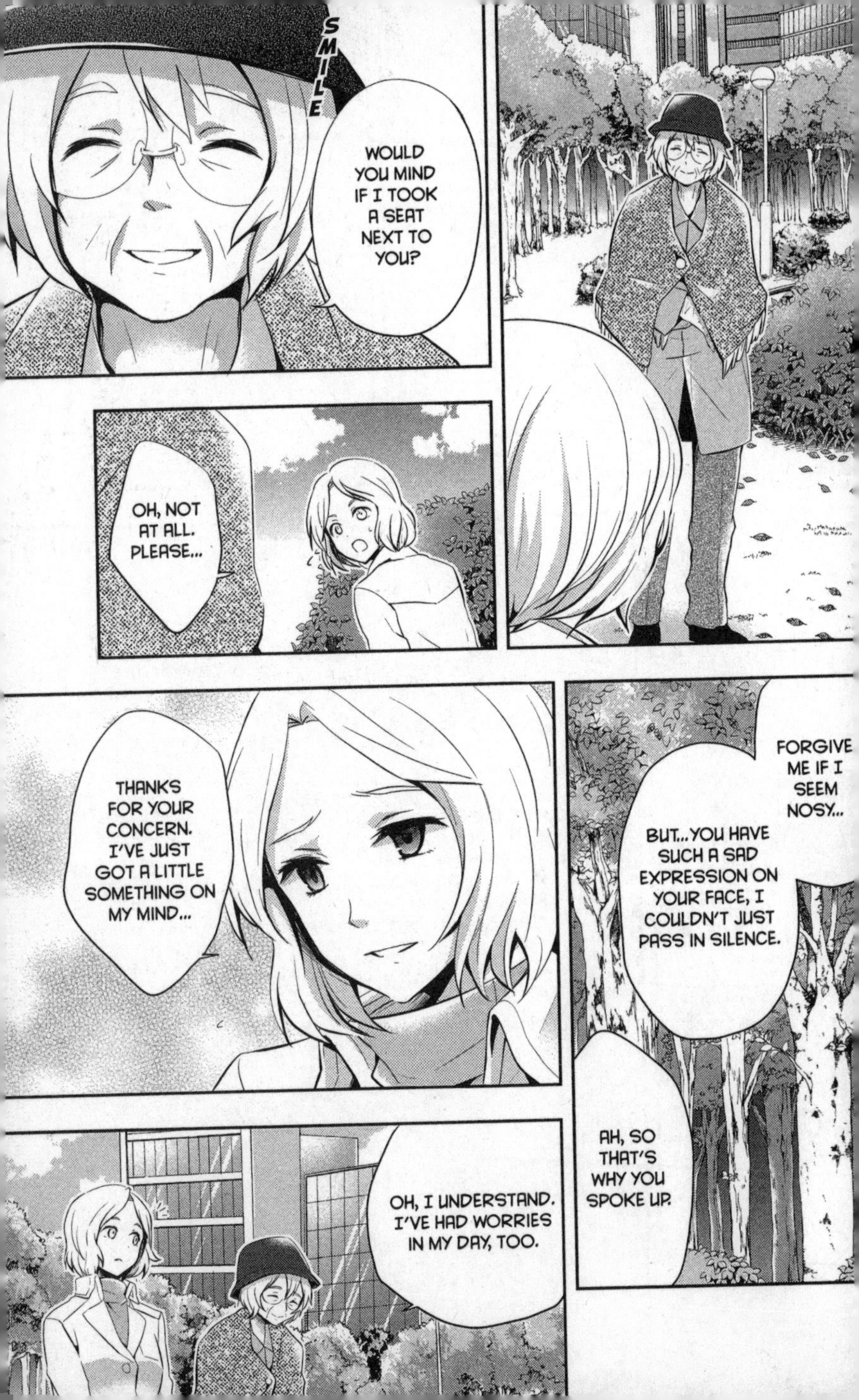
SMILE
WOULD YOU MIND IF I TOOK A SEAT NEXT TO YOU?
OH, NOT AT ALL. PLEASE...
FORGIVE ME IF I SEEM NOSY...
BUT...YOU HAVE SUCH A SAD EXPRESSION ON YOUR FACE, I COULDN'T JUST PASS IN SILENCE.
AH, SO THAT'S WHY YOU SPOKE UP.
THANKS FOR YOUR CONCERN. I'VE JUST GOT A LITTLE SOMETHING ON MY MIND...
OH, I UNDERSTAND. I'VE HAD WORRIES IN MY DAY, TOO.

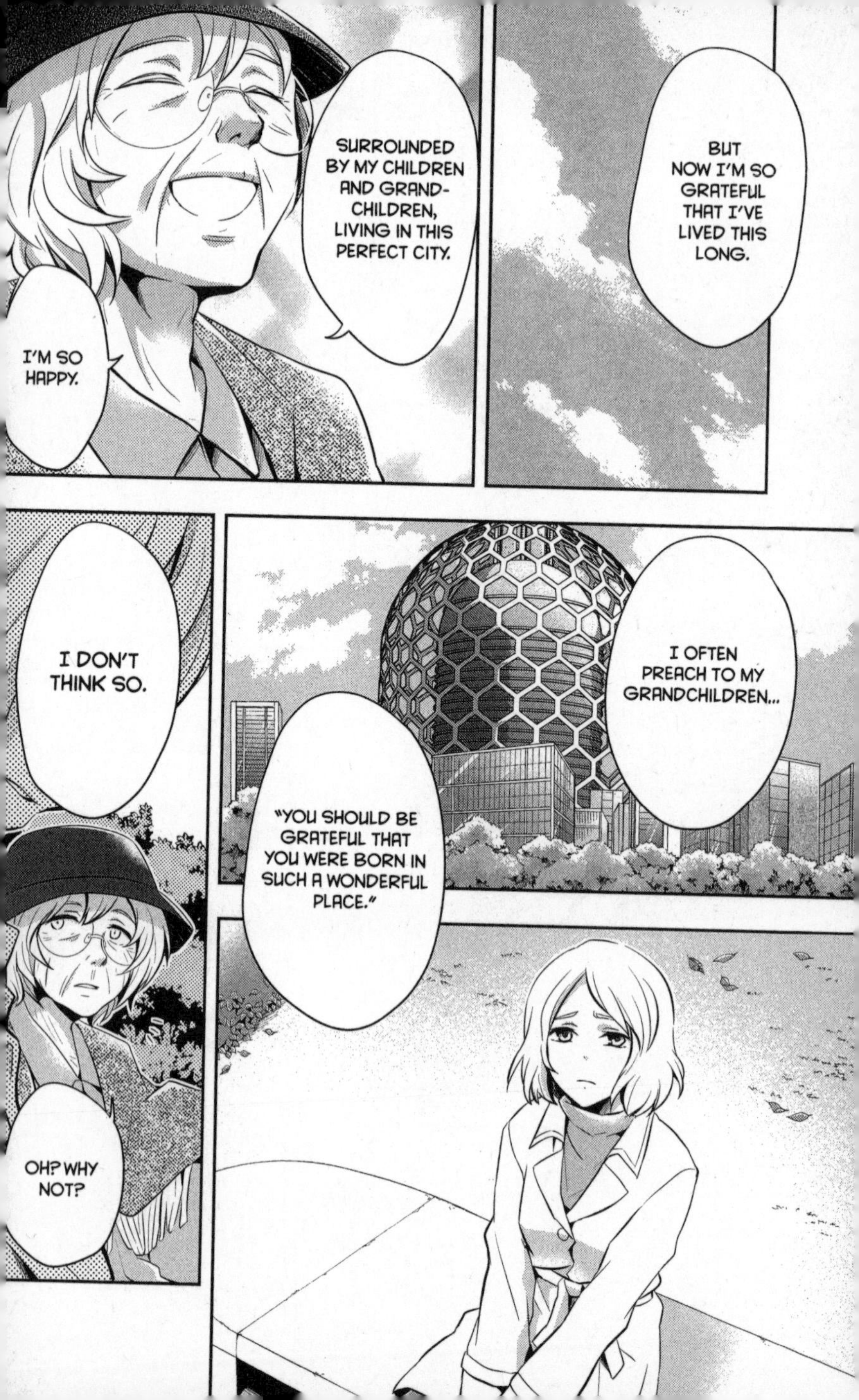
BUT NOW I'M SO GRATEFUL THAT I'VE LIVED THIS LONG.
SURROUNDED BY MY CHILDREN AND GRAND-CHILDREN, LIVING IN THIS PERFECT CITY.
I'M SO HAPPY.
I OFTEN PREACH TO MY GRANDCHILDREN...
"YOU SHOULD BE GRATEFUL THAT YOU WERE BORN IN SUCH A WONDERFUL PLACE."
I DON'T THINK SO.
OH? WHY NOT?

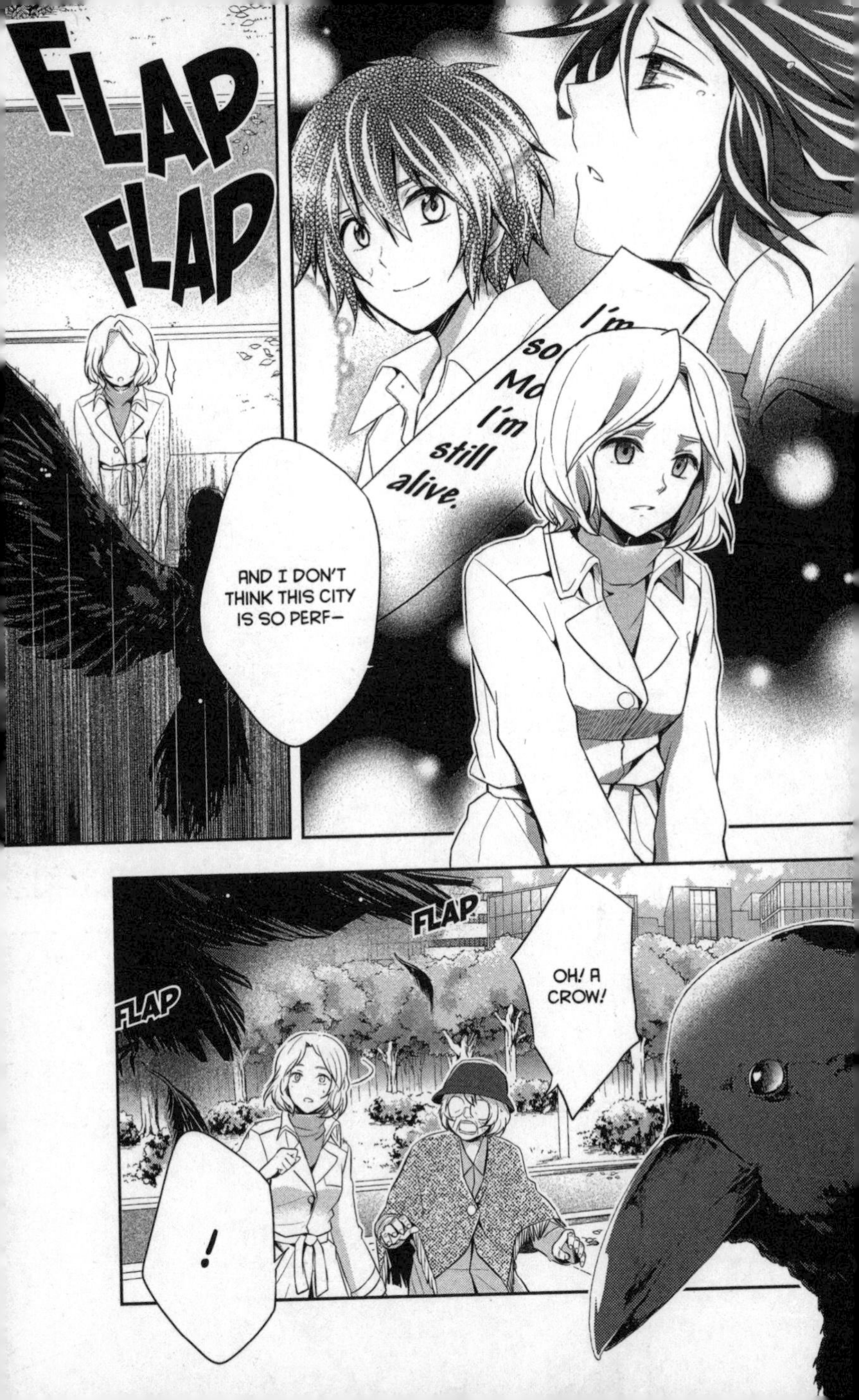
I'm
so
Mo
I'm
still
alive.
AND I DON'T THINK THIS CITY IS SO PERF—
FLAP
FLAP
OH! A CROW!
FLAP
FLAP
!

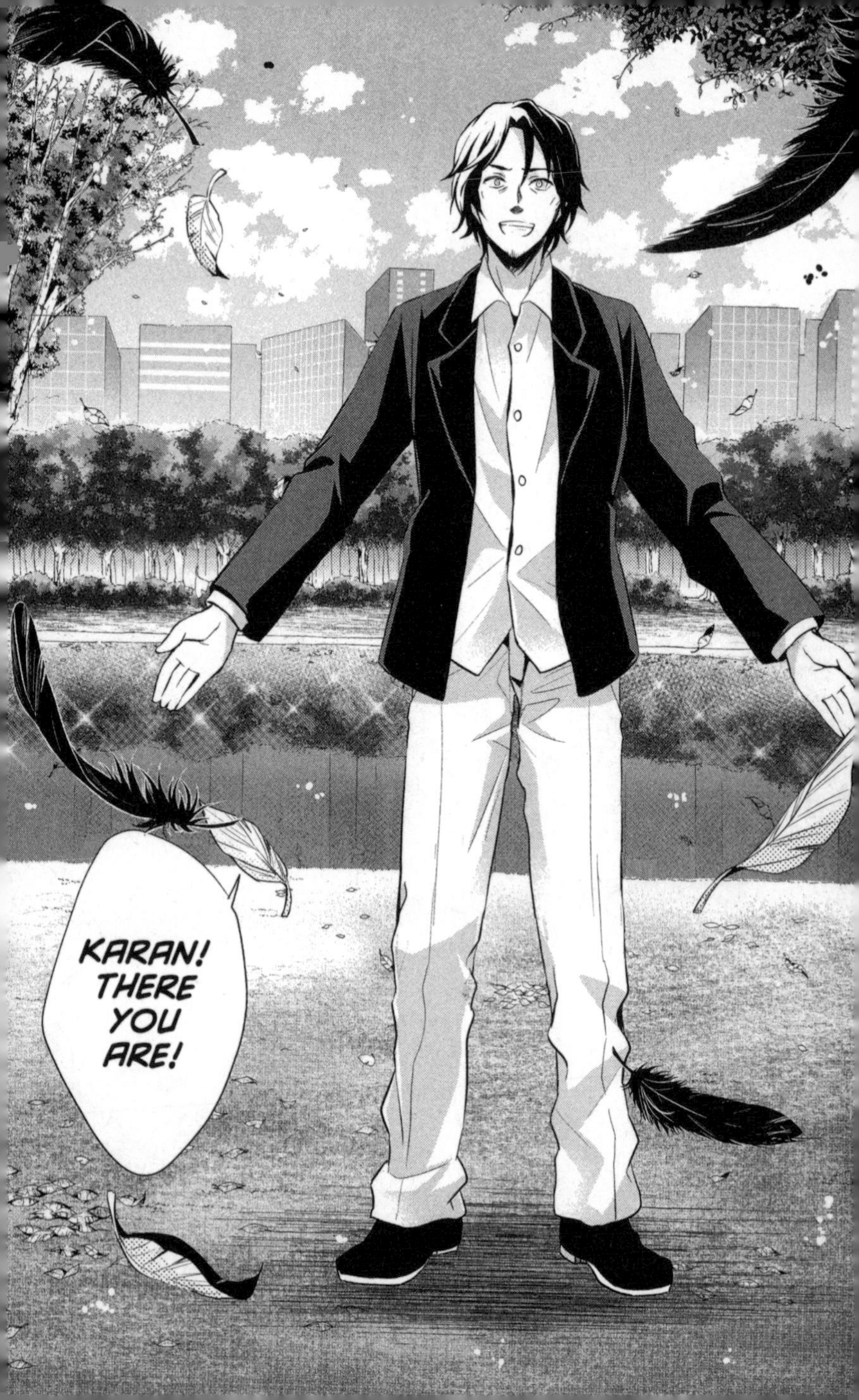
KARAN! THERE YOU ARE!

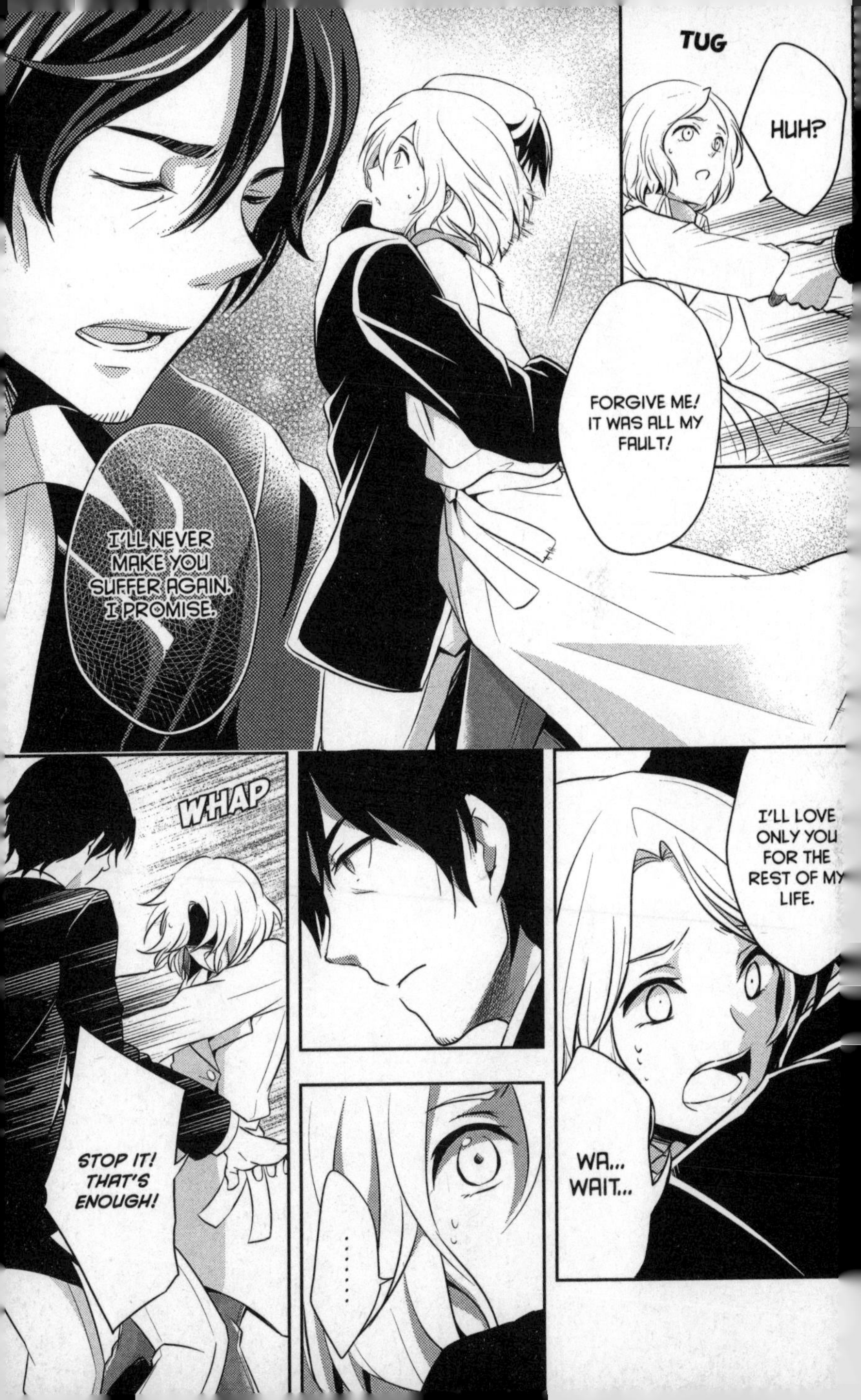
TUG
HUH?
FORGIVE ME! IT WAS ALL MY FAULT!
I'LL NEVER MAKE YOU SUFFER AGAIN. I PROMISE.
I'LL LOVE ONLY YOU FOR THE REST OF MY LIFE.
WA... WAIT...
......
WHAP
STOP IT! THAT'S ENOUGH!

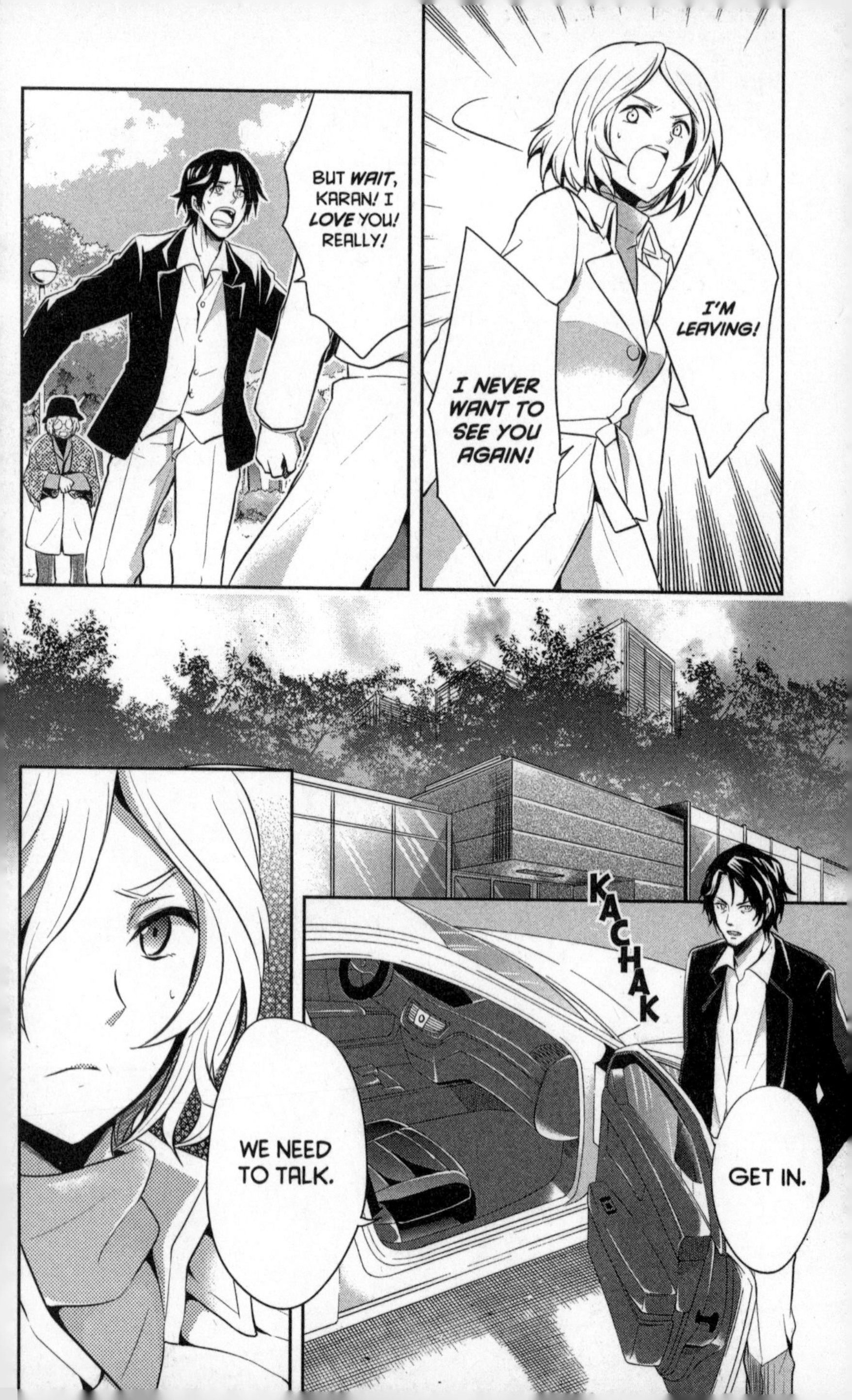
I'M LEAVING!
I NEVER WANT TO SEE YOU AGAIN!
BUT WAIT, KARAN! I LOVE YOU! REALLY!
KACHAK
GET IN.
WE NEED TO TALK.

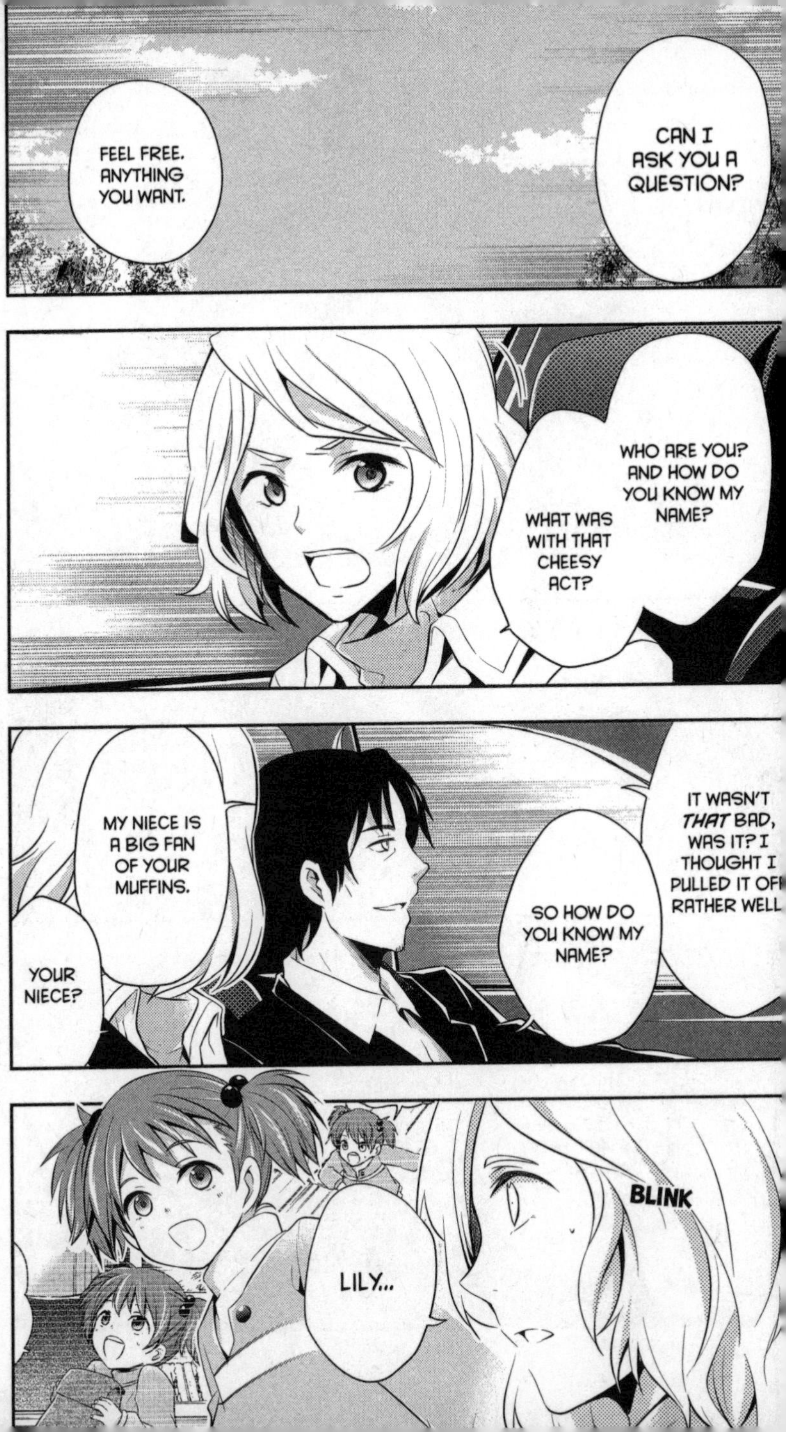
CAN I ASK YOU A QUESTION?
FEEL FREE. ANYTHING YOU WANT.
WHO ARE YOU? AND HOW DO YOU KNOW MY NAME?
WHAT WAS WITH THAT CHEESY ACT?
IT WASN'T *THAT* BAD, WAS IT? I THOUGHT I PULLED IT OF RATHER WELL.
SO HOW DO YOU KNOW MY NAME?
MY NIECE IS A BIG FAN OF YOUR MUFFINS.
YOUR NIECE?
BLINK
LILY...

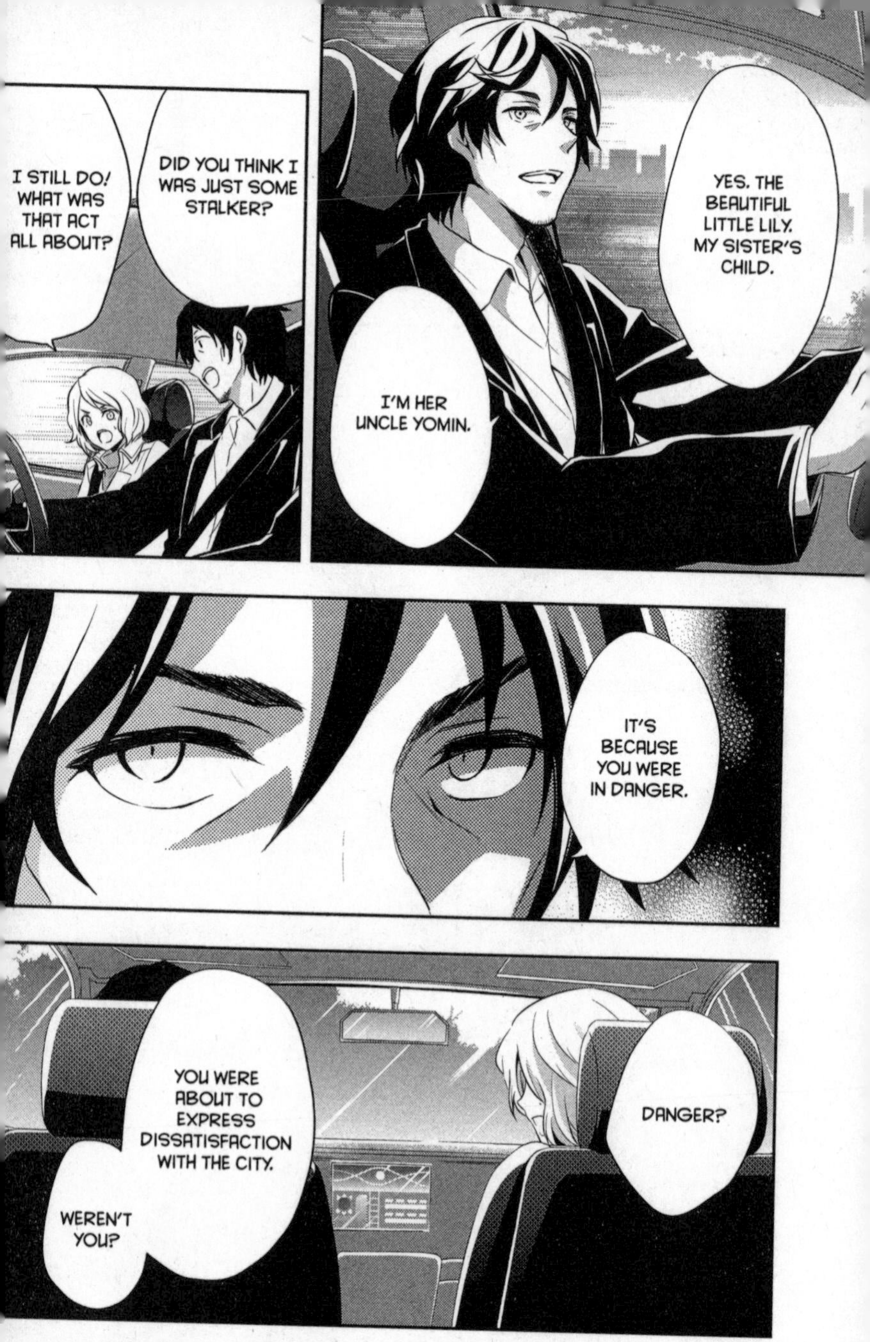
YES. THE BEAUTIFUL LITTLE LILY. MY SISTER'S CHILD.
I'M HER UNCLE YOMIN.
DID YOU THINK I WAS JUST SOME STALKER?
I STILL DO! WHAT WAS THAT ACT ALL ABOUT?
IT'S BECAUSE YOU WERE IN DANGER.
DANGER?
YOU WERE ABOUT TO EXPRESS DISSATISFACTION WITH THE CITY.
WEREN'T YOU?

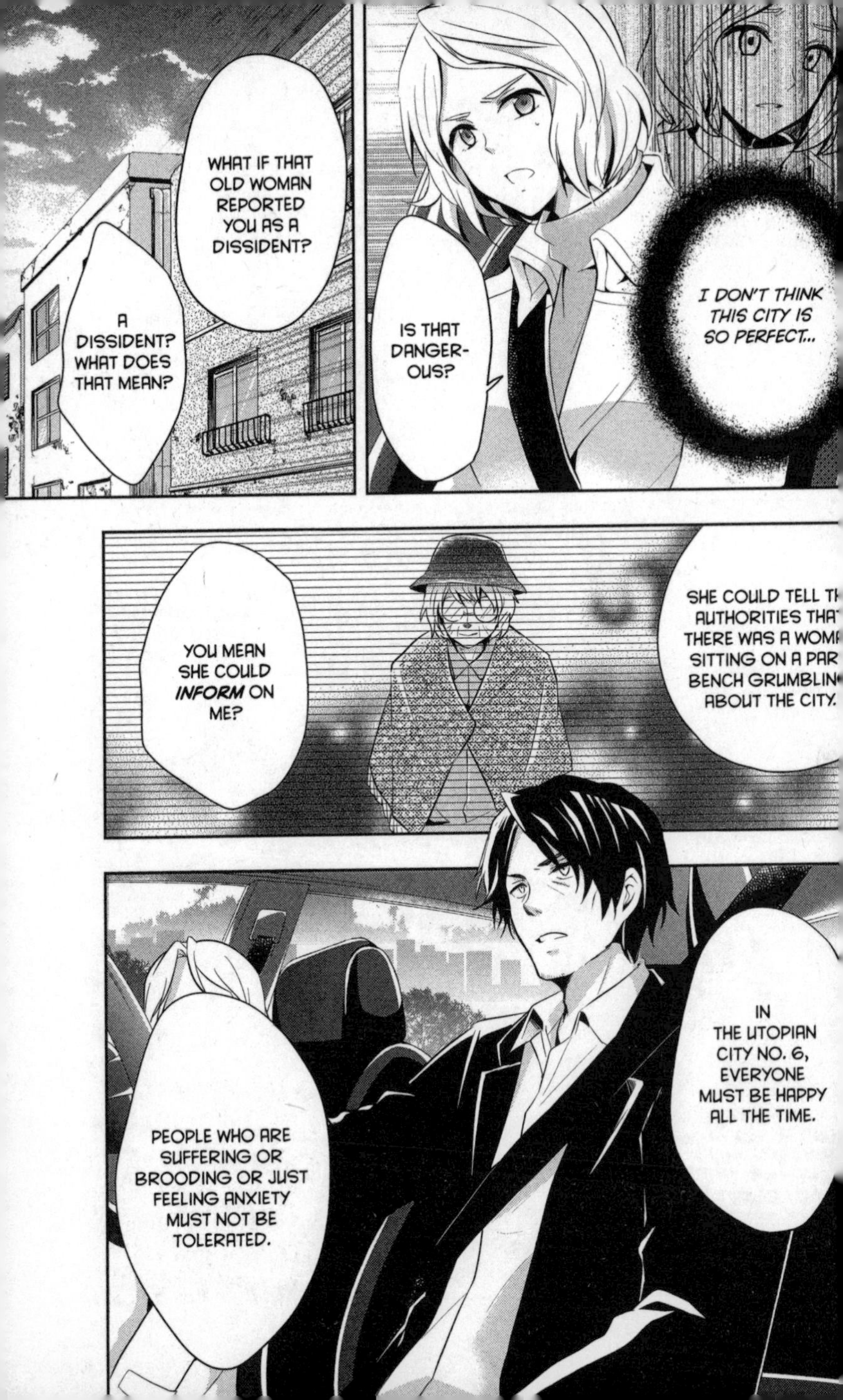
I DON'T THINK THIS CITY IS SO PERFECT...
IS THAT DANGER-OUS?
WHAT IF THAT OLD WOMAN REPORTED YOU AS A DISSIDENT?
A DISSIDENT? WHAT DOES THAT MEAN?
SHE COULD TELL TH AUTHORITIES THAT THERE WAS A WOMA SITTING ON A PAR BENCH GRUMBLIN ABOUT THE CITY.
YOU MEAN SHE COULD *INFORM* ON ME?
IN THE UTOPIAN CITY NO. 6, EVERYONE MUST BE HAPPY ALL THE TIME.
PEOPLE WHO ARE SUFFERING OR BROODING OR JUST FEELING ANXIETY MUST NOT BE TOLERATED.

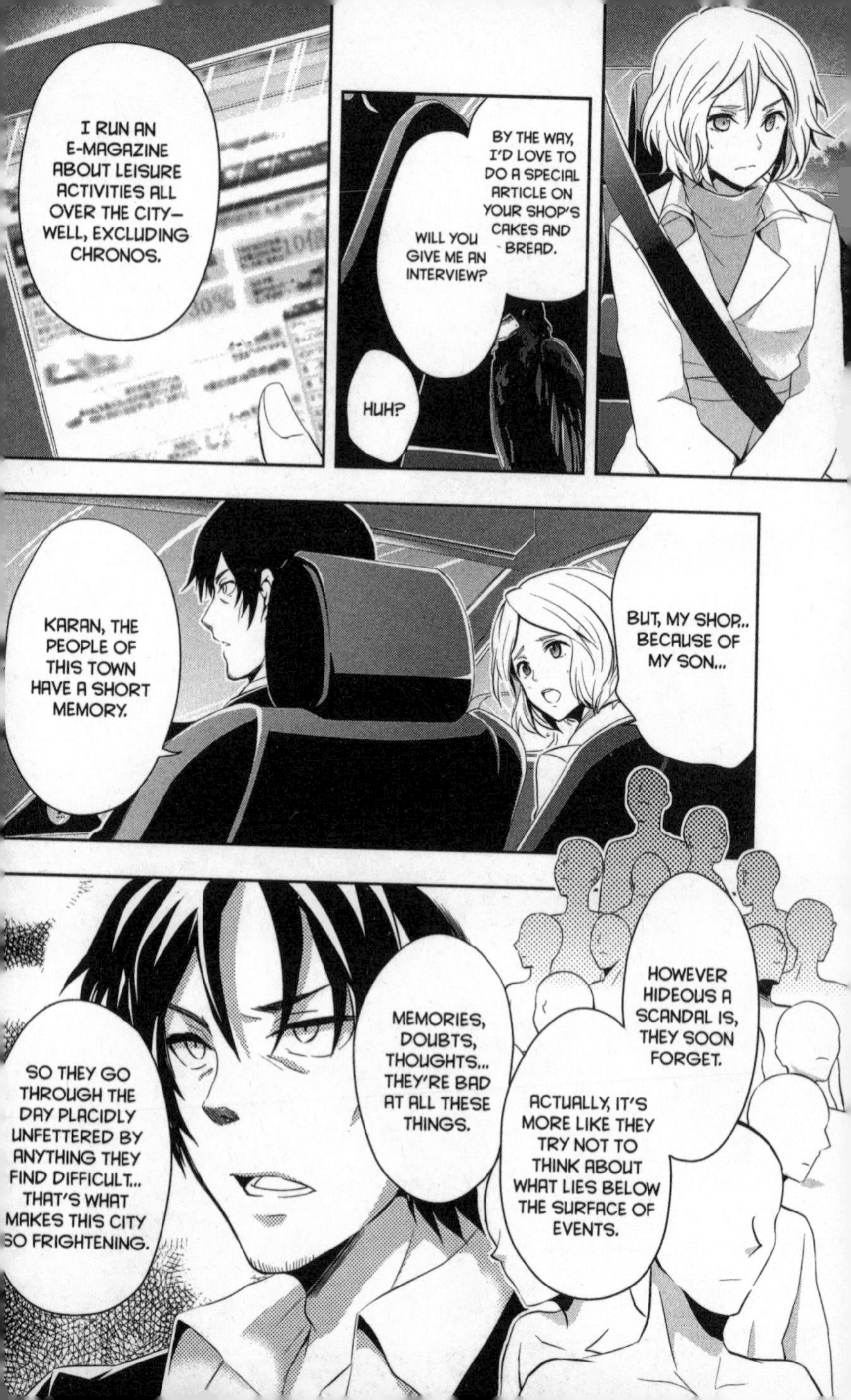
BY THE WAY, I'D LOVE TO DO A SPECIAL ARTICLE ON YOUR SHOP'S CAKES AND BREAD.
WILL YOU GIVE ME AN INTERVIEW?
HUH?
I RUN AN E-MAGAZINE ABOUT LEISURE ACTIVITIES ALL OVER THE CITY—WELL, EXCLUDING CHRONOS.
BUT, MY SHOP... BECAUSE OF MY SON...
KARAN, THE PEOPLE OF THIS TOWN HAVE A SHORT MEMORY.
HOWEVER HIDEOUS A SCANDAL IS, THEY SOON FORGET.
ACTUALLY, IT'S MORE LIKE THEY TRY NOT TO THINK ABOUT WHAT LIES BELOW THE SURFACE OF EVENTS.
MEMORIES, DOUBTS, THOUGHTS... THEY'RE BAD AT ALL THESE THINGS.
SO THEY GO THROUGH THE DAY PLACIDLY UNFETTERED BY ANYTHING THEY FIND DIFFICULT... THAT'S WHAT MAKES THIS CITY SO FRIGHTENING.

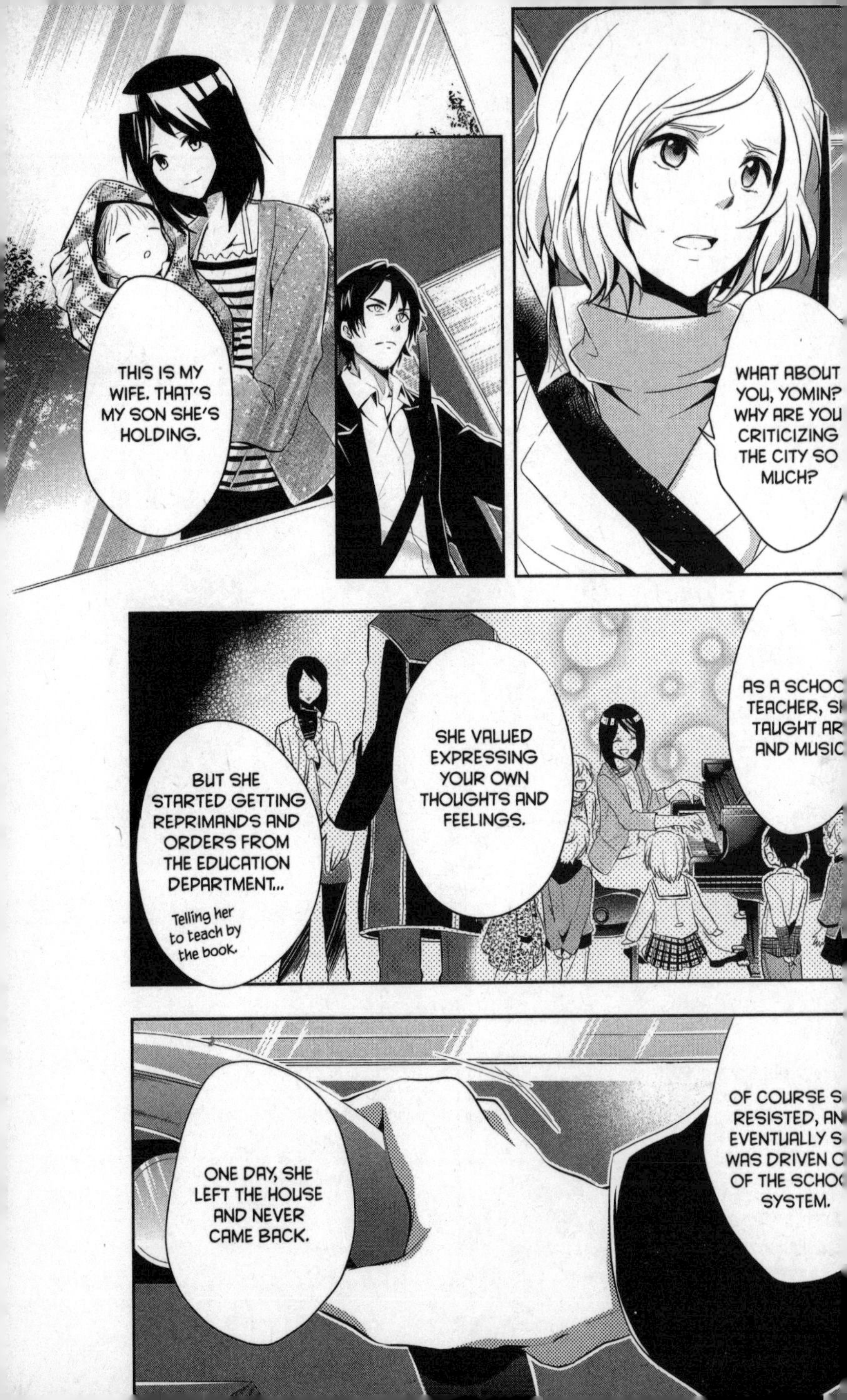
WHAT ABOUT YOU, YOMIN? WHY ARE YOU CRITICIZING THE CITY SO MUCH?
THIS IS MY WIFE. THAT'S MY SON SHE'S HOLDING.
AS A SCHOC TEACHER, SH TAUGHT AR AND MUSIC
SHE VALUED EXPRESSING YOUR OWN THOUGHTS AND FEELINGS.
BUT SHE STARTED GETTING REPRIMANDS AND ORDERS FROM THE EDUCATION DEPARTMENT...
Telling her to teach by the book.
OF COURSE S RESISTED, AN EVENTUALLY S WAS DRIVEN C OF THE SCHOC SYSTEM.
ONE DAY, SHE LEFT THE HOUSE AND NEVER CAME BACK.

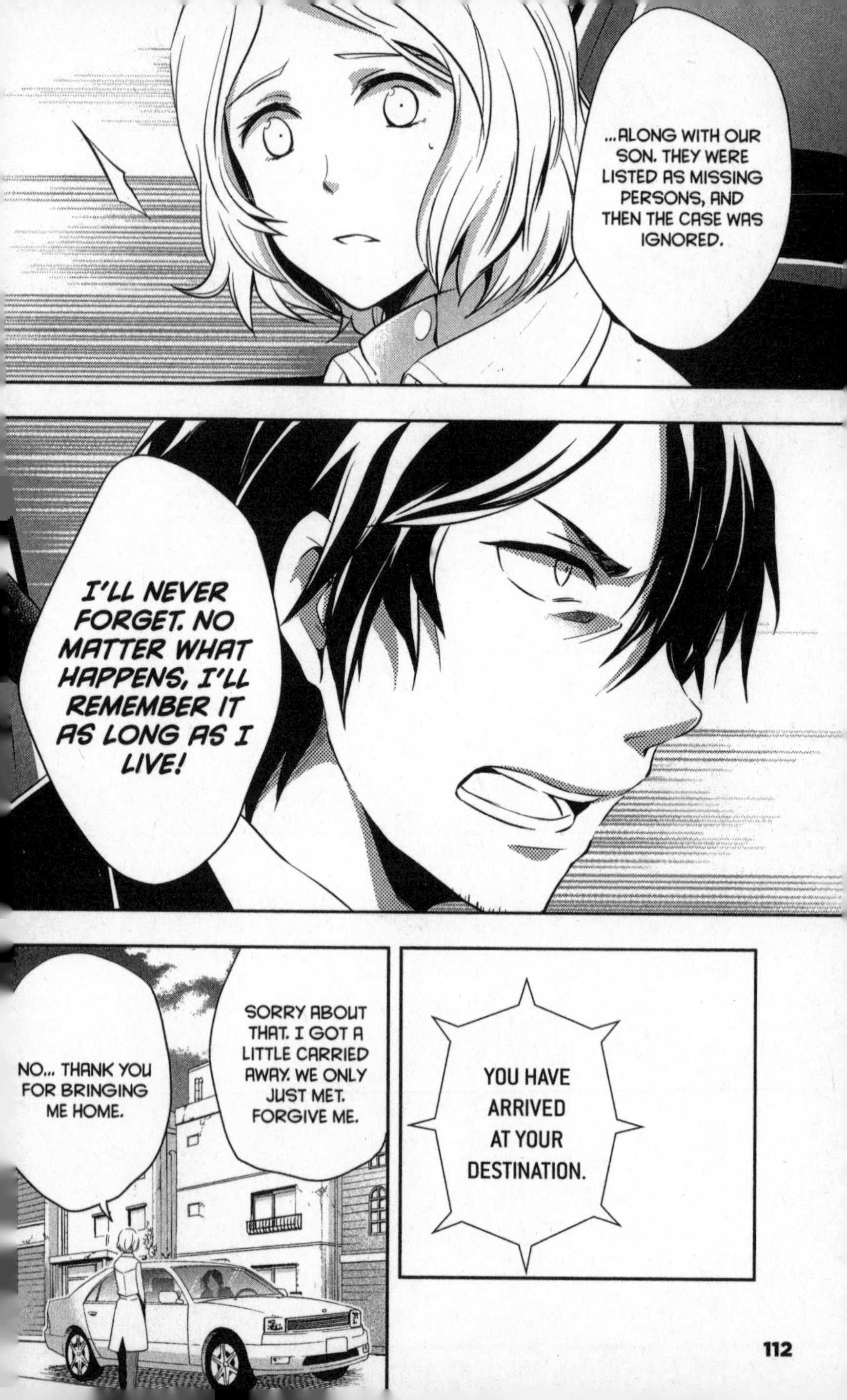
...ALONG WITH OUR SON. THEY WERE LISTED AS MISSING PERSONS, AND THEN THE CASE WAS IGNORED.
I'LL NEVER FORGET. NO MATTER WHAT HAPPENS, I'LL REMEMBER IT AS LONG AS I LIVE!
YOU HAVE ARRIVED AT YOUR DESTINATION.
SORRY ABOUT THAT. I GOT A LITTLE CARRIED AWAY. WE ONLY JUST MET. FORGIVE ME.
NO... THANK YOU FOR BRINGING ME HOME.

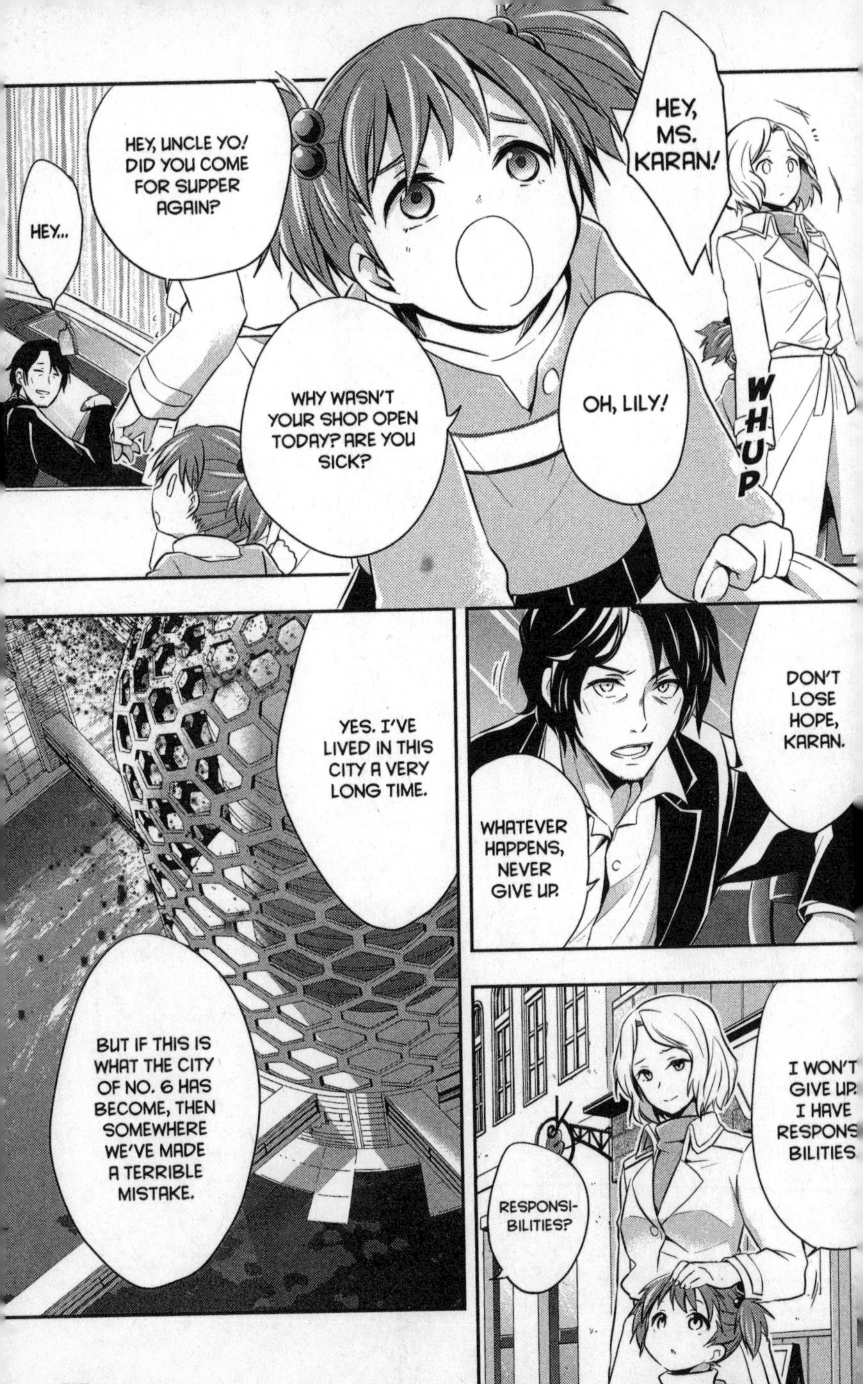
HEY, MS. KARAN!
WHUP
OH, LILY!
WHY WASN'T YOUR SHOP OPEN TODAY? ARE YOU SICK?
HEY, UNCLE YO! DID YOU COME FOR SUPPER AGAIN?
HEY...
DON'T LOSE HOPE, KARAN.
WHATEVER HAPPENS, NEVER GIVE UP.
I WON'T GIVE UP. I HAVE RESPONSIBILITIES.
RESPONSI-BILITIES?
YES. I'VE LIVED IN THIS CITY A VERY LONG TIME.
BUT IF THIS IS WHAT THE CITY OF NO. 6 HAS BECOME, THEN SOMEWHERE WE'VE MADE A TERRIBLE MISTAKE.

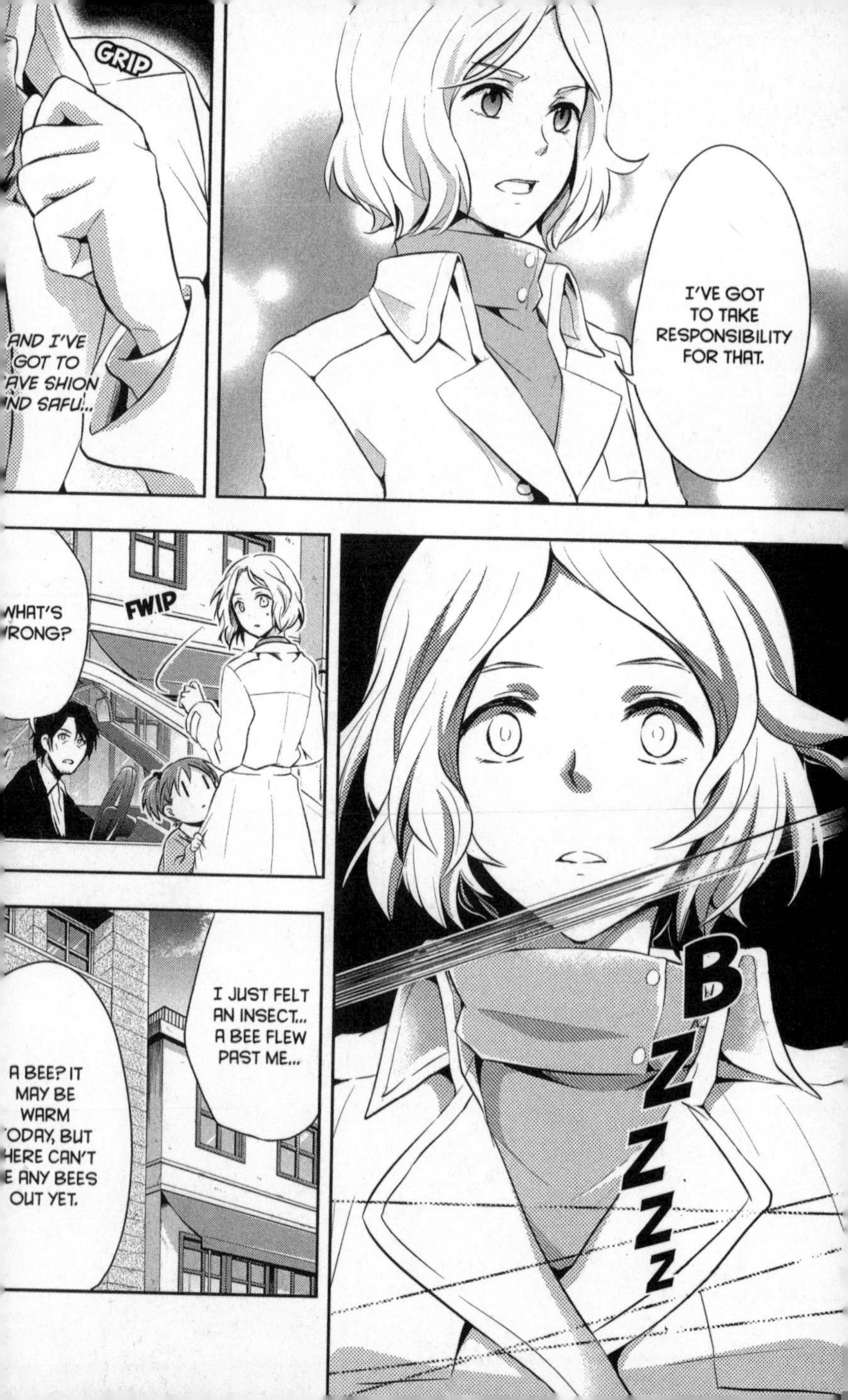

I'VE GOT TO TAKE RESPONSIBILITY FOR THAT.
GRIP
AND I'VE GOT TO AVE SHION ND SAFU...
BZZZZ
FWIP
WHAT'S RONG?
I JUST FELT AN INSECT... A BEE FLEW PAST ME...
A BEE? IT MAY BE WARM ODAY, BUT HERE CAN'T E ANY BEES OUT YET.

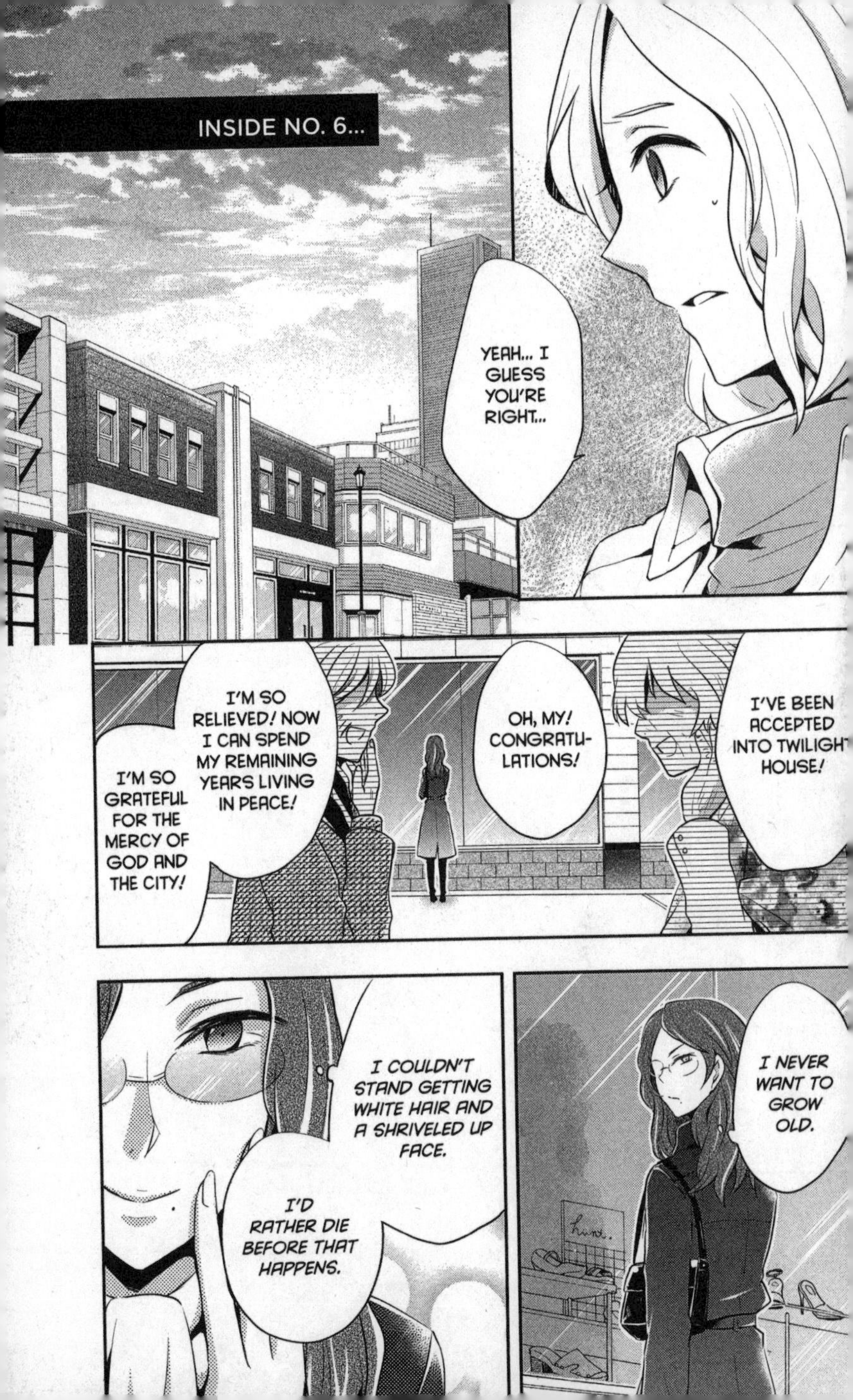
YEAH... I GUESS YOU'RE RIGHT...
INSIDE NO. 6...
I'VE BEEN ACCEPTED INTO TWILIGHT HOUSE!
OH, MY! CONGRATU-LATIONS!
I'M SO RELIEVED! NOW I CAN SPEND MY REMAINING YEARS LIVING IN PEACE!
I'M SO GRATEFUL FOR THE MERCY OF GOD AND THE CITY!
I NEVER WANT TO GROW OLD.
I COULDN'T STAND GETTING WHITE HAIR AND A SHRIVELED UP FACE.
I'D RATHER DIE BEFORE THAT HAPPENS.

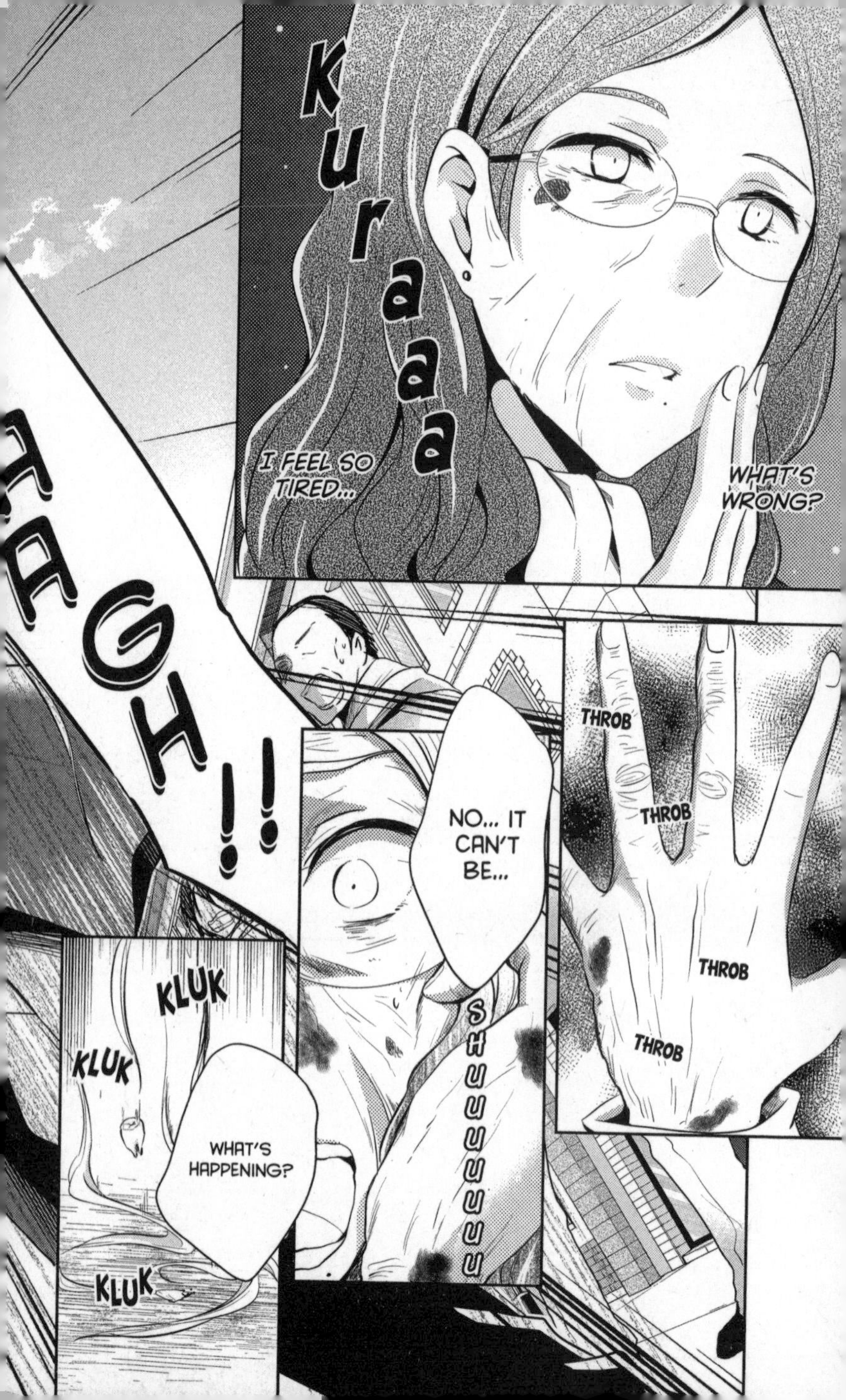

WHAT'S WRONG?
Kuraaa
I FEEL SO TIRED...
AAGH!!
THROB
THROB
THROB
THROB
NO... IT CAN'T BE...
SHUUUUUUUUUU
KLUK
KLUK
WHAT'S HAPPENING?
KLUK

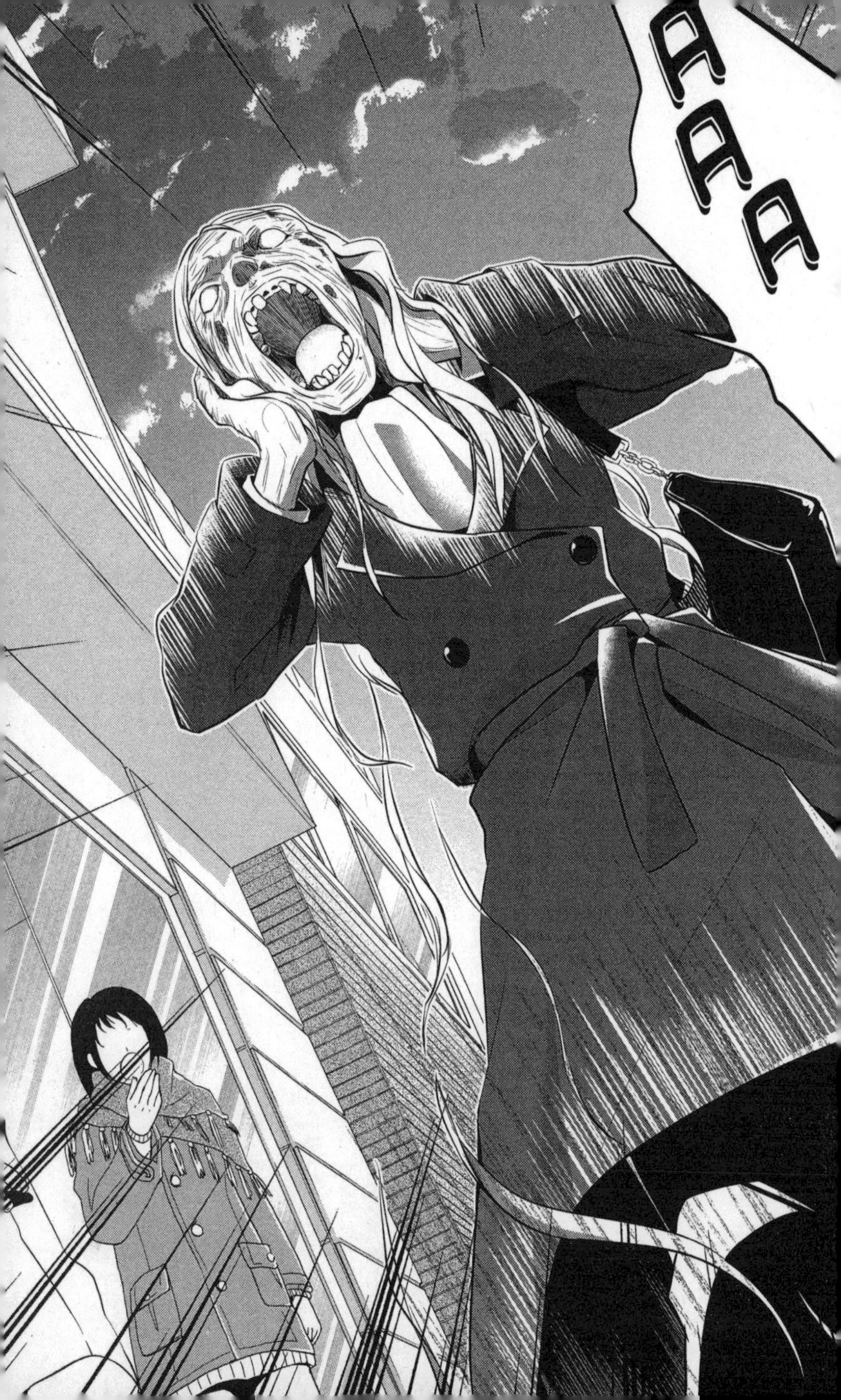
AAAA

NO.6

Chapter 11: The Netherworld

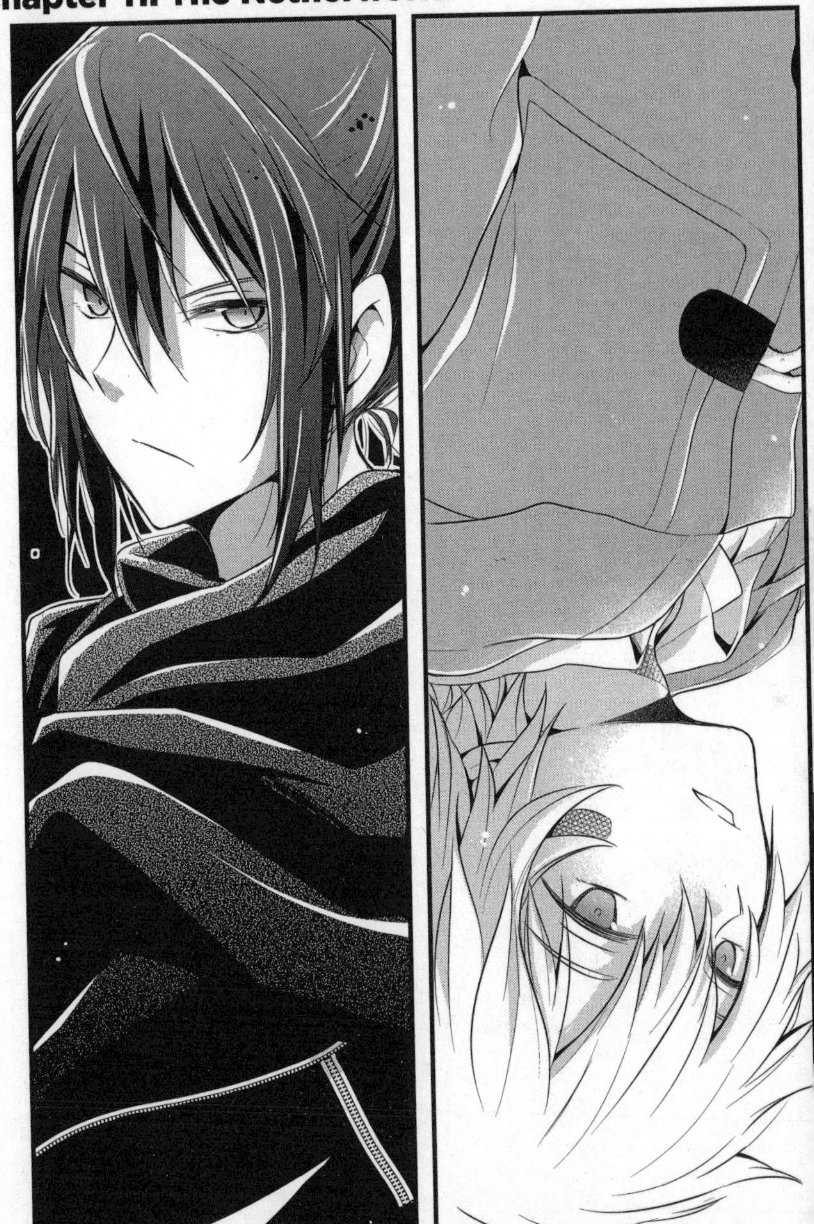

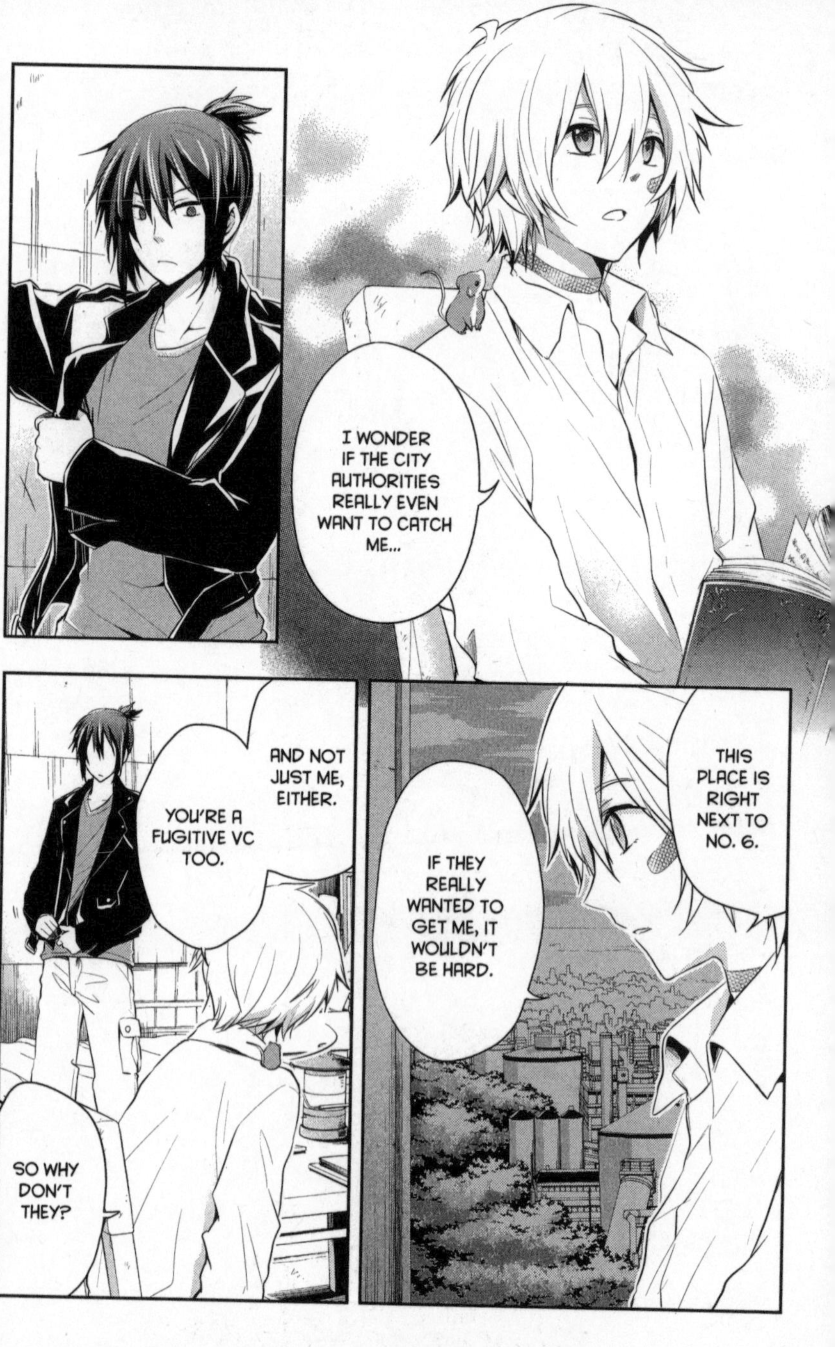
I WONDER IF THE CITY AUTHORITIES REALLY EVEN WANT TO CATCH ME...
THIS PLACE IS RIGHT NEXT TO NO. 6.
IF THEY REALLY WANTED TO GET ME, IT WOULDN'T BE HARD.
AND NOT JUST ME, EITHER.
YOU'RE A FUGITIVE VC TOO.
SO WHY DON'T THEY?

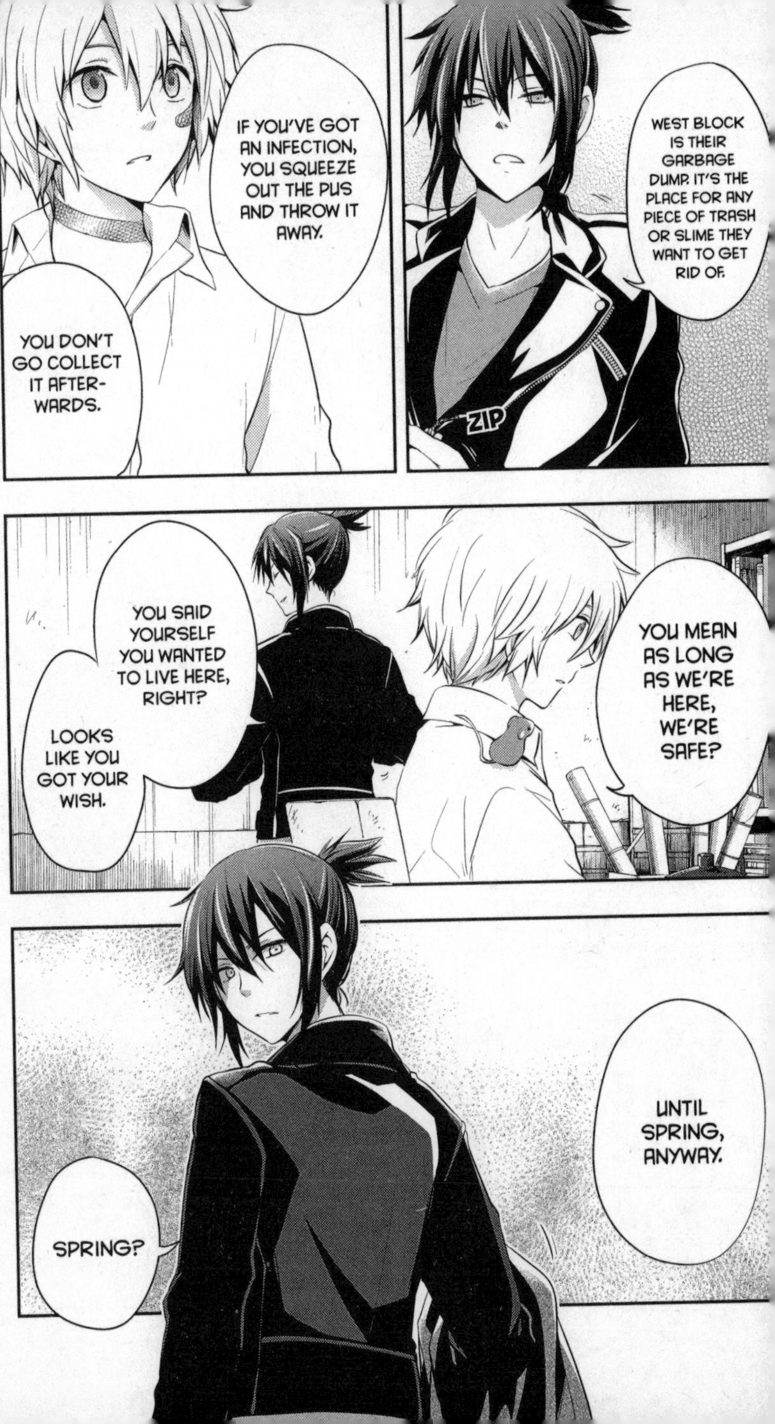
WEST BLOCK IS THEIR GARBAGE DUMP. IT'S THE PLACE FOR ANY PIECE OF TRASH OR SLIME THEY WANT TO GET RID OF.
ZIP
IF YOU'VE GOT AN INFECTION, YOU SQUEEZE OUT THE PUS AND THROW IT AWAY.
YOU DON'T GO COLLECT IT AFTER-WARDS.
YOU MEAN AS LONG AS WE'RE HERE, WE'RE SAFE?
YOU SAID YOURSELF YOU WANTED TO LIVE HERE, RIGHT?
LOOKS LIKE YOU GOT YOUR WISH.
UNTIL SPRING, ANYWAY.
SPRING?

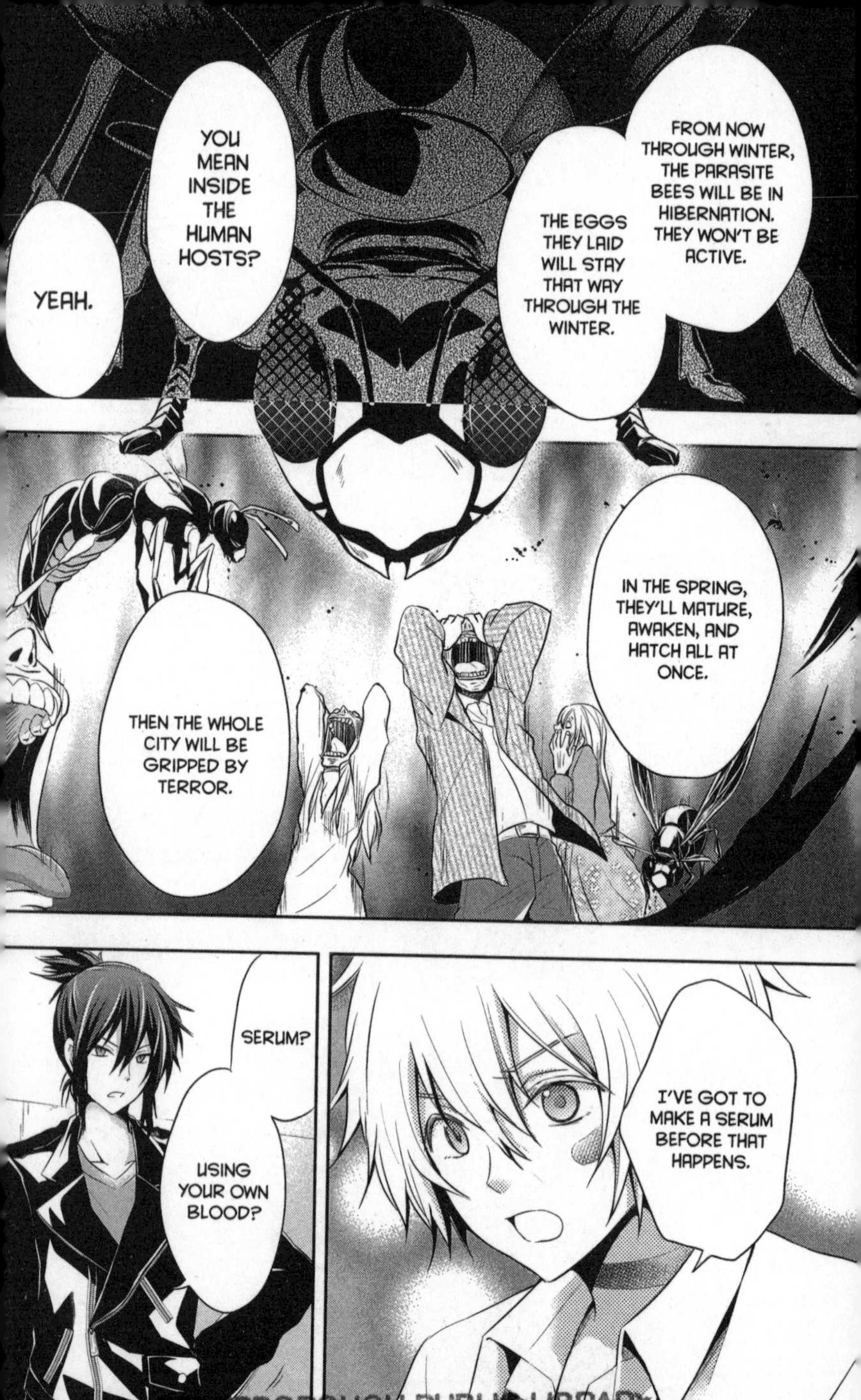
FROM NOW THROUGH WINTER, THE PARASITE BEES WILL BE IN HIBERNATION. THEY WON'T BE ACTIVE.
THE EGGS THEY LAID WILL STAY THAT WAY THROUGH THE WINTER.
YOU MEAN INSIDE THE HUMAN HOSTS?
YEAH.
IN THE SPRING, THEY'LL MATURE, AWAKEN, AND HATCH ALL AT ONCE.
THEN THE WHOLE CITY WILL BE GRIPPED BY TERROR.
I'VE GOT TO MAKE A SERUM BEFORE THAT HAPPENS.
SERUM?
USING YOUR OWN BLOOD?

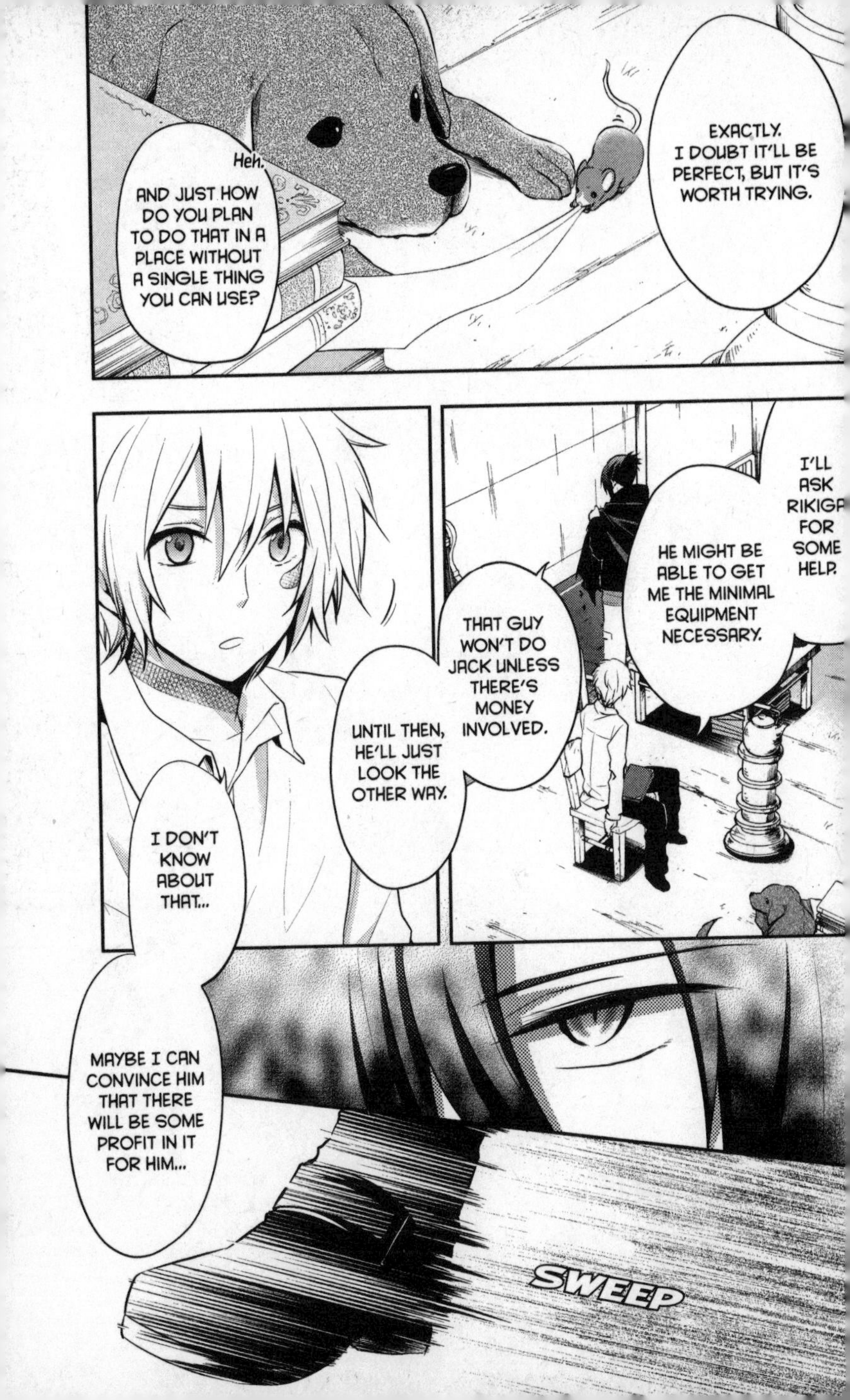
EXACTLY. I DOUBT IT'LL BE PERFECT, BUT IT'S WORTH TRYING.
Heh.
AND JUST HOW DO YOU PLAN TO DO THAT IN A PLACE WITHOUT A SINGLE THING YOU CAN USE?
I'LL ASK RIKIGA FOR SOME HELP.
HE MIGHT BE ABLE TO GET ME THE MINIMAL EQUIPMENT NECESSARY.
THAT GUY WON'T DO JACK UNLESS THERE'S MONEY INVOLVED.
UNTIL THEN, HE'LL JUST LOOK THE OTHER WAY.
I DON'T KNOW ABOUT THAT...
MAYBE I CAN CONVINCE HIM THAT THERE WILL BE SOME PROFIT IN IT FOR HIM...
SWEEP

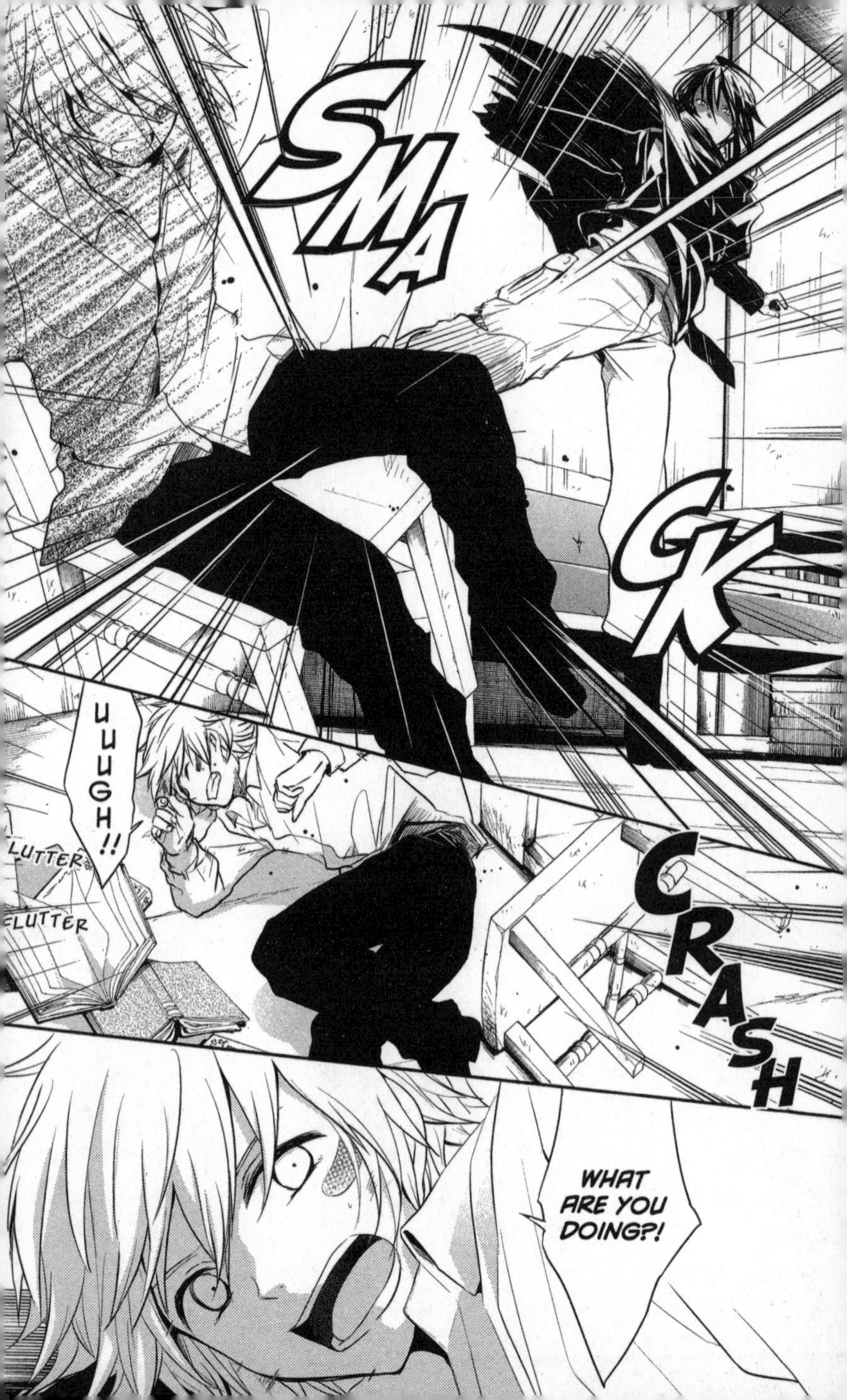
SMA
GK
CRASH
UUUGH!!
FLUTTER
FLUTTER
WHAT ARE YOU DOING?!

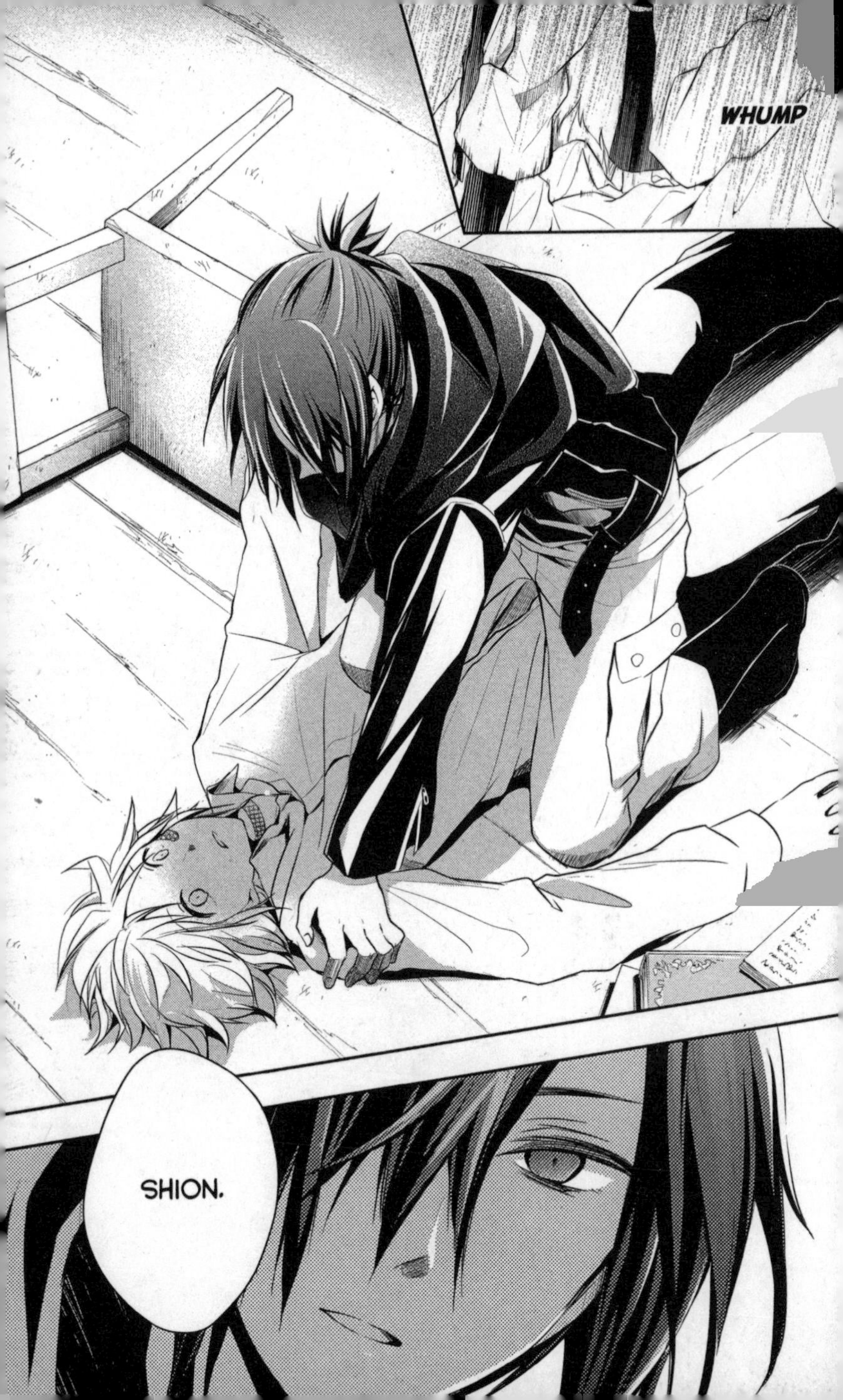
WHUMP
SHION.

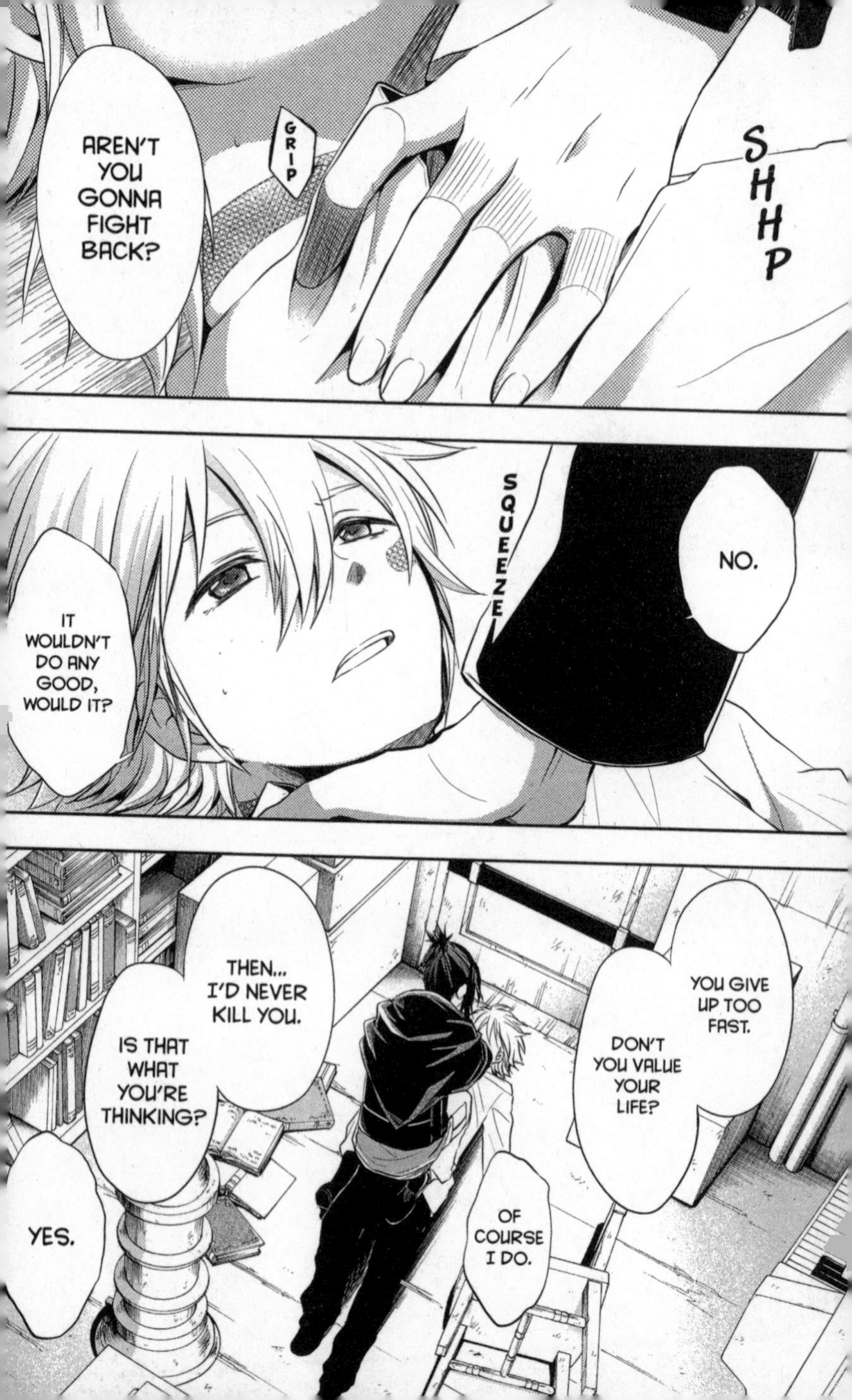
SHHP
GRIP
AREN'T YOU GONNA FIGHT BACK?
NO.
SQUEEZE
IT WOULDN'T DO ANY GOOD, WOULD IT?
YOU GIVE UP TOO FAST.
DON'T YOU VALUE YOUR LIFE?
OF COURSE I DO.
THEN... I'D NEVER KILL YOU.
IS THAT WHAT YOU'RE THINKING?
YES.

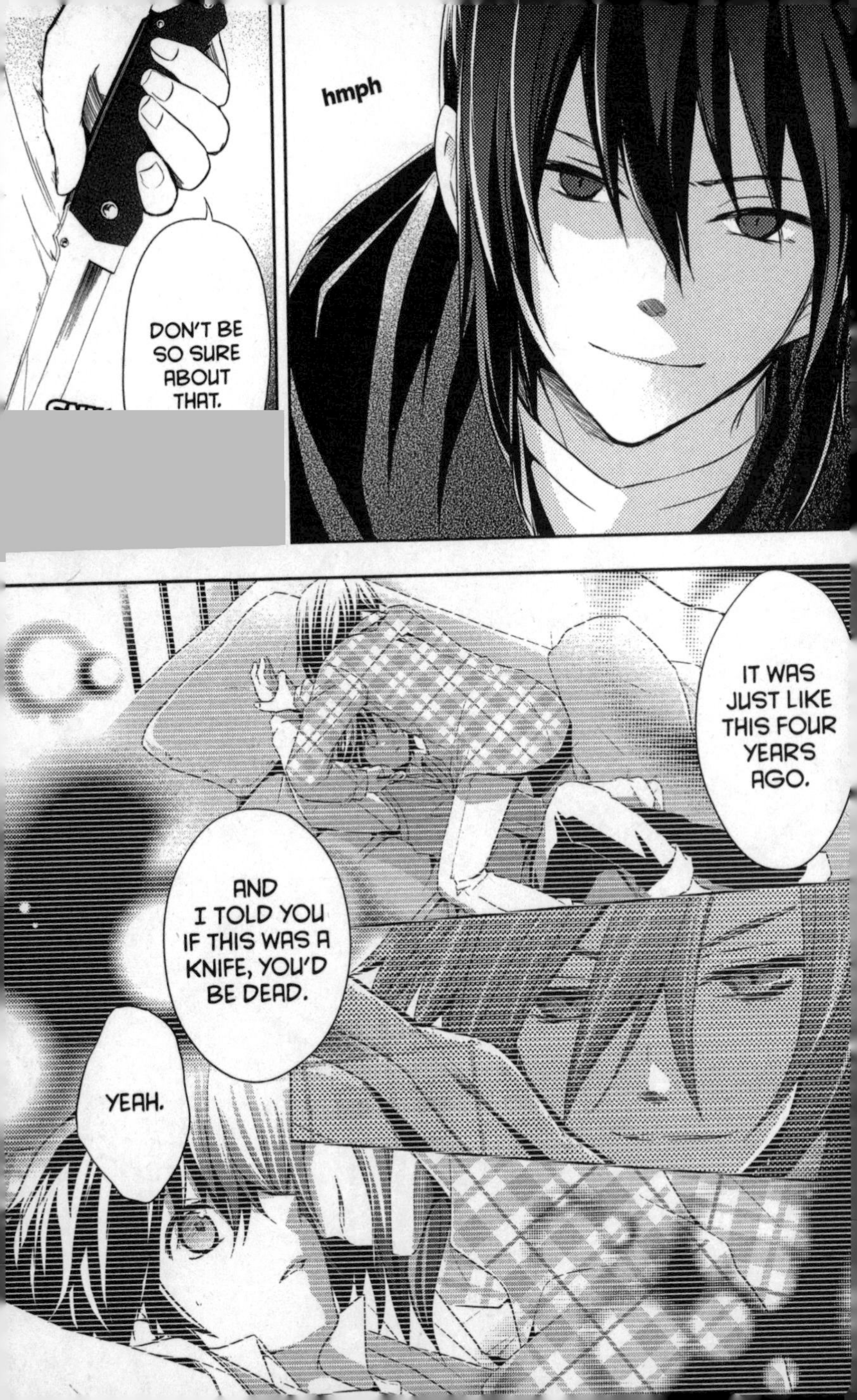
hmph
DON'T BE SO SURE ABOUT THAT.
IT WAS JUST LIKE THIS FOUR YEARS AGO.
AND I TOLD YOU IF THIS WAS A KNIFE, YOU'D BE DEAD.
YEAH.

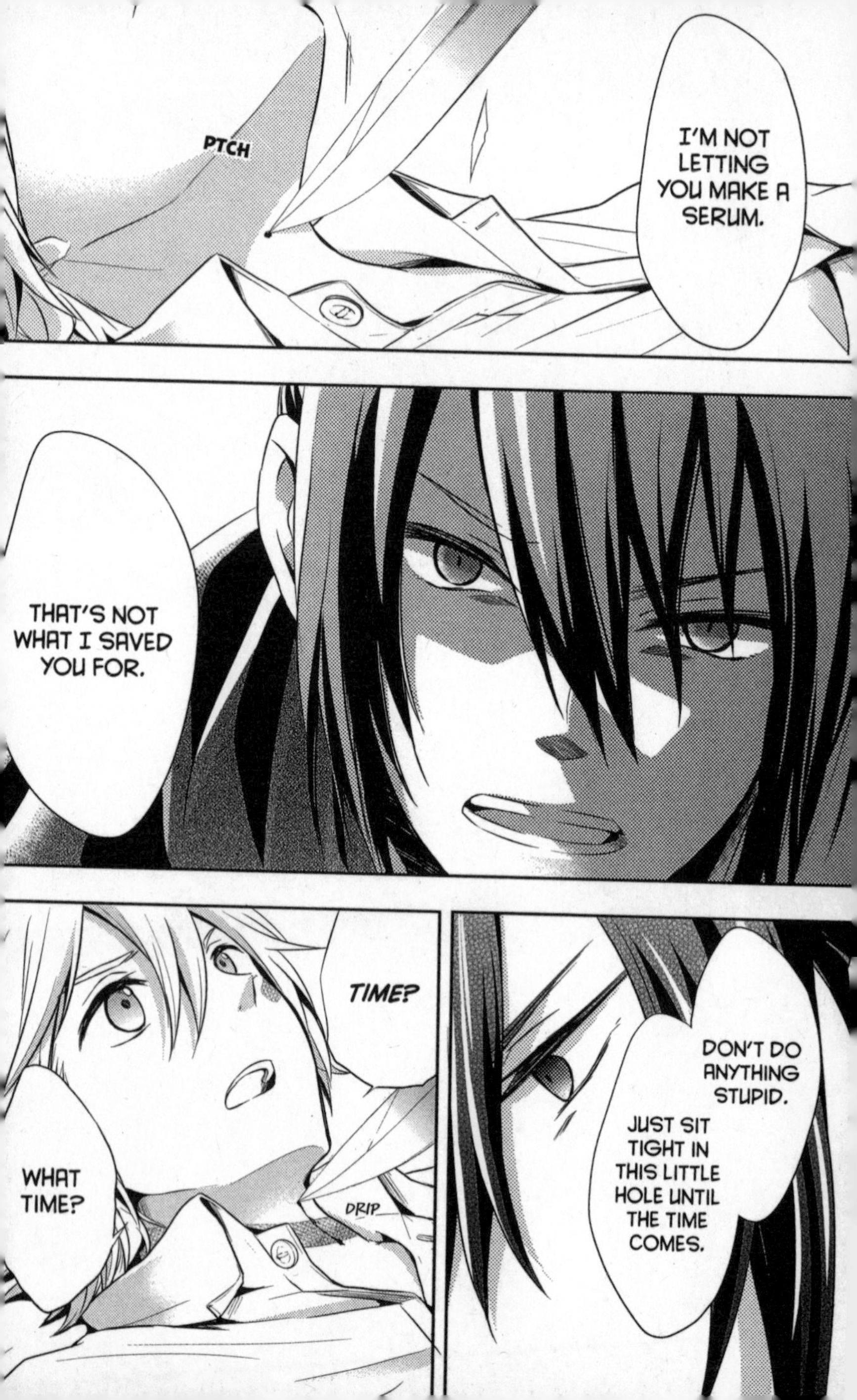
I'M NOT LETTING YOU MAKE A SERUM.
PTCH
THAT'S NOT WHAT I SAVED YOU FOR.
DON'T DO ANYTHING STUPID.
JUST SIT TIGHT IN THIS LITTLE HOLE UNTIL THE TIME COMES.
TIME?
DRIP
WHAT TIME?

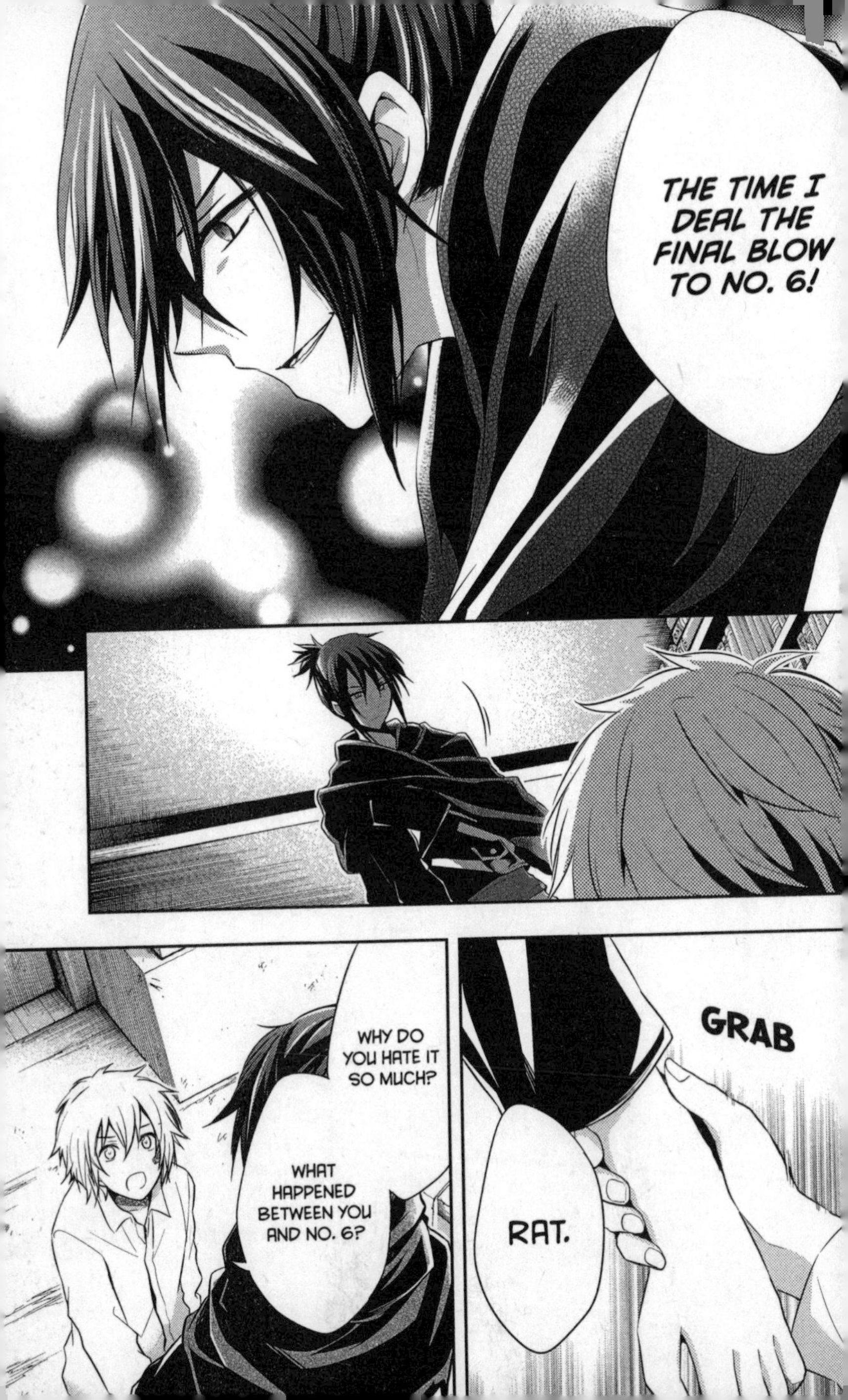
THE TIME I DEAL THE FINAL BLOW TO NO. 6!
GRAB
RAT.
WHY DO YOU HATE IT SO MUCH?
WHAT HAPPENED BETWEEN YOU AND NO. 6?

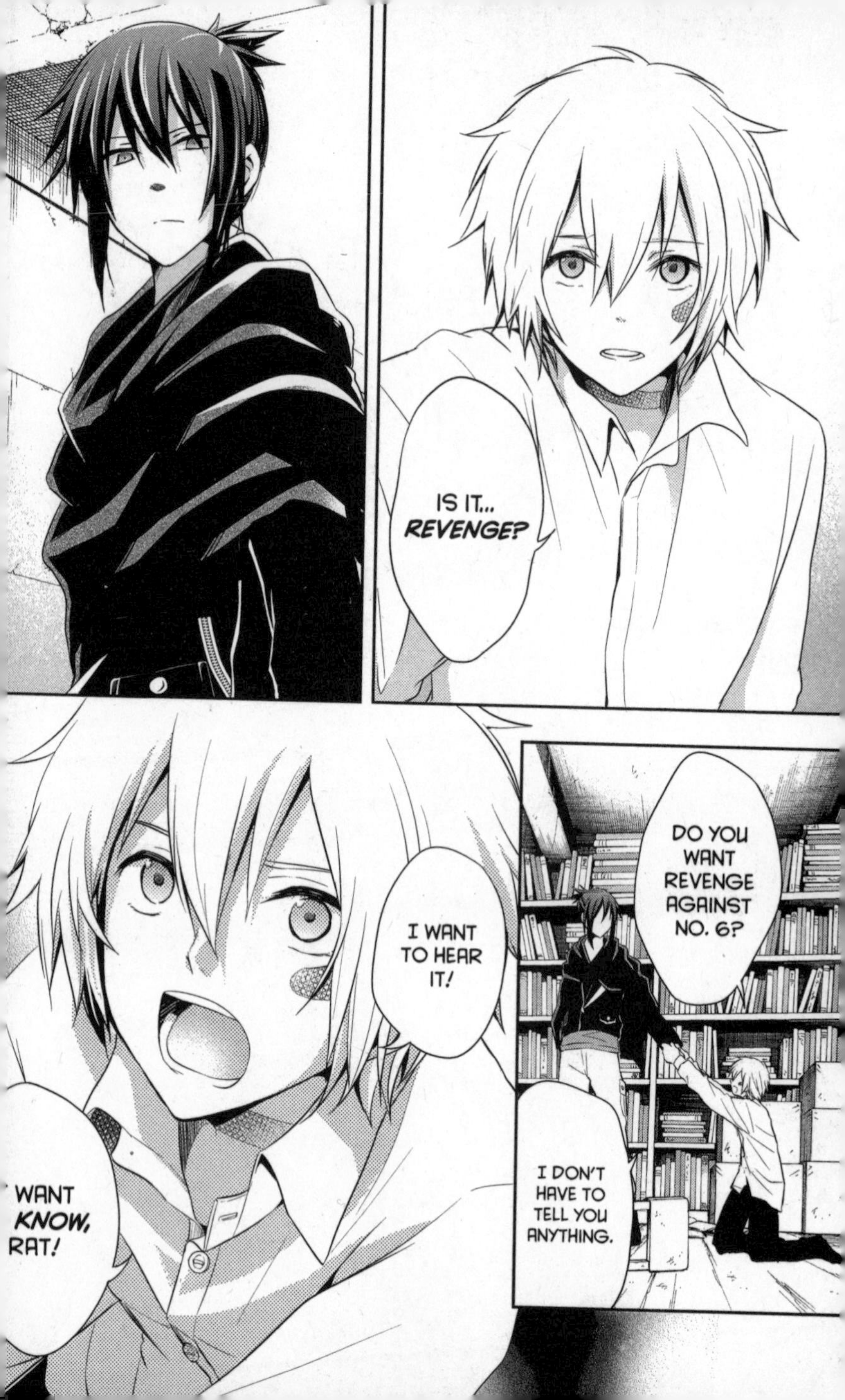
IS IT... *REVENGE?*
DO YOU WANT REVENGE AGAINST NO. 6?
I DON'T HAVE TO TELL YOU ANYTHING.
I WANT TO HEAR IT!
WANT *KNOW,* RAT!

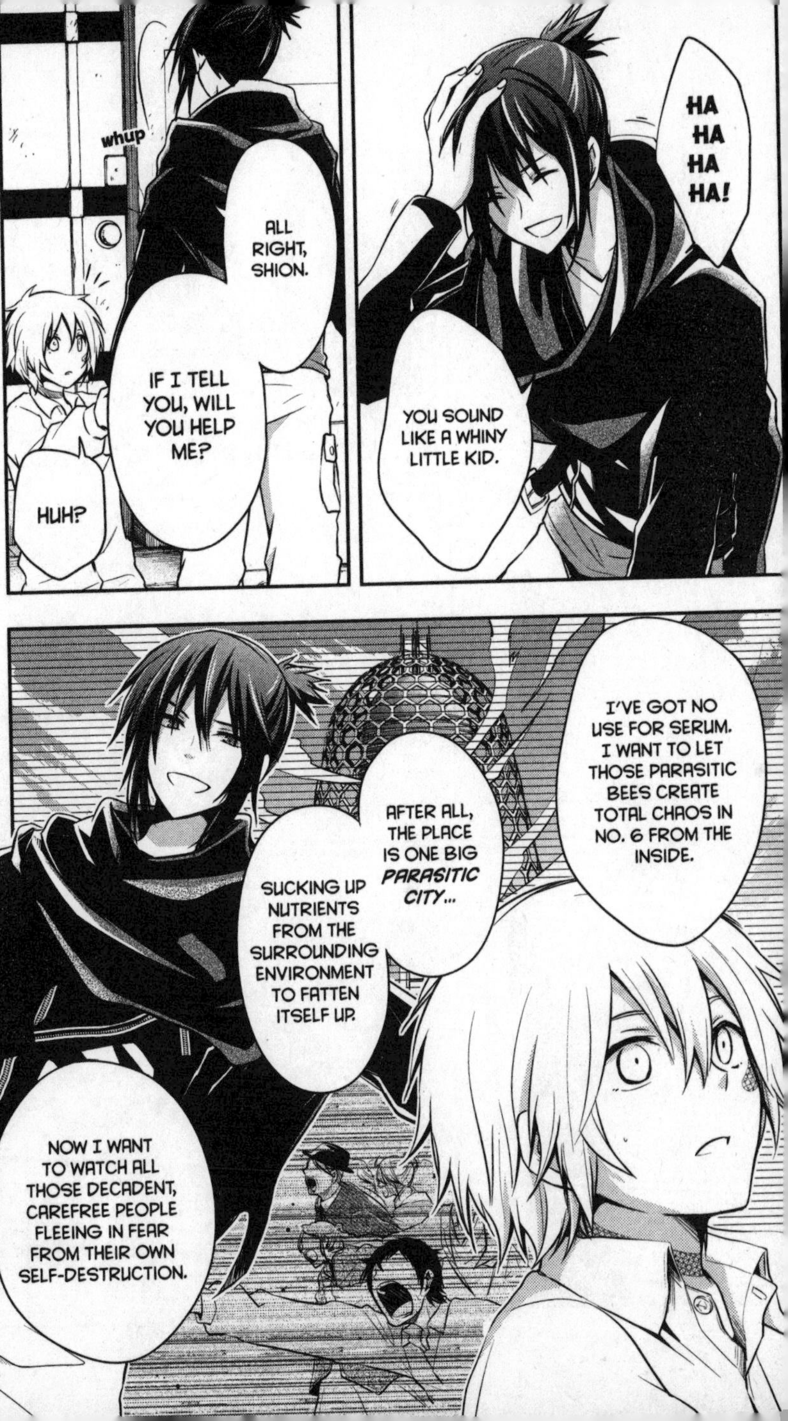
HA HA HA HA!
YOU SOUND LIKE A WHINY LITTLE KID.
whup
ALL RIGHT, SHION.
IF I TELL YOU, WILL YOU HELP ME?
HUH?
I'VE GOT NO USE FOR SERUM. I WANT TO LET THOSE PARASITIC BEES CREATE TOTAL CHAOS IN NO. 6 FROM THE INSIDE.
AFTER ALL, THE PLACE IS ONE BIG PARASITIC CITY...
SUCKING UP NUTRIENTS FROM THE SURROUNDING ENVIRONMENT TO FATTEN ITSELF UP.
NOW I WANT TO WATCH ALL THOSE DECADENT, CAREFREE PEOPLE FLEEING IN FEAR FROM THEIR OWN SELF-DESTRUCTION.

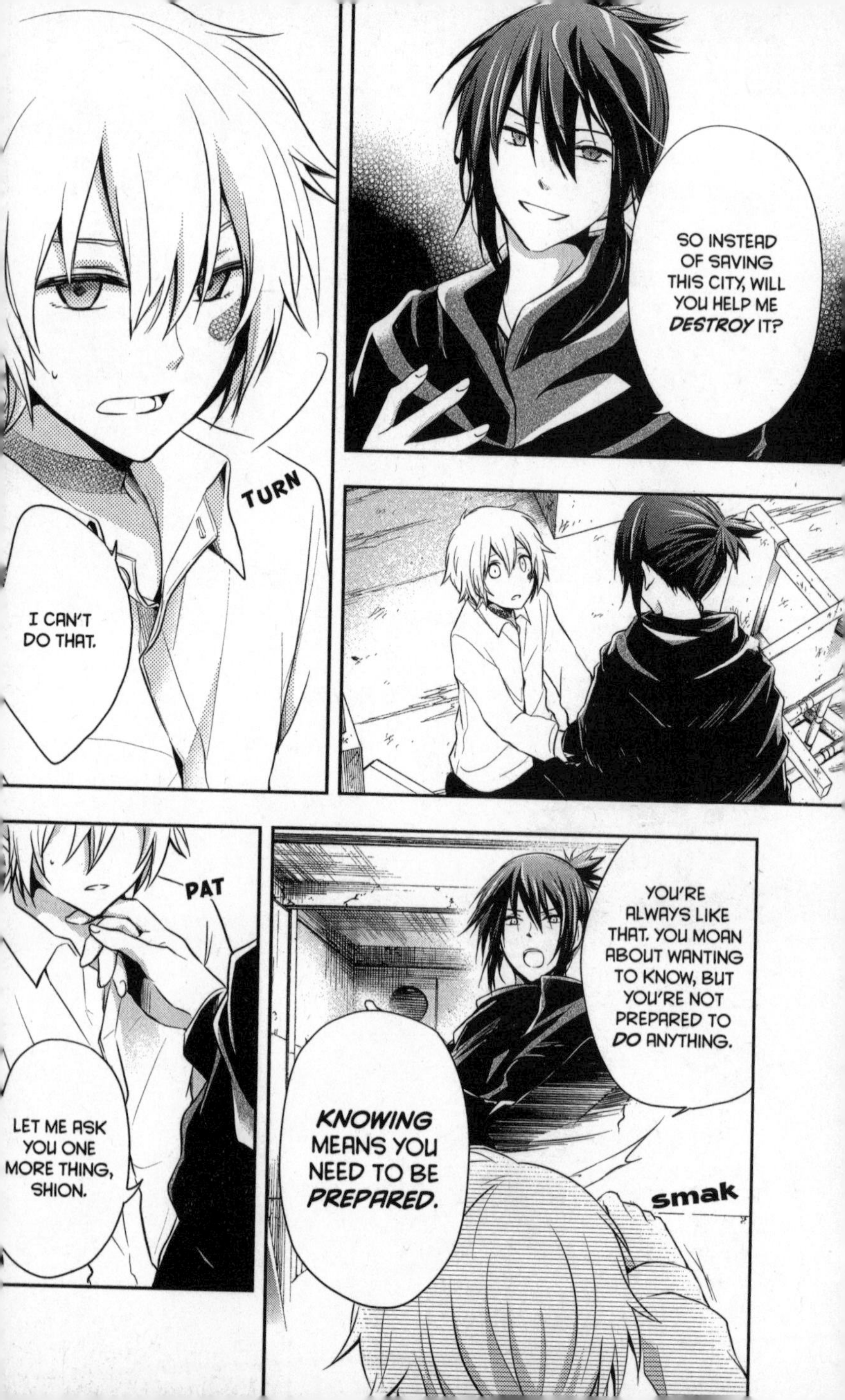
SO INSTEAD OF SAVING THIS CITY, WILL YOU HELP ME DESTROY IT?
TURN
I CAN'T DO THAT.
YOU'RE ALWAYS LIKE THAT. YOU MOAN ABOUT WANTING TO KNOW, BUT YOU'RE NOT PREPARED TO DO ANYTHING.
KNOWING MEANS YOU NEED TO BE PREPARED.
smak
PAT
LET ME ASK YOU ONE MORE THING, SHION.

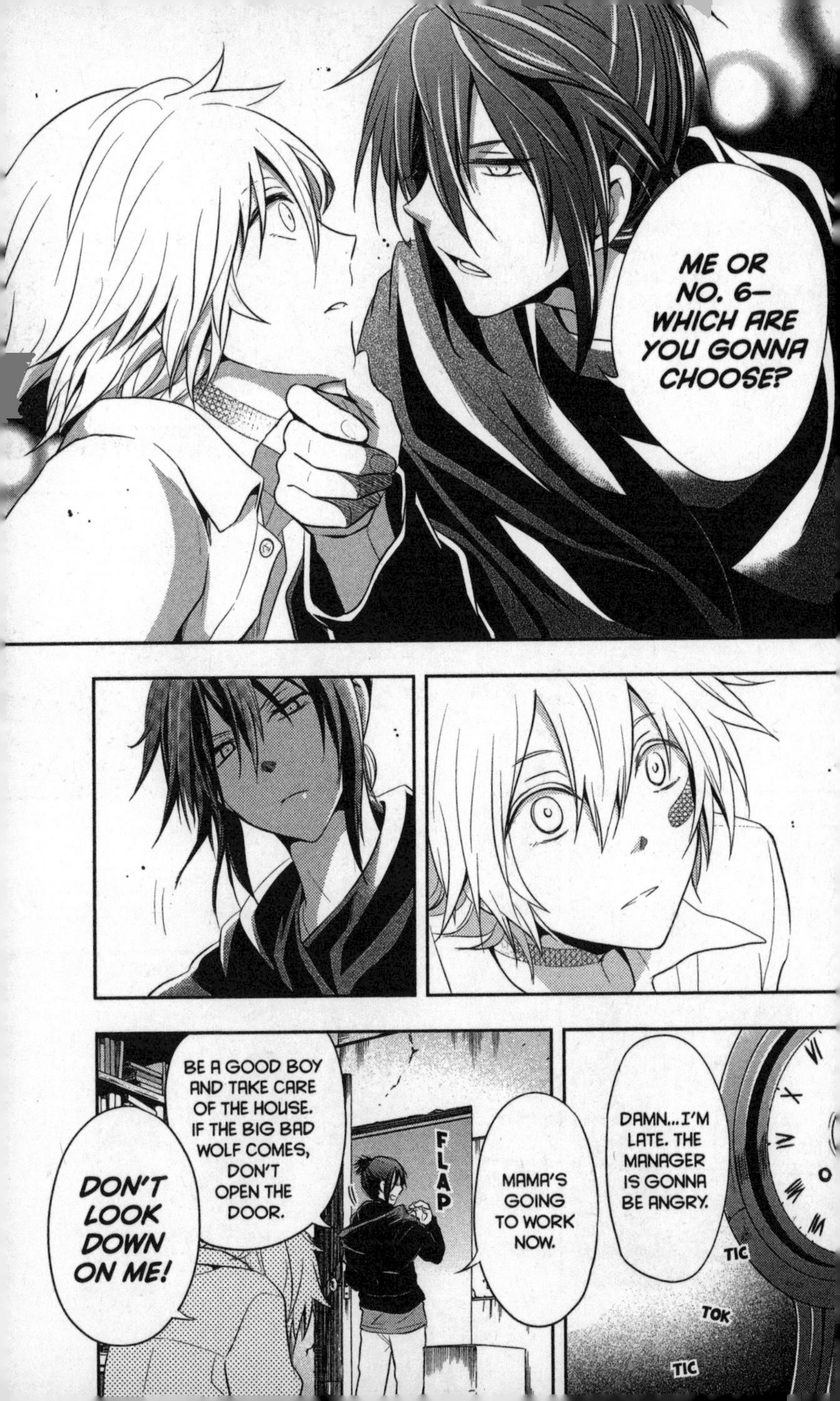
ME OR NO. 6—WHICH ARE YOU GONNA CHOOSE?
DAMN...I'M LATE. THE MANAGER IS GONNA BE ANGRY.
TIC
TOK
TIC
MAMA'S GOING TO WORK NOW.
FLAP
BE A GOOD BOY AND TAKE CARE OF THE HOUSE. IF THE BIG BAD WOLF COMES, DON'T OPEN THE DOOR.
DON'T LOOK DOWN ON ME!

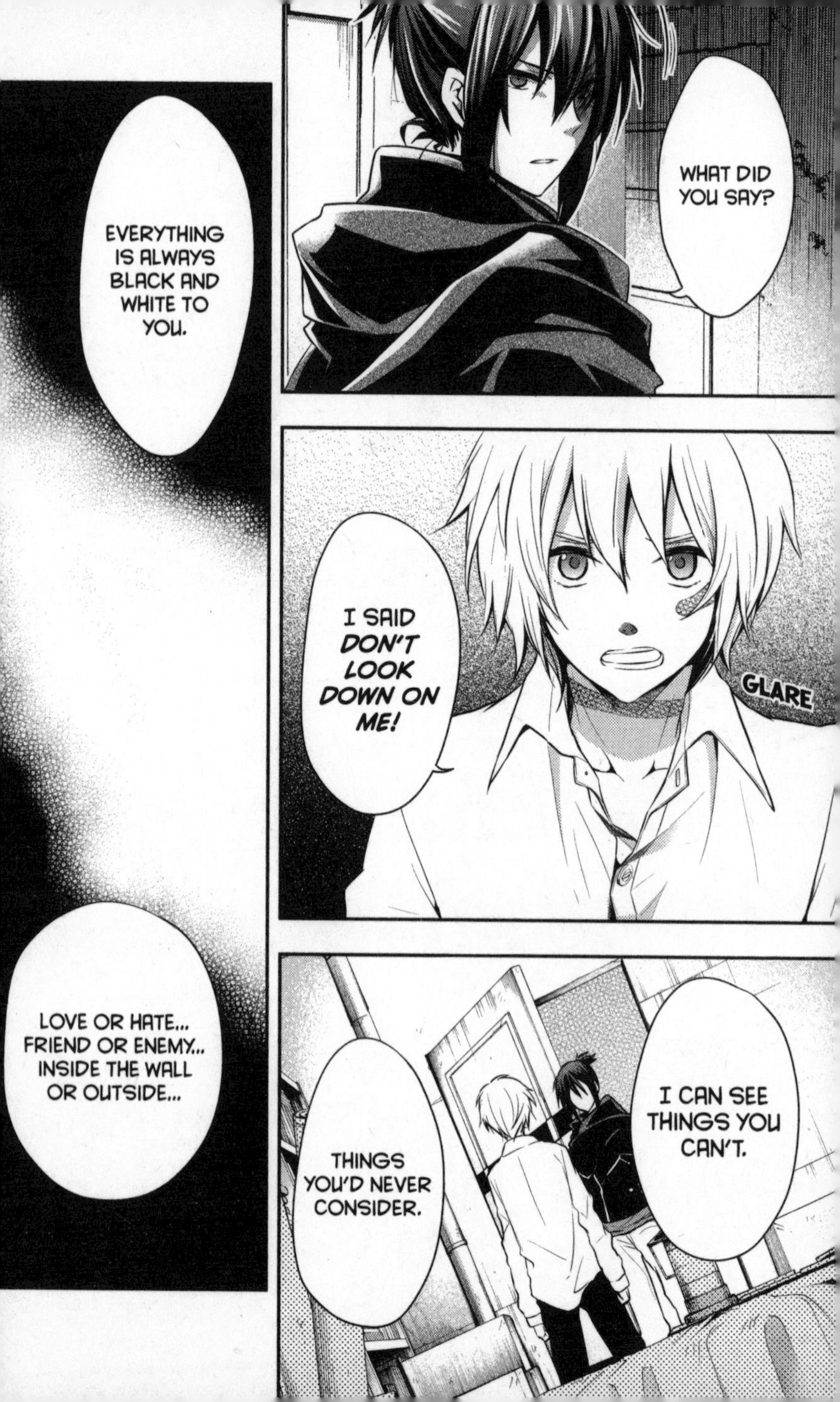
WHAT DID YOU SAY?
I SAID *DON'T LOOK DOWN ON ME!*
GLARE
I CAN SEE THINGS YOU CAN'T.
THINGS YOU'D NEVER CONSIDER.
EVERYTHING IS ALWAYS BLACK AND WHITE TO YOU.
LOVE OR HATE... FRIEND OR ENEMY... INSIDE THE WALL OR OUTSIDE...

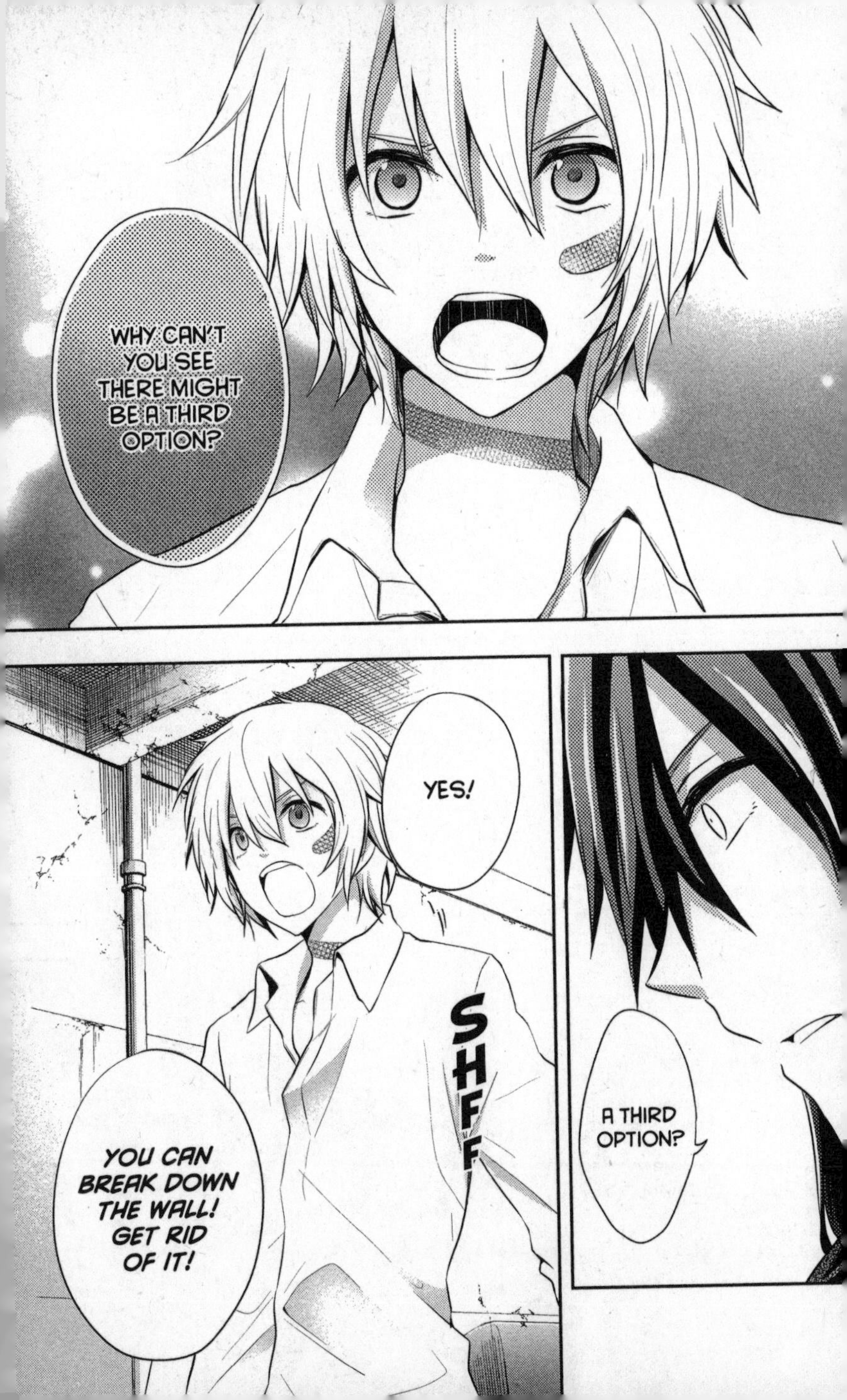
WHY CAN'T YOU SEE THERE MIGHT BE A THIRD OPTION?
A THIRD OPTION?
YES!
SHFF
YOU CAN BREAK DOWN THE WALL! GET RID OF IT!

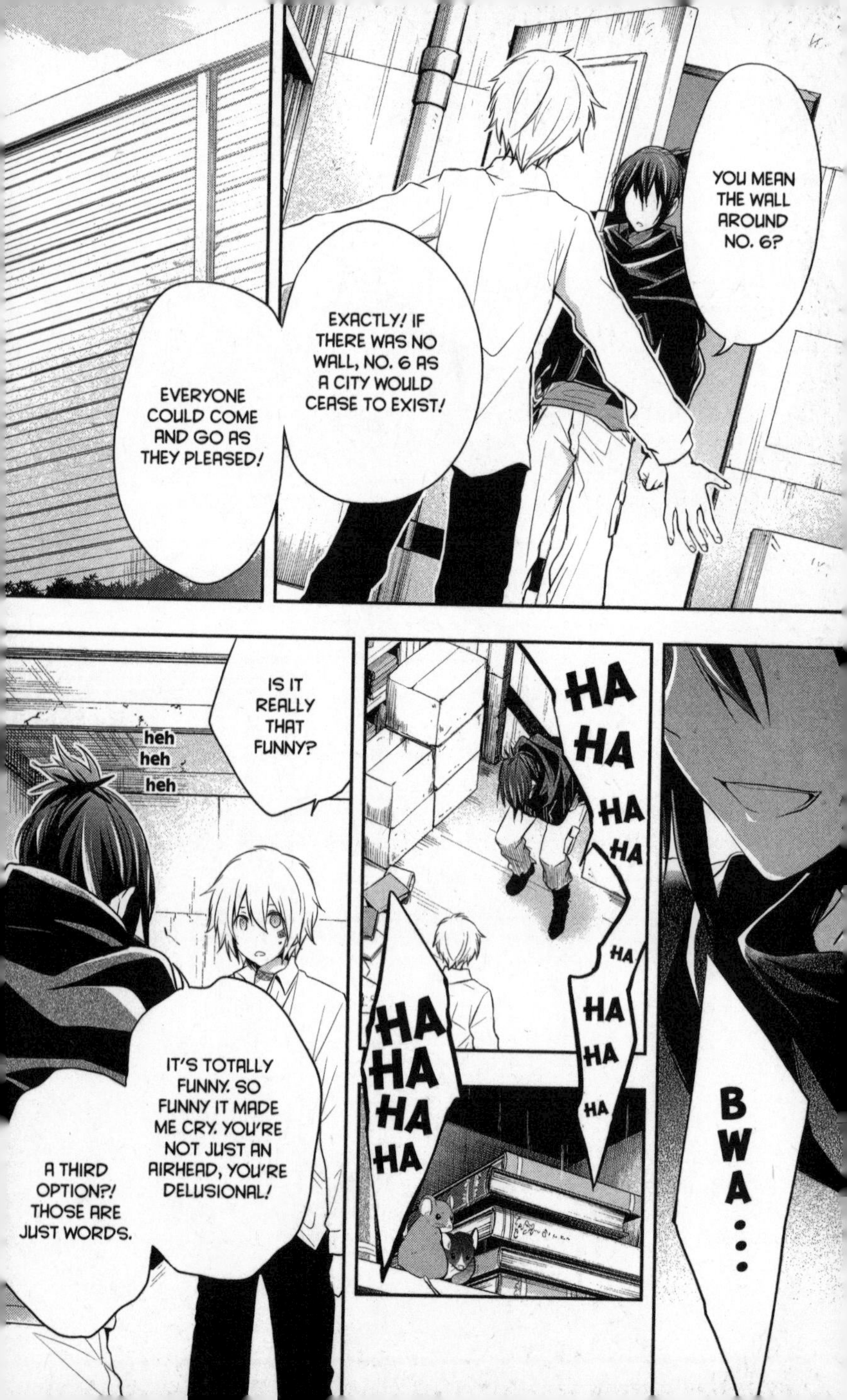
YOU MEAN THE WALL AROUND NO. 6?
EXACTLY! IF THERE WAS NO WALL, NO. 6 AS A CITY WOULD CEASE TO EXIST!
EVERYONE COULD COME AND GO AS THEY PLEASED!
BWA...
HA HA HA HA HA HA HA HA
HA HA HA HA
IS IT REALLY THAT FUNNY?
heh heh heh
IT'S TOTALLY FUNNY. SO FUNNY IT MADE ME CRY. YOU'RE NOT JUST AN AIRHEAD, YOU'RE DELUSIONAL!
A THIRD OPTION?! THOSE ARE JUST WORDS.

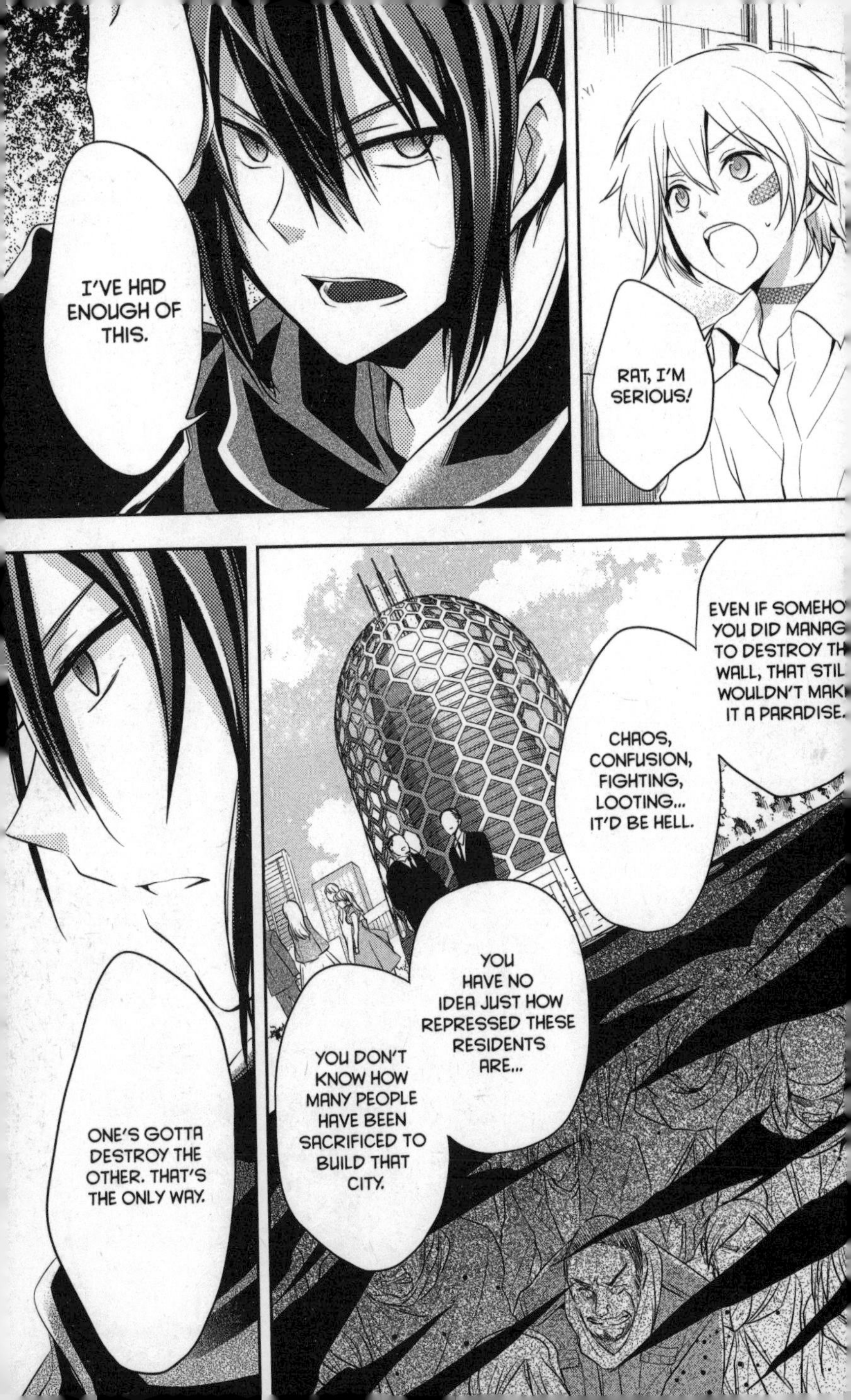
RAT, I'M SERIOUS!
I'VE HAD ENOUGH OF THIS.
EVEN IF SOMEHO YOU DID MANAG TO DESTROY TH WALL, THAT STIL WOULDN'T MAK IT A PARADISE.
CHAOS, CONFUSION, FIGHTING, LOOTING... IT'D BE HELL.
YOU HAVE NO IDEA JUST HOW REPRESSED THESE RESIDENTS ARE...
YOU DON'T KNOW HOW MANY PEOPLE HAVE BEEN SACRIFICED TO BUILD THAT CITY.
ONE'S GOTTA DESTROY THE OTHER. THAT'S THE ONLY WAY.

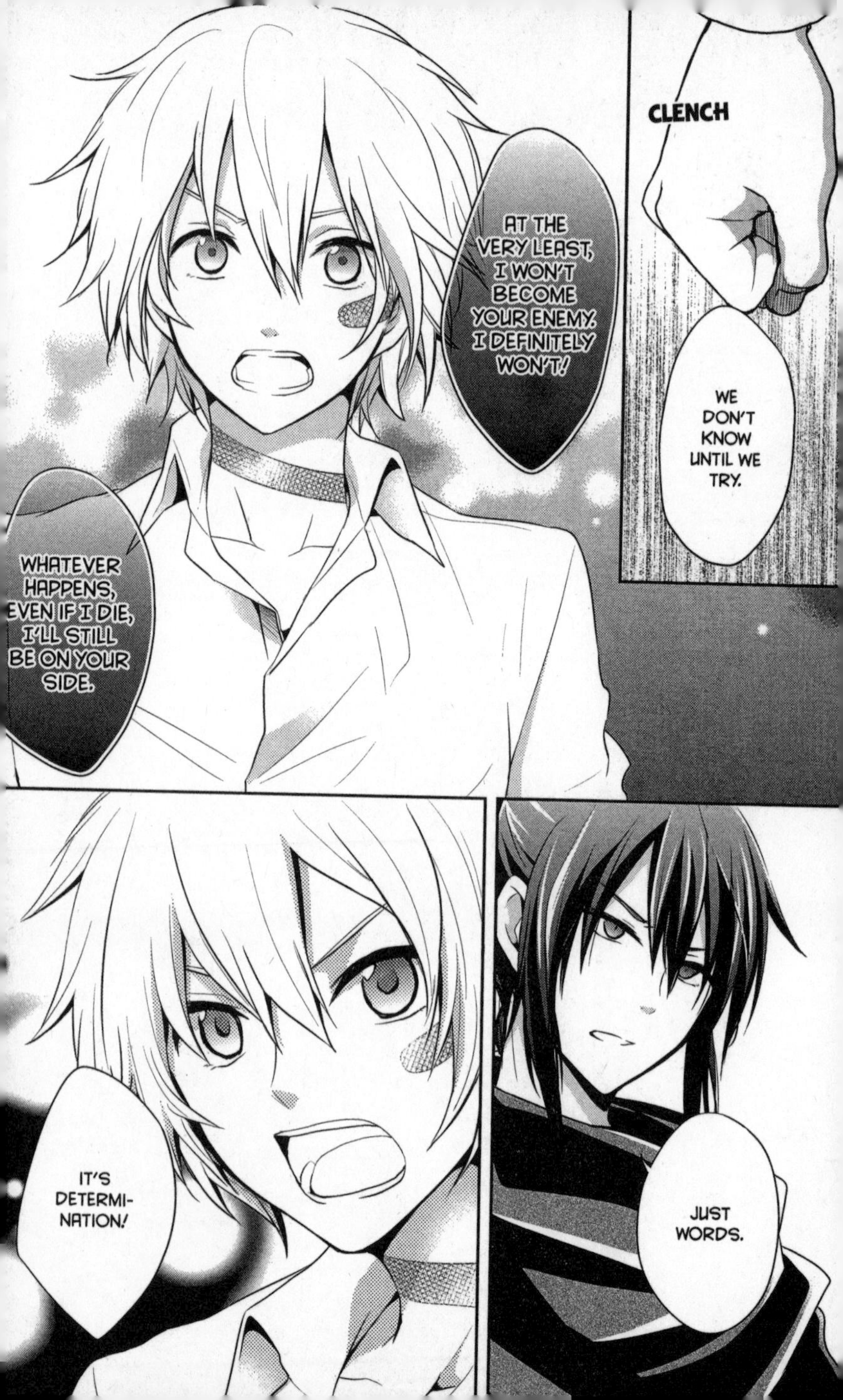
CLENCH
WE DON'T KNOW UNTIL WE TRY.
AT THE VERY LEAST, I WON'T BECOME YOUR ENEMY. I DEFINITELY WON'T!
WHATEVER HAPPENS, EVEN IF I DIE, I'LL STILL BE ON YOUR SIDE.
JUST WORDS.
IT'S DETERMI-NATION!

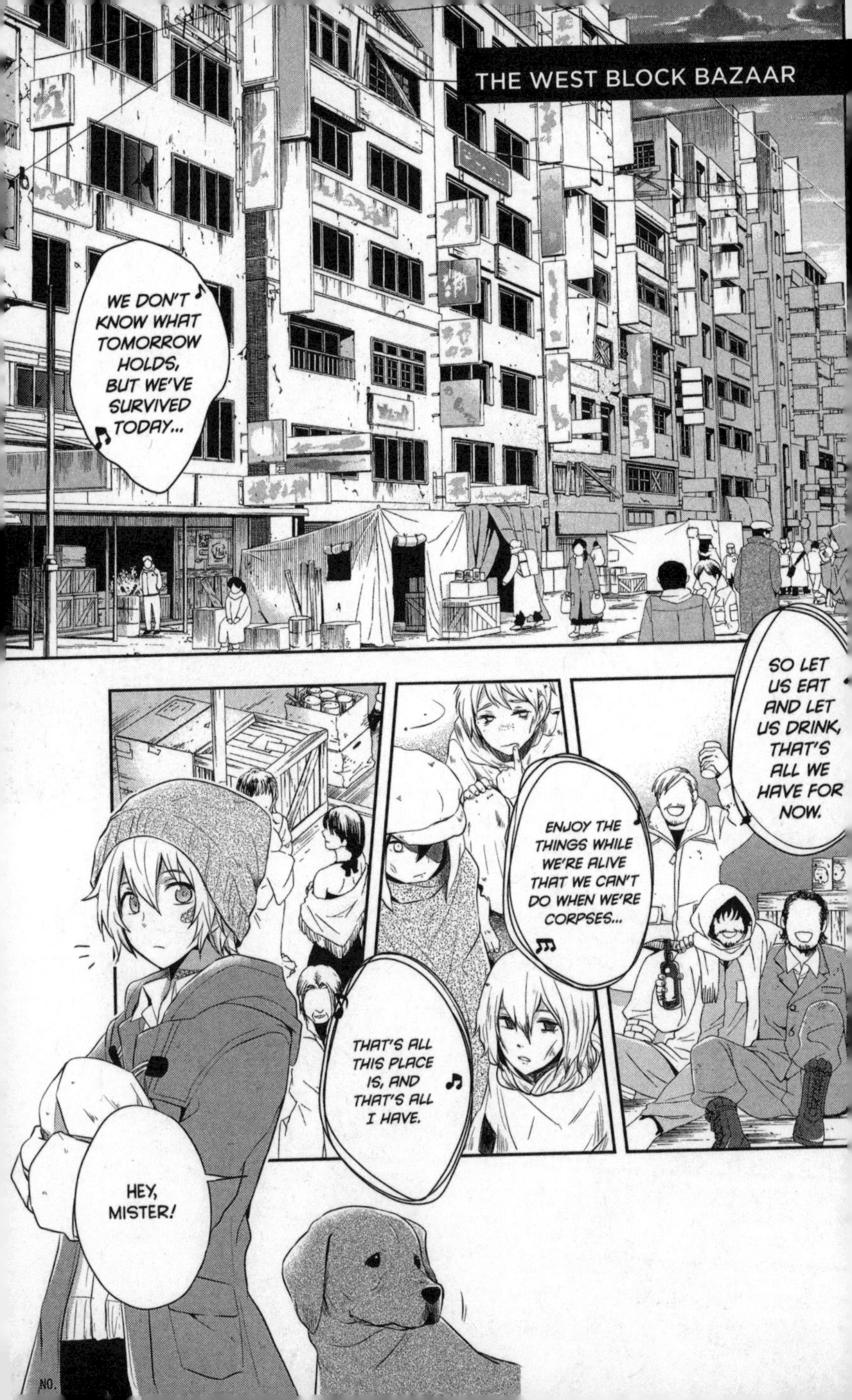
THE WEST BLOCK BAZAAR
WE DON'T KNOW WHAT TOMORROW HOLDS, BUT WE'VE SURVIVED TODAY...
SO LET US EAT AND LET US DRINK, THAT'S ALL WE HAVE FOR NOW.
ENJOY THE THINGS WHILE WE'RE ALIVE THAT WE CAN'T DO WHEN WE'RE CORPSES...
THAT'S ALL THIS PLACE IS, AND THAT'S ALL I HAVE.
HEY, MISTER!

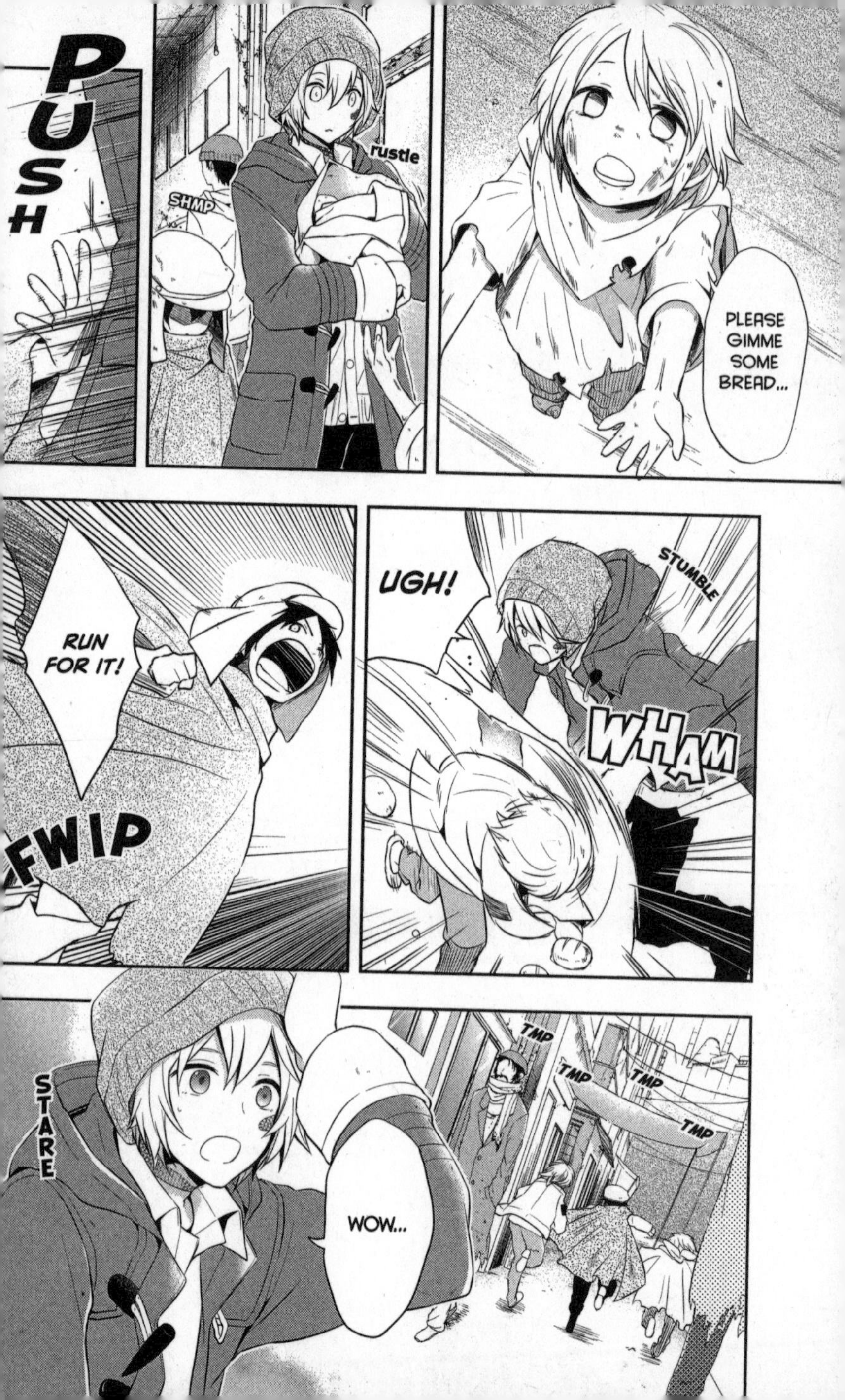
PLEASE GIMME SOME BREAD...
rustle
SHMP
PUSH
UGH!
STUMBLE
WHAM
RUN FOR IT!
FWIP
TMP
TMP
TMP
TMP
STARE
WOW...

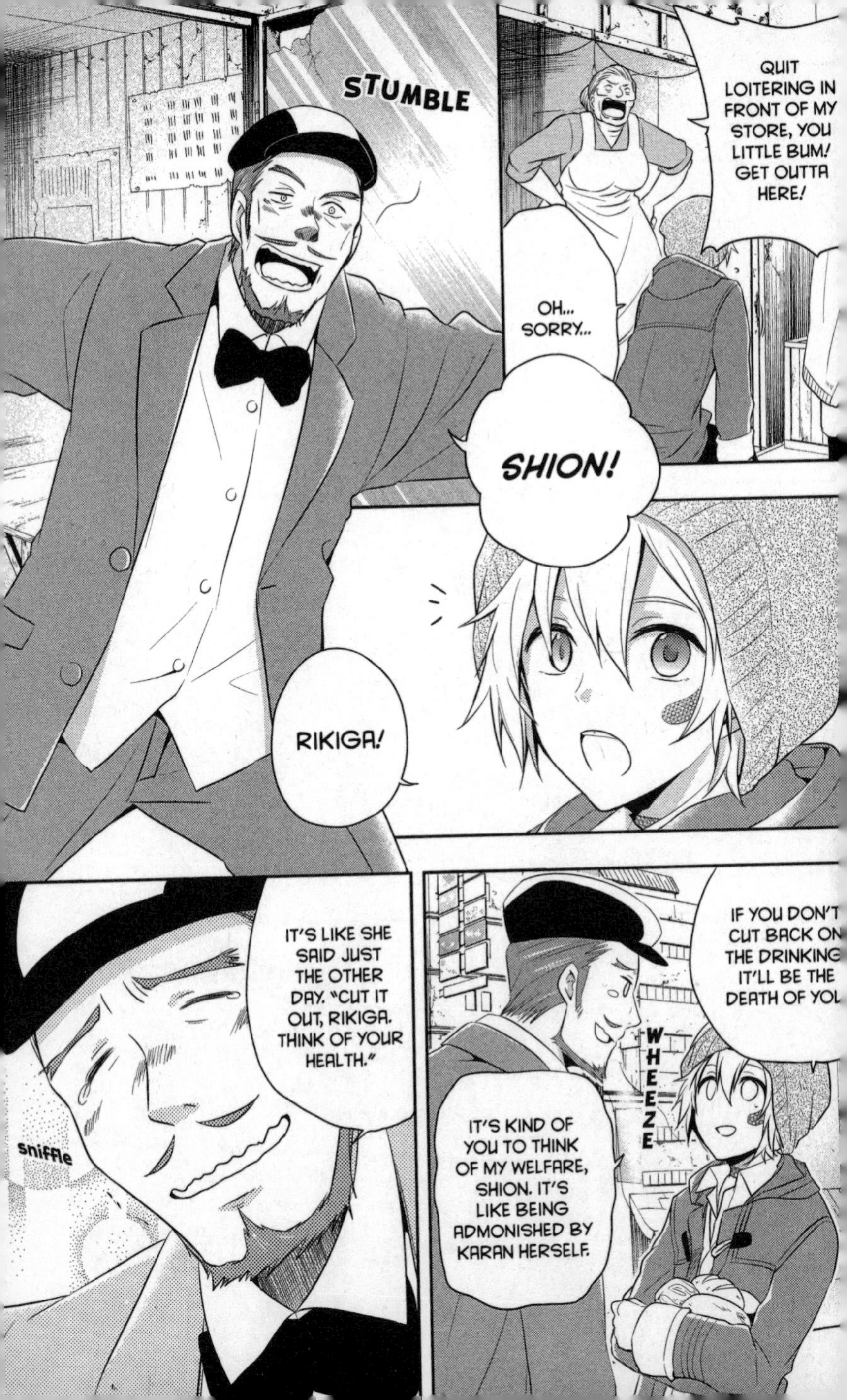
QUIT LOITERING IN FRONT OF MY STORE, YOU LITTLE BUM! GET OUTTA HERE!
OH... SORRY...
SHION!
RIKIGA!
STUMBLE
IF YOU DON'T CUT BACK ON THE DRINKING IT'LL BE THE DEATH OF YO
WHEEZE
IT'S KIND OF YOU TO THINK OF MY WELFARE, SHION. IT'S LIKE BEING ADMONISHED BY KARAN HERSELF.
IT'S LIKE SHE SAID JUST THE OTHER DAY. "CUT IT OUT, RIKIGA. THINK OF YOUR HEALTH."
sniffle

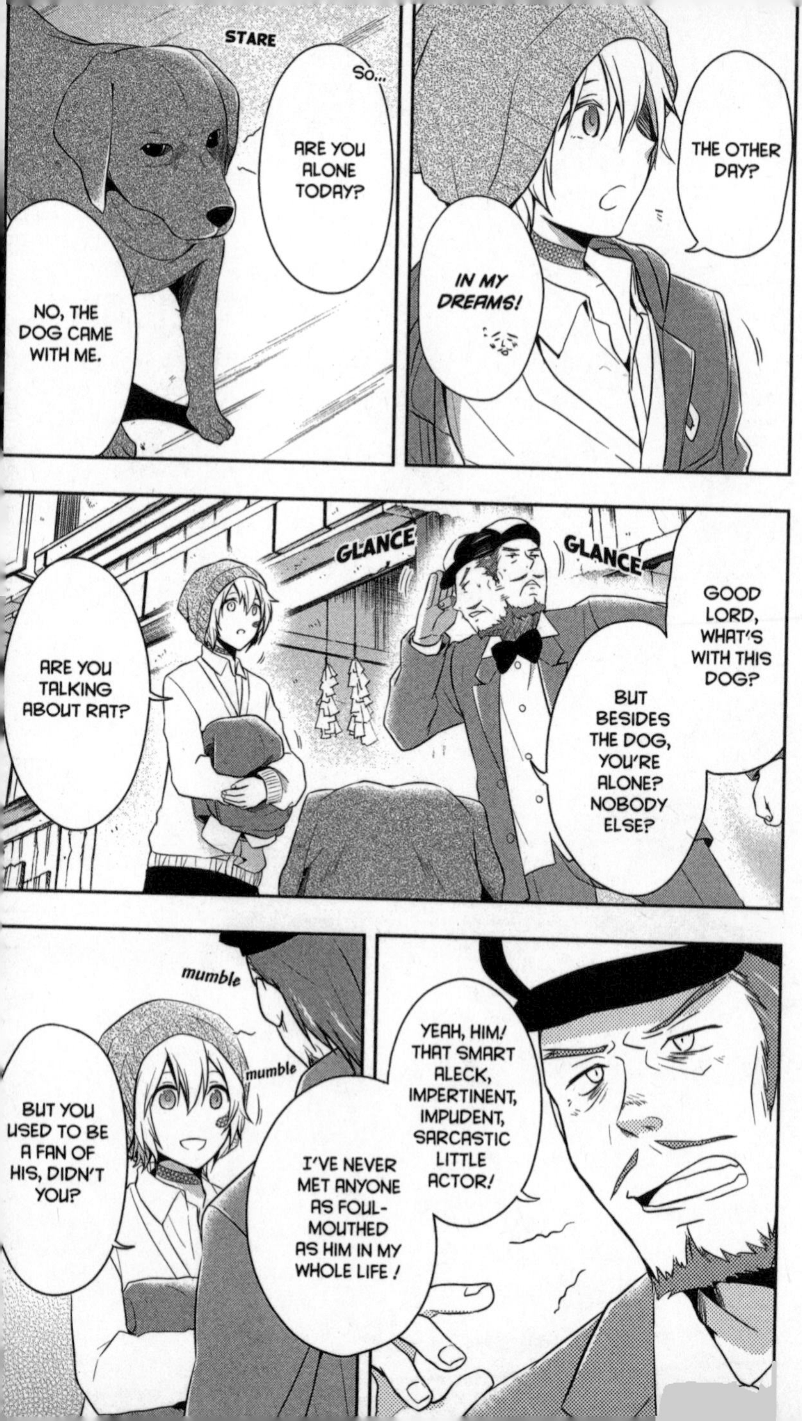
THE OTHER DAY?
IN MY DREAMS!
STARE
SO...
ARE YOU ALONE TODAY?
NO, THE DOG CAME WITH ME.
GOOD LORD, WHAT'S WITH THIS DOG?
GLANCE
GLANCE
BUT BESIDES THE DOG, YOU'RE ALONE? NOBODY ELSE?
ARE YOU TALKING ABOUT RAT?
YEAH, HIM! THAT SMART ALECK, IMPERTINENT, IMPUDENT, SARCASTIC LITTLE ACTOR!
I'VE NEVER MET ANYONE AS FOUL-MOUTHED AS HIM IN MY WHOLE LIFE!
mumble
mumble
BUT YOU USED TO BE A FAN OF HIS, DIDN'T YOU?

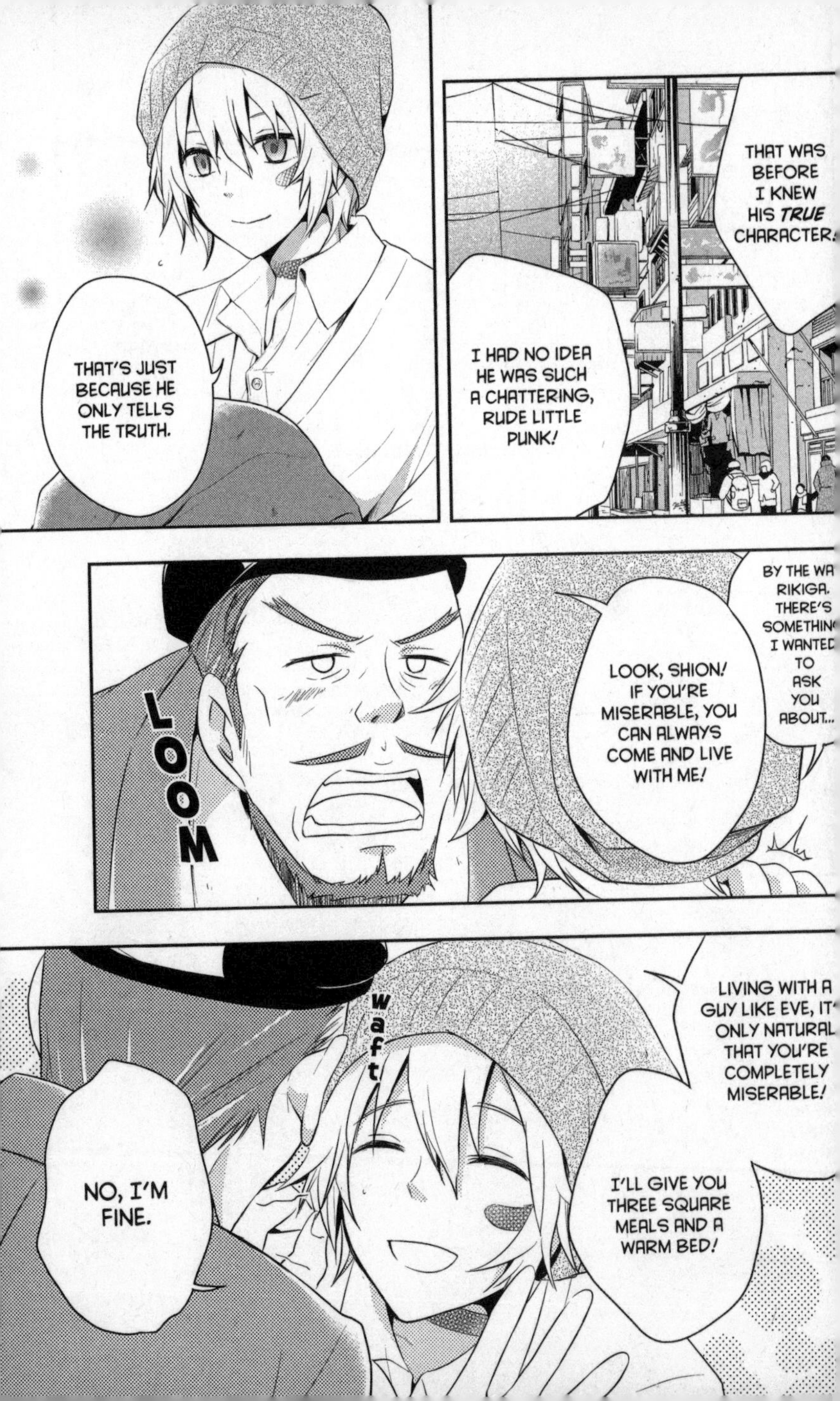
THAT WAS BEFORE I KNEW HIS *TRUE* CHARACTER.
I HAD NO IDEA HE WAS SUCH A CHATTERING, RUDE LITTLE PUNK!
THAT'S JUST BECAUSE HE ONLY TELLS THE TRUTH.
BY THE WA RIKIGA. THERE'S SOMETHIN I WANTED TO ASK YOU ABOUT...
LOOK, SHION! IF YOU'RE MISERABLE, YOU CAN ALWAYS COME AND LIVE WITH ME!
LOOM
LIVING WITH A GUY LIKE EVE, IT' ONLY NATURAL THAT YOU'RE COMPLETELY MISERABLE!
I'LL GIVE YOU THREE SQUARE MEALS AND A WARM BED!
waft
NO, I'M FINE.

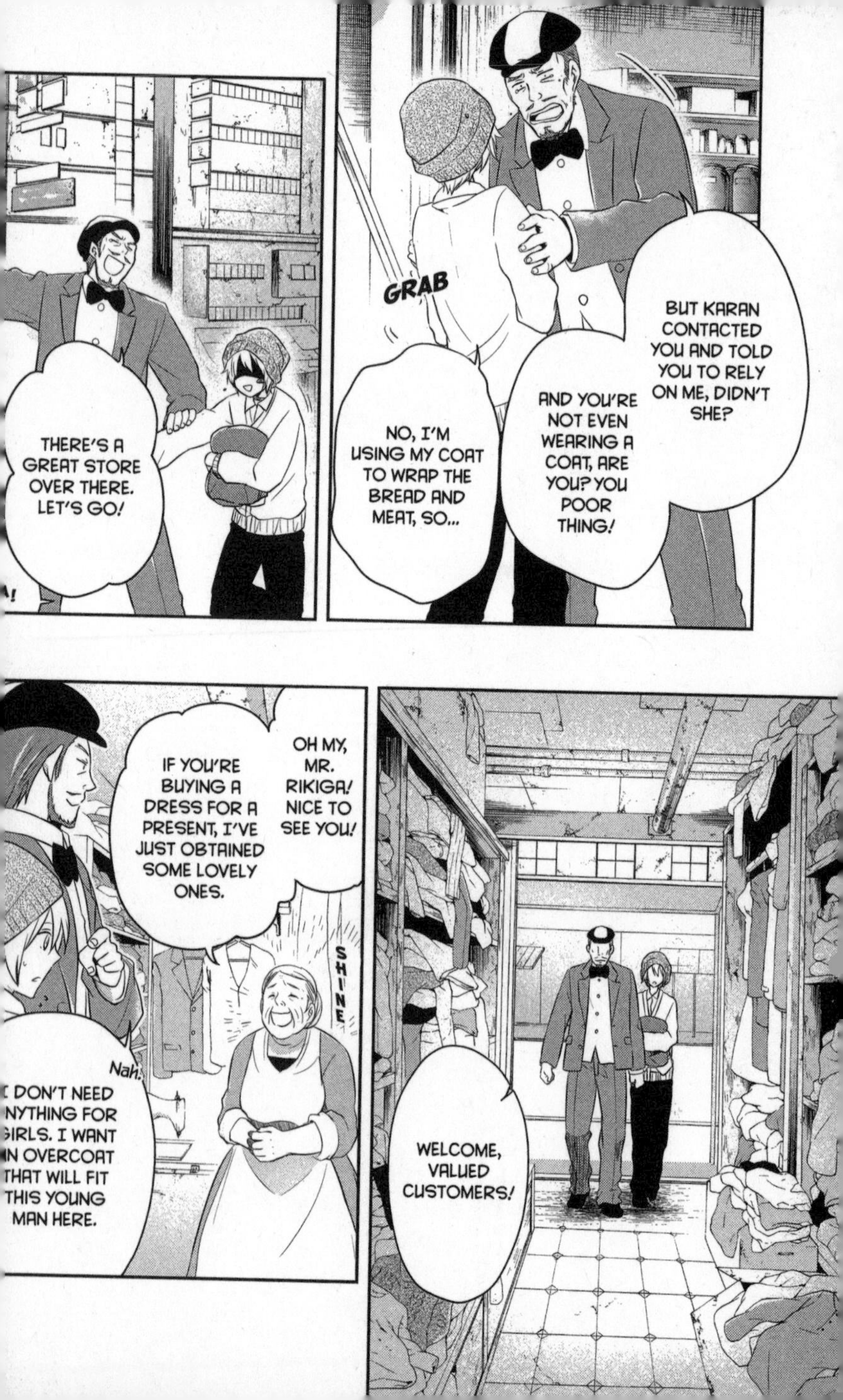
BUT KARAN CONTACTED YOU AND TOLD YOU TO RELY ON ME, DIDN'T SHE?
AND YOU'RE NOT EVEN WEARING A COAT, ARE YOU? YOU POOR THING!
GRAB
NO, I'M USING MY COAT TO WRAP THE BREAD AND MEAT, SO...
THERE'S A GREAT STORE OVER THERE. LET'S GO!
WELCOME, VALUED CUSTOMERS!
OH MY, MR. RIKIGA! NICE TO SEE YOU!
IF YOU'RE BUYING A DRESS FOR A PRESENT, I'VE JUST OBTAINED SOME LOVELY ONES.
SHINE
Nah.
DON'T NEED NYTHING FOR IRLS. I WANT N OVERCOAT THAT WILL FIT THIS YOUNG MAN HERE.

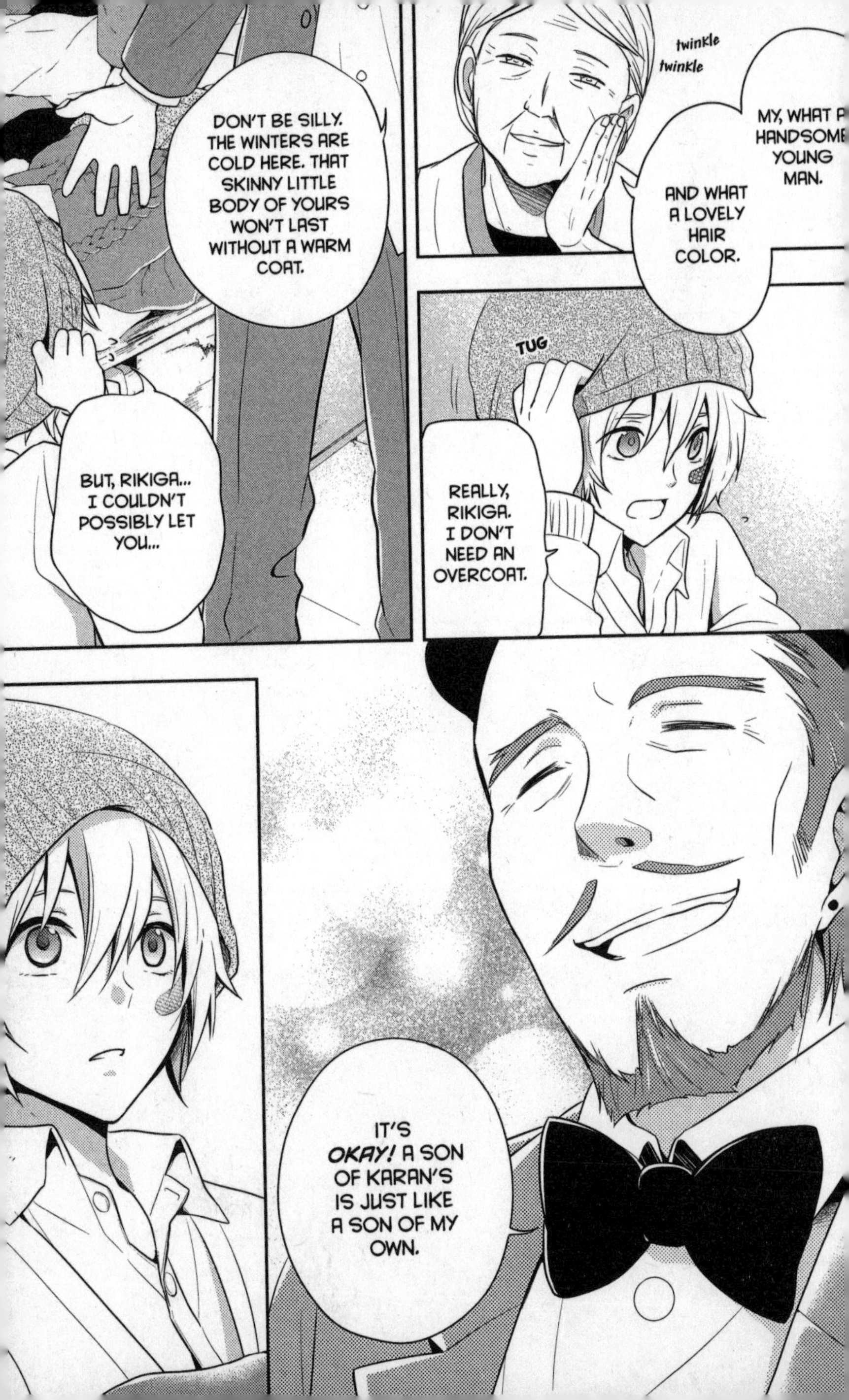
twinkle twinkle
MY, WHAT A HANDSOME YOUNG MAN.
AND WHAT A LOVELY HAIR COLOR.
TUG
REALLY, RIKIGA. I DON'T NEED AN OVERCOAT.
DON'T BE SILLY. THE WINTERS ARE COLD HERE. THAT SKINNY LITTLE BODY OF YOURS WON'T LAST WITHOUT A WARM COAT.
BUT, RIKIGA... I COULDN'T POSSIBLY LET YOU...
IT'S *OKAY!* A SON OF KARAN'S IS JUST LIKE A SON OF MY OWN.

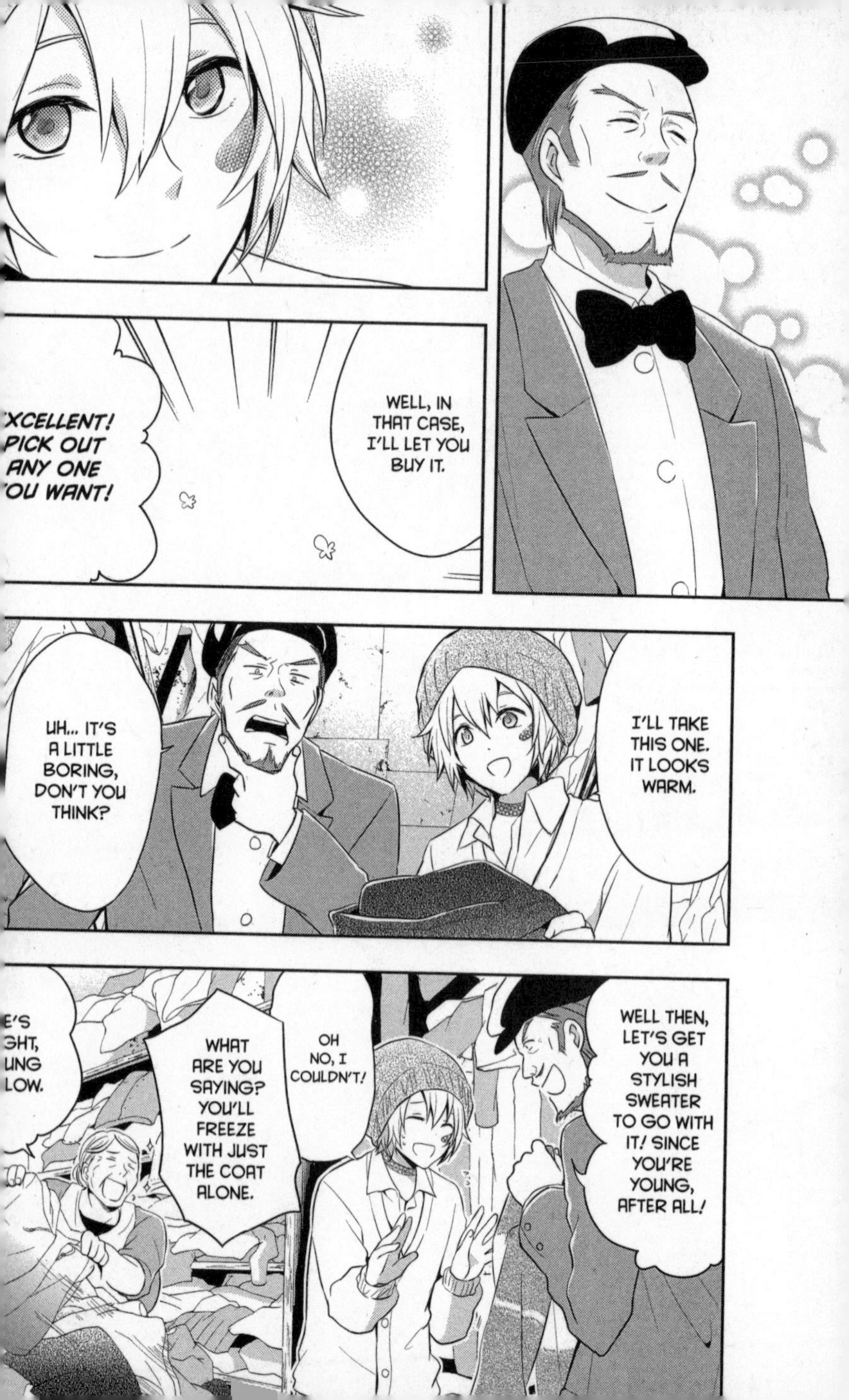
WELL, IN THAT CASE, I'LL LET YOU BUY IT.
XCELLENT! PICK OUT ANY ONE OU WANT!
I'LL TAKE THIS ONE. IT LOOKS WARM.
UH... IT'S A LITTLE BORING, DON'T YOU THINK?
WELL THEN, LET'S GET YOU A STYLISH SWEATER TO GO WITH IT! SINCE YOU'RE YOUNG, AFTER ALL!
OH NO, I COULDN'T!
WHAT ARE YOU SAYING? YOU'LL FREEZE WITH JUST THE COAT ALONE.
E'S GHT, UNG LOW.

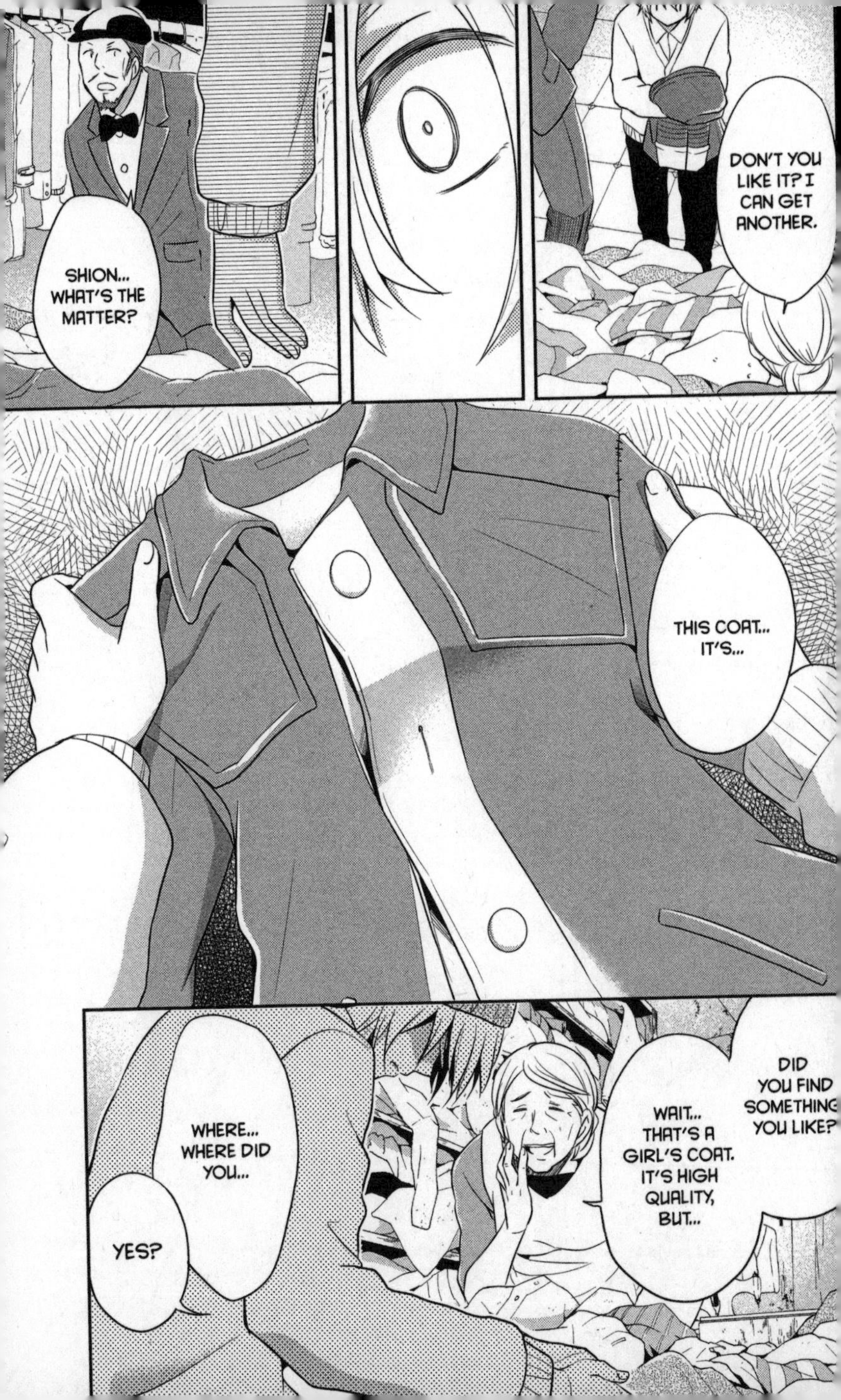
DON'T YOU LIKE IT? I CAN GET ANOTHER.
SHION... WHAT'S THE MATTER?
THIS COAT... IT'S...
DID YOU FIND SOMETHING YOU LIKE?
WAIT... THAT'S A GIRL'S COAT. IT'S HIGH QUALITY, BUT...
WHERE... WHERE DID YOU...
YES?

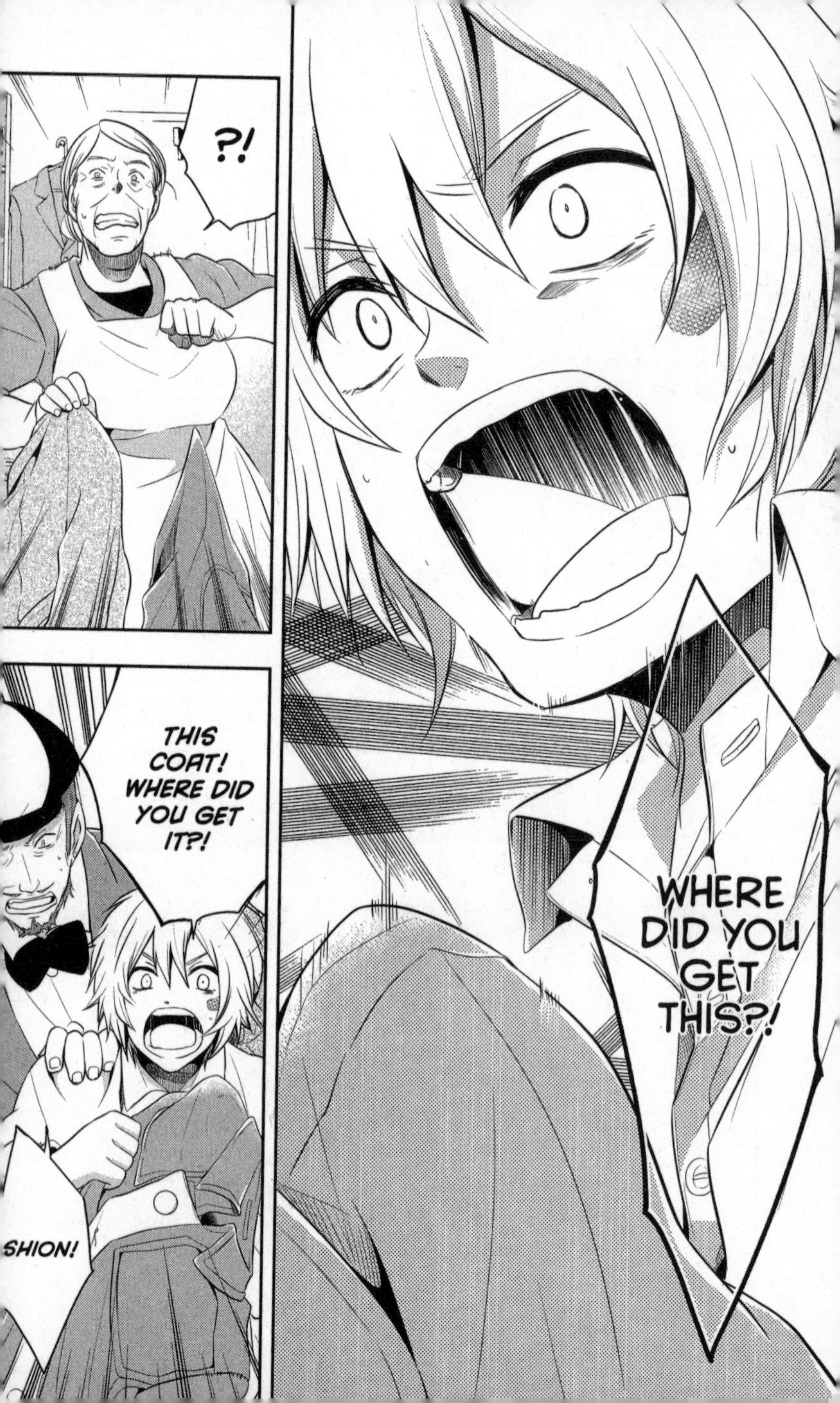
WHERE DID YOU GET THIS?!
?!
THIS COAT! WHERE DID YOU GET IT?!
SHION!

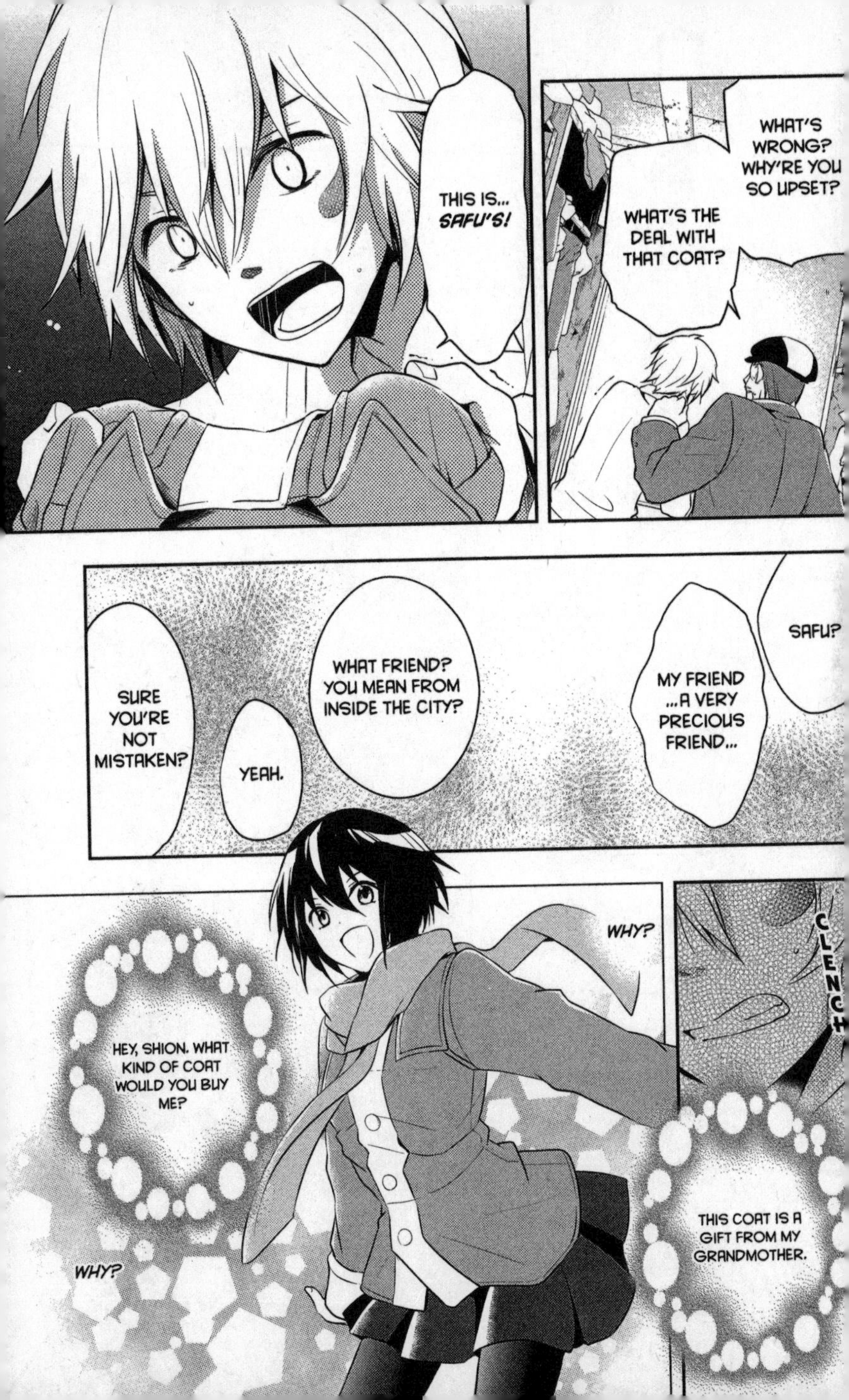
WHAT'S WRONG? WHY'RE YOU SO UPSET?
WHAT'S THE DEAL WITH THAT COAT?
THIS IS... SAFU'S!
SAFU?
MY FRIEND ...A VERY PRECIOUS FRIEND...
WHAT FRIEND? YOU MEAN FROM INSIDE THE CITY?
YEAH.
SURE YOU'RE NOT MISTAKEN?
CLENCH
WHY?
HEY, SHION. WHAT KIND OF COAT WOULD YOU BUY ME?
THIS COAT IS A GIFT FROM MY GRANDMOTHER.
WHY?

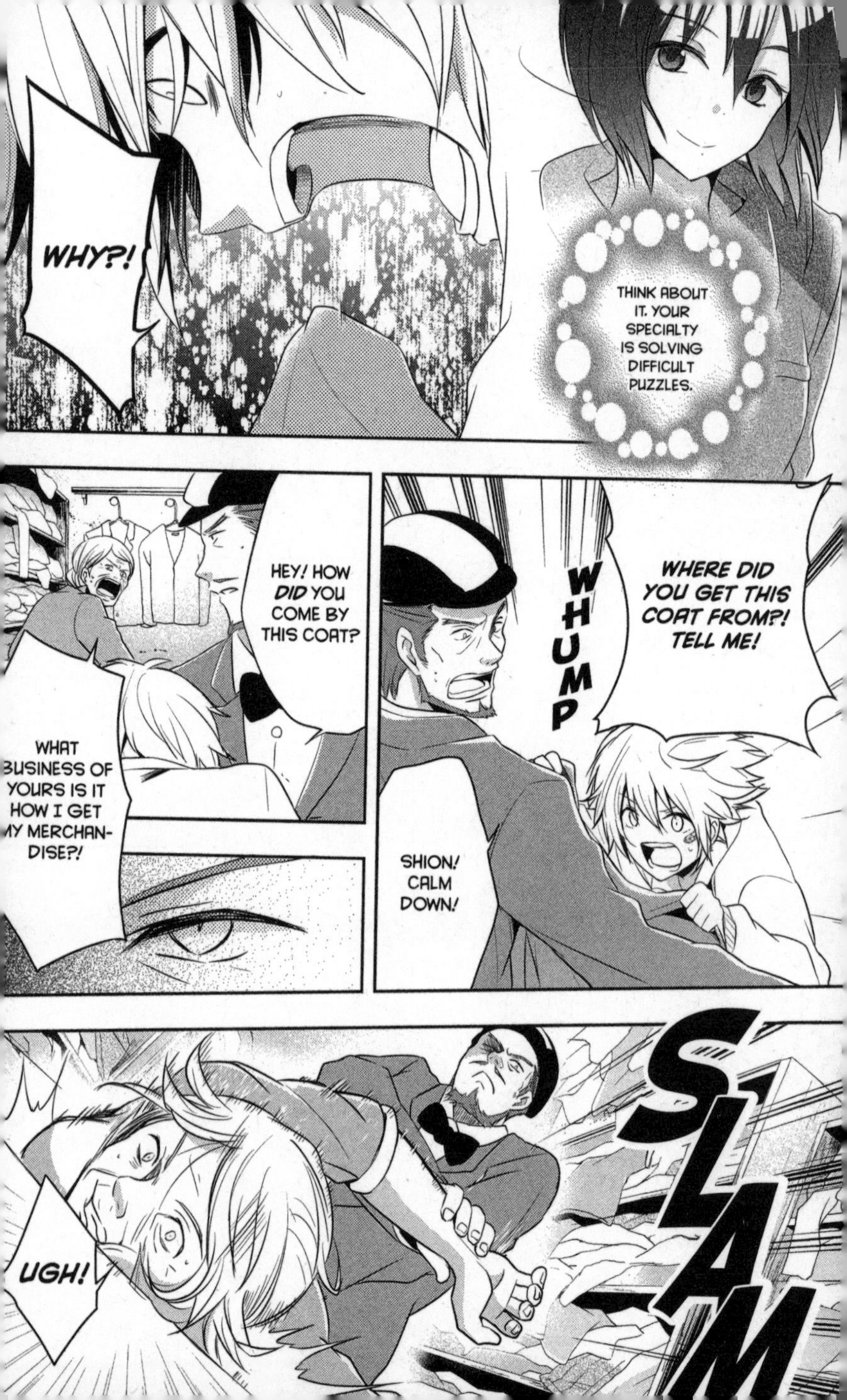
THINK ABOUT IT. YOUR SPECIALTY IS SOLVING DIFFICULT PUZZLES.
WHY?!
WHERE DID YOU GET THIS COAT FROM?! TELL ME!
WHUMP
SHION! CALM DOWN!
HEY! HOW *DID* YOU COME BY THIS COAT?
WHAT BUSINESS OF YOURS IS IT HOW I GET MY MERCHANDISE?!
SLAM
UGH!

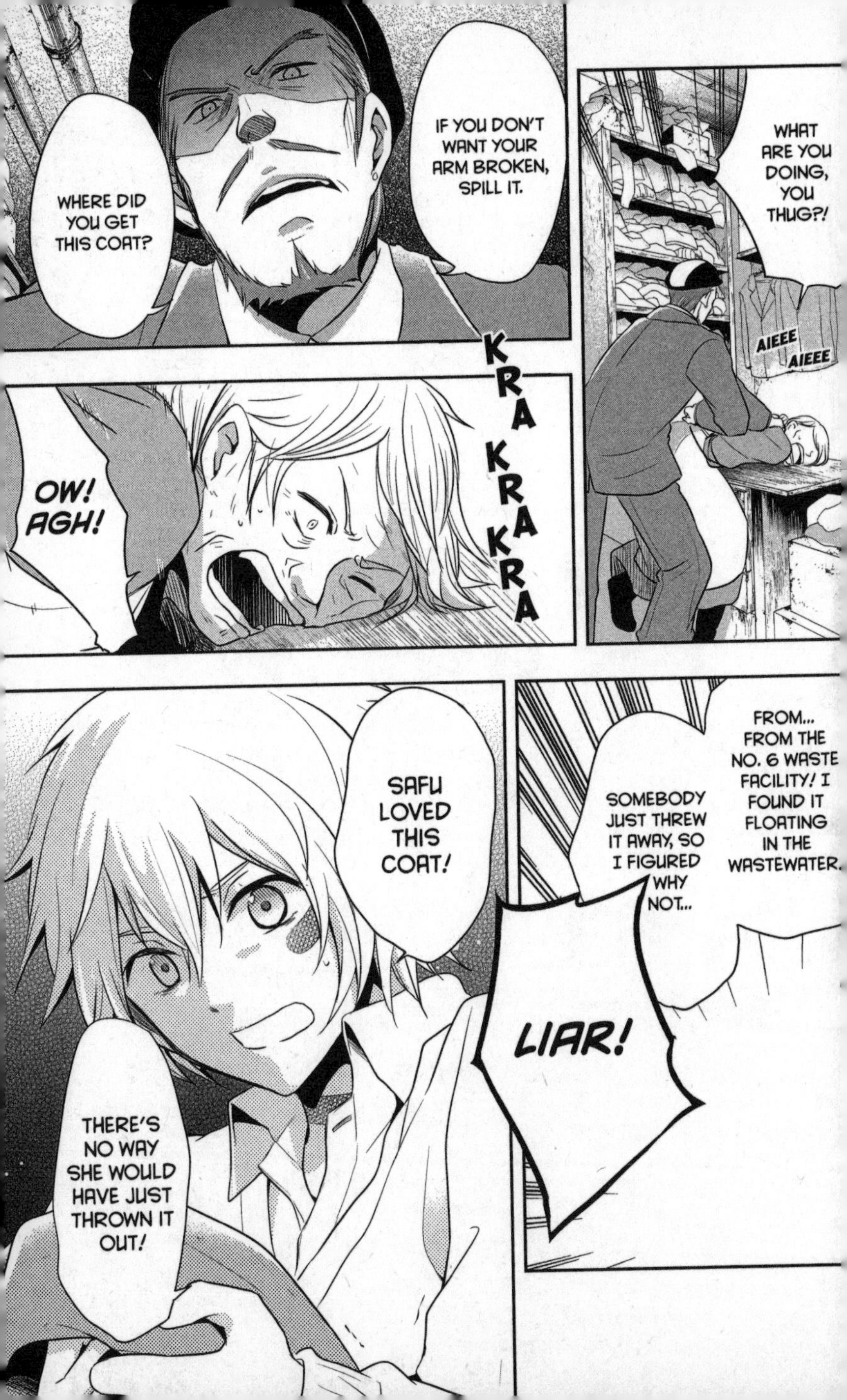

WHAT ARE YOU DOING, YOU THUG?!
AIEEE
AIEEE
IF YOU DON'T WANT YOUR ARM BROKEN, SPILL IT.
WHERE DID YOU GET THIS COAT?
KRA KRA KRA
OW! AGH!
FROM... FROM THE NO. 6 WASTE FACILITY! I FOUND IT FLOATING IN THE WASTEWATER.
SOMEBODY JUST THREW IT AWAY, SO I FIGURED WHY NOT...
LIAR!
SAFU LOVED THIS COAT!
THERE'S NO WAY SHE WOULD HAVE JUST THROWN IT OUT!

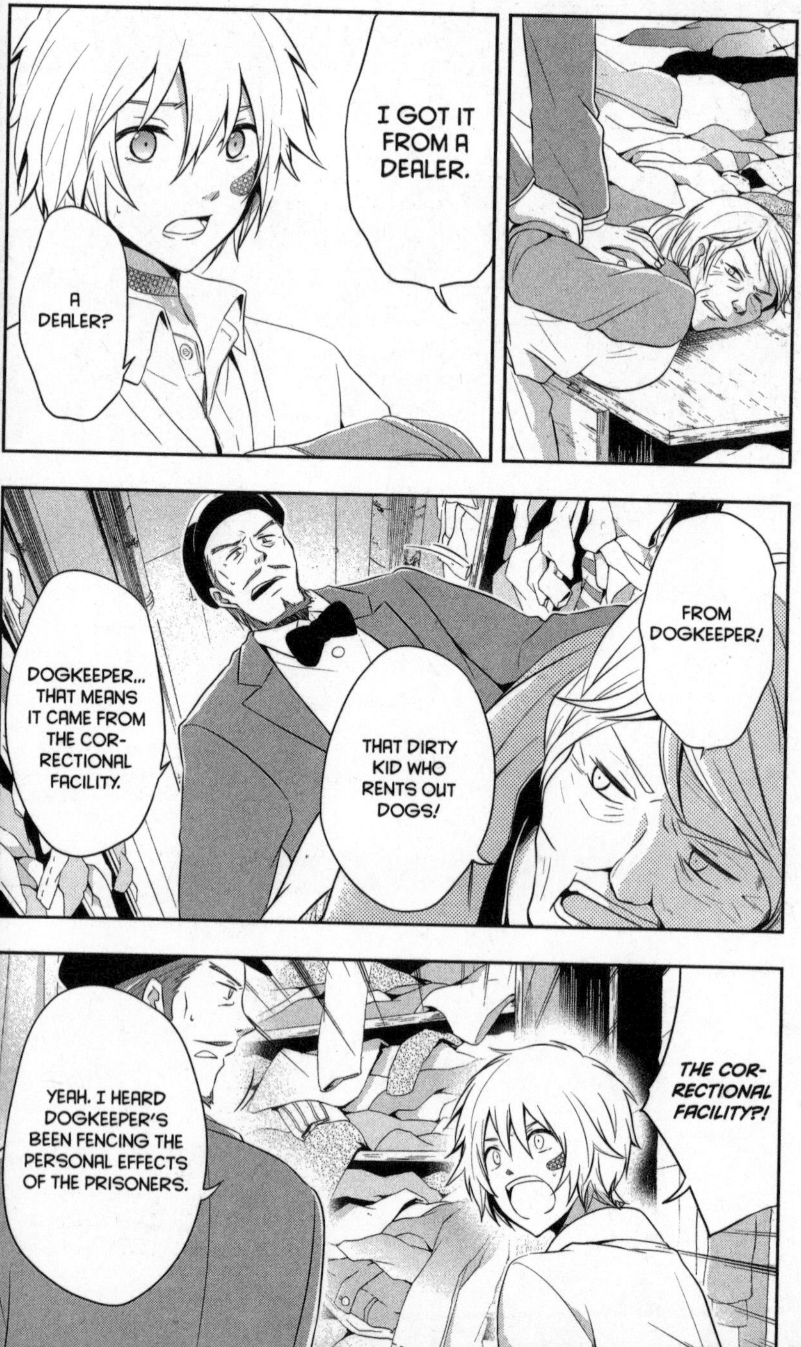
I GOT IT FROM A DEALER.
A DEALER?
FROM DOGKEEPER!
THAT DIRTY KID WHO RENTS OUT DOGS!
DOGKEEPER... THAT MEANS IT CAME FROM THE COR-RECTIONAL FACILITY.
THE COR-RECTIONAL FACILITY?!
YEAH. I HEARD DOGKEEPER'S BEEN FENCING THE PERSONAL EFFECTS OF THE PRISONERS.

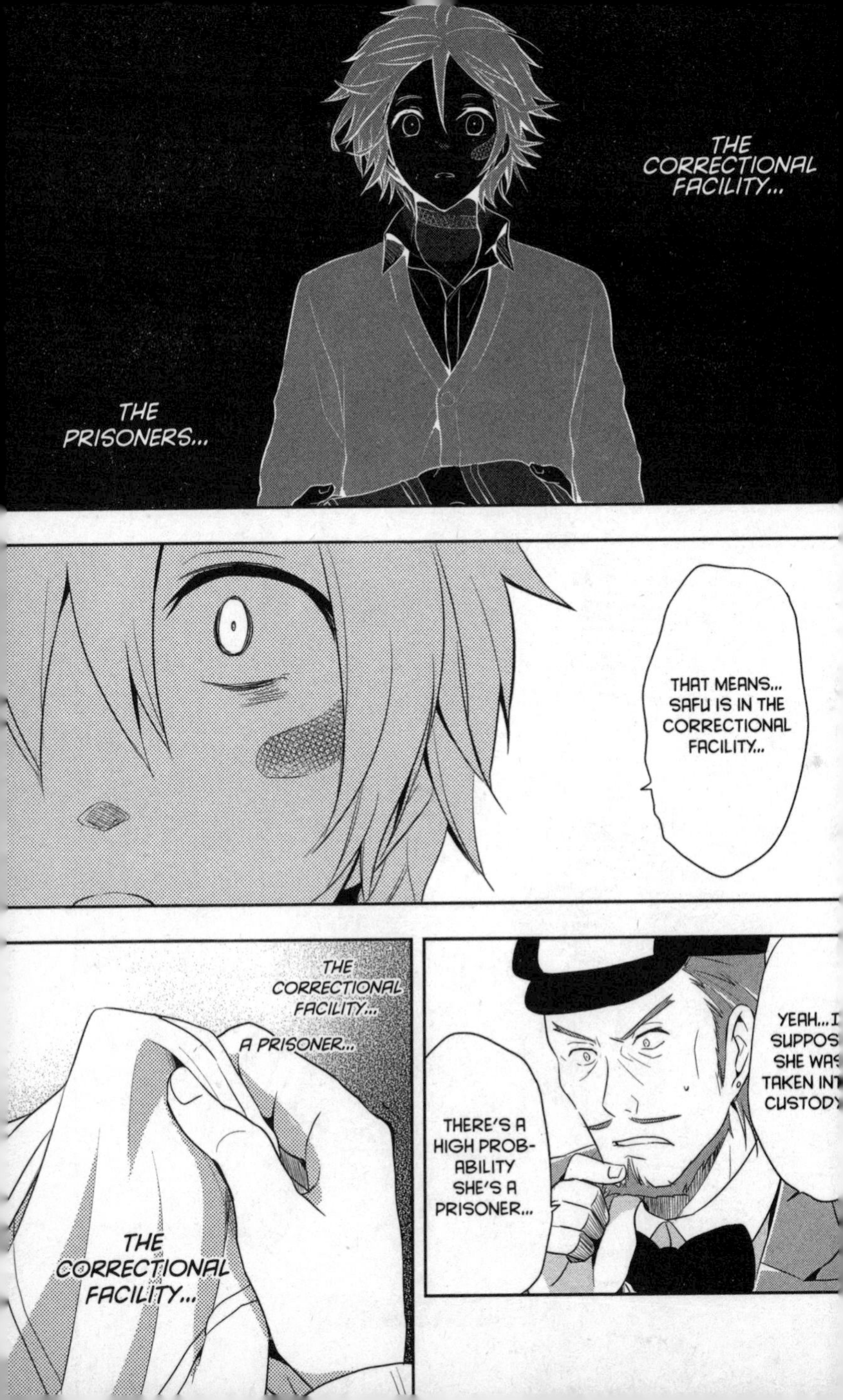
THE CORRECTIONAL FACILITY...
THE PRISONERS...
THAT MEANS... SAFU IS IN THE CORRECTIONAL FACILITY...
YEAH...I SUPPOS SHE WAS TAKEN INT CUSTODY
THERE'S A HIGH PROB-ABILITY SHE'S A PRISONER...
THE CORRECTIONAL FACILITY...
A PRISONER...
THE CORRECTIONAL FACILITY...

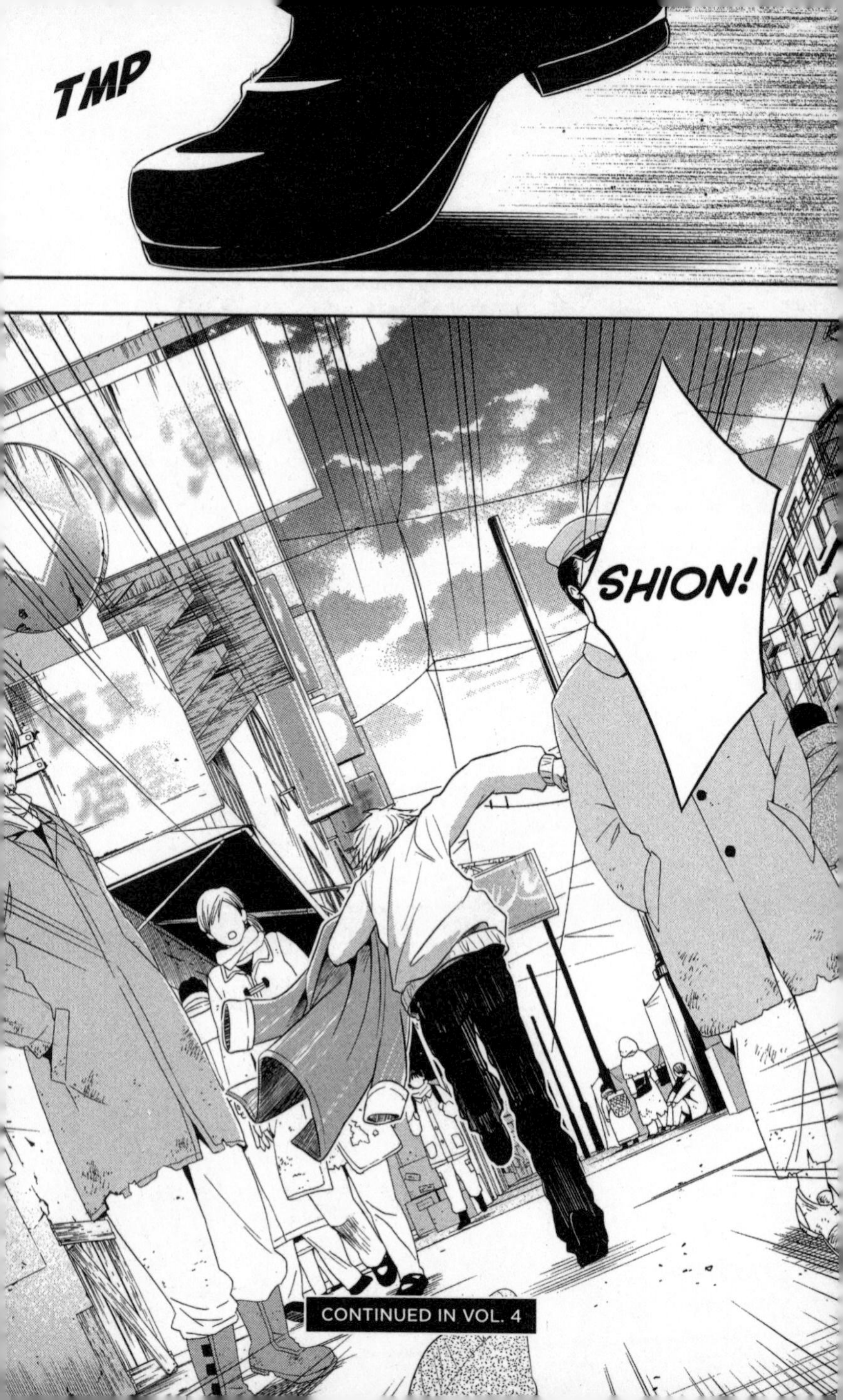
TMP
SHION!
CONTINUED IN VOL. 4

NO.6

Hello. Hinoki Kino here. Here we are at volume 3 of "No. 6." How did it happen so fast? We're still fumbling around over the rough spots, but as long as you enjoy it, we're happy.

In terms of the original novels, we're somewhere between volume 2 and the middle of volume 3. The action takes place in West Block. Dogkeeper's scenes are so cute! I just love them!

Compared to volumes 1 and 2, this volume unfolded a little more slowly. Shion and Rat, Karan and Safu, Shion and Dogkeeper, Shion and Rikiga, Rat and Dogkeeper—I hoped to establish these relationships. How do you think it went? And from now on, I'm really hoping you keep your eyes on what changes are coming, what influences are unfolding, and in particular, what's going to happen with the newly introduced characters like Yomin and the two mystery men.

And then there's Eve's scene. From the moment we saw the character design, the editor and I got so excited, we wanted to draw everything. Without hesitation, we dove into the original story (?). Thanks so much for that.

Now that he knows about Safu, what will Shion do? What has happened to Safu? What will Rat do? What about Dogkeeper and Rikiga and Karan? Within the churning chaos at the heart of "No. 6," we'll meet up with you again in volume 4. Until then...

Hinoki Kino

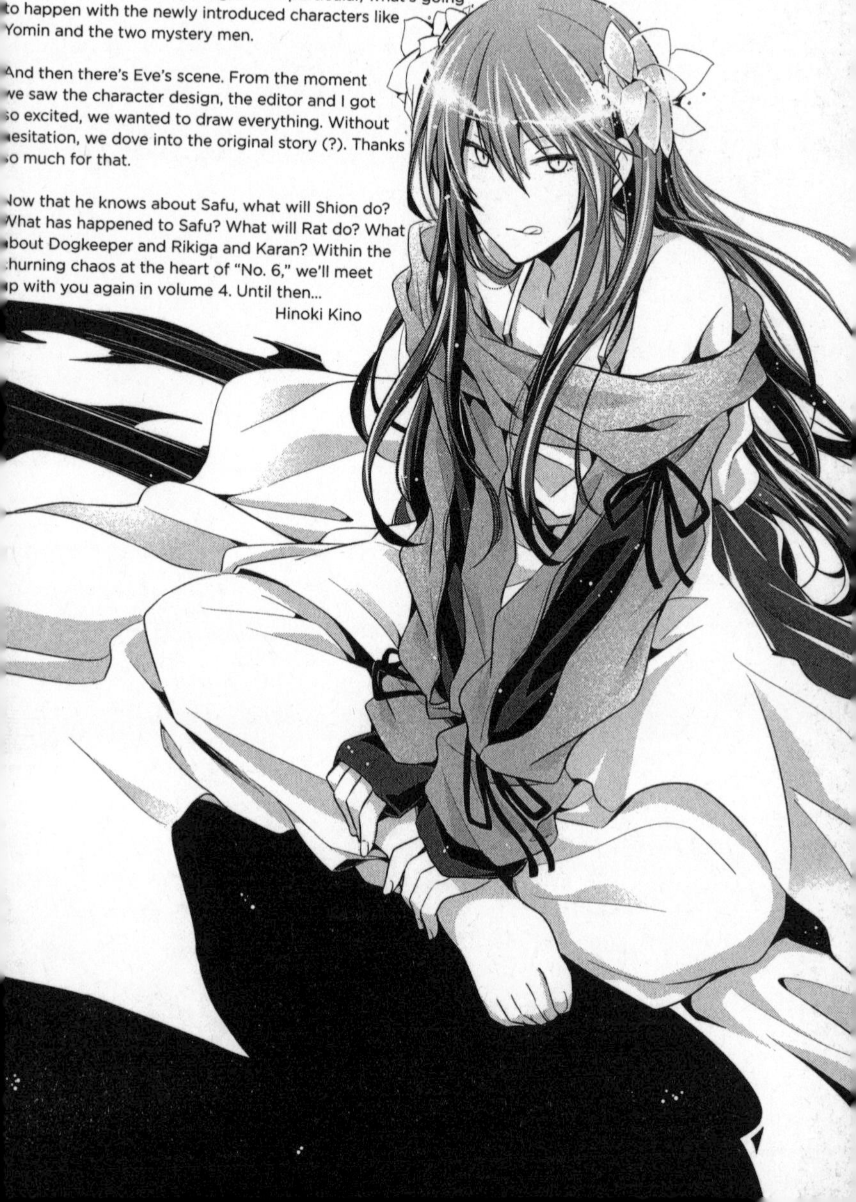

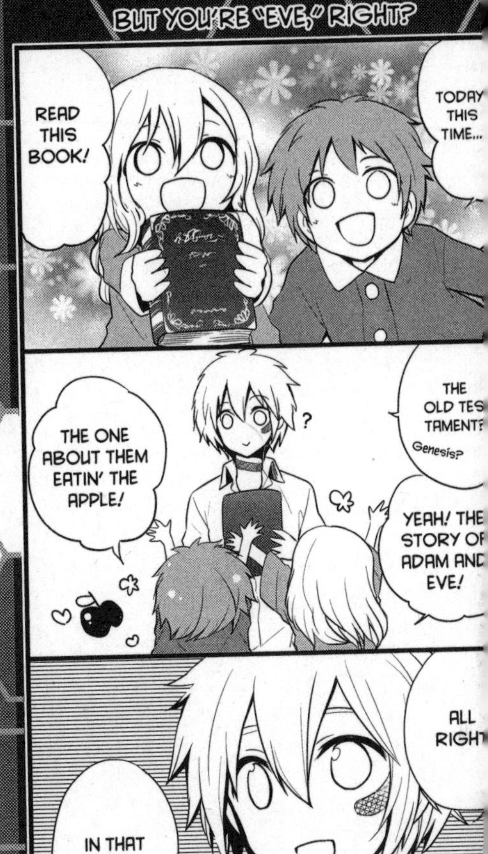
BUT YOU'RE "EVE," RIGHT?
TODAY THIS TIME...
READ THIS BOOK!
THE OLD TES TAMENT?
Genesis?
YEAH! THE STORY OF ADAM AND EVE!
THE ONE ABOUT THEM EATIN' THE APPLE!
ALL RIGHT
IN THAT CASE...
"EVE".
NO WAY.
BUT I HAVEN'T ASKED ANYTHING YET...
NO WAY.
Hey.

Atsuko Asano

Everyone in the Kodansha
Aria editorial department

Everyone on the No. 6 Team
My editor K-gata
toi8
Everyone on the anime staff
Everyone at NARTi;S
Ginkyo

* Production Cooperation
Honma
Megi
Netanon
Yamamoto
Noguchi (#5)

* Finishing
Tsunocchi

* 3D
Kei Rinkan

* Color Backgrounds
Mr. dominori (Big Brother)
My family
And everyone else who
helped out

Also, all you readers!

Thank you all so very much!

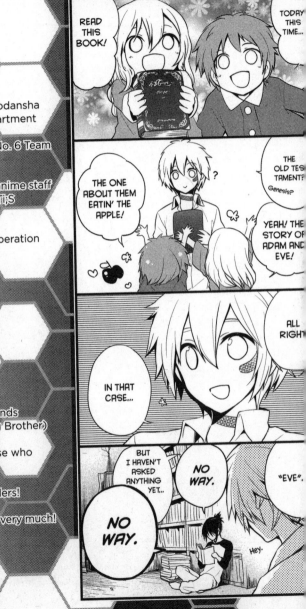

NO.6

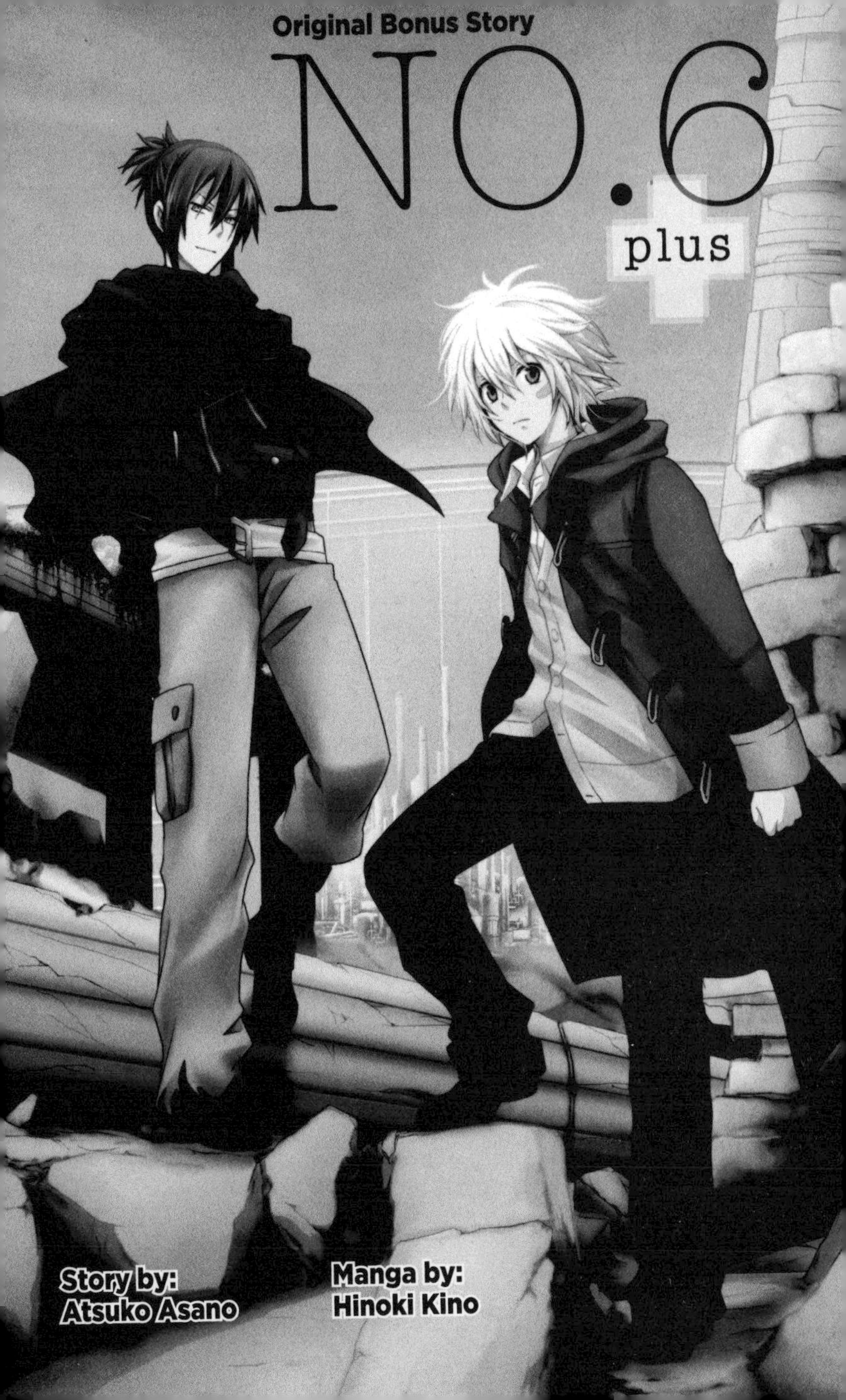
Original Bonus Story
NO.6
plus
Story by:
Atsuko Asano
Manga by:
Hinoki Kino

NO.6

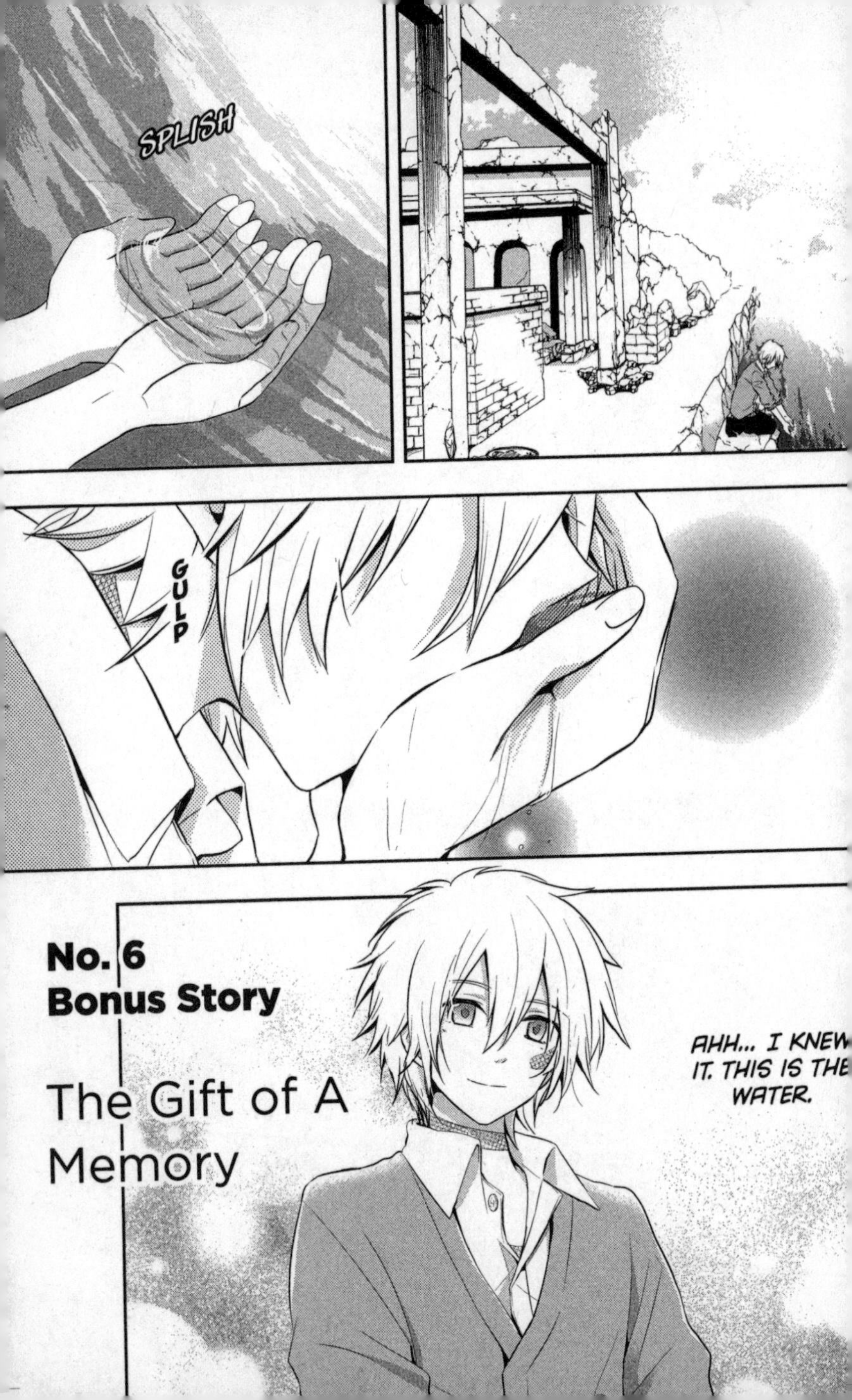
SPLISH
GULP
AHH... I KNEW IT. THIS IS THE WATER.
No. 6
Bonus Story
The Gift of A Memory

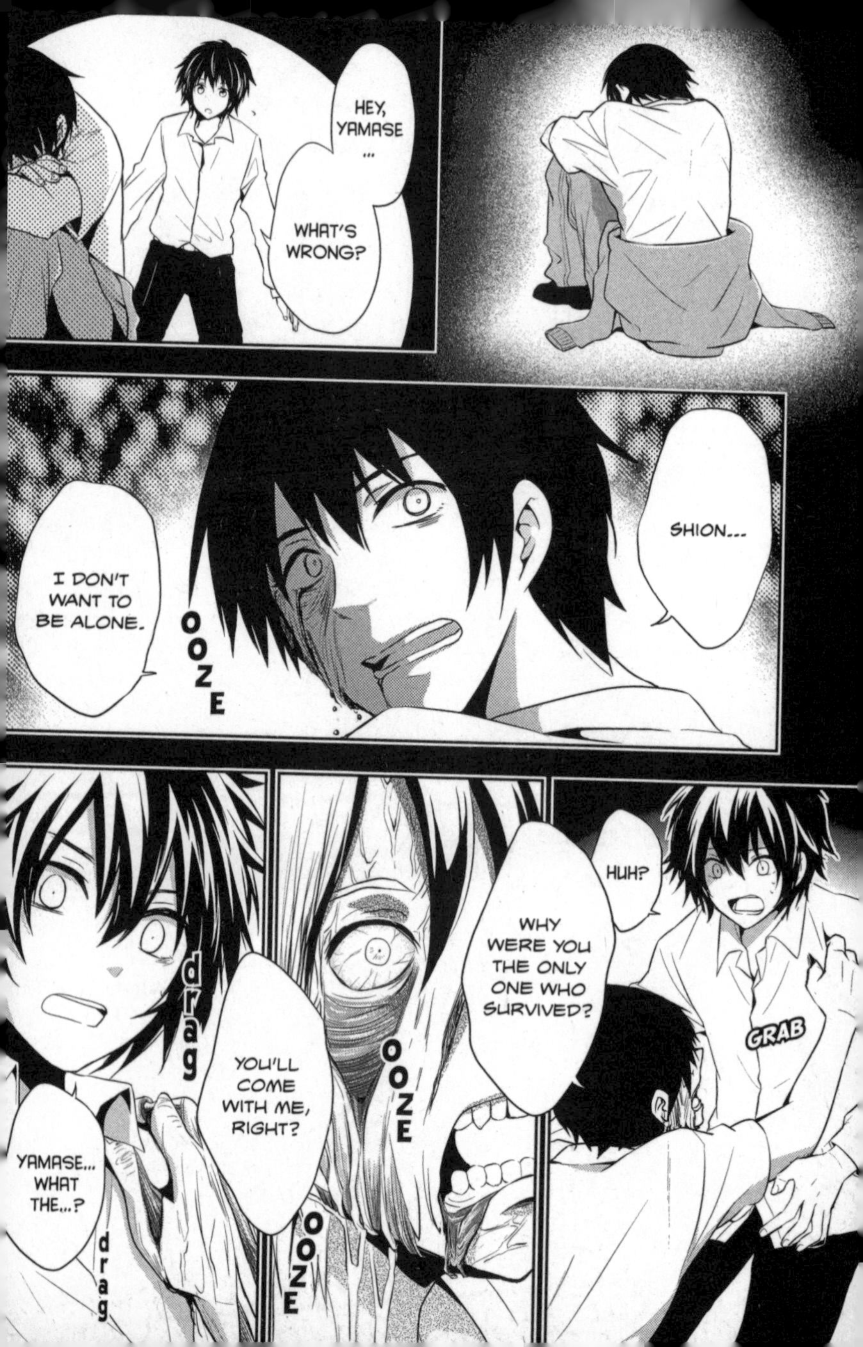
HEY, YAMASE ...
WHAT'S WRONG?
SHION...
OOZE
I DON'T WANT TO BE ALONE.
HUH?
WHY WERE YOU THE ONLY ONE WHO SURVIVED?
GRAB
OOZE
YOU'LL COME WITH ME, RIGHT?
OOZE
drag
YAMASE... WHAT THE...?
drag

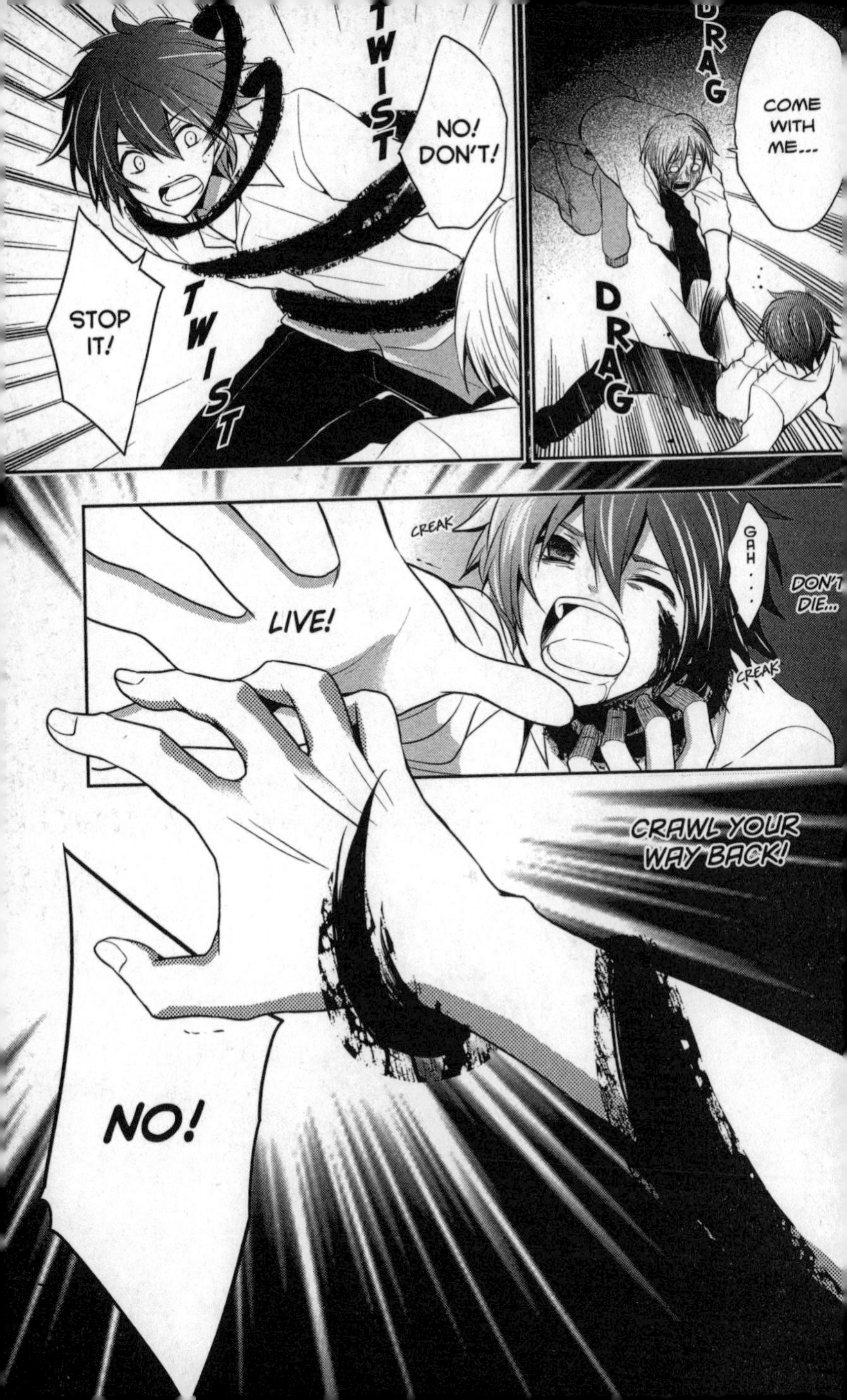
DRAG
COME WITH ME...
DRAG
TWIST
NO! DON'T!
STOP IT!
TWIST
DON'T DIE...
GAH...
CREAK
CREAK
LIVE!
CRAWL YOUR WAY BACK!
NO!

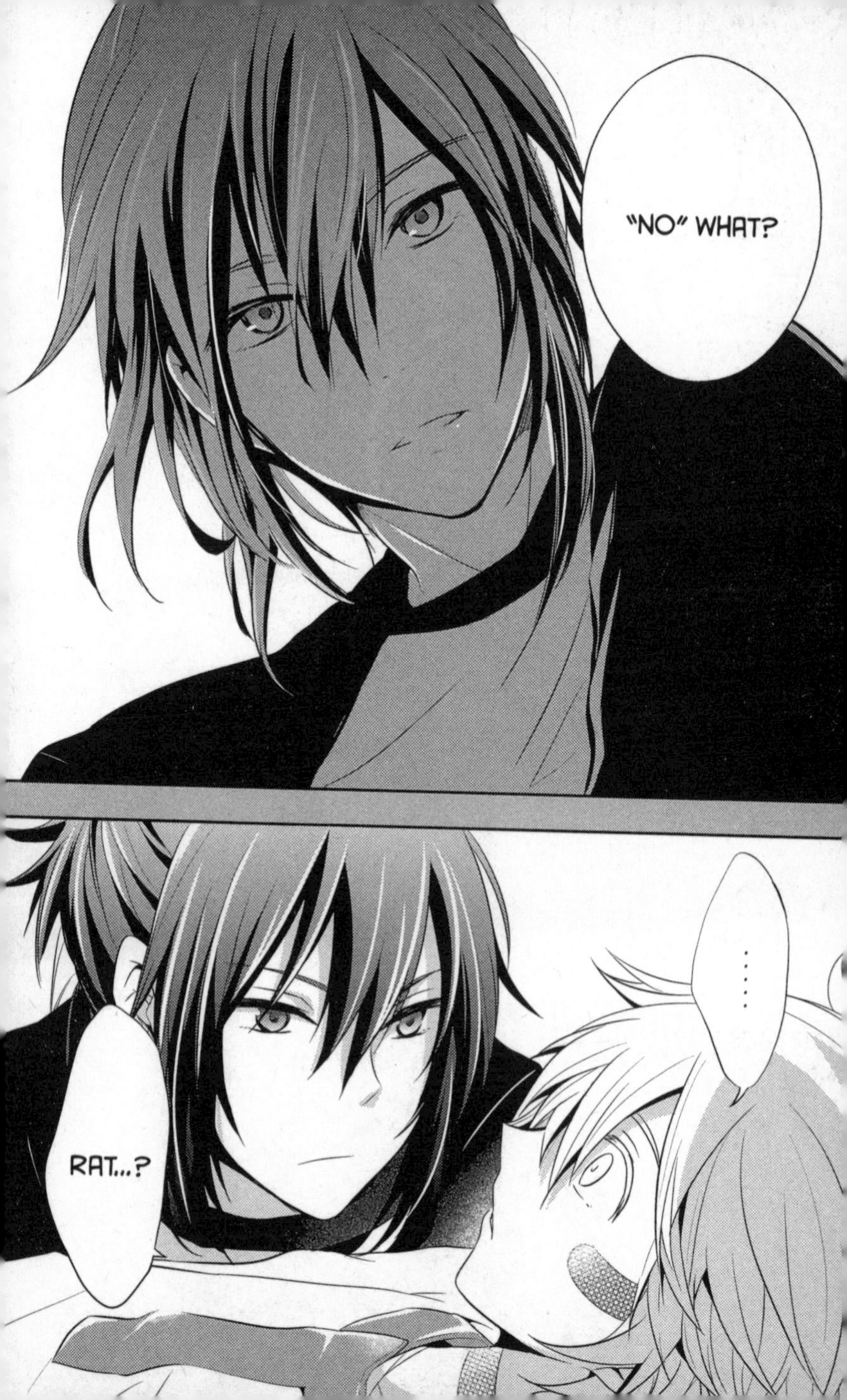
"NO" WHAT?
.....
RAT...?

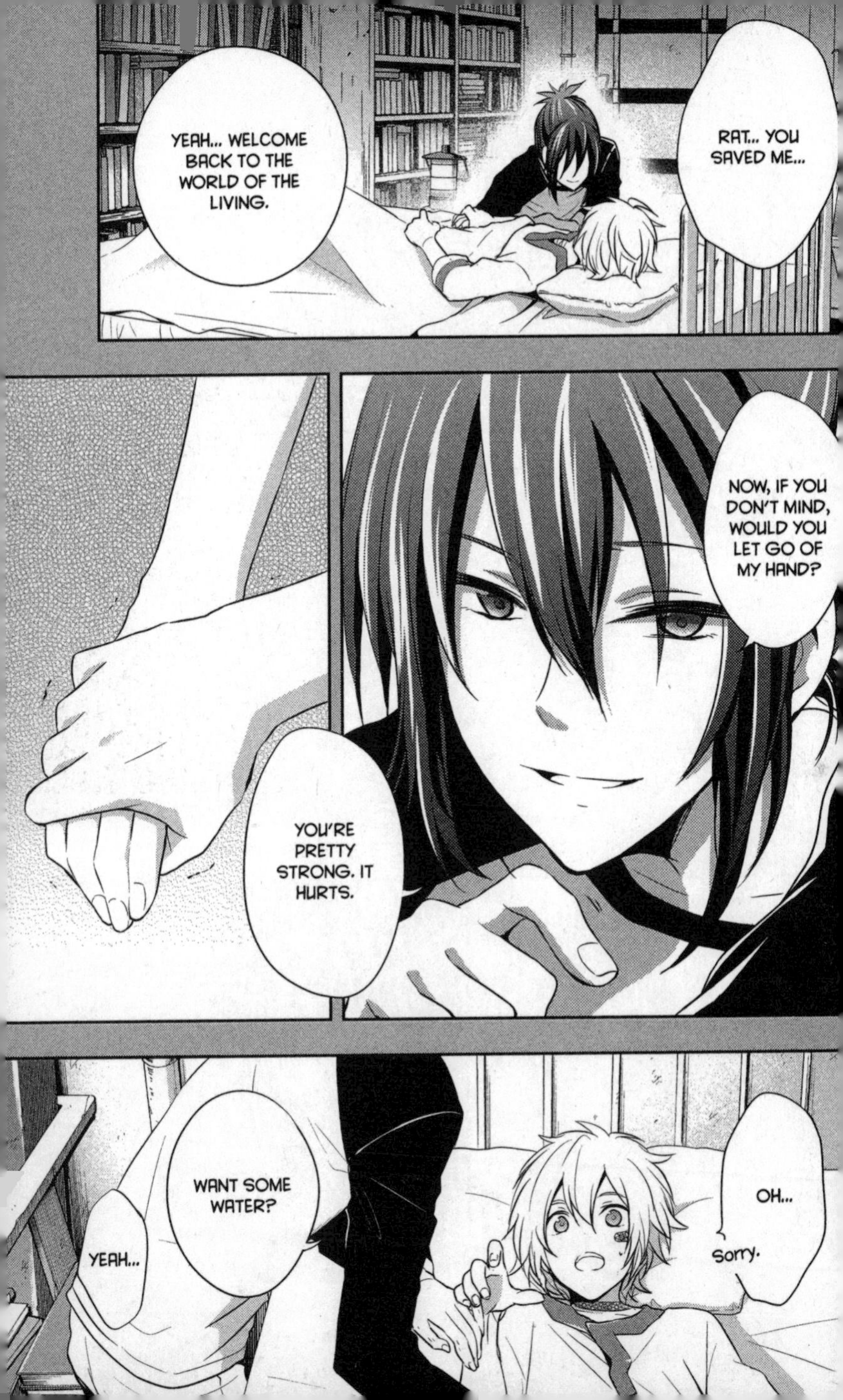
RAT... YOU SAVED ME...
YEAH... WELCOME BACK TO THE WORLD OF THE LIVING.
NOW, IF YOU DON'T MIND, WOULD YOU LET GO OF MY HAND?
YOU'RE PRETTY STRONG. IT HURTS.
OH...
Sorry.
WANT SOME WATER?
YEAH...

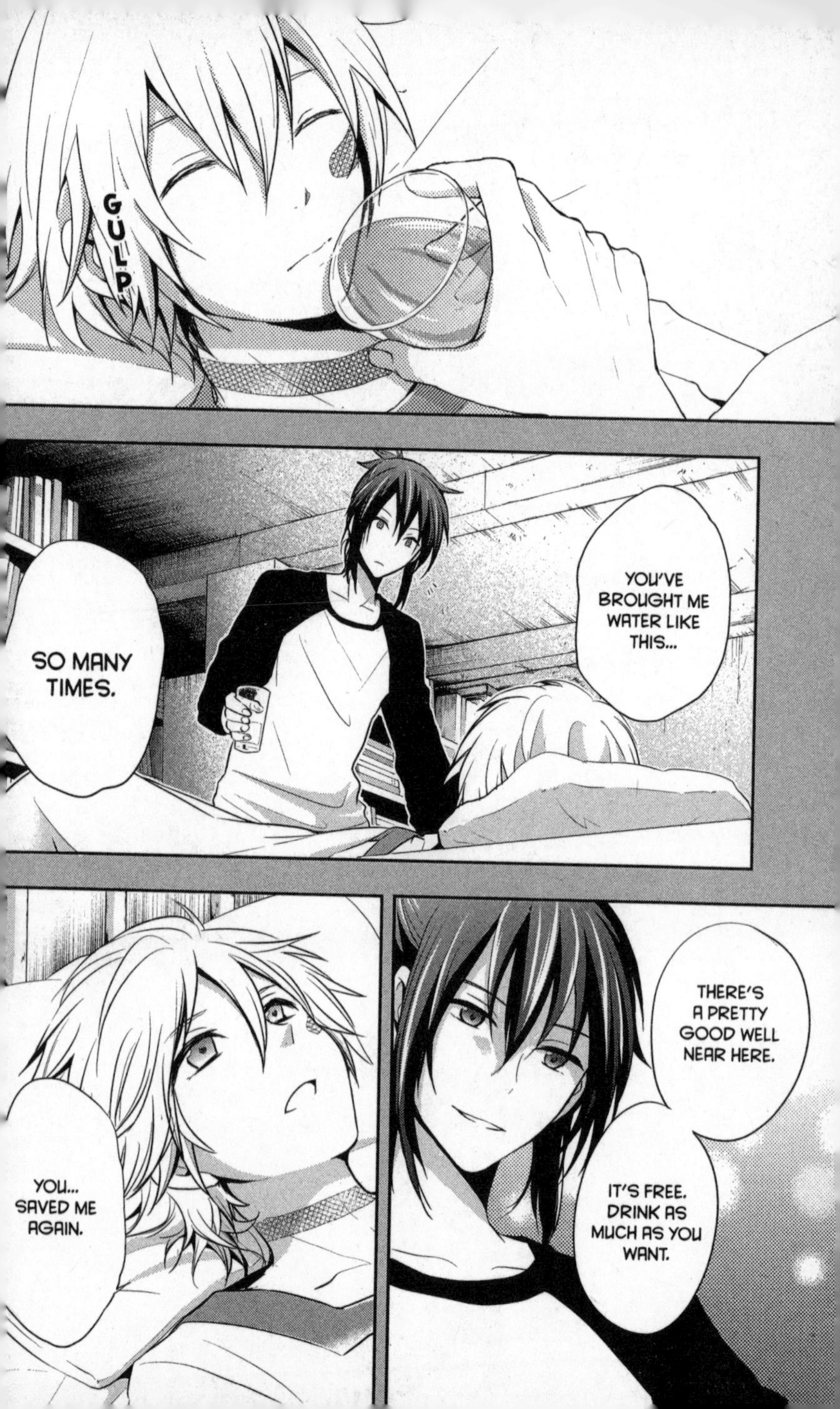
GULP
YOU'VE BROUGHT ME WATER LIKE THIS...
SO MANY TIMES.
THERE'S A PRETTY GOOD WELL NEAR HERE.
IT'S FREE. DRINK AS MUCH AS YOU WANT.
YOU... SAVED ME AGAIN.

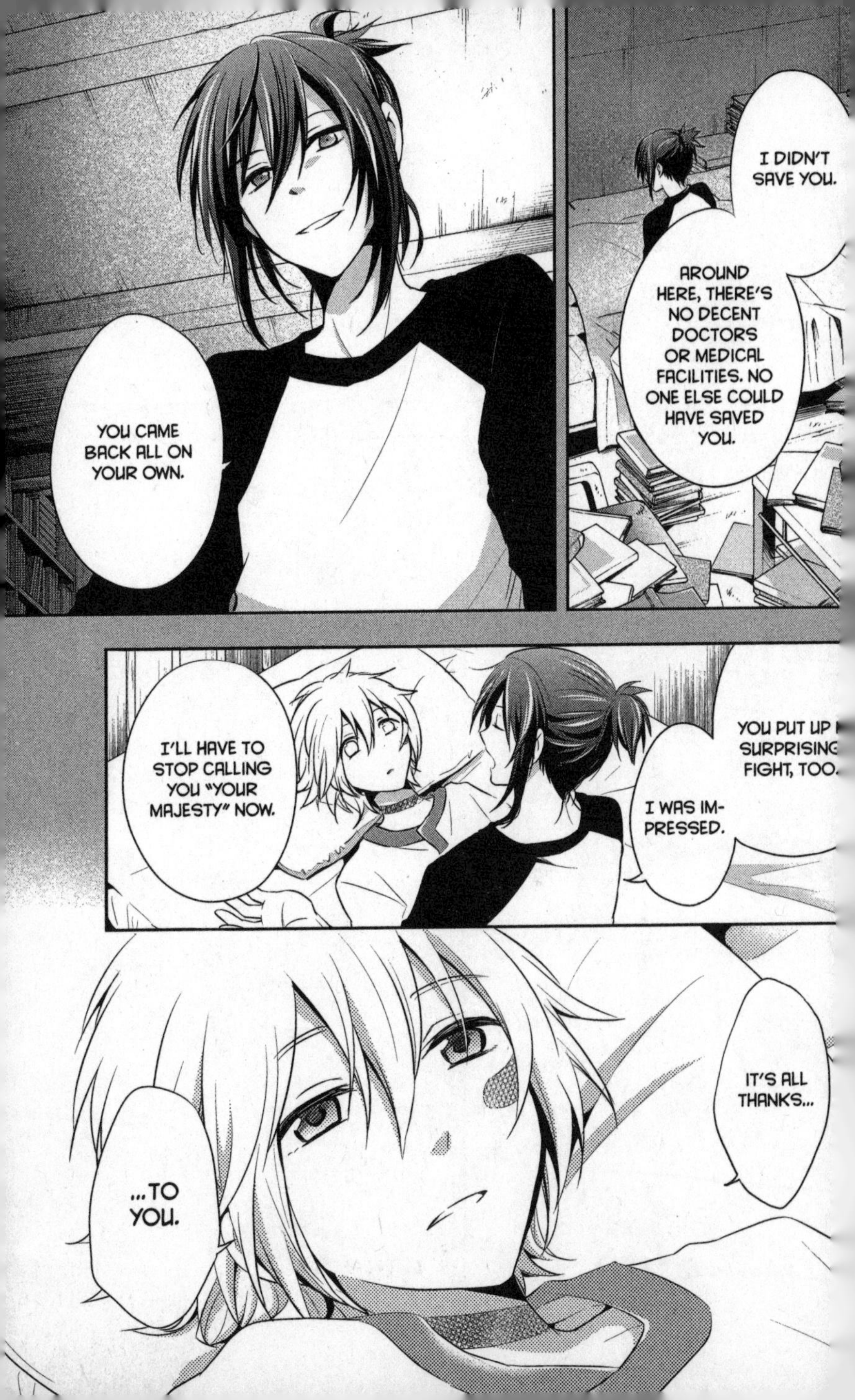
I DIDN'T SAVE YOU.
AROUND HERE, THERE'S NO DECENT DOCTORS OR MEDICAL FACILITIES. NO ONE ELSE COULD HAVE SAVED YOU.
YOU CAME BACK ALL ON YOUR OWN.
YOU PUT UP SURPRISING FIGHT, TOO.
I WAS IMPRESSED.
I'LL HAVE TO STOP CALLING YOU "YOUR MAJESTY" NOW.
IT'S ALL THANKS...
...TO YOU.

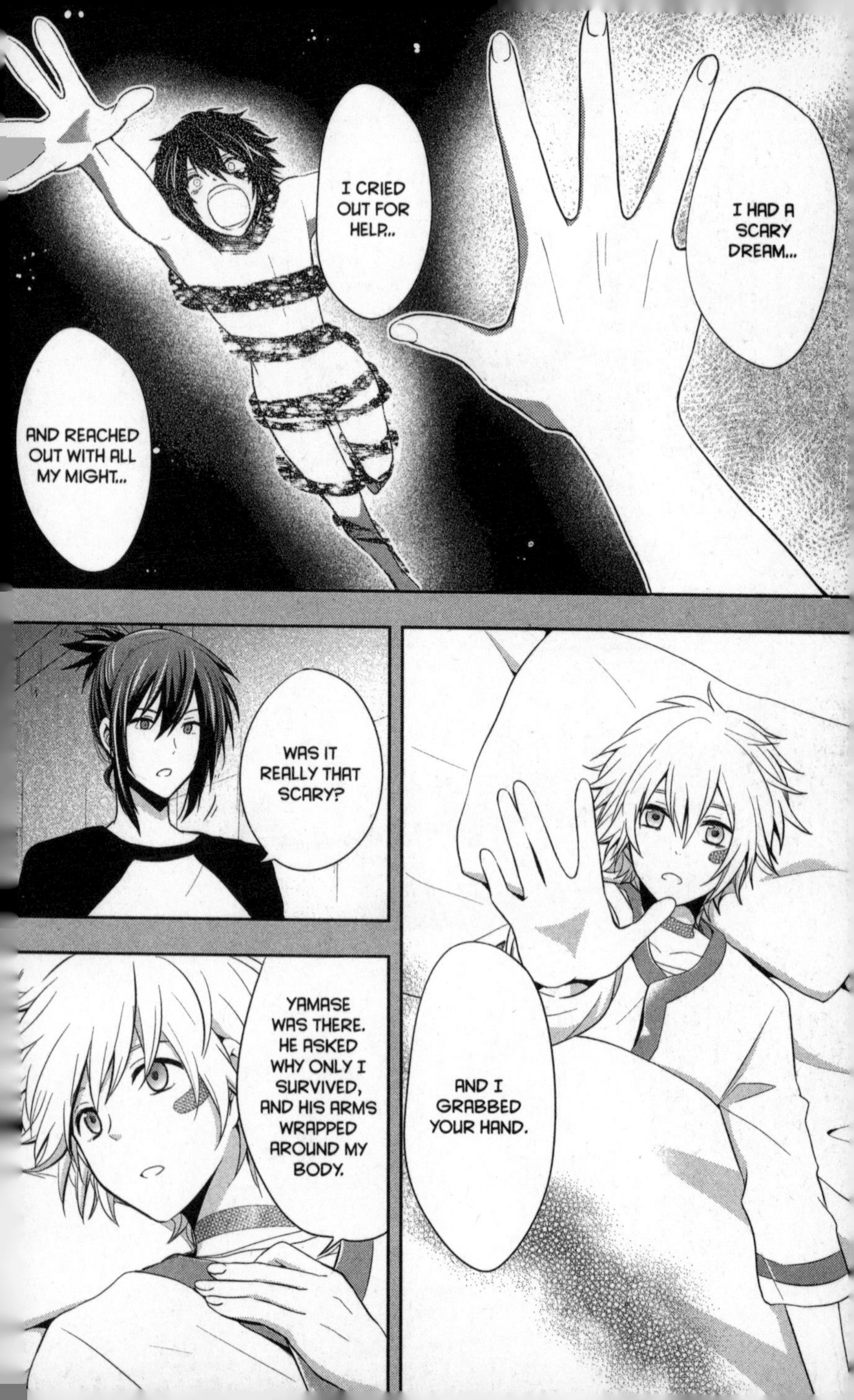
I HAD A SCARY DREAM...
I CRIED OUT FOR HELP..
AND REACHED OUT WITH ALL MY MIGHT...
AND I GRABBED YOUR HAND.
WAS IT REALLY THAT SCARY?
YAMASE WAS THERE. HE ASKED WHY ONLY I SURVIVED, AND HIS ARMS WRAPPED AROUND MY BODY.

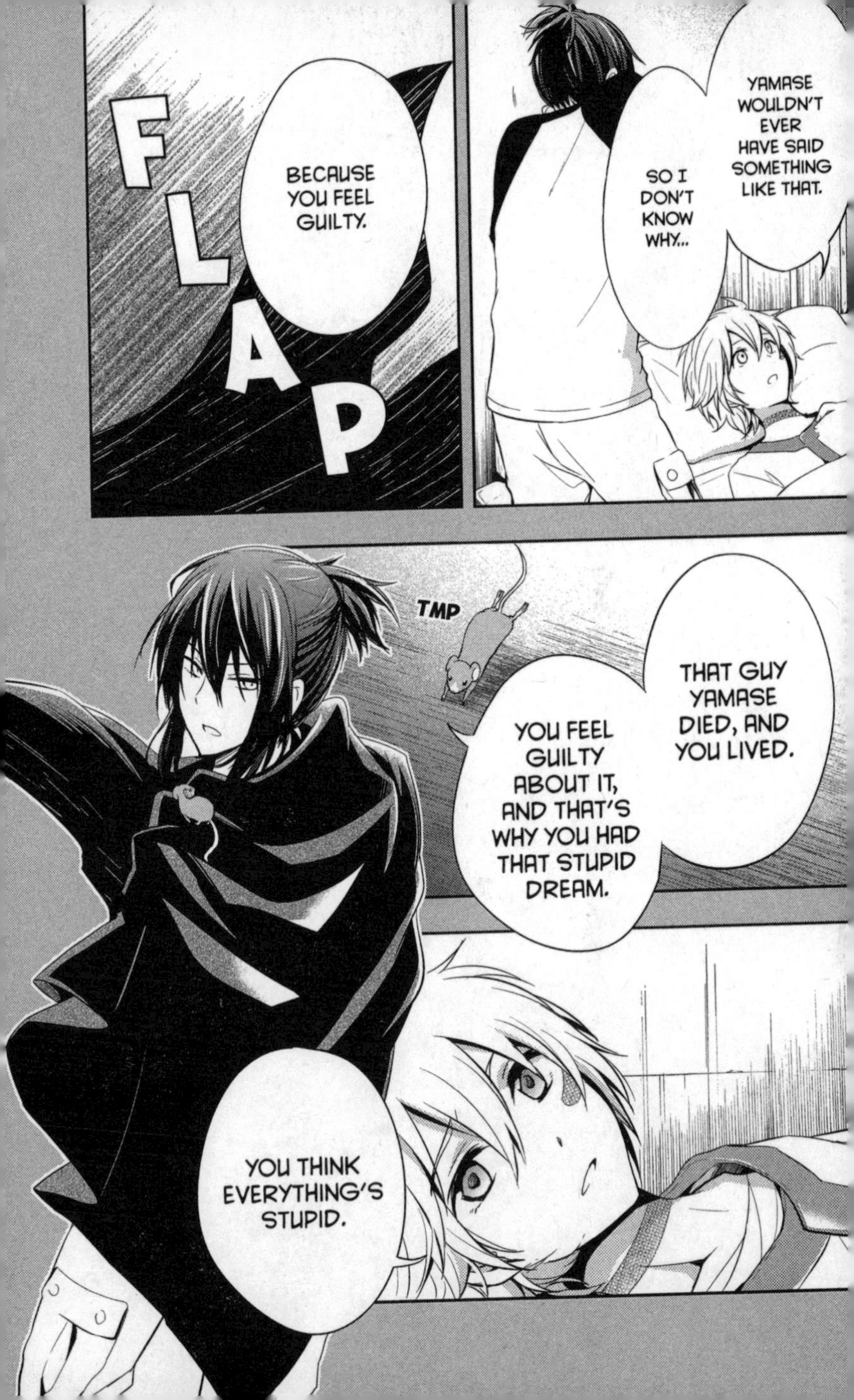

YAMASE WOULDN'T EVER HAVE SAID SOMETHING LIKE THAT.
SO I DON'T KNOW WHY...
FLAP
BECAUSE YOU FEEL GUILTY.
THAT GUY YAMASE DIED, AND YOU LIVED.
YOU FEEL GUILTY ABOUT IT, AND THAT'S WHY YOU HAD THAT STUPID DREAM.
TMP
YOU THINK EVERYTHING'S STUPID.

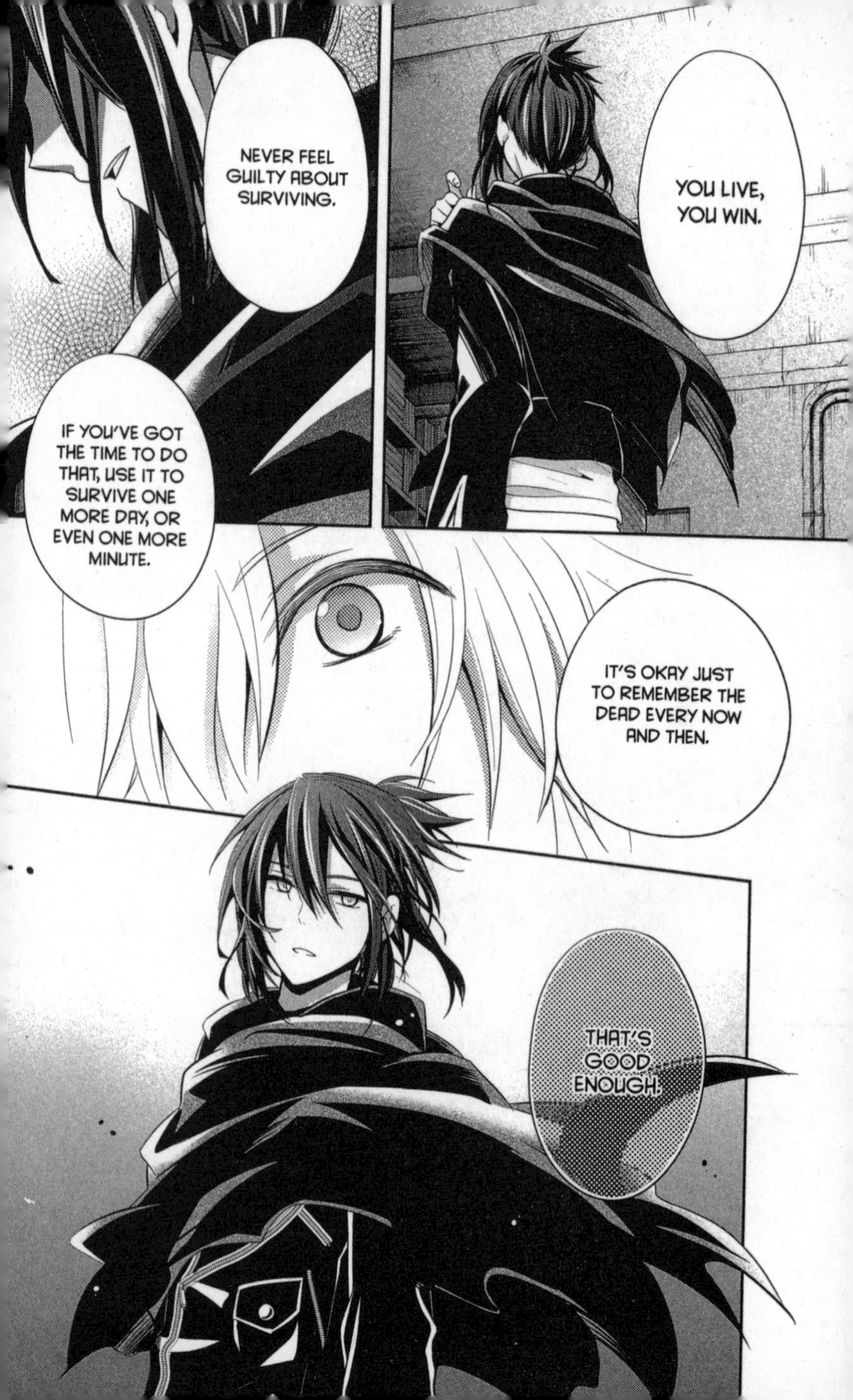
YOU LIVE, YOU WIN.
NEVER FEEL GUILTY ABOUT SURVIVING.
IF YOU'VE GOT THE TIME TO DO THAT, USE IT TO SURVIVE ONE MORE DAY, OR EVEN ONE MORE MINUTE.
IT'S OKAY JUST TO REMEMBER THE DEAD EVERY NOW AND THEN.
THAT'S GOOD ENOUGH.

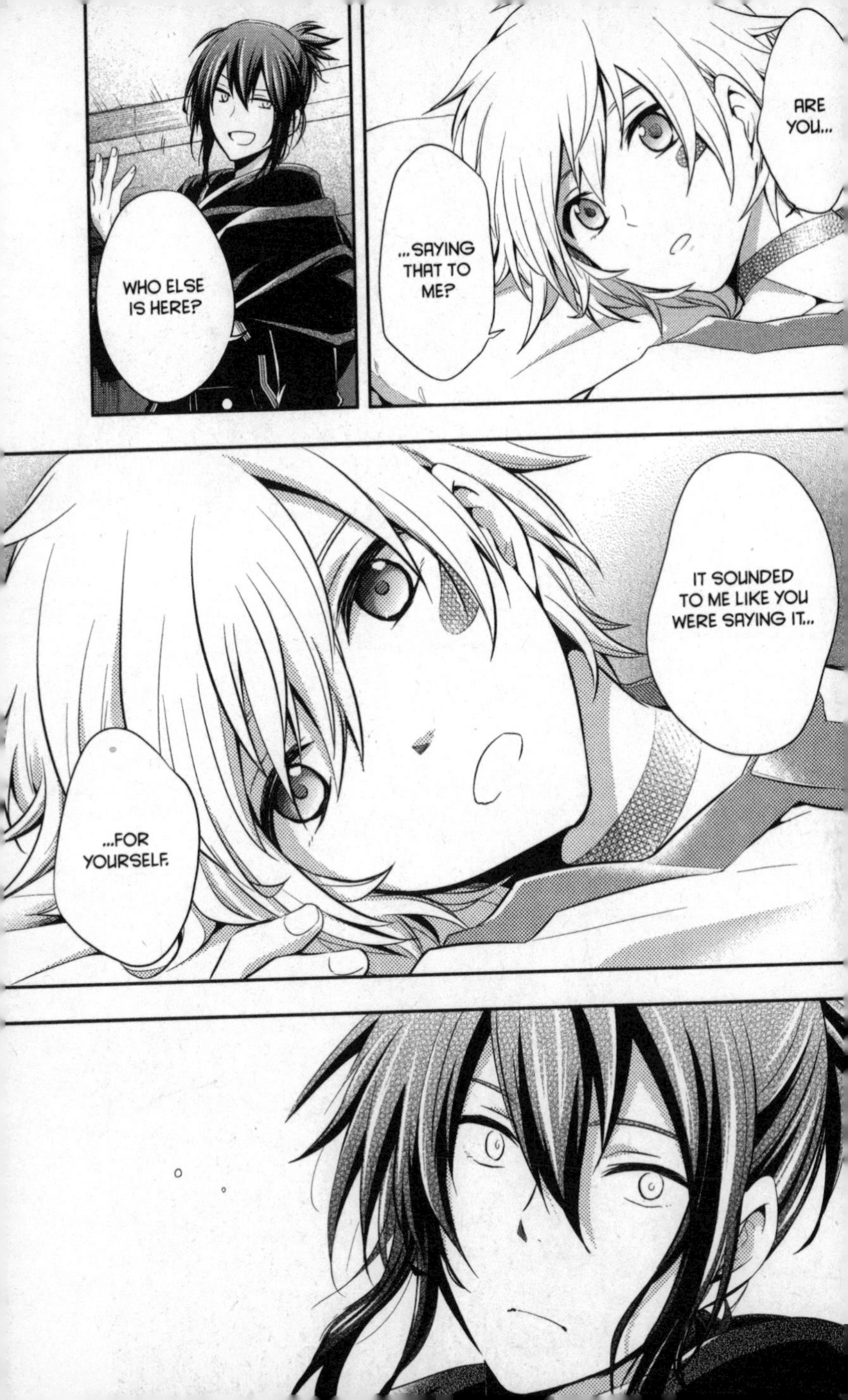
ARE YOU...
...SAYING THAT TO ME?
WHO ELSE IS HERE?
IT SOUNDED TO ME LIKE YOU WERE SAYING IT...
...FOR YOURSELF.

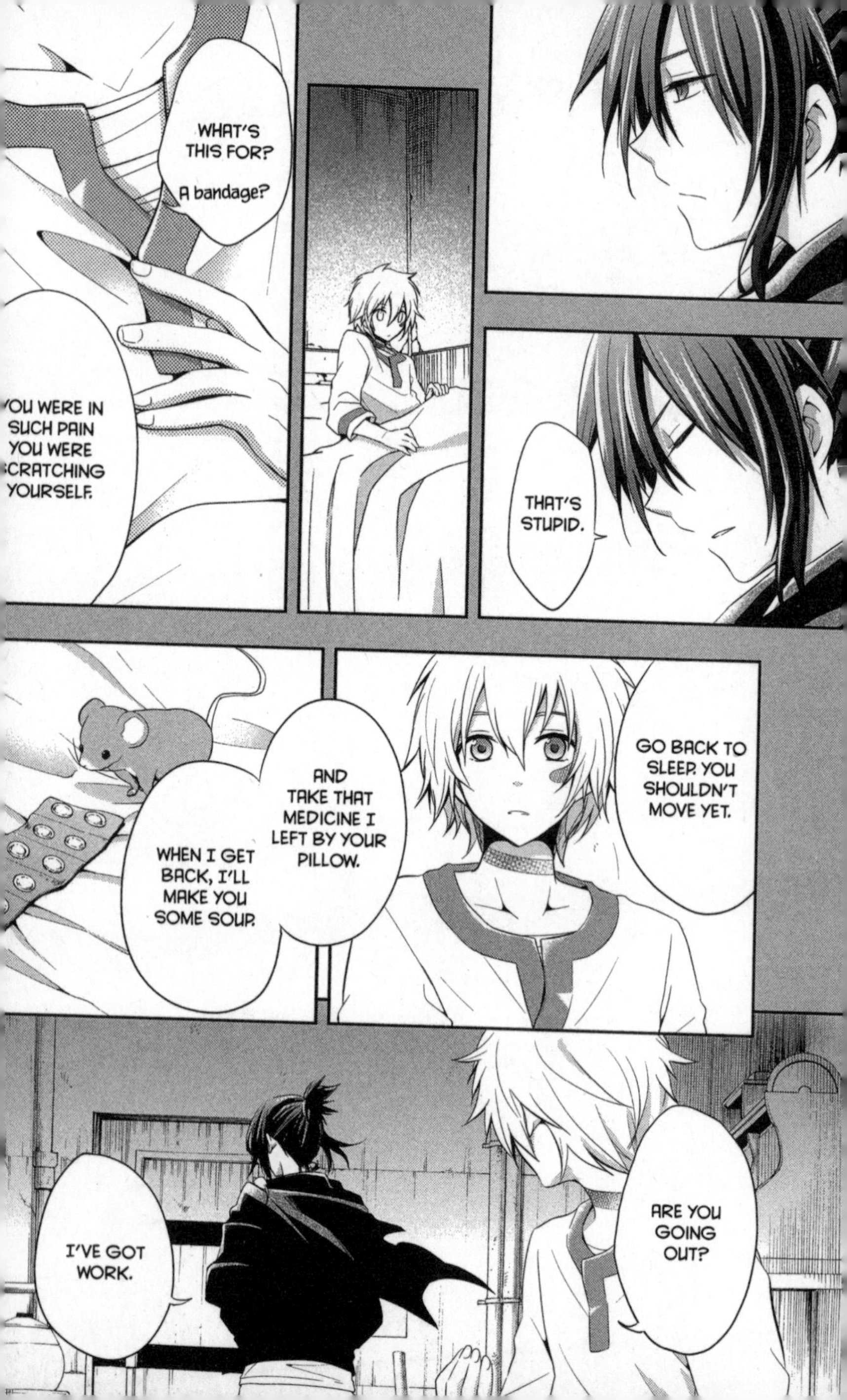
THAT'S STUPID.
WHAT'S THIS FOR?
A bandage?
YOU WERE IN SUCH PAIN YOU WERE SCRATCHING YOURSELF.
GO BACK TO SLEEP. YOU SHOULDN'T MOVE YET.
AND TAKE THAT MEDICINE I LEFT BY YOUR PILLOW.
WHEN I GET BACK, I'LL MAKE YOU SOME SOUP.
ARE YOU GOING OUT?
I'VE GOT WORK.

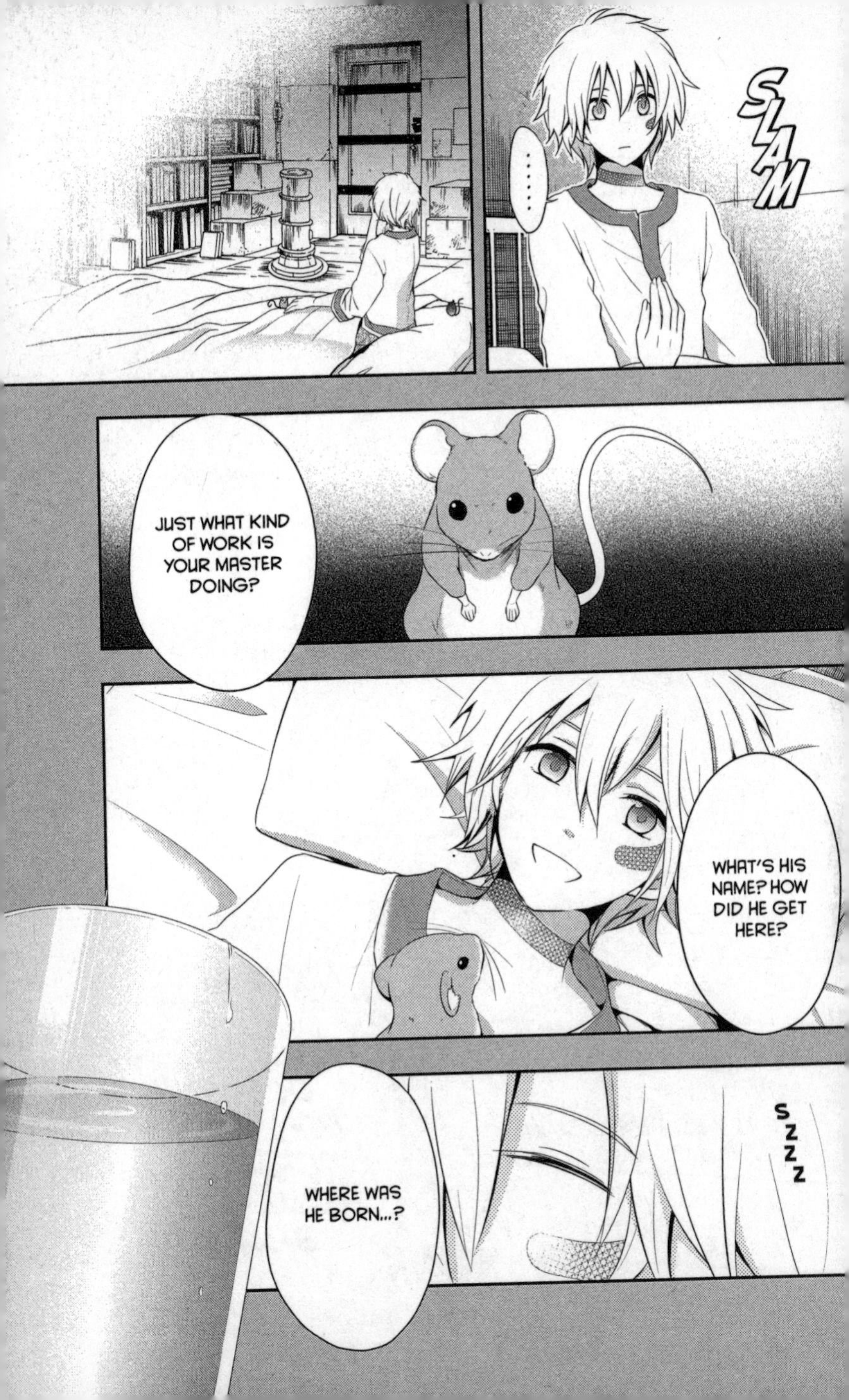
SLAM
......
JUST WHAT KIND OF WORK IS YOUR MASTER DOING?
WHAT'S HIS NAME? HOW DID HE GET HERE?
SZZZ
WHERE WAS HE BORN...?

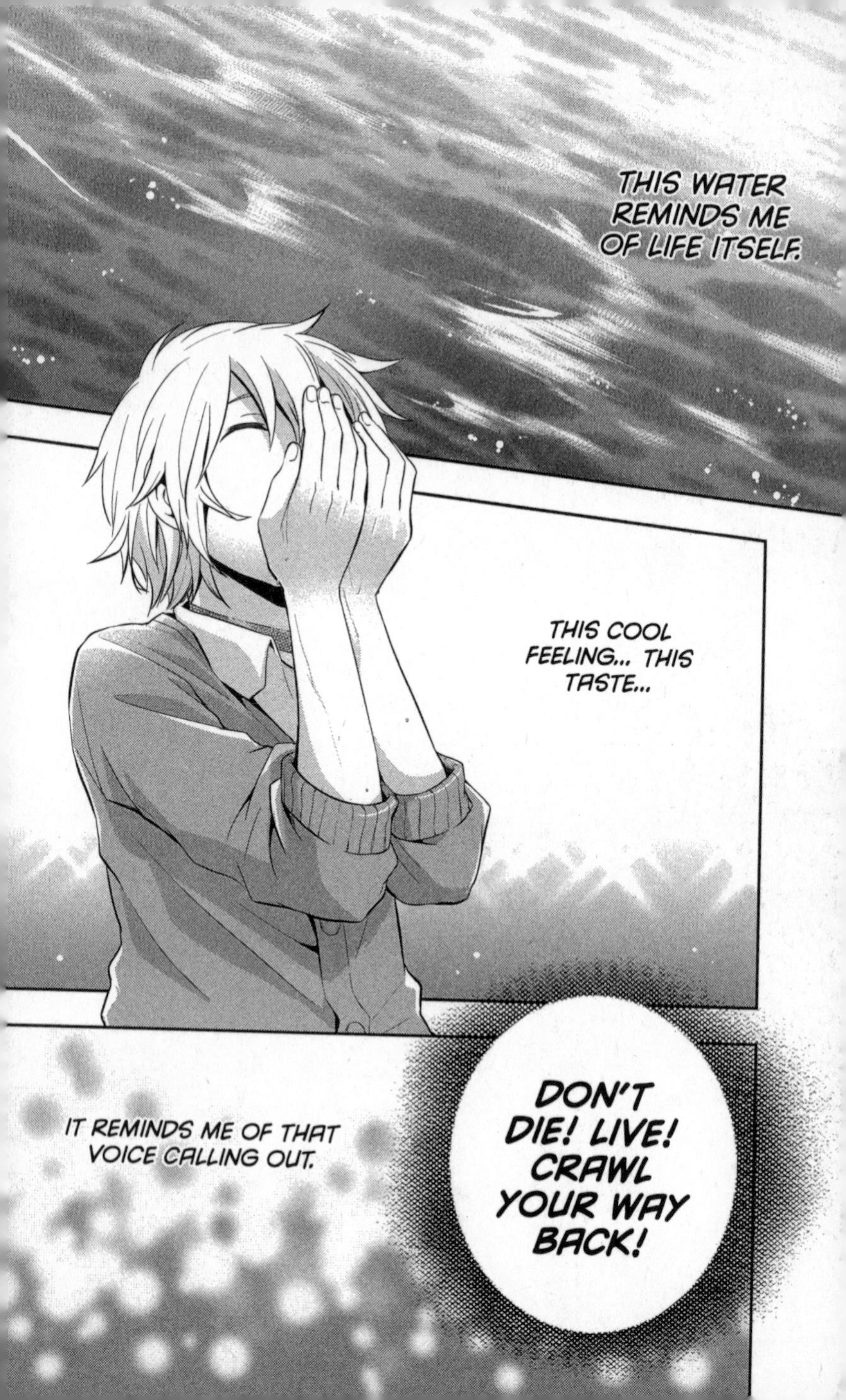
THIS WATER REMINDS ME OF LIFE ITSELF.
THIS COOL FEELING... THIS TASTE...
DON'T DIE! LIVE! CRAWL YOUR WAY BACK!
IT REMINDS ME OF THAT VOICE CALLING OUT.

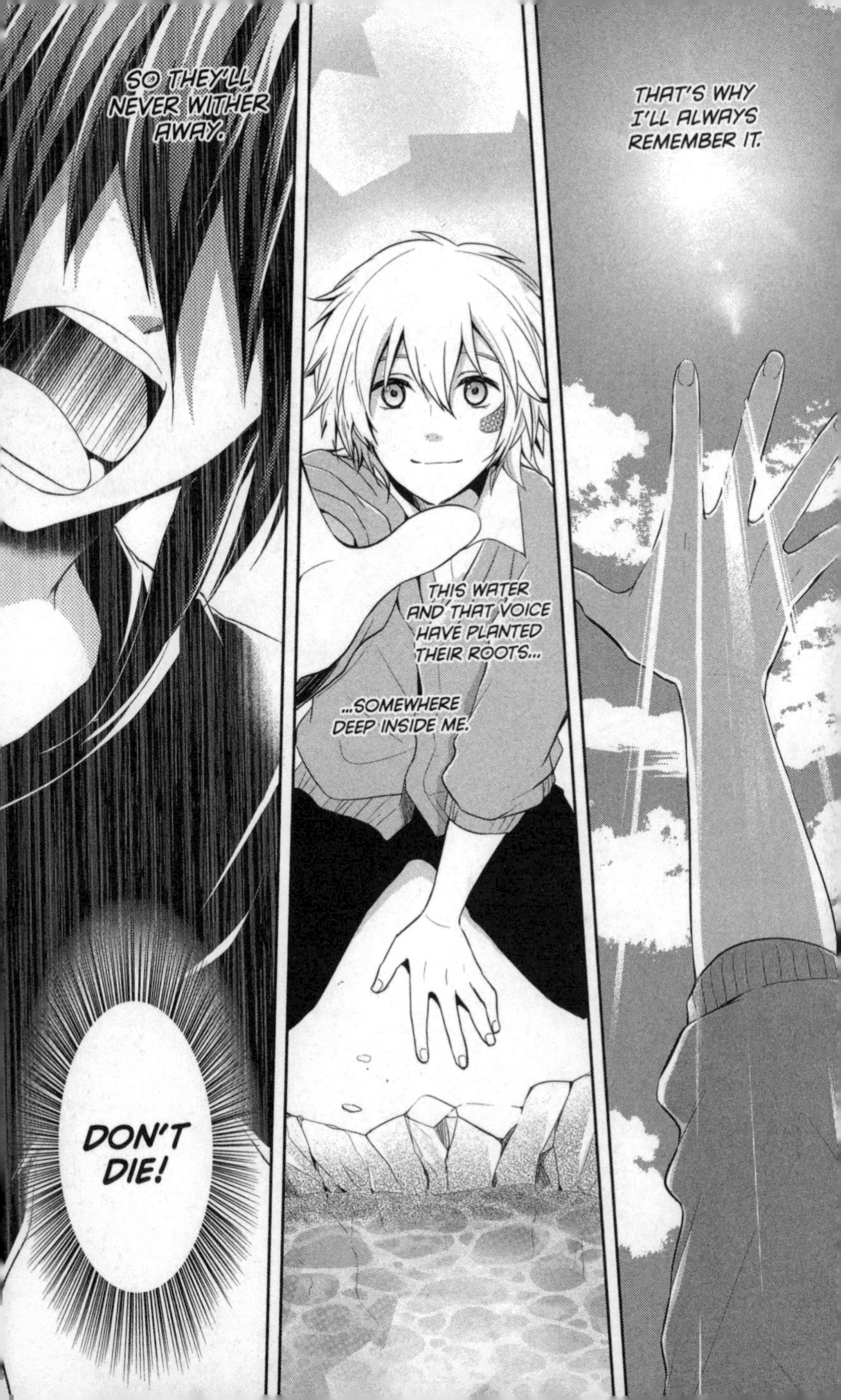
THAT'S WHY I'LL ALWAYS REMEMBER IT.
THIS WATER AND THAT VOICE HAVE PLANTED THEIR ROOTS...
...SOMEWHERE DEEP INSIDE ME.
SO THEY'LL NEVER WITHER AWAY.
DON'T DIE!

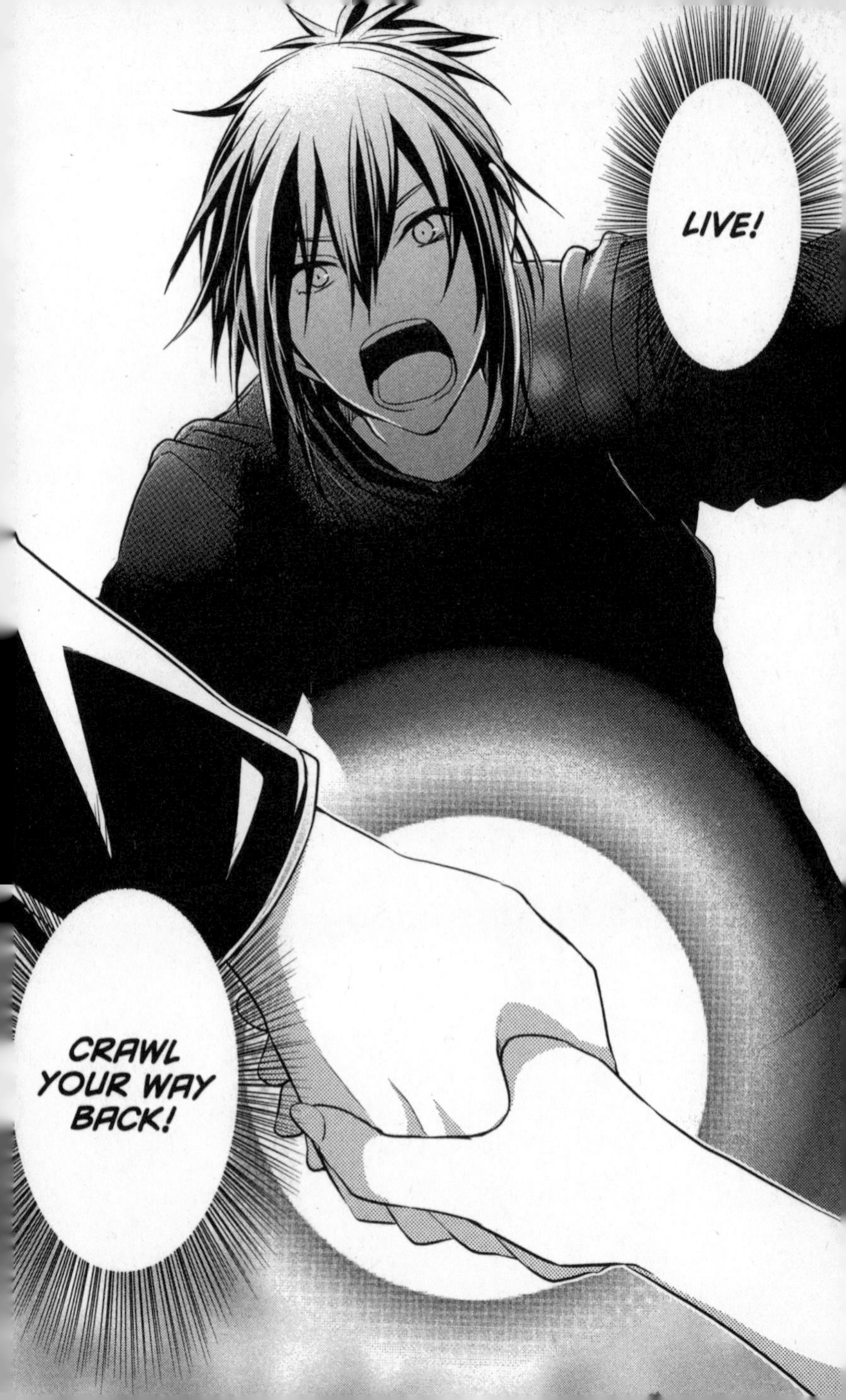
LIVE!
CRAWL YOUR WAY BACK!

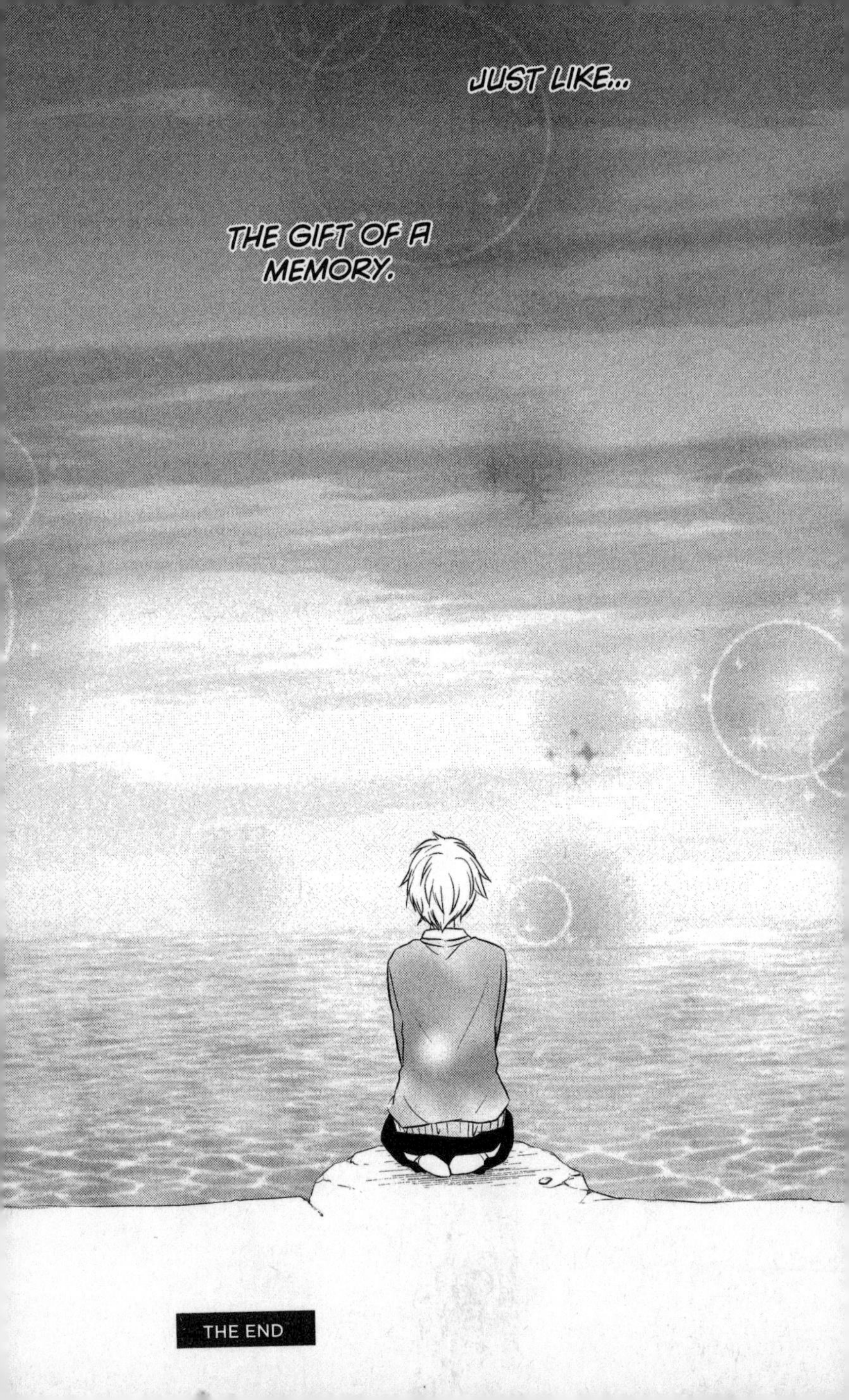
JUST LIKE...
THE GIFT OF A MEMORY.
THE END

Bonus Strip #1: Hairstyle

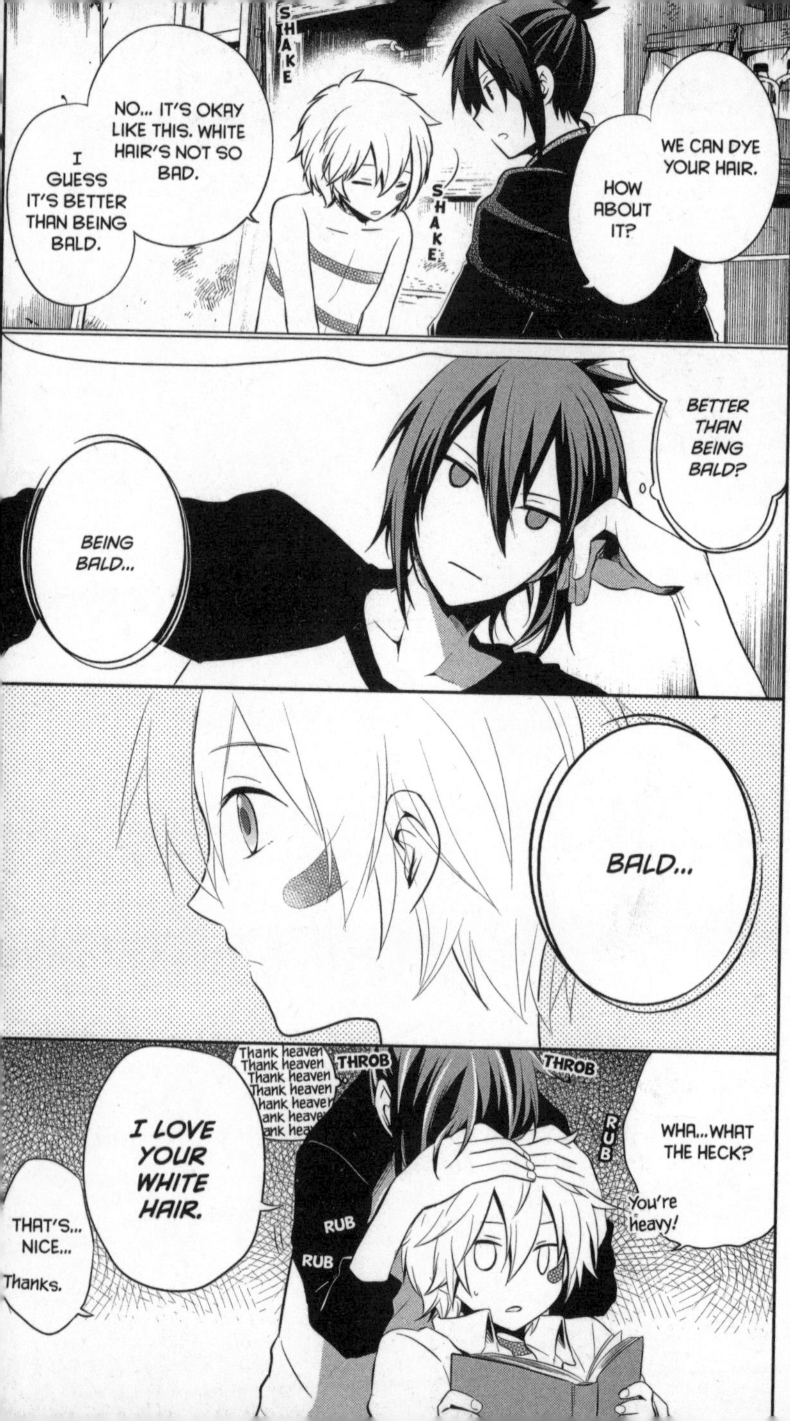
WE CAN DYE YOUR HAIR.
HOW ABOUT IT?
SHAKE
SHAKE
NO... IT'S OKAY LIKE THIS. WHITE HAIR'S NOT SO BAD.
I GUESS IT'S BETTER THAN BEING BALD.
BETTER THAN BEING BALD?
BEING BALD...
BALD...
THROB
THROB
WHA...WHAT THE HECK?
RUB
You're heavy!
Thank heaven
Thank heaven
Thank heaven
Thank heaven
hank heave
ank heave
ank hea
I LOVE YOUR WHITE HAIR.
RUB
RUB
THAT'S... NICE...
Thanks.

#2: Disguise

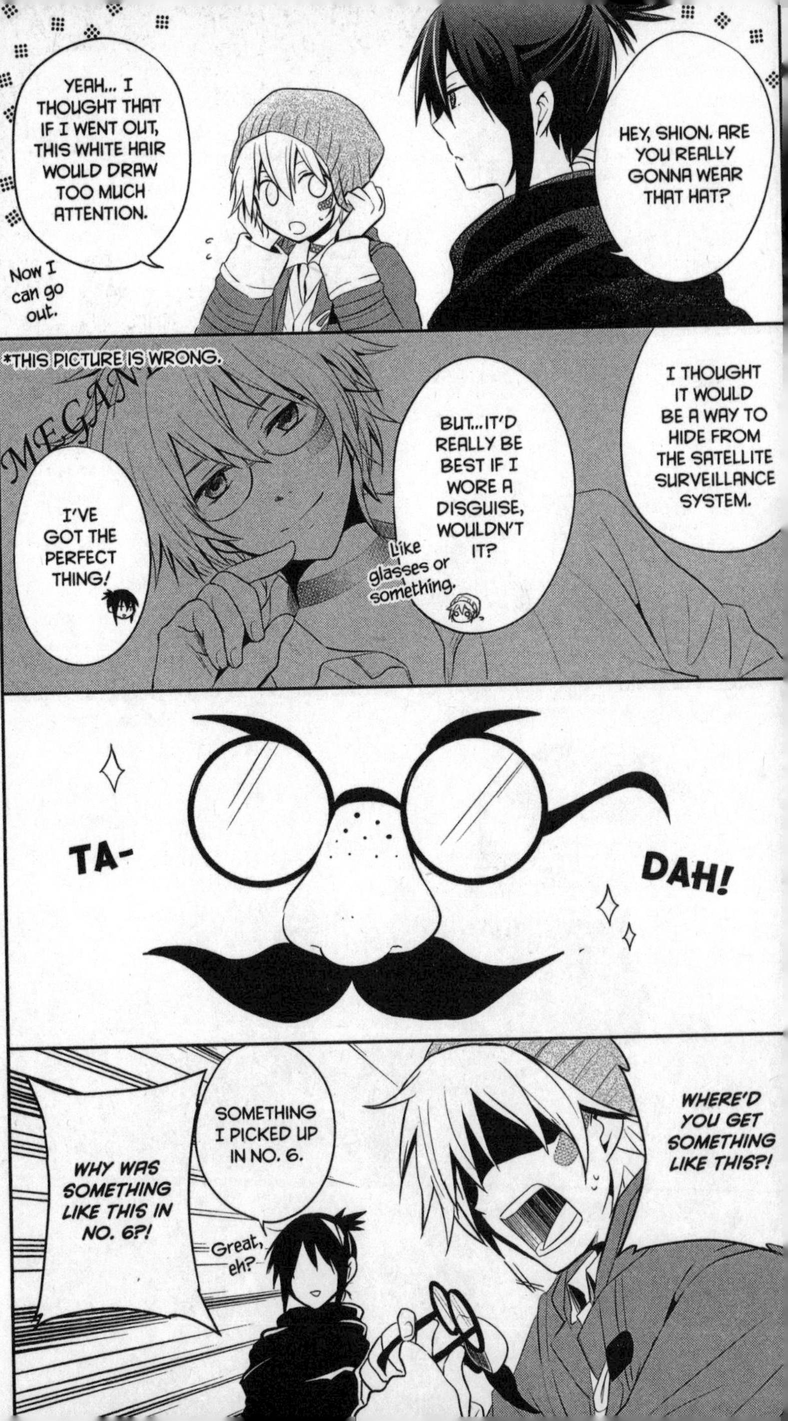
HEY, SHION. ARE YOU REALLY GONNA WEAR THAT HAT?
YEAH... I THOUGHT THAT IF I WENT OUT, THIS WHITE HAIR WOULD DRAW TOO MUCH ATTENTION.
Now I can go out.
I THOUGHT IT WOULD BE A WAY TO HIDE FROM THE SATELLITE SURVEILLANCE SYSTEM.
BUT...IT'D REALLY BE BEST IF I WORE A DISGUISE, WOULDN'T IT?
Like glasses or something.
*THIS PICTURE IS WRONG.
I'VE GOT THE PERFECT THING!
TA- DAH!
WHERE'D YOU GET SOMETHING LIKE THIS?!
SOMETHING I PICKED UP IN NO. 6.
Great, eh?
WHY WAS SOMETHING LIKE THIS IN NO. 6?!

#3: Monster

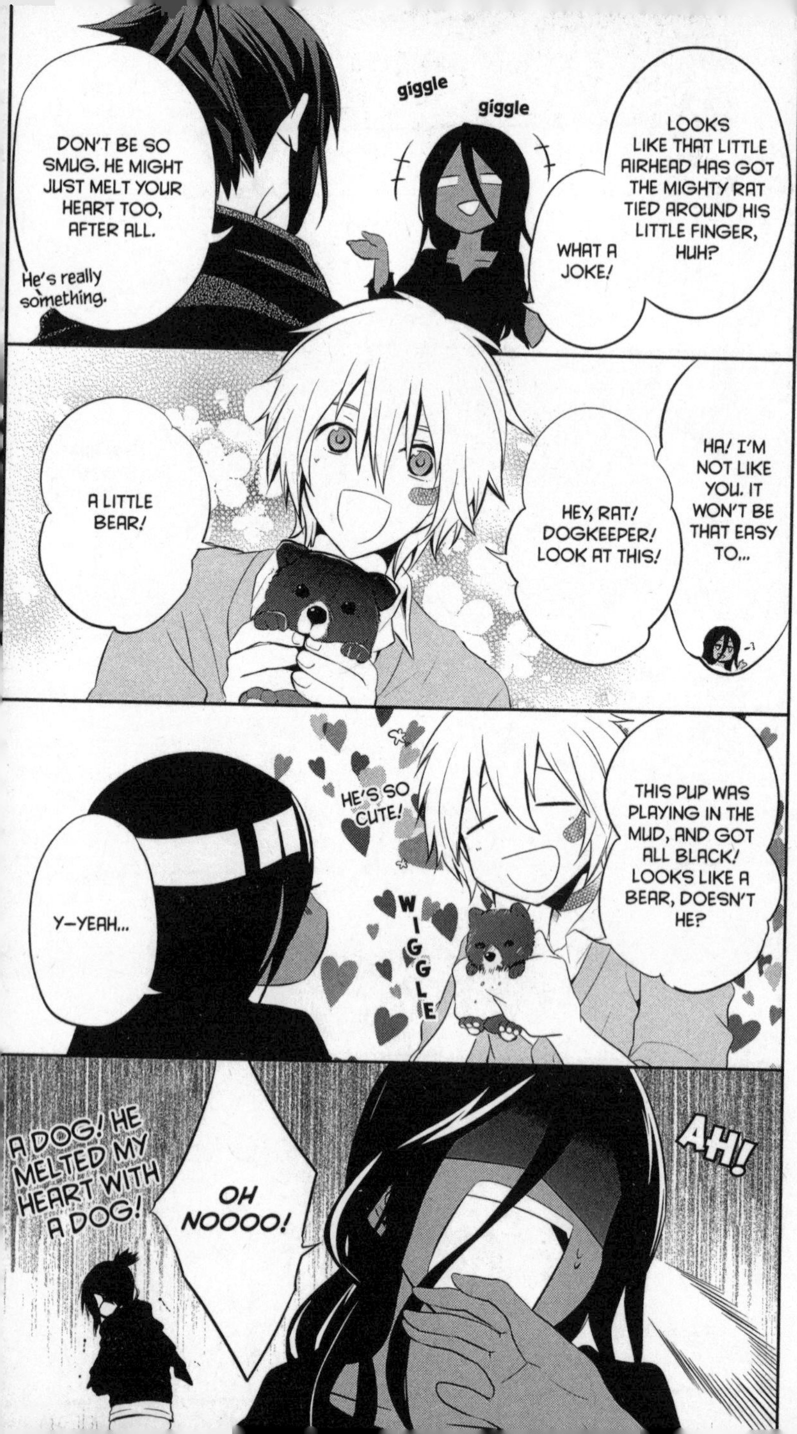

giggle
giggle
LOOKS LIKE THAT LITTLE AIRHEAD HAS GOT THE MIGHTY RAT TIED AROUND HIS LITTLE FINGER, HUH?
WHAT A JOKE!
DON'T BE SO SMUG. HE MIGHT JUST MELT YOUR HEART TOO, AFTER ALL.
He's really something.
HA! I'M NOT LIKE YOU. IT WON'T BE THAT EASY TO...
HEY, RAT! DOGKEEPER! LOOK AT THIS!
A LITTLE BEAR!
THIS PUP WAS PLAYING IN THE MUD, AND GOT ALL BLACK! LOOKS LIKE A BEAR, DOESN'T HE?
WIGGLE
HE'S SO CUTE!
Y–YEAH...
AH!
OH NOOOO!
A DOG! HE MELTED MY HEART WITH A DOG!

#4: Discussion

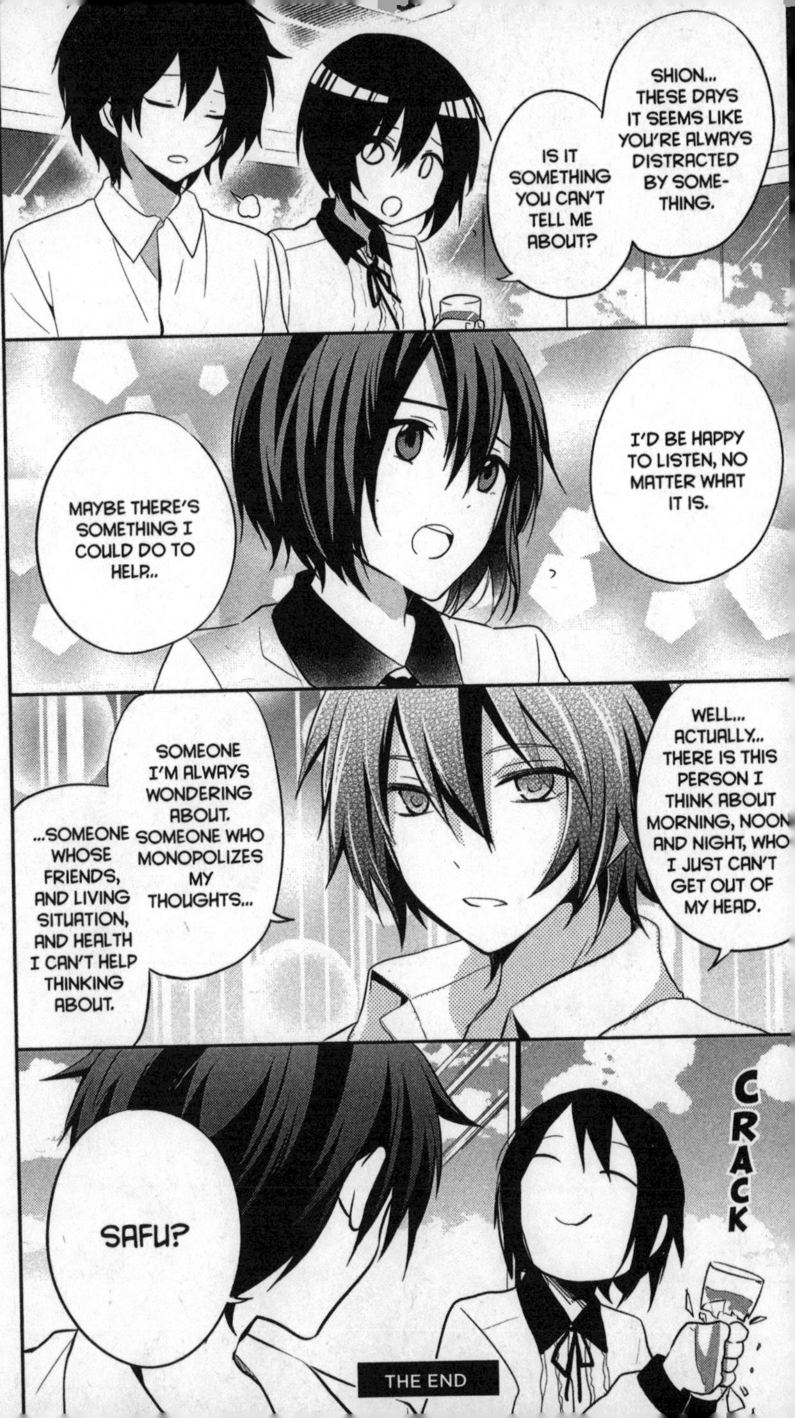
SHION... THESE DAYS IT SEEMS LIKE YOU'RE ALWAYS DISTRACTED BY SOME-THING.
IS IT SOMETHING YOU CAN'T TELL ME ABOUT?
I'D BE HAPPY TO LISTEN, NO MATTER WHAT IT IS.
MAYBE THERE'S SOMETHING I COULD DO TO HELP...
WELL... ACTUALLY... THERE IS THIS PERSON I THINK ABOUT MORNING, NOON AND NIGHT, WHO I JUST CAN'T GET OUT OF MY HEAD.
SOMEONE I'M ALWAYS WONDERING ABOUT. SOMEONE WHO MONOPOLIZES MY THOUGHTS...
...SOMEONE WHOSE FRIENDS, AND LIVING SITUATION, AND HEALTH I CAN'T HELP THINKING ABOUT.
CRACK
SAFU?
THE END

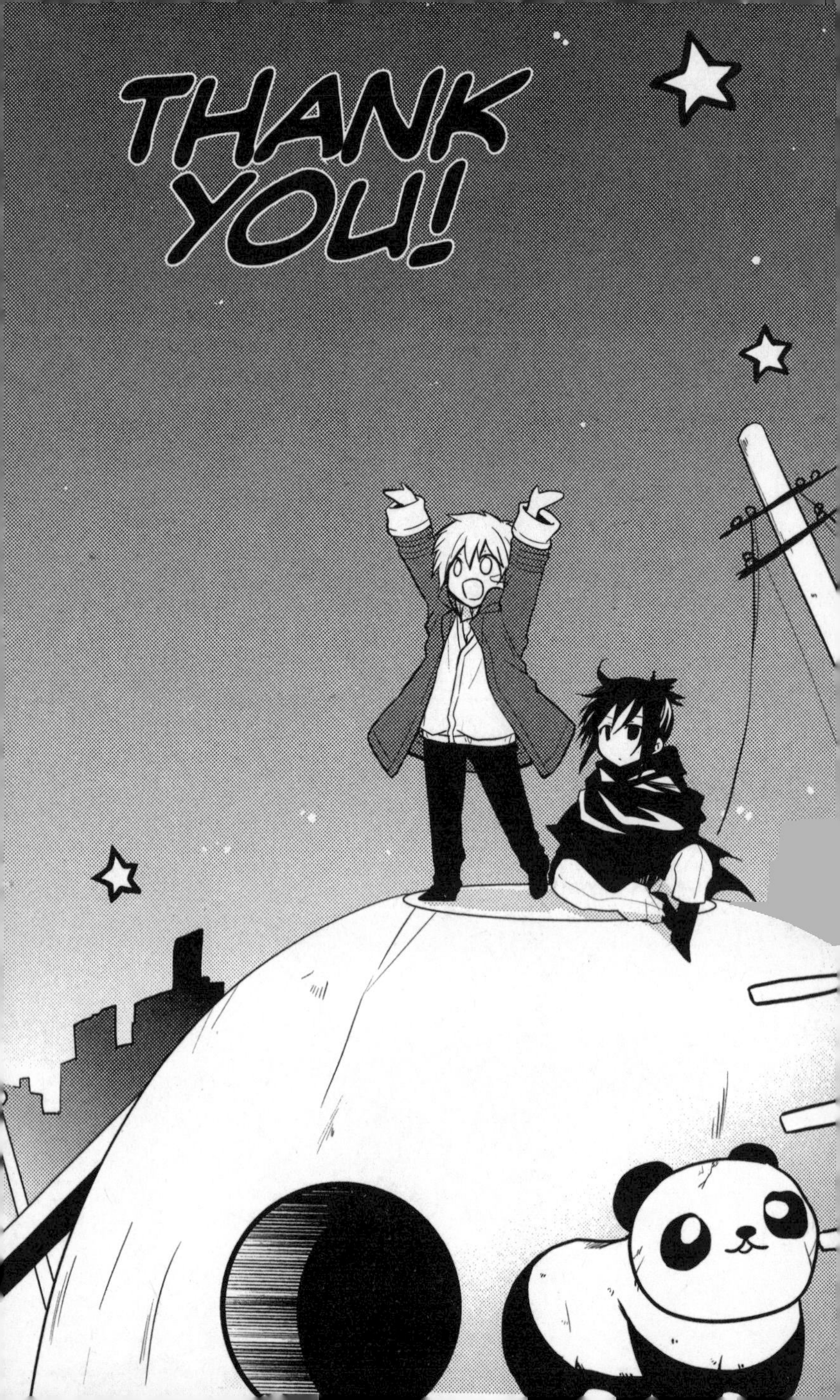
THANK YOU!

NO.6
plus

Atsuko Asano & Hinoki Kino present
NO.6 special edition "NO.6 plus".

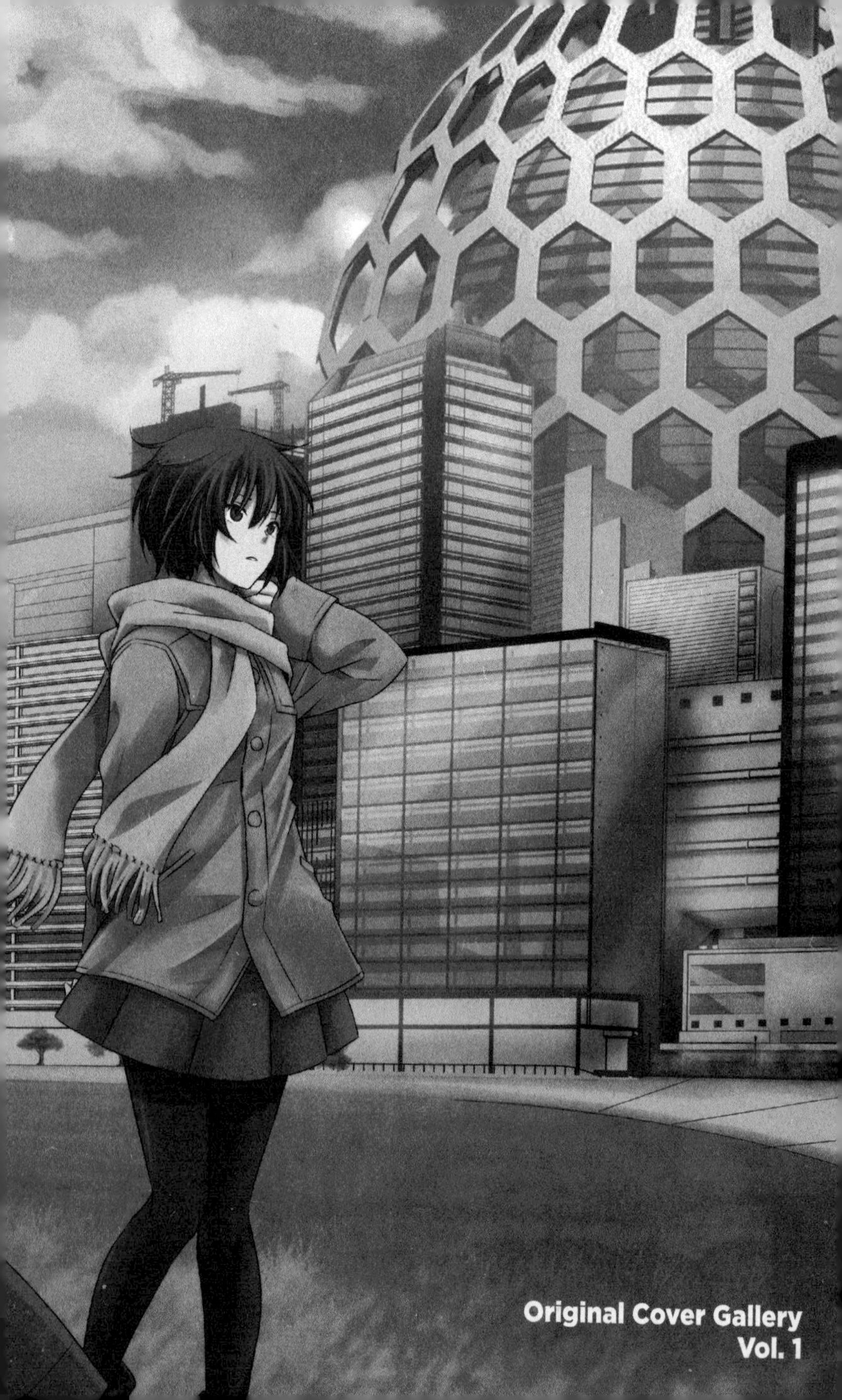

Original Cover Gallery
Vol. 1

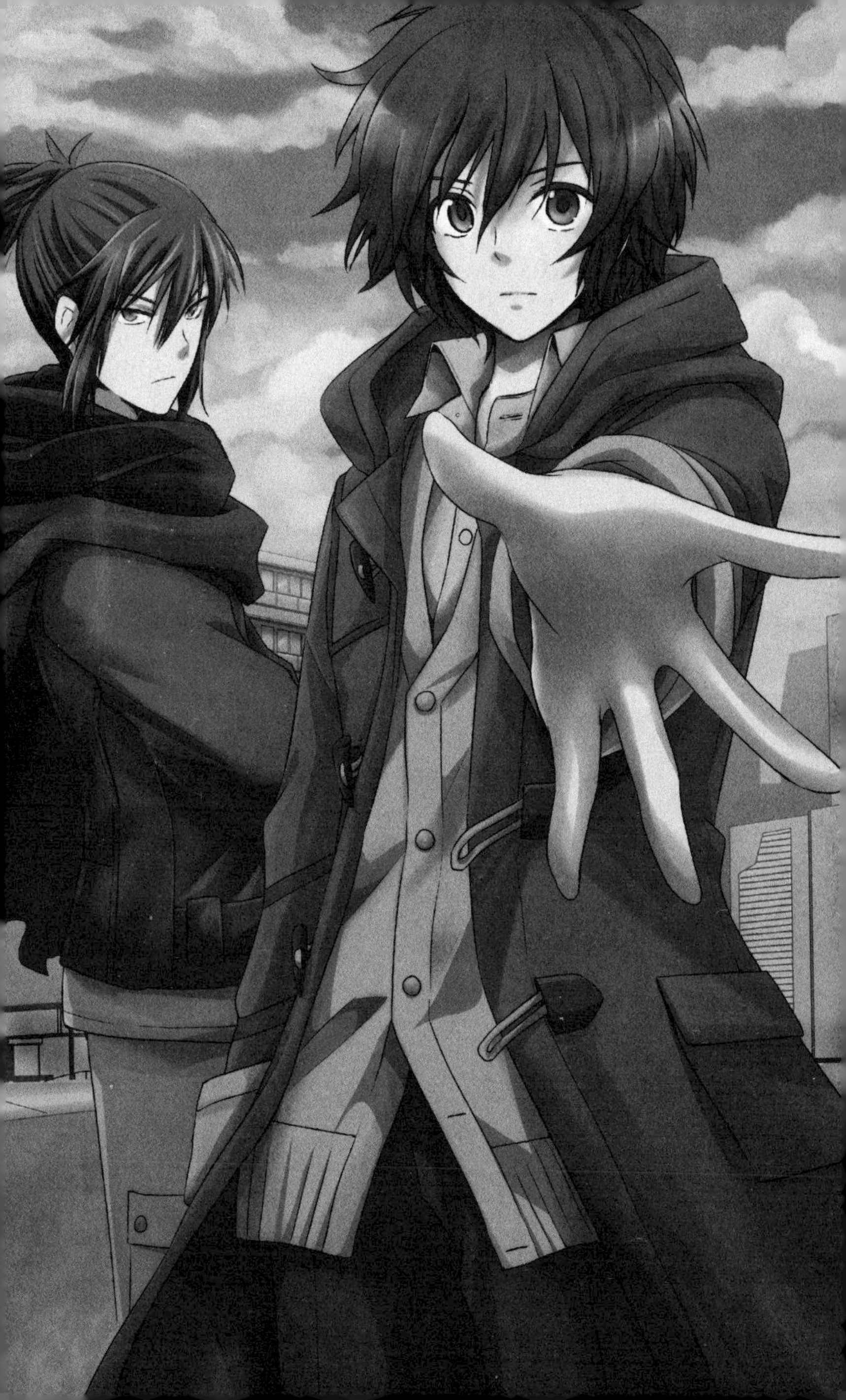

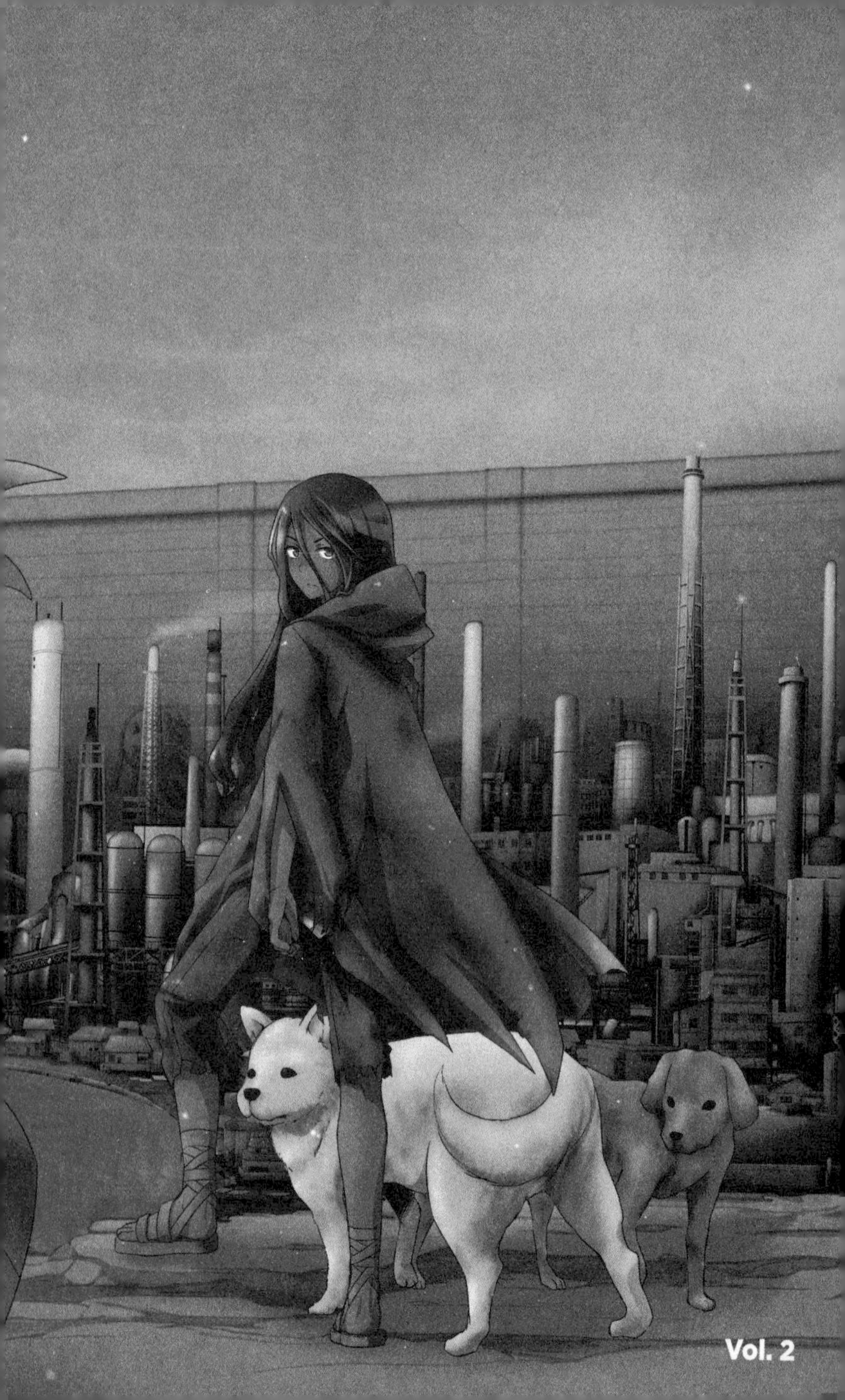
Vol. 2

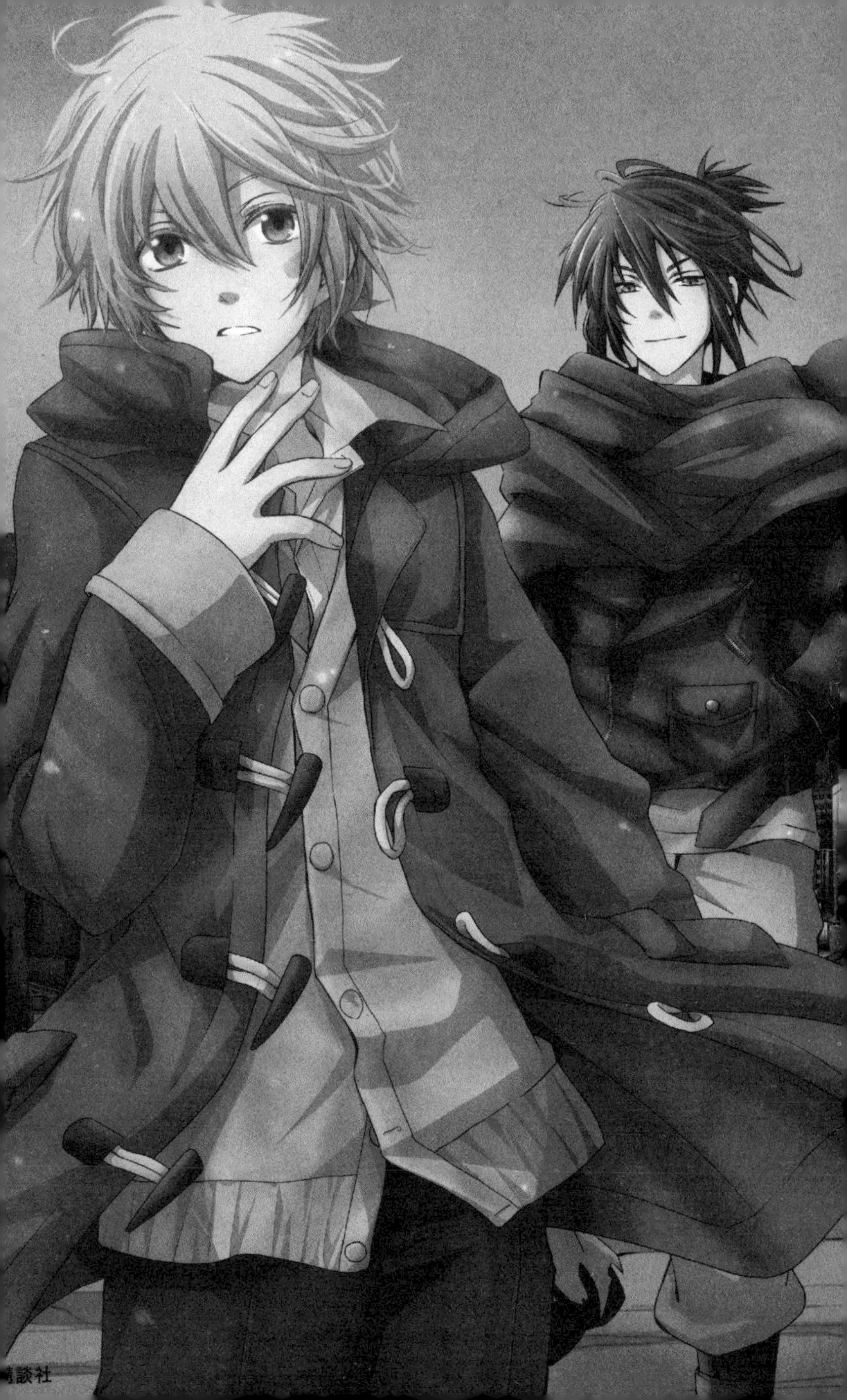
談社

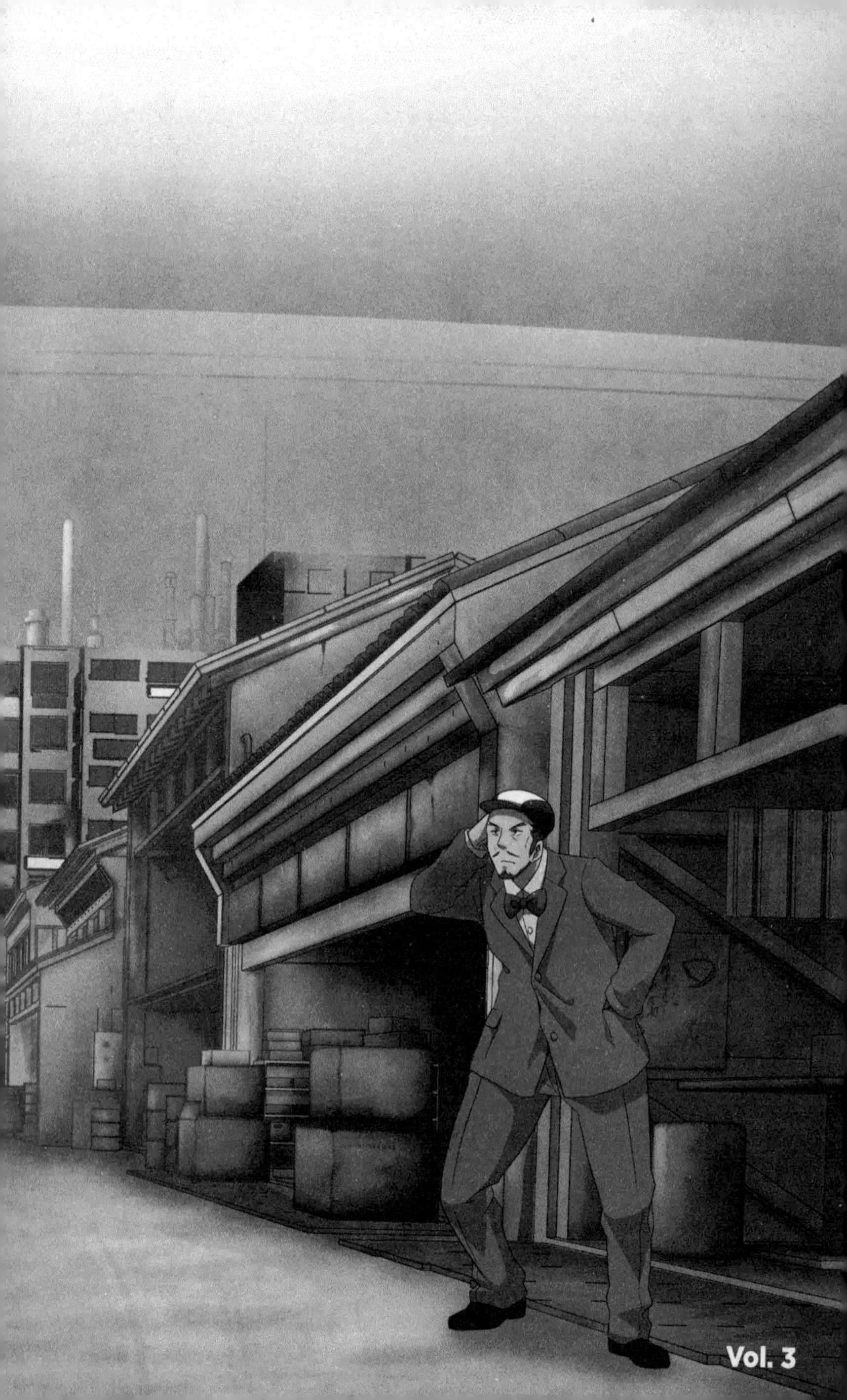
Vol. 3

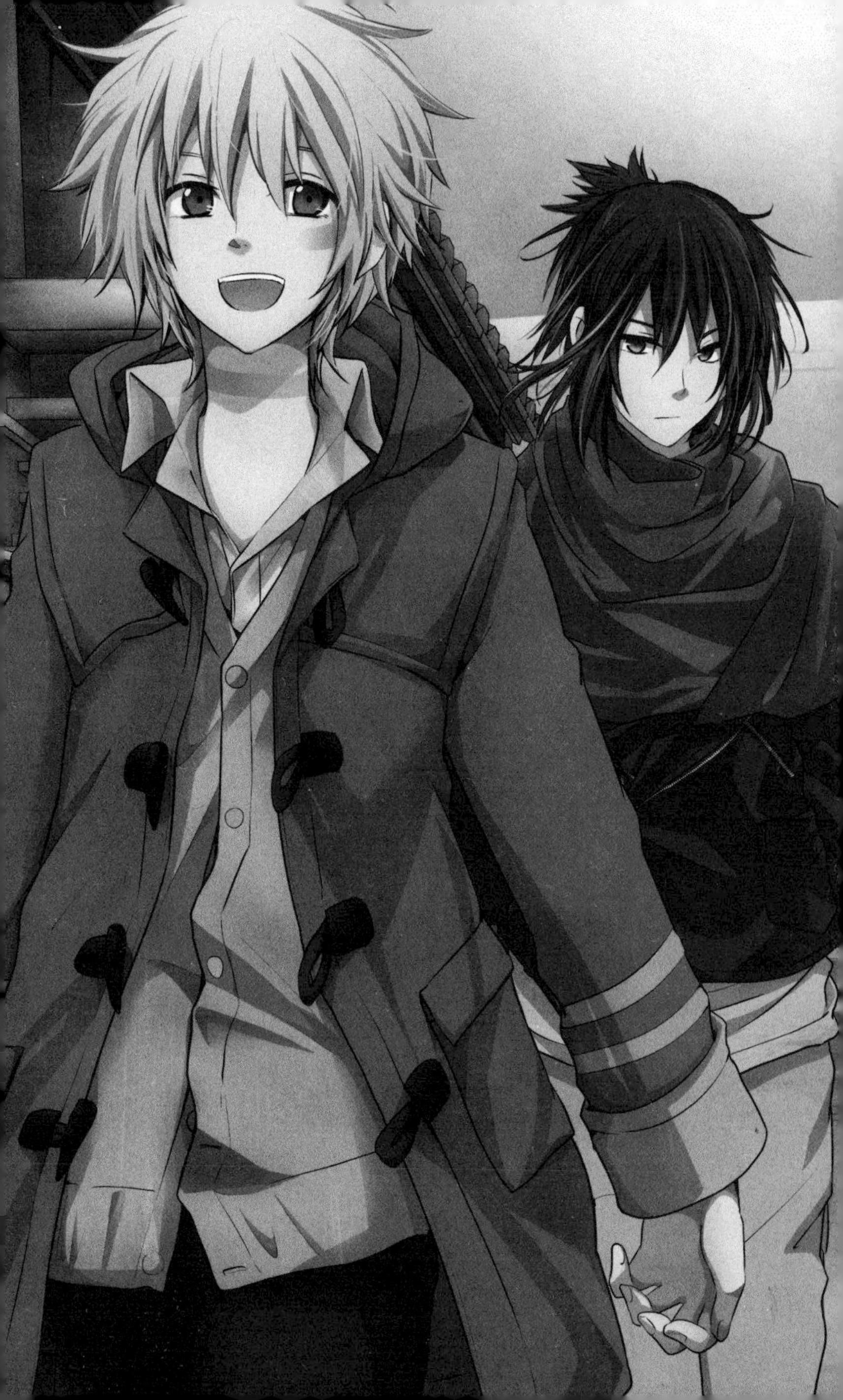

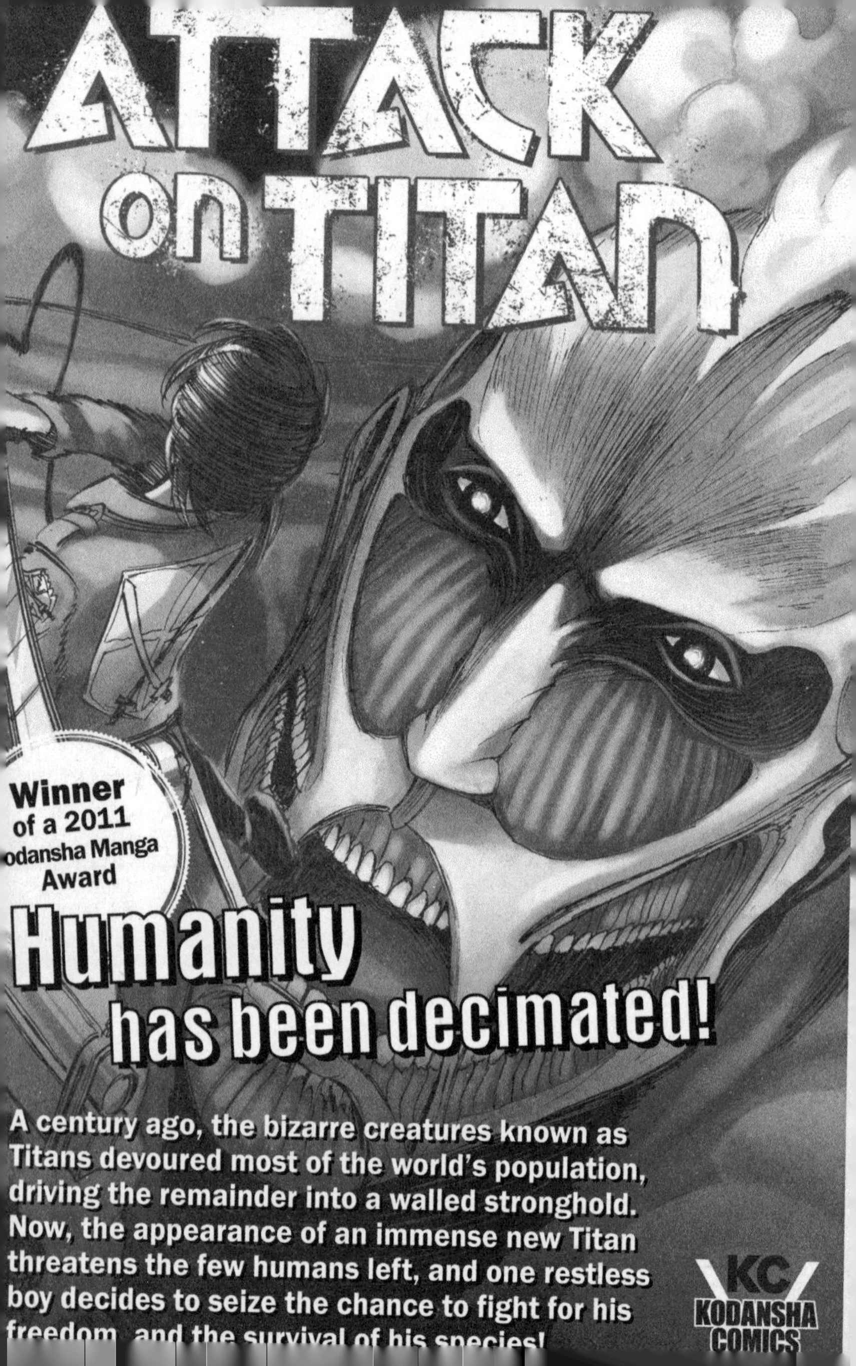
ATTACK on TITAN
Winner of a 2011 Kodansha Manga Award
Humanity has been decimated!
A century ago, the bizarre creatures known as Titans devoured most of the world's population, driving the remainder into a walled stronghold. Now, the appearance of an immense new Titan threatens the few humans left, and one restless boy decides to seize the chance to fight for his freedom, and the survival of his species!
KC KODANSHA COMICS

Kodansha Comics Trade Paperback Original.

o. 6 volume 3 copyright © 2012 Atsuko Asano, Hinoki Kino
glish translation copyright © 2013 Atsuko Asano, Hinoki Kino

blished in the United States by Kodansha Comics, an imprint of Kodansha
A Publishing, LLC, New York.

blication rights for this English edition arranged through Kodansha Ltd.,
kyo.

st published in Japan in 2012 by Kodansha Ltd., Tokyo
N 978-1-61262-357-3

nted in the United States of America.

w.kodanshacomics.com

7 6 5 4 3

nslation: Jonathan Tarbox and Kazuko Shimizu
tering: Christy Sawyer
ting: Ben Applegate